Eastern Africa Series

GENDER,
HOME
& IDENTITY

Eastern Africa Series

Women's Land Rights & Privatization in Eastern Africa
BIRGIT ENGLERT & ELIZABETH DALEY (EDS)

War & the Politics of Identity in Ethiopia KJETIL TRONVOLL

Moving People in Ethiopia
ALULA PANKHURST & FRANÇOIS PIGUET (EDS)

Living Terraces in Ethiopia ELIZABETH E. WATSON

Eritrea GAIM KIBREAB

Borders & Borderlands as Resources in the Horn of Africa
DEREJE FEYISSA & MARKUS VIRGIL HOEHNE (EDS)

After the Comprehensive Peace Agreement in Sudan
ELKE GRAWERT (ED.)

Land, Governance, Conflict & the Nuba of Sudan
GUMA KUNDA KOMEY

Ethiopia JOHN MARKAKIS

Resurrecting Cannibals HEIKE BEHREND

Pastoralism & Politics in Northern Kenya & Southern Ethiopia
GŰNTHER SCHLEE & ABDULLAHI A. SHONGOLO

Islam & Ethnicity in Northern Kenya & Southern Ethiopia
GŰNTHER SCHLEE with ABDULLAHI A. SHONGOLO

Foundations of an African Civilisation DAVID W. PHILLIPSON

Regional Integration, Identity & Citizenship
in the Greater Horn of Africa
KIDANE MENGISTEAB & REDIE BEREKETEAB (EDS)

Dealing with the Government in South Sudan CHERRY LEONARDI

The Quest for Socialist Utopia BAHRU ZEWDE

Disrupting Territories
JÖRG GERTEL, RICHARD ROTTENBURG & SANDRA CALKINS (EDS)

The African Garrison State
KJETIL TRONVOLL & DANIEL R. MEKONNEN

The State of Post-conflict Reconstruction
NASEEM BADIEY

Gender, Home & Identity: Nuer Repatriation to Southern Sudan
KATARZYNA GRABSKA

Remaking Mutirikwi*
JOOST FONTEIN

*forthcoming

Gender,
Home
& Identity

NUER REPATRIATION
TO SOUTHERN SUDAN

KATARZYNA GRABSKA

Research Fellow,
Dept of Anthropology & Sociology of Development
Graduate Institute of International
& Development Studies, Geneva

James Currey
is an imprint of Boydell & Brewer Ltd
PO Box 9, Woodbridge, Suffolk IP12 3DF (GB)
www.jamescurrey.com

and of

Boydell & Brewer Inc.
668 Mt Hope Avenue, Rochester, NY 14620-2731 (US)
www.boydellandbrewer.com

British Library Cataloguing in Publication Data

A catalogue record for this book is available from the British Library

ISBN 978-1-84701-099-5 (James Currey Cloth)

This publication is printed on acid-free paper

Typeset in 10 on 12pt Cordale with Gill Bold display
by Avocet Typeset, Somerton, Somerset

Contents

List of Maps and Photographs   vii
Preface   viii
Acknowledgements   x
Glossary of Nuer Terms   xii
Acronyms   xv

1.   Returnee Dilemmas: Dangerous Trousers and Threatening
      Mini-skirts   1
      Gender and generational relations in flux   4
      Gendered displacement: why does it matter?   6
      Historical and feminist ethnography across places and spaces   8
      Gender relations in displacement and emplacement   18
      Nuer women and men's gendered encounters with
         displacement, emplacement and 'modernities'   22
      Transforming gendered self through seasons   25

2.   *Jiom* – Season of Fighting and Running: Conflict, Mobility,
      Gender   28
      'Which wars do you want me to talk about?': narratives of wars   28
      War costs: mass displacement and diverse mobility   30
      Women and men: war and violence   45
      The wind and the change   62

3.   *Mai* – Season of Displacement: Becoming 'Modern' in Kakuma   64
      'Modernity', global humanitarianism, gender and
         generations   66
      Kakuma and arrival of a new custom: cieng mi pai ben   67
      People who have awoken: gendered and generational
         identities   80
      Contesting gender power, ideology and 'our culture'   95
      Aspirations and contradictions   101

4. *Rwil* – Season of 'Returns'   104
    Nyakuol and Kuok   104
    Movement, place and gendered emplacement   106
    Diasporic returns, place and 'home'   110
    We cannot be the same Nuer as our parents: the irreversibility
        of displacement, home and being in flux   121

5. Season of Settling-in: Land and Livelihoods   126
    Nyakuol: becoming men   126
    Imagined and lived 'homes' and return   128
    Nyuuri piny: gendered settling-in   132
    'When women become men': accessing livelihoods   140
    Are women really becoming men?   149

6. *Tot* – Gendered Emplacement Identities, Ideologies and
        Marriage   152
    Kuem and Nyarial: suits, trousers, mini-skirts and learning to
        wear a tuac   152
    Gender identities, ideologies and 'self' in flux: the experience of
        'homecoming' and settling-in   155
    Settling-in and marriage   167
    Gendered emplacement: gender relations in-flux   181
    Changing the landscapes of post-war communities   187

7. Returnees as Visitors and the Nuer Community: Where Do We
        Go From Here?   189
    Dilemmas about social life in flux   189
    Anthropology of disorder and social theory   190
    'Homemaking' and implications for the study of return migration   191
    Gendered displacement, emplacement and implications for theories
        of social change   194
    Gender theories, displacement and implications for gender-
        mainstreaming policies   198
    Refugees and home in flux   201

    Epilogue   203
    Bibliography   206
    Index   219

Maps and Photographs

Maps

1.1 South Sudan   2

3.1 Kakuma Refugee Camp, UNHCR 2006   71

Photographs

2.1 Returnee boy in military uniform, Lɛr 2007   55

2.2 Military parade in Lɛr, southern Sudan, January 2007   56

3.1 Women's rights campaign in Kakuma refugee camp, 2006   65

3.2 Signpost – NGO compound, Kakuma, 2006   65

3.3 'New' young men, Kakuma, 2006   82

3.4 Nuer court elders in Kakuma, 2006   87

3.5 Female role models in the Angelina Jolie boarding school
     for girls, Kakuma, 2006   91

4.1 Repatriation flight of Nuer refugees from Kakuma to Bentiu,
     December 2006   105

6.1 Returnee young men, 'Lost Boys' at a marriage ceremony in
     Lɛr, 2007   153

6.2 'New' Nuer young women, Lɛr, 2007   165

Preface

The stories of lives fragmented by wars, experienced in several contexts and pieced together in the aftermath are seldom told. This book follows the efforts of seventeen Nuer families and over fifty additional individuals who fled their homes due to the violence and wars that tore their communities apart, were displaced throughout Sudan and East Africa and eventually settled in a refugee camp in Kenya. In the process, their lives were irreversibly changed, and in unexpected and differentiated ways. Many years later, in the aftermath of repatriation, they and their relatives and friends who were displaced elsewhere, or who had stayed behind, have come together to (re)create and (re)build a home, a community and a nation. The narratives of those displaced and those who had stayed behind reveal the complexity of social change in the context of forced displacement and nation-building.

Since the mid-1990s, I have been following the developments in Sudan and consequently in South Sudan, first during my MA studies, later as a researcher of Sudanese refugees' livelihoods in Cairo and subsequently as a doctoral student between 2005 and 2010. Based mainly on multi-sited ethnographic research in Kakuma refugee camp in Kenya and in South Sudan between April 2006 and September 2007, which formed the fieldwork for my DPhil in Development Studies, this book narrates and analyses the experience of gendered and generational displacement of the group of Nuer women and men whom I followed.

In Chapter 1, I explain in more detail the methodology on which the fieldwork was based as well as the choice of interviewees. The three main characters whose narratives constitute the backbone of the story line in the book were chosen deliberately. I became very familiar with the lives of these three individuals and their families throughout my research, meeting them first in Kakuma and then throughout my time in South Sudan. I have also kept in touch with them since 2006. I felt that their individual stories presented a set of diverse experiences of single mothers, young women and men who were the main groups of refugees I encountered in Cairo or in Kakuma. My respondents insisted that I refer to them using their real names as they wanted their experiences to be shared with others. To honour them, I have kept parts of their names unchanged while not providing them in full to protect their identity to some extent.

The research for this book took place mainly before South Sudan's independence. I use the term 'southern Sudan' to refer to the area of Sudan before the South's 2011 independence. To reflect the fragile situation of post-war southern Sudan, I use the term 'after-fire' fieldwork. This term refers to the book *Fieldwork Under Fire* which discusses ethnographic fieldwork in the context of war and violence.[1] My 'after-fire' fieldwork was carried out in the wake of decades of conflict in southern Sudan.

In this preface, I set out a few explanations for the readers related to the use of names, transliteration, and the use of language in the citation. The spelling of the primary location of my research in South Sudan is often confusing and is used in a variety of ways. Lɛr is the transliteration from the Nuer. Ler is the English version of the term. Leer is NGO-speak, a transcription of the way Lɛr is written in Arabic where it appears either with a long vowel (Leer) or a diphthong (Lair). I follow the Nuer original transliteration and use Lɛr throughout the book.

The informants sometimes spoke in Nuer and sometimes in English, and at times Dinka or Arabic. Sometimes they also mixed words from one language into conversation in the other. I have thus standardised the use of the two main languages for quotes. I use English with significant words only in Nuer in brackets. I use square brackets for any of my own interpolations in quoted passages. Some English terms have been adopted as loan words in Nuer. These words are placed within single quotation marks in the translation. Conversely, if the respondents were speaking in English and used a Nuer word, that word is also marked by quotation marks.

[1] Carolyn Nordstrom and Antonius C. G. M. Robben, eds, *Fieldwork Under Fire: Contemporary Studies of Violence and Survival* (Berkeley, 1995).

Acknowledgements

A long journey of new discoveries, adventures, new encounters, frustrations, hardship and new friendships have accompanied the creation of this book. I would not have been able to embark on this project, let alone to complete it, without the wonderful support of so many dedicated individuals and institutions. First and foremost, my deepest gratitude goes to my two dedicated DPhil supervisors, Professor Ann Whitehead and Dr Lyla Mehta who accompanied me on this journey from its very beginning and were there for me during difficult moments of fieldwork and writing-up. They both challenged me every step of the way and encouraged me to think critically and in new ways. I have learned a lot from them – thank you!

This book is also inspired by the wonderful opportunity to collaborate with Professor Barbara Harrell-Bond. Her dedication to seek justice for those who have been deprived of protection and their rights grounded my commitment to forced migration issues. She made me believe that through academic work it is possible to contribute to those whose lives have been torn apart by wars and conflicts. Thank you for believing in me.

I am also indebted to Professor Richard Black and Dr Meera Warrier of the Development Research Centre on Migration, Globalisation and Poverty (DRC Migration) for their support, friendship and many insightful conversations about my work. My gratitude goes to the DRC Migration and Alan Sverrisson Fund whose grants allowed me to carry out fieldwork research. Thanks also go to the Institute of Development Studies at the University of Sussex where I undertook my doctoral degree for its logistical support and, especially to Angela Dowman and Sue Ong for their administrative assistance. I also wanted to extend my thanks to those who provided comments for this manuscript, including Dr Laura Hammond, Professor Andrea Cornwall, Dr Cathrin Brun, Dr Cindy Horst, Dr Douglas Johnson and Professor Signe Arnfred. Thanks also go to Tim Morris, Jenny Edwards and Frances Marks for their wonderful editing skills.

This book would not have been possible without the special support of many people, new and old friends, who were there for me throughout the entire process. Special thanks go to my Turkana hosts in Kakuma Guest house, to John from JRS for his readiness to help, to IRC Kakuma staff for their generous logistical support, Jane Ndungu for her generosity and help in Kakuma and to Seeda for her friendship. In southern Sudan, Dr Luka Deng Bol – the ex-presidential Minister of southern Sudan, Rein-ooth Wanrooj of UNOCHA, Care International, IRC and MSF-Holland staff offered wonderful assistance during my stay. John, Carmen, the Comboni sisters and brothers took care of me when I fell sick with malaria. Erica De Piero offered her home as a warm refuge during my stays in Nairobi.

My host family in Lɛr, Nyajuc, NyaBol, Nyakuma, Gatchang and their children opened up their home to me and I will never forget their trust, generosity and friendship. My friends at IDS and the University of Sussex were there to share our doctoral journeys through struggle and laughter. They lifted me up in moments of doubt. Louise, Sally, Cawo, Gail, Julie and Joon-Wong, I will always treasure your friendship. Special thanks go to Professor Sharon Hutchinson who shared with me her immense knowledge of the Nuer people, provided me with a copy of the Kiggen Nuer dictionary, offered generous comments on my work in progress and her friendship. I am also grateful to Professor Ethixia Voutira who inspired my first reflections on my data.

Most of all, I am indebted to all of the Nuer women and men who generously opened up their lives and homes to me in Kakuma and Nuer-land. I am grateful for having had the opportunity to learn from you and about you. I am honoured that you allowed me to share your lives during your journeys through displacement. This book is a small tribute to your courage and determination to survive in the face of the tormented winds of history. My thanks go to Nyakuoth for her friendship and for standing up for her beliefs. I am grateful to Kuok for his dedication, openness and for sharing the journey in Nuerland. Your struggles to make a place for yourselves in the world will remind me of the beauty, strength and resis-tance of human beings.

Finally, my very special thanks go to my family. Mama, for your love and unending support of my 'insubordination' and zeal to explore. Grand-mom, for your belief in me and for always standing by me. Agata, for putting up with your wandering sister. Dad, for giving me a chance to pursue my dreams. Foremost, I thank Karim for sharing the journey of life with me; for his love, patience, friendship and understanding that inspired me and allowed me to get through this project. During its course, two new lives were born. Samir and Maxim, you have become my new inspiration and teachers of the wonders and beauties of life! I dedicate this book to my Nuer friends, my loved ones and especially the women of my life. You have made me who I am today.

Glossary of Nuer Terms

adab	propriety
beben cieng	coming home/returning home
buth	sharing of sacrificial meat
buul	dance around fire
ca ker/raan ca ker/ nei ti cike ker	I have awoken (translated as I am civilised/ modern)/ person who has seen light/people who have seen light, are 'modern' 'civilised'
ciang, pl. *cieng*	village, community, home, culture
ciek, man	woman-wife (fertile), women
ciek nuära	Nuer woman-wife, 'real Nuer woman'
cieng Kume	government laws, customs
cieng mi pai ben	a new custom/mode of life has arrived; used to describe 'modernity' and 'civilisation' by the Nuer
cieng nuära	Nuer village, community, culture
cuong, cung	right, rights
duang	old woman
dhool/dholi	boy/boys
diel	aristocrat
dit	elder
dual	fear
duel (dueel)	house(s), hut(s)
duël g∂arä	school
duëlkuoth	church
fuul	fried beans
gaar	initiation for boys, sacrificial marks on the forehead
g∂ar	education
gallaba	Arab
gεεr ro	change
guankuoth	earth priest
jääl	traveller, guest ,visitor
jiäke	bad
Jieng	Dinka
Jiom	wind

jiluäk kuoth	Christianity
jut	old unmarried girl
(ha)kume	from Arabic, government
kau	young wife without children
keaagh	unmarried concubine, spoilt girl, 'prostitute'
khaway	white foreigners (from Arabic)
koor	war
koor cieng	community war, intra-Nuer
koor kume	government war
kuäar	chief, leader, elder
kuong-yong	drunkards
kuoth Nhial	Divinity, God
luak (luaak)	cattle byre(s)
luth	respect
mac	gun
mai	drought
maar	kinship
mut	spear
nei ti cike ker	people who have awoken, seen light (metaphor for 'modern' people)
nei ti naath	people of the people, the Nuer
nei ti ngac ke ngoani	people who are knowledgeable, who have deeper insights into the workings of the world, who are 'modern'/'civilised'
nueer	pollution
nyabor	daughter of a white man (from Nuer)
nyakhaway	daughter of a foreigner (mixed of Nuer and Arabic)
nyal/nyieri	girl/girls/dauther/daughters
nyal duël gɘarä	schoolgirl
nyal nuära	Nuer girl
nyuuri piny	sitting on the ground/earth, meaning settled in
qahwa	coffee (in Arabic)
pöc	respect
pöth	small gift (wedding gift) for the bride's mother
raan	human (being), citizen, person
rek	town
ric	age set
riem	blood
rool Nuärä	Nuerland
ruok	cattle-based fine
ruon	year
rwil	movement from camp to village
thak	oxen
thok	language
tot	rain

tuac	leopard skin
tuoc	wedding dance
tut	bull
wa loorä	walk/go aimless, 'loose'
walwal	sorghum (porridge)
wa nhiam	moving forward; signifies development, progress
waraqa	paper
wic	responsible, wise
wec	cattle camp
wur/wutni	man/men
wur nuära	Nuer man
wur nuära pany	'real Nuer man'
yang	cattle
yiou	money
yodh	migration

The following English words and phrases have entered the Nuer language, and for some a Nuer word is used:

children rights	(*cung gaat*)
civilised	(*ca ker/raan ca ker/nei ti cike ker*)
culture	(*cieng*)
development	(*wa nhiam*)
gender	–
gender awareness	–
gender equality	–
human right/s	(*coung raan/cung naath*)
modern person/people	(*ca ker/raan ca ker/nei ti cike ker*)
progress	(*wa nhiam*)
woman right/women/ women's rights	(*cuong ciek/cung man*)

Acronyms

AGDM	Age, Gender and Diversity Mainstreaming
CPA	Comprehensive Peace Agreement
GoS	Government of Sudan
GoSS	Government of Southern Sudan
ICG	International Crisis Group
ICRC	International Committee of the Red Cross
IDPs	Internally Displaced Population/Persons
IGAD	Intergovernmental Authority on Development
IOM	International Organization for Migration
IRC	International Rescue Committee
JRS	Jesuit Refugee Services
LWF	Lutheran World Federations
MSF	Médecins Sans Frontières (Doctors Without Borders)
NCCK	National Council of Churches of Kenya
OCHA	United Nations Office of Coordination of Humanitarian Affairs
OLS	Operation Lifeline Sudan
OSIEA	Open Society Initiative for Eastern Africa
SAF	Sudanese Armed Forces
SGBV	Sexual and Gender Based Violence
SPLA/M	Sudanese People's Liberation Army/Movement
SSCCSE	Southern Sudan Centre for Census, Statistics and Evaluation
SSDF	South Sudan Defence Forces
SSIM	South Sudan Independence Movement
SSLS	South Sudan Law Society
SSRRC	South Sudan Relief and Rehabilitation Commission
UNHCR	United Nations High Commissioner for Refugees
UNDP	United Nations Development Programme
UNICEF	United Nations Children's Fund
UNMIS	United Nations Mission in Sudan
WFP	World Food Programme

I

Returnee Dilemmas: Dangerous Trousers and Threatening Mini-skirts

When, after years of displacement Nyakuol, Nyariek and Kuok arrived in Lɛr, a Nuer town in southern Sudan's Greater Upper Nile region,[1] they were faced with the dilemma of finding long-lost relatives, settling in and confronting local expectations of proper behaviour as 'real' Nuer women and men. Like many others displaced during the 22-year-long second civil war in southern Sudan (1983–2005),[2] they had spent most of their lives in refugee camps. In the aftermath of the 2005 peace agreement between the Sudanese government in Khartoum and the Sudan People's Liberation Army/Movement (SPLA/M) – the main southern Sudanese rebel organisation that had fought against northern domination since 1983 – they repatriated to post-war Nuerland. This place, which they barely remembered or knew, was supposed to become 'home'. Yet, due to their diverse experiences during wars and flight and the changes that had taken place in southern Sudan, they often felt estranged within their own homes.

Nyakuol, a widow in her forties, Kuok, a slim, boyish-looking young man in his late twenties, and Nyariek, an 18-year-old woman, stood out. Nyakuol wore a wig purchased in Nairobi and was always elegantly dressed in Kenyan-made clothes. Kuok wore a bright green shirt and well-ironed trousers, while Nyariek sported tight trousers and red hair extensions. This was unprecedented in Lɛr, where men mostly wore torn sports clothes or cast-off military uniforms and carried spears or guns, and women, hidden in their homesteads, had shaved heads and wore long dresses.

It was not only their appearance that distinguished Nyakuol, Kuok and Nyariek. Daughter of the first ever chief of Lɛr, Nyakuol had married a high-ranking SPLA officer at the age of fifteen and joined him in the military camps in Ethiopia in 1998. Her husband was one of the SPLA's founding members. She and her children moved frequently, following her husband, eventually finding refuge in Kenya's Kakuma refugee camp in 1994. After her husband died in what she described as 'unexplained

---

[1] Historically, Unity state of Greater Upper Nile region, where I carried out the fieldwork, has been referred to as Western Upper Nile, a term still used in post-independence South Sudan. I use the terms of Unity state and Western Upper Nile interchangeably in the text.
[2] The first civil war took place between 1963 and 1972.

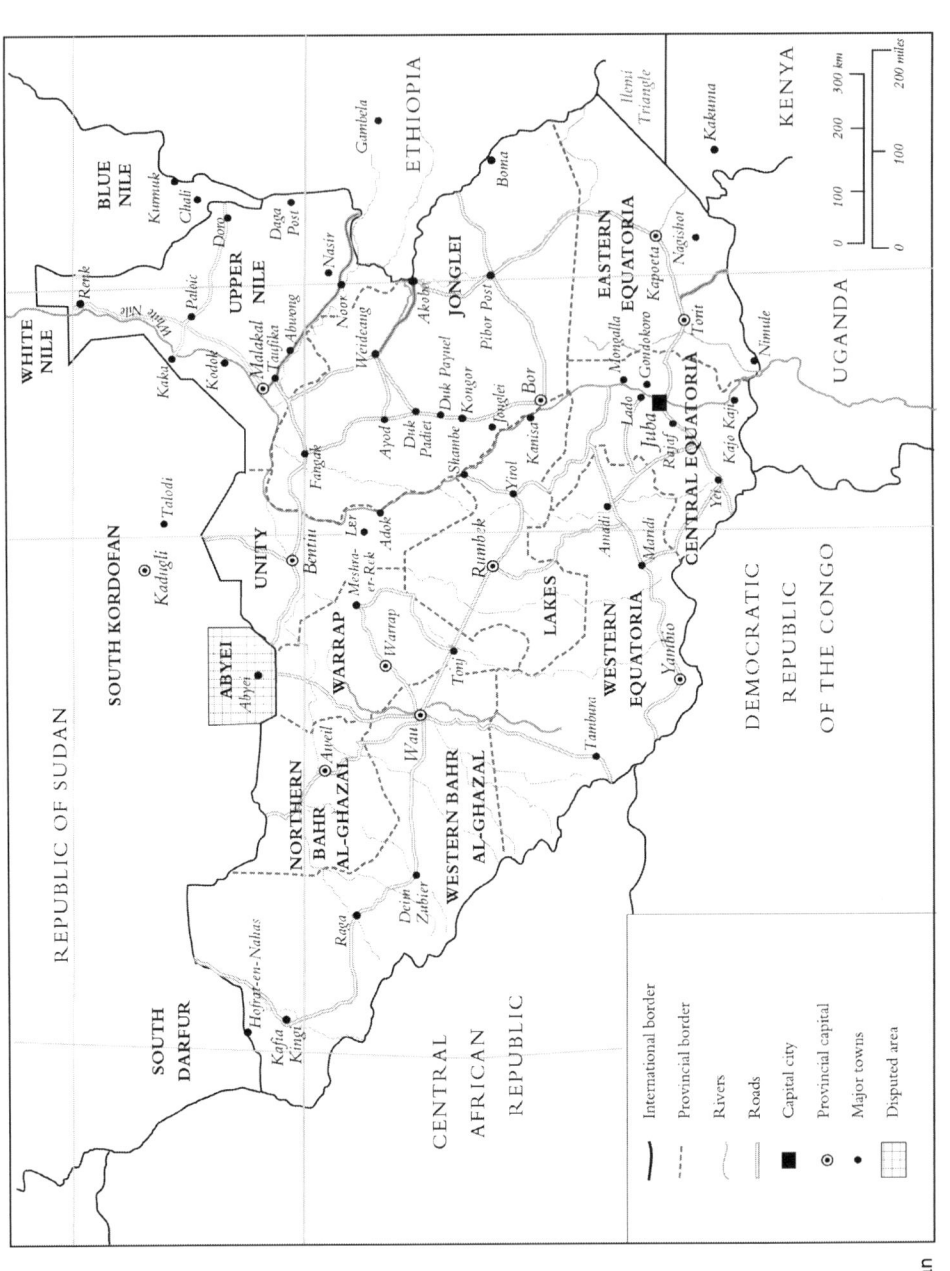

Map 1.1 South Sudan

circumstances', she stayed in Kenya so that her children could continue to access education and health services. Becoming a camp leader, she attended income-generating and gender-awareness training courses and started her own brewing business to sustain her family. In December 2006, she and most of her children to repatriated to Lɛr with the assistance of the Office of the United Nations High Commissioner for Refugees (UNHCR). 'I missed my family and wanted to see my home. Kakuma was not a home, and you can only be free in your land,' she told me.

Also born in a village near Lɛr, Kuok spent his childhood herding goats and cattle. However, in the late 1980s, when aged about seven, the SPLA recruited him and other local boys, sending them to training camps in Ethiopia. Thus began a 20-year journey of multiple displacements and family separation for Kuok. Following the expulsion of SPLA forces and Sudanese refugees from Ethiopia in 1991, Kuok, together with sixteen thousand other boy soldiers, walked through southern Sudan to Kenya, where he became a refugee. In Kakuma he spent fifteen years sharing a house with other boys. I met him there in August 2006 as he was graduating from the Teachers' Training College, the first higher education institute set up for refugees in Africa. In April 2007, Kuok decided to go to Lɛr to visit his home.

In the late 1990s, eight-year-old Nyariek was taken by her aunt, a niece of a Nuer SPLA commander, to Ethiopia in order to escape northern Sudanese military bombardments. In 2001, they moved to Kakuma, where, like Kuok, she went to school. Nyariek finished Grade Seven, a remarkable achievement for Nuer girls as they are largely denied education. In February 2007, her father, who had stayed behind in Sudan, asked her to come home. Worried about her safety, he wanted her to marry, a plan of which she was unaware.

I followed the lives of Nyakuol, Kuok and Nyariek first in the Kakuma refugee camp and then during their homecoming and settlement in Lɛr. Their narratives and those of other refugees and returnees who repatriated to southern Sudan form the foundation of this book.

During my stay in Lɛr there was continuous controversy around the social norms and dress codes of the returnees, which seemed to cause a moral panic among those who stayed behind. Matters came to a head in September 2008 when around thirty women and girls were rounded up and beaten by police in Juba, the southern Sudanese capital, for wearing tight trousers, mini-skirts and fitted t-shirts. Administrators condemned them for their 'indecent clothing' and adherence to a 'Nigger illicit culture' that was banned.[3] The cultural debate that erupted was not an isolated event, for across southern Sudan there has been much controversy over

---

[3] Several articles appeared in the local Sudanese press following the arrests in Juba (*Sudan Tribune*, 9 October and 15 October 2008) and on the SPLM website (11 October 2008). The Juba Commissioner's Local Order No. 4/2008 referred to a section of the Social and Cultural Affairs of Local Government Act 2003 that criminalised 'all bad behaviours, activities and imported illicit cultures'. The order specifically mentioned 'Niggers' in Juba County as potential targets, without explaining who qualified as a 'Nigger'.

the new cultures introduced by those returning from Khartoum, East Africa and elsewhere. As the *Sudan Tribune* noted, '[T]he incident[s] ha[ve] revealed the dilemma south Sudanese are in after the peace in the region' (15 October 2008). The author of this article called on politicians to speak out on social issues such as dress codes, abortion and racism. He warned that hip-hop was a form of cultural pollution for 'undeveloped cities like Juba', and distracted children from their studies:

> unregulated culture norms will destroy our social fabric. I believe special measures like Juba city ordinance[4] are needed to safe guard [sic] our social way of life and democracy... We are all for change (positive one) but spreading hazardous behaviours like seen in Juba should be treated as a crime, because if not brought into an end ultimately it will infest the entire nation.

The local morality initiative in Juba sparked debates around changes caused by the second civil war, the conflict-induced massive displacement in southern Sudan and the different social norms, relations and values brought in by those returning from years, or decades, spent in exile. The moral panic caused by baggy trousers and mini-skirts shows how gender, power and identity are key underlying issues in the contestation of social change embedded in the return of displaced populations. They are the axes of this book. Conceptualising conflict-induced displacement and emplacement as catalysts of social change, this book explores the transformation of gender and generational relations among the South Sudanese Nuer in the context of refugee return and settling-in in the aftermath of civil war.

GENDER AND GENERATIONAL RELATIONS IN FLUX

I define gender relations as the social, economic and political exchanges between women and men as well as within genders in different arenas such as the household, community and the state. They are dynamic, undergoing transformation according to the historical, political, economic, cultural and social environment. Gender is also intertwined with age as power relations change throughout the life-cycle. Acute to the voices and dilemmas expressed by Nuer women and men whom I encountered, I consider the production of particular changes in gender and generational relations as the result of the abrupt nature and traumatic gendered experiences of conflict-induced displacement.

Nuer gender and generational relations were already in transition before the second civil war, due to colonisation, emergence of markets and government chiefs, development of courts, and changing notions of bridewealth.[5] Yet the war-time experiences of women and men, which were often differentiated by age, place of origin, social class and length and trajectory, show a different set of complexities of social change

---

[4] Juba Commissioner's Local Order No. 4/2008.
[5] See Sharon E. Hutchinson, *Nuer Dilemmas, Coping with Money, War and the State* (Berkeley, CA, 1996).

and have shaped individuals and communities and affected gender and generational relations in fundamentally dissimilar ways.

In my analysis, women coming from privileged social groups (wives and daughters of chiefs, commanders, priests, government officials) were more likely to be displaced to refugee camps in Kenya or Ethiopia, where they would have access to education, training and limited-income generation activities. As a result, their social position increased vis-à-vis men and other women who had stayed behind or were displaced within Sudan. Moreover, due to their social and physical mobility, young men had relatively easier access to refugee camps than their elders and young women. In the refugee camps, they gained a higher social status through education, their conversion to Christianity and changing notions of masculinity, seniority and leadership, hence challenging the position of their (male) elders.

Those who had been displaced within Sudan, and especially to Khartoum, were faced with a substantially different context. Harsh living conditions in the squatter camps around Khartoum provided fewer opportunities for education and work. Confrontation with Islamic codes and norms for mostly Christian southern Sudanese Nuer shaped gender relations in increasingly more conservative ways. Such displacement for women was thus less emancipating than for their sisters, mothers, and co-wives who were in Kenya or Ethiopia. The subsequent coming together of displaced populations from the variety of exile contexts, and their encounters with those who had stayed behind, exposes the tensions in the visions of (re)making of Nuer community and the South Sudanese nation.

In this book, I ask whether war and displacement can have empowering and emancipating impacts, questioning gender asymmetries existing within societies. How does being in flux between war, prolonged displacement – sometimes for decades – belonging, not belonging and returning to a supposed 'home' affect people's lives and the practice and negotiation of gender relations? Here, 'in flux' refers not only to being out of place from one's own environment due to war, but also to transforming cultural practices in refugee camps and after return. A closer look at the experiences of displacement and emplacement after return reveals how women and men continuously negotiate and reshape their gender identities and generational relations in and between the different settings. In particular, I analyse how Nuer women and men, old and young, navigated the social conditions of war and violence and used their agency to adjust, adapt and negotiate their place in exile and after their return home.

As the narratives and experiences of the women and men encountered demonstrate, during violent civil conflicts masculine and feminine identities change in multiple ways. Gender asymmetrical relations are challenged differently in conflict-zones, refugee camps and in the processes of emplacement and nation-building after return. I argue that women's subordination was partially reversed as a result of the Sudanese civil wars. Consequently, multiple forms of gender identities emerged showing creative ways in which women and men cope with war-time displacement, beyond being either only victims or perpetrators of violence. In post-war South Sudan, militarised forms of masculinities and violence-affected femininities are juxtaposed with the educated, pro-women men and empowered, educated women who emerged as a result of to their experiences in refugee camps. While there are fewer opportunities for women to reverse their subordination upon return to South Sudan, they actively contest, resist and (re)negotiate old and new hegemonies of male privilege. Returnee women from Kakuma continue to carve out a place for greater autonomy for themselves by creating autonomous households.

This book represents a nuanced analysis of women's and men's agency when faced with traumatic experiences of war and displacement. There is a need to go beyond the simplified view of women as victims of wars and displacement. By bringing in the pre-war historical perspective, it underscores the constant motion of gender relations with the younger men, especially those who took part in military struggle, who continue to gain in power and privilege at the expense of younger women and elders.

GENDERED DISPLACEMENT: WHY DOES IT MATTER?

Why is such focus important? Forced displacement, exile and uprootedness due to conflict, natural disasters, so-called development and climate change are conditions that mark the lives of millions of people throughout the world. In 2009, 43.3 million people were forcibly displaced worldwide, the highest number of people uprooted by conflict and persecution since the mid-1990s.[6] In that year, in Pakistan alone, three million people became displaced due to conflict within a few months. New forms of displacement due to natural disasters such as the January 2011 tsunami in Japan, the 2010 Haitian earthquake and the 2004 Indian Ocean tsunami have prompted the international community to consider the emergence of 'ecological refugees'. Yet the focus on war-time displacement is of particular importance due to the urgency and violent affects of wars that tear families and communities apart, and the power politics of international humanitarian enterprises to which displaced women and men are subjected.

Violent displacement involves people living on the edge of urban slums or in refugee camps. Such settings create particular problems where the deserving poor are faced with the gendering effects of humanitarian assistance. For years, they live outside of state protection, in a state of suspension. Such drastic displacement affects (albeit differently) women and men, old and young, and changes their lives dramatically. The visions for the future and the imagined homes that women and men long for are shaped according to their experiences in the specific framework of refugee camps. In recent years, the forced mobility of populations, whether in the context of displacement or return, has become more prev-

---

[6] UNHCR policy on refugee protection and solutions in urban areas, UNHCR (2009).

alent. There needs to be careful considerations of the role of the humanitarian community in creating the refugee subjects and shaping their visions of return and long-term nation-building. Part of my focus here is on the particularities of NGO and UN humanitarianism and their long-term impact on returnees' efforts to (re)create a community and a nation.

On 9 July 2011, South Sudan became the newest independent nation. It is thus timely to consider the gendered dimension of the state and society formation in the aftermath of conflict and displacement. Sudan gained its independence from Egypt in 1956, as part of the British–Egyptian condominium. It has been at war almost continually since 1963, with numerous periods of displacement affecting the population.[7] The political and civil turmoil that re-erupted in southern Sudan in 1983 due to conflict between the Khartoum government and southern rebels claimed an estimated two million lives and resulted in one of world's largest ever displacements. Over five million people were internally displaced and another estimated five hundred thousand sought refuge in neighbouring countries.[8] In January 2005, the signing of a peace agreement between the government in Khartoum and the SPLA enabled the possible return of refugees and internally displaced persons (IDPs) to South Sudan, both spontaneous and organised by international organisations and the government.

While this book focuses mainly on the example of Lɛr as a microscope of return dilemmas, issues raised in this book are also relevant to other parts of South Sudan, Sudan and the African continent. In South Sudan, Juba experienced a large influx of returning and migrating populations who had been struggling to make a place for themselves while battling some of the prevailing post-war gender norms. The woman-as-a-nation discourse still prevails in South Sudan, and among the South Sudanese diaspora, thus creating major challenges for change in gender relations.[9] Other major urban settings in the South, such as Bor, Rumbek and Malakal, have faced similar problems concerning returnees and the local population. K.L. Ringera also mentions the issues of exclusion of women from peace-building and settlement processes.[10] Questions around return and settling-in processes have been raised by the large number of returning southern Sudanese from the North and Khartoum. Some key problems relate to access to land, as this vital resource has proved to be a major dynamic in post-conflict situations.[11]

[7] See Chapter 2 and John Ryle, Baldo Willing and Madut Jok, *The Sudan Handbook* (James Currey, 2011).
[8] International Crisis Group, *God, Oil and Country, Changing the Logic of War in Sudan* (Brussels, 2002).
[9] See Caroline Faria, 'Contesting Miss Sudan: Gender and Nation Building in Diasporic Discourse', *International Feminist Journal of Politics*, 2010, Vol. 2, pp. 222–43; L.G. Riaka, 'Miss Malaika is a Threat to Southern Sudanese Cultures', *Sudan Tribune*, 7 December 2007, http://www.sudantribune.com/spip.php?
[10] K.L. Ringera, 'Excluded Voices: Grassroots Women and Peacebuilding in Southern Sudan', PhD thesis, Department of Human Communication Studies, University of Denver, 2007.
[11] See Sara Pantuliano, *Uncharted Territory: Land, Conflict and Humanitarian*

The narratives of Nyakuol, Kuok and Nyariek, as well as other South Sudanese women and men, reveal gender and generational differences in the experiences and memories of forced displacement and emplacement. Although, since the 1970s, there has been increased attention paid to women's experiences of migration, war and displacement, the gender and generational dynamics remain under-researched. The dominant view is that the focus is 'on refugees who happen to be women rather than on women and men who happen to be refugees'.[12] With my strong commitment to feminist transformative politics, gender and generational analysis of displacement, the refugee experience and emplacement after refugee return was the departure point of my research and involved looking at 'how both men and women [young and old] (re)construct social relations and renegotiate gender identities and relations in the process of coping with forced migration',[13] both in the place of displacement and post-return emplacement. Despite increased attention being paid to the effects of displacement and migration on women, they are still largely perceived as victims rather than active agents.

To rectify this, the analyses of Nyakuol, Kuok, Nyariek's and many other Nuer women and men's narratives, experiences, practices and memories of violence and displacement focus on how forced displacement affects gender and intergenerational power structures embedded in the social institutions of marriage, gender identity and division of labour and how gender relations are being (re)negotiated upon the return of refugees. These narratives point to a set of very specific transformations in gender and generational relations. These include the emergence of diversified masculinities as a result of war-time militarisation, emerging women's autonomous households, women's access to income through education and paid work, changes in marriage and divorce practices, changes in livelihoods, control over resources and discourse around rights. I do not attempt to simply document the latter, but rather show how Nuer women and men, young and old are coping with the transformative nature of these events in refugee camps and after return.

HISTORICAL AND FEMINIST ETHNOGRAPHY ACROSS PLACES AND SPACES

My inquiry into gendered experiences of war, displacement and post-return settlement was conducted among the Nuer communities of

(cont.) *Action* (Rugby, 2009) and Samir Elharaway and Sara Pantuliano, 'Land Issues in Post-Conflict Return and Recovery' in J. Unruh and R. Williams (eds) *Land and Post-Conflict Peacebuilding* (London, 2013) pp. 115–20.

[12] Doreen Indra, *Engendering Forced Migration: Theory and Practice* (New York, 1999), p. 224.

[13] Roos Willems, 'Embedding the Refugee Experience: Forced Migration and Social Networks in Dar Es Salaam, Tanzania', PhD thesis, University of Florida, Miami, 2003, p. 19.

Western Upper Nile. The Nuer people are, after the Dinka, the largest ethnic group in South Sudan and one of the most celebrated peoples in anthropology. Since my aim was to provide a historic account for the changes and continuities in gender relations, I initially thought that previous anthropological writings about the Nuer communities (as controversial and provocative as they might have been due to their close links to the colonial powers and interests at the time, see, for example, Evans-Pritchard's seminal work, among others[14]) would provide me a historical anchor for studying long-term social transformations. However, these insights about Nuer lives, institutional and social organisation, livelihood strategies, religious beliefs, kinship and marriage have to be put in a historical and political specific perspective. At times, they had little to do with the people whose lives I was interested in understanding. As Rogaia Abu-Sharaff argues, 'in the Sudan there is no static "before", no golden era of peace and stability that was suddenly interrupted by armed conflict, as many analyses of the impact of war on civilian populations assumes'.[15] Indeed, it is rather the certainty of upheaval, conflicts, and numerous and multiple displacements that marked the lives of the communities and individuals that I was trying to understand.

Sharon Hutchinson's writings provided some of the most crucial insights into the continuous change instigated by wars. In the 1980s and 1990s, she examined the changing nature of Nuer gender relations as a result of war, the emerging market economy and the transformative influence of the state. Her historical ethnography, *Nuer Dilemmas: Coping with Money, War, and the State* (1996), demonstrates how myriad global and local forms of power and knowledge are empirically intertwined in the everyday experiences of the Nuer communities. Piecing together these historical accounts and combining them with my in-depth interviews with men and women elders in Kenya and southern Sudan gave me a glimpse into the ever-changing and fluctuating gender and generational relations and identities.

This book captures a particular moment in the lives of the contemporary Nuer communities, one that is marked by rapid social transformation resulting from wars, encounters with particular forms of modernity in Kakuma forged by UN humanitarianism, massive refugee repatriation and the gradual creation of a southern Sudanese state in the aftermath of the Comprehensive Peace Agreement (CPA). These transformations are situated against a backdrop of globalisation and changing notions of modernities in Africa.[16] In this way, it contributes to Sudanese, African and forced displacement scholarship by providing a gender and generational perspective on the effects of conflict-induced displacement.

---

[14] Edward E. Evans-Pritchard, *The Nuer: A Description of the Modes of Livelihood and Political Institutions of a Nilotic People* (Oxford, 1940); *Kinship and Marriage among the Nuer* (Oxford, 1951); and *Nuer Religion* (Oxford, 1956).
[15] Rogaia Abu-Sharaff (2009), p. 3.
[16] See Dorothy L. Hodgson and Sherry McCurdy (eds) *"Wicked" Women and the Reconfiguration of Gender in Africa* (Portsmouth, NH, 2001).

Fieldwork and methods

My 'after-fire' fieldwork was carried out between April 2006 and September 2007, in the wake of decades of conflict in southern Sudan. The study is situated in feminist anthropology, which emphasises difference as its starting point,[17] and the study of gender in its social, political, economic and cultural construction and practice. This commitment to a transformative feminist politics shaped my approach to formulating research questions, research focus, fieldwork, data analysis and writing-up. It also resulted in some of the ethical, personal, academic and political feminist dilemmas in fieldwork revolving around power and the position of the researcher described by Diane Wolf and Sondra Hale.[18] I chose to follow feminist methodologies because of their central commitment to reflexivity and making biases and stands on issues visible and explicit.[19] Working in volatile conditions of the grey area between war and peace, among conflict-ridden communities and people whose lives have been shaped by violence and displacement, required constant questioning of my own positionality. Feminist methodologies allowed me to bring my own preconceptions and interpretations to the subject under study, resulting in the production of 'partial truths' rather than one overarching hegemonic interpretation.[20]

In order to capture the displaced and fragmented trajectories of the lives of the people whom I encountered and understand the changing practice of gender and generational relations, I followed their lives as refugees in Kakuma camp in northern Kenya and then in southern Sudan. I accompanied Nuer returnees to Lɛr, which is inhabited by the Dok Nuer in Unity state of the Greater Upper Nile,[21] studying and observing how

---

[17] See, for example, Henrietta Moore, *A Passion for Difference. Essays in Anthropology and Gender* (London, 1994); Marilyn Strathern, *The Gender of the Gift* (Berkeley, CA, 1988); and Donna Haraway, 'A Manifesto for Cyborgs: Science, Technology, Socialist Feminism in the 1980s', *Socialist Review*, Vol. 80, pp. 65–107.

[18] Diane L. Wolf, 'Situating Feminist Dilemmas in Fieldwork', in D.L. Wolf (ed.), *Feminist Dilemmas in Fieldwork* (Boulder, CO, 1996); Sondra Hale, 'Feminist Method, Process and Self-Criticism: Interviewing Sudanese Women', in S. Berger Gluck and D. Patai (eds), *Women's Words*, (New York, 1991), pp. 121–36.

[19] Sandra Harding (ed.) *Feminism and Methodology* (Bloomington, IN, 1987); Wolf, 'Situating Dilemmas in Fieldwork'.

[20] See Chandra T. Mohanty, 'Categories of Struggle: Third World Women and the Politics of Feminism', *The Third World Women and the Politics of Feminism*, C.T. Mohanty, A. Russo and L. Torres (eds) (Bloomington, 1991); and Liz Stanley and Sue Wise, *Breaking out again: Feminist Ontology and Epistemology* (London, 1993).

[21] The Nuer people are divided into tribes and *cieng*, or sections (primary and secondary, see Evans-Pritchard, *The Nuer*). I focus mainly on the impact of forced displacement and return among the western Nuer, especially the Dok, Jagei and Nyuong groupings. The dominant section or tribe of Lɛr is Dok or Adok, subdivided into seven *cieng*. Unity (Arabic: الوحدة, transliterated: al-Wahda), with Bentiu as its capital, was one of the 26 *wilayat* or states of Sudan. It now represents one of the ten states in South Sudan which are located within three regions: Equatoria, Bahr Ghazal, and Greater Upper Nile. An area of 35,956 km², in 2000 it had approximately 175,000 inhabitants, mostly Nuer, with a Dinka minority. It has nine counties – comprising Mayom, Rubkona, Parieng, Lɛr, Guit, Koch, Abiemnhom,

the returning displaced pieced their lives together (see Map 1.1). Thus, this book is about journeys, survival, (re)creation and change, transformations and continuities. To this extent, what follows is an ethnography of displacement and emplacement.

Displacement, emplacement and change

In order to understand the transformations of the social relations of the Nuer people, it is necessary to briefly present their social organisation. Much of the social organisation suggested by Evans-Pritchard was transformed throughout the twentieth century, a result of colonialism, education, encroaching of government and Christianity. The recent conflicts further transformed Nuer social structures, although some of the terms are still relevant today and give us an insight into the meanings attached to social transformations as seen by the Nuer people themselves. Four terms are central: *buth, maar, thok duel* and *cieng. Buth* (the sharing of sacrificial meat) is translated by Evans-Pritchard as relations that link lineage groups through ties of agnation.[22] *Maar*, or *mar* (literally means 'my mother'), signifies relations that link individuals through ties of marriage and bilateral kinship.[23] *Thok mac* – 'the doorway to the hearth' or 'the entrance to the hut' (*thok duel*) – is referred to by Evans-Pritchard as lineage.[24] My respondents also translated this as 'clan'. *Cieng*, literally meaning 'home' or 'community',[25] is translated as a tribal territorial section, i.e., 'homestead, hamlet, village and tribal sections of various dimensions'.[26] At times, however, it was translated and used by my respondents as 'culture'.[27] Nuer images of themselves as distinct people (*nei ti naath*) with a unique language (*thok*) and culture (*ciaŋ*, pl. *cieŋ*) became even stronger in the context of civil wars and life in refugee camps.

(cont.) Mayendit and Panyiajiar – and is the location of some rich oil fields.

[22] Evans-Pritchard, *The Nuer*, pp. 193–4.

[23] Ibid.

[24] Ibid., p. 195.

[25] J. Kiggen, *Nuer English Dictionary* (London, 1948).

[26] Evans-Pritchard, *The Nuer*, p. 136.

[27] Nuer acephalous (or 'stateless') organisation was based on kinship and residency affiliations affirmed through mutual obligations 'to combine in warfare against outsiders and acknowledge the rights of their members to compensation for injury' (ibid). They were divided into eleven loose major territorially bound groupings: Bul, Leek [Leeγ], western Jikany [Jikäny ciëŋ], Nyuong [Nyuoŋ], Dok, Jagei [Jagɛi], Gaawär, Thiäng [Thiäŋ], Lak [Laak], Lou and eastern Jikany Nuer [Jikäny door]. Hutchinson shows some of the linguistic, cultural, social, ecological and political differences between the eastern and the western Nuer (*Nuer Dilemmas*, p. 37). My own research among the eastern and western Nuer refugees in Kakuma concurs with Hutchinson's observations that contemporary easterners see themselves as more open and adaptable, and hence, in their words, more 'modern' than their western cousins. The eastern and western Nuer respondents in Kakuma stressed that the Nuer originated from the west, and in the nineteenth century migrated to the east. The western Nuer, they argued, are the 'real Nuer', whereas the easterners 'got mixed up with Dinka and Anuak'.

A particular problem from the outset of my research was the difficulty of conceptualising change or *gɛɛr ro* (see below) and making it methodologically meaningful in the contexts of the disjunctions and ruptures due to conflict, displacement and emplacement after return. I also faced difficulties in distinguishing between general social change and change due to displacement and conflict. This was especially difficult given my core interest in often-invisible negotiations and practices of gender relations. I decided that I could only begin to understand some of the transformations while being embedded in two places: a place of displacement and a place of emplacement after return.

Lɛr, a place in flux, illustrated the ongoing dilemmas facing South Sudanese emerging from long-term conflict. This place was a melting pot of those who had been displaced to different parts of Sudan and across its borders and who had undergone different experiences during the war. Processes of homecoming and settling in either involved making a foreign space (for those who had settled elsewhere or who had been born in exile) or a war-changed familiar space into a familial and comfortable environment. Women and men described emplacement as *nyuuri piny*, which literally means sitting on the ground/earth. It is a metaphor for a process of settling-in and becoming part of a community.

Emplacement in Lɛr was performed through a myriad of activities such as accessing land, building a house, farming, finding a job, cooking, reconnecting with and visiting friends and relatives, and taking part in community events. In addition, emplacement was linked to the practice, negotiation and (re)production of gender relations, including starting a marriage process. It also entailed being and becoming (again) a Nuer, a congruent identity that linked the personal experiences of 'place' and *cieng* to wider gendered and generational social and communal obligations, rights and networks of mutual support. Emplacement of the Nuer communities involved both material and moral aspects of practice, including the negotiation, practice and (re)construction of social, economic and cultural activities and social, especially gender, relations. In this way, I see emplacement as a dialectic and negotiation between the 'stayees' and the displaced that is influenced by the latter's capacities to put themselves and others into a place and the power relations that unequally distribute this capacity.[28] As such, emplacement is inevitably intertwined with changes in social relations.

Locations and my positionalities: Kakuma and Lɛr

On 17 April 2006, after landing in Nairobi, I waited in a long queue of khaki-clad tourists ready for their safari adventure in the Masaai Mara plains. I felt rather out of place. Greeting me in a British accent, the immigration officer asked if I was coming to see animals. 'No,' I replied, somewhat perplexed. 'I am a student and will be doing research in the refugee camp in Kakuma. Later, I will follow Sudanese refugees returning to southern Sudan and will do my research there.' 'Oh, so you are with

[28] See Stef Jansen and Löfving, *Struggles for Home: Violence, Hope and the Movement of People* (Berghan Books, 2009), p. 13.

the UN, the humanitarian business, right? You are coming to see the refugees'. Suddenly, I became a refugee tourist, rather than somebody on safari – clearly the two known categories of visitors in a country with many animals and refugees.

Eight months later, on a flight to the South Sudanese capital Juba, I found myself one of the few female passengers. The men represented different aspects of the humanitarian post-war world: South African de-miners, UN peacekeepers, representatives of donor and aid agencies and South Sudanese politicians. Again, immigration officials could not understand the purpose of my visit and quickly categorised me as a humanitarian worker. These assumptions both in Kenya and in South Sudan were to dog me throughout my fieldwork.

Both Kakuma and southern Sudan challenge the notion of 'the field' as unitary and complete.[29] They are complex due to the interaction of many worlds – the tourist, humanitarian and oil industries, the host and the refugee communities in Kakuma, and the stayee and returnee worlds in Sudan. The idiosyncrasies of the field became clear to me on my first day in the region.

An important aspect that influenced my access was my own positionality as researcher, which is often presented as the 'insider/outsider' dilemma.[30] Before embarking on the fieldwork research, I was conscious that as a young, white, female European, my position in the research process exemplified for many South Sudananese the world of humanitarian assistance and thus might obscure my understanding of the nuanced local relations. However, positionalities as knowledge are both multiple and mobile, relational and context-specific. As I moved from one setting to another, my core as a white woman remained static, but axes of difference (gender, age, race and social status) were reinterpreted by those whom I encountered depending on the context and environment.

Kakuma proved a highly challenging place to establish my credibility as a researcher. Although sited within Kenya, the camp is overseen by the UNHCR, managed by the Lutheran World Federation (LWF) and serviced by a number of international NGOs and missionaries. It has also been a focus of numerous studies and hosts many international and Kenyan NGOs and missionary groups, complicating the establishment of my own position. In this highly politicised and internationalised environment that was showing signs of research fatigue,[31] it was crucial to establish my credibility. I often had to manoeuvre between the different worlds of the aid workers, missionaries, the local population and the refugees. I was also in the middle of the institutional power politics in the camp (see

[29] See Akhil Gupta and James Ferguson (eds), *Culture, Power, Place: Explorations in Critical Anthropology* (Durham, NJ, 1997).

[30] See Jayati Lal, 'Situating Locations: The Politics of Self, Identity, and "Other" in Living and Writing the Text', in D.L. Wolf (ed.), *Feminist Dilemmas in Fieldwork* (Boulder, CO, 1996); Daphne Patai, 'US Academics and Third World Women: Is Ethical Research Possible?', in S. Berger Gluck and D. Patai (eds) *Women's Words: The Feminist Practice of Oral History* (New York, 1991), pp. 137–53.

[31] Many refugees complained about the number of researchers, NGO and UN workers coming to gather information and never sharing their findings.

Chapter 3), and I often felt isolated, lonely and depressed after having witnessed horrifying living conditions, violence and abuse of rights.

In order to disassociate myself from the aid industry's highly politicised tensions and acquire a better understanding of refugees' lives, I turned down accommodation offers from UNHCR and some NGOs. Instead, I stayed at a local guesthouse[32] on the outskirts of Kakuma, at the far end of the refugee camp. Staying there gave me an opportunity to learn more about the local host Turkana population and the impact of the refugee presence on their lives.[33] Other examples of my manoeuvring included maintaining good relations through socialising with, and seeking input from, NGO workers by maintaining physical distance from the NGO compound and by spending most of my time in refugees' houses.

Despite my attempts to distance myself from international humanitarians, many refugees had high expectations of being rewarded for sharing information. Thok, a research assistant in Kakuma and himself a young Nuer man, explained to me: 'They see you as a white person who is here to help others. That's why they are also very interested in talking to you because they think you came with a mission to help.' My gender, race, social status, class and age were all determinants of how I was perceived by refugees and at the same time influenced the type of information that they would share. Since some refugees saw me in the camp with NGO gender workers, they assumed that I was working for the well-known gender-equality programme (see Chapter 3). Some women started their stories with complaints about domestic violence and abuse committed by their husbands and male relatives, hoping that this would enhance prospects of resettlement to western countries. I continuously explained my position and research interests to research participants and minimised contact with the humanitarian workers in order to reinforce my credibility.

Southern Sudan proved to be similarly divided. With a large contingent of foreign, mostly European and American, humanitarian and development workers, as a white woman I was once again initially perceived as part of the humanitarian enterprise. This was understandable, given my dependence on securing access to my research site from international organisations with resources and infrastructure. I had to rely on the World Food Programme (WFP) to board the only aircraft regularly flying to remote areas in southern Sudan. I occasionally used the facilities of one of the few NGOs present in the area in order to check my email, type notes, get a ride to town, participate in some of their community training workshops and share a meal. Thus, I often had to manoeuvre between

---

[32] UNHCR and LWF cited 'high insecurity in the camp' as grounds for rejecting my request to live in the refugee camp.

[33] The focus of the aid organisations and researchers on refugees, with almost complete neglect of the situation of the local population despite the fact they are among the most impoverished and marginalised groups in Kenya, made me question my own moral stance. By living in the guesthouse I was at least able to interact with local population.

being perceived as an aid worker, a missionary, a politician bearing aid and a neighbour.

My concern was how to get beyond the label of *nyakhaway* (from Arabic – the daughter of a foreigner or a white man) or *nyabor* (in Nuer – the daughter of a white man), terms the local population used when referring to me. I decided that the only way to arrive at some understanding of community life and the experiences of return and settling-in of refugees was to follow some of the families from the refugee camp in Kenya on their journey back to Sudan and to live among the population. In Lɛr, I stayed with one of the families whom I befriended through my connections from Kakuma and built a small *duël* (a mud and grass hut) on their land. I lived with a wife of a young man and their four children. Her husband, Gatchang, lived with his second wife in Rubkona, about a four-hour drive away. As I started building my house and learning the Nuer language, I quickly became known as *ciek Gatchang* – the wife/woman of my host. Even Nyakuma, my hostess, referred to me as her 'co-wife', *nyakhda* (the daughter of jealousy).

How do we know what we know?
This book is based on participation and observation, in-depth interviews, life (hi)stories of individuals and families, semi-structured interviews, court cases, two surveys and a review of secondary materials and arrives at an in-depth understanding of changes in gender and generational relations and social order. In addition, I used video and photography as supporting tools. However, the best method of gathering information was not through questioning but rather through conversation. I often engaged in vivid conversations with women and men, friends, acquaintances, or almost anyone whom I met on the road during my daily ventures out in the community. I posed controversial questions, expressing my surprise or disagreement in order to learn more about the views of the people with whom I was sharing my life. In a feminist fashion, and against the positivist notions of 'scientific distancing from the object of research',[34] through sharing my own stories and living with a host family in Lɛr I attempted to minimise the distance between the researcher and the researched.

I also learned a lot about gender practices and relations through conversations about my own culture, as many people I encountered were curious about marriage practices and the position of girls, women and men in my own society. It was through dialogue that I attempted to arrive at 'negotiated truths',[35] which involved both equalising power relations between myself as a researcher and those whose narratives I was trying to capture, as well as acknowledging bias.

Family life stories allowed for an in-depth inquiry into the complexities of people's personal trajectories and changes in social relations.

[34] Adler and Adler cited in Uwe Flick, *An Introduction of Qualitative Research* (London, 2002).
[35] Barry P. Michrina and Cherylanne Richards, *Person to Person: Fieldwork, Dialogue, and the Hermeneutic Method* (Albany, NY, 1996), p. 29.

During the war, family members were dispersed throughout the region and hence subjected to different experiences which in turn influenced the strategies and experiences of homecoming and emplacement in the context of family (re)unification. I followed seventeen families, mapping their life stories from refugee camps in Kenya to settling in Lɛr. I interviewed and documented the experiences of women, girls, boys and men from different age groups who had been displaced or had stayed behind. I found that gathering family life stories was useful both in identifying moments of personal change and how views on appropriate gender practices have evolved due to experiences of war, displacement and return. It also helped me to understand the complexity of people's experiences as individuals and family and community members. This was, however, a challenging method due to the high mobility of Nuer communities.

Narrative methods have been used in forced migration research as useful tools to examine 'how people themselves as "experiencing subjects", make sense out of violence and turbulent change'.[36] Personal accounts give a more in-depth and diversified image of the over-generalised refugee experience. The life stories method in refugee settings is particularly suitable to researching marginalised populations and has proved very useful in illuminating views of, and providing space for refugees' voices.[37] Life (hi) story research allowed me to untangle some of the historical elements of identity, which is particularly important in terms of gender identity and ideology constructions. The method also created space for personal narratives and reflection on past experiences, including traumatic experiences of war, family separation and death, and helps to situate the current transformation of gender relations in a wider historical framework.

Gaining respondents' trust is not only about building rapport, breaking the ice and confounding prejudices; it is as much about breaking down one's own prejudice and the barrier of fear and misunderstanding and learning about oneself. As the proud and secluded Nuer women intimidated me at the beginning, the challenge for me was to reach out to them and try to understand their own positions. I did this by carrying out the same daily activities of the women and girls and by honouring elder women and including their voices in the stories. In this way, I became more of a 'woman' and less of a *nyakhaway*. I also made it clear to women that I wanted to learn from them and that I was interested in women's views on life. At the end, without jeopardising my close friendships and wide access to male respondents, I not only broke the ice, but also became known in Lɛr as a supporter of women and girls. I was regularly visited by female neighbours and acquaintances who either came for a chat or advice, or to share intimate stories and jokes. Some discretely

[36] Marita Eastmond 'Transnational Returns and Reconstruction in Post-war Bosnia and Herzegovina', *International Migration*, 2006, Vol. 44, pp. 141–66.

[37] Ibid.; Julia Powles, 'Life History and Personal Narrative: Theoretical and Methodological Issues Relevant to Research and Evaluation in Refugee Contexts', *New Issues in Refugee Research Working Paper* 106 (UNHCR Geneva, 2004); Halleh Ghorashi, 'Giving Silence a Chance: The Importance of Life Stories for Research on Refugees', *Journal of Refugee Studies*, 2008, Vol. 21.

asked for help with abortion or escaping an arranged marriage. As with other women researchers, by playing my gender card and doing what the local women did, I was able to establish close and intimate relations.

By being engaged in local issues, sharing people's concerns, participating in decision-making and contributing to the family budget, I got a glimpse into the life of the community and individuals among whom I lived. My presence was recognised by a local young woman, Nyapiliny, who established a special friendship with me through offering me a cow, a Nuer custom. Even so, I managed to become more 'part of' rather than 'apart from' the community in but a few instances, and often only when the research participants saw the benefits of having me around. Mostly, I remained an outsider, not only due to my ethnic and racial background, but also because of my social status, class and ability to transgress the gender- and age-separated worlds of the Nuer communities. I continued to study their lives from outside, but as an outsider and someone from a different cultural background, I created an opportunity for some to share experiences and views that they would not normally be able to discuss with family and friends.

The narratives of displacement and emplacement surfaced in a variety of contexts, offered by familiar respondents and by strangers. They emerged in the distribution centre in Kakuma, during school breaks, in the market over coffee, in local buses and on lorries, in dugout canoes or on days-long walks, while starting a fire, preparing an evening meal, during cultivation, at burials, at weddings and after a Sunday prayer. As in the case of Malkki's research among Burundian refugees in Tanzania,[38] these conversations about different aspects of lives helped to contextualise and put wider reflections and findings in a historical context.

One of my many ethical considerations was how my writing would do justice to the lives of those who had survived the experience of traumatic conflict. I felt, and continue to feel, that I have a duty to write their stories for others to understand the meaning of war and displacement as lived experiences. Yet how do I write about these gendered experiences without taking away the rupture and profound suffering from people's stories? How can I do justice through my writings to lives fractured and fragmented by war, displacement, family separation, death and violence? I often found myself unable to find the words to accurately convey the stories. This is the biggest ethical dilemma that I face, not only as a researcher, but also as a person.

Ethnography is a form of representation and what follows is a partial story. Despite my endeavour to follow narratives of Nuer women and men and minimise the power imbalance between the researcher and the research participants, I had to make often uncomfortable choices about which stories to tell. This was particularly difficult when analysing the fragmented stories of families separated during the wars. Often, these experiences were marked by silences and interruptions, not only due to

---

[38] Liisa H. Malkki, *Purity and Exile: Violence, Memory, and National Cosmology among Hutu Refugees in Tanzania* (Chicago, 1995).

constant and abrupt movement resulting from the ensuing violence and insecurity, but more importantly as a result of death that has constantly accompanied the lives of people whom I encountered for the past two and a half decades. The storytelling, and what follows – a re-creation of people's lives and experiences during conflict, flight and 'return' – is not simply a matter of creating either personal or social meanings. Here, I concur with Michael Jackson's interpretation of Hannah Arendt's view of the politics of storytelling, where 'the multiplicity of private and public interests' are intertwined and simultaneously at play, where the story becomes an aspect of 'the subjective in-between'.[39] Cautioned by their attention to the violent and hegemonic nature of storytelling and the role of the researcher who has the power to decide which stories to reveal, I remain conscious that apart from the stories shared with me and told here, there are many that lingered and linger in the shadows.

GENDER RELATIONS IN DISPLACEMENT AND EMPLACEMENT

Much of the literature on gender analyses women's subordination in isolation from men, thus ignoring the relational nature of gender. I agree with Ann Whitehead that we 'cannot start from the viewpoint that the problem is women, but rather men and women, and more specifically the socially constituted relations between them'.[40] This book is *not* about women, but about how gender is a constraining social concept for both women and men, boys and girls. It determines relations not only between, but also among, the same sex.

I am interested in the everyday practice and (re)negotiation of gender relations embedded in gender identities, marriage process and household relations. I conceptualise gender as the analysis of social relations. This framework allows for examining change, transformation and continuity of gender relations by taking a holistic approach and including other forms of social differentiation. These transformations might affect the allocation of tasks and the dynamics of appropriation and control over resources and labour in gendered spheres. Analysing social relations allows the investigation of social constructions, meanings and prac-tices of gender relations in a wide set of arenas. It allowed me to consider issues of rights, norms and values that sustain social relations, which Pearson, Whitehead and Young refer to as 'practice of everyday life'.[41] This approach allowed me to ask what the precise terms are under which men and women co-operate in the specific institutions through which social groups acquire resources and entitlements based on gender iden-

[39] Michael Jackson, *The Politics of Story Telling* , p. ii; Hannah Arendt (1958), pp. 182–4.
[40] Ann Whitehead, 'Some Preliminary Notes on the Subordination of Women', *IDS Bulletin*, 1979, Vol. 10.
[41] Ruth Pearson, Ann Whitehead and Kate Young, 'The Continued Subordination of Women in the Development Process', in K. Young, C. Wolkowitz and R. McCul-lagh (eds), *Of Marriage and the Market* (London, 1984).

tity (marriage, household, the community, the market and the state), and through which such co-operation is structured. This approach allows me to go beyond the domestic and household analysis of power relations 'to wider institutions of social, political, cultural and economic organisation'.[42] Put simply, it lets us enter the realm of gender politics. Consequently, feminist analysis unpacks and provides avenues for addressing the problems of women's subordination.

What emerged in a number of the conversations was the endurance of women's subordination as linked to its embeddedness in social institutions, structures and everyday practices that normalise and reproduce asymmetrical relations between women and men. As the women often pointed out, their subordination is embedded in the institution of marriage and linked to bridewealth that determines their responsibilities, entitlements and status within the household and the wider community (see Chapter 3). Many of my respondents were already asking themselves whether, and how, changes prompted by war, displacement and mobility undermine, re(configure) and challenge the material basis of gender asymmetry.

War and conflict-induced displacement and migration often produce accelerated social change.[43] They also greatly impact gender asymmetrical configurations. Daniz Kandiyoti points out that 'patriarchal bargains' have normal and crisis phases.[44] During normal phases, there might be little questioning of the asymmetrical gender relations that subordinate women to men, as its gender system is depicted as 'everyday life' and legitimised through the discourse of 'our culture'. However:

> at the point of breakdown ... every order reveals its systematic contradictions. The impact of contemporary socio economic transformations upon marriage and divorce, on household formation, and on the gendered division of labour inevitably lead to a questioning of the fundamental, implicit assumptions behind the arrangements between men and women. (Kandiyoti, 1988, pp. 285–6)

Depending on the society in question, the result of these crises might take different forms. During times of dramatic social change, affirmations and/or (re)negotiations of gender relations may lead to dramatic, minimal or no changes. At times they may even reverse autonomy previously exercised by women and lead to the imposition of much stricter gender norms. During war in Guatemala, former Yugoslavia and Eritrea, women became involved as combatants and as primary breadwinners in exile. Although this led to strengthening their economic positions in the household and in the community, these gains were often reversed at the end of the conflicts. Such transformations are even more pronounced among those women and men who were resettled to western countries

[42] Naila Kabeer (1994), p. xiii.

[43] See, for example, Laura Hammond, *This Place will become Home: Refugee Repatriation to Ethiopia* (Ithaca, NY, 2004); Barbara Harrell-Bond and Efthixia Voutira, 'Anthropology and the Study of Refugees', *Anthropology Today*, 1992, Vol. 8, pp. 6–10.

[44] Deniz Kandiyoti, 'Bargaining with Patriarchy', *Gender and Society*, 1988, Vol. 2, pp. 274–90.

and were exposed to different gender ideas and economic possibilities.[45] Hence, crises might either undermine or reinforce women's subordination. As Nuer women and men who experienced exile in Khartoum, Ethiopia and or in Kenya indirectly pointed out, local and global conditions as linked to specific gender relations play an important role in these transformations.

The experiences of forcibly displaced populations offer considerable insight into the theoretical debates on social change and its gender repercussions. Multi-dimensional change is often provoked by specific political, social and economic conditions.[46] Social changes might either reinforce and/or re-configure gender ideology. Much of the recent gender and development literature focuses on the changed economic conditions and the entry of women into the labour market and their impact on power relations within the household and community.[47] While these arrangements might challenge the former terms of the 'conjugal bargain', women's access to income does not necessarily lead to greater empowerment.

However, even in dramatic circumstances, women and men retain their agency and affect the outcome of social transformations. While men have a vested interest in perpetuating the male breadwinner ideal (or, in the case of Nuer communities, the provider of bridewealth and protector of the household) and thus maintaining gendered hegemonic hierarchies, women are not passive bystanders. They actively participate in resisting/perpetuating these arrangements. As Kandiyoti notes, 'women become experts in maximising their own life chances'.[48] In highly patriarchal structures women, and men, might become agents of resistance, which might ultimately lead to further subordination of women.

To describe the points of transformation in Nuer social relations and in gender relations in particular I will employ the concept of 'being in flux' or 'being part and apart', partly adopted from the writings of Trinh Minh Ha.[49] I also use the Nuer term '*gɛɛr ro*', which means 'to change', while the transitive verb convening the meaning of action indicates separation. Hence, the Nuer metaphor for change relates to 'splitting away, separating oneself from the past'.[50] Although some of the narratives of the displaced

---

[45] See Lucia A. McSpadden, 'Negotiating Masculinity in the Reconstruction of Social Place: Eritrean and Ethiopian Refugees in the United States and Sweden', in D. Indra (ed.), *Engendering Forced Migration: Theory and Practice* (New York, 1999), pp. 242–61; Hellen Moussa, *Storm and Sanctuary: The Journey of Ethiopian and Eritrean Women Refugees* (Dundas, 1993).

[46] See Andrea Cornwall, Elizabeth Harrison and Ann Whitehead (eds), *Feminisms in Development: Contradictions, Contestations and Challenges* (London, 2007); Naila Kabeer, *Power to Choose* (London, 2000); Amartya K. Sen, 'Gender and Cooperative Conflicts', in I. Tinker (ed.), *Persistent Inequalities: Women and World Development* (Oxford, 1990), pp. 123–49.

[47] See Naila Kabeer, *Power to Choose*; Deniz Kandiyoti, 'Bargaining with Patriarchy'.

[48] Kandiyoti, 'Bargaining with Patriarchy'.

[49] Trinh Minh Ha, *Woman, Native, Other: Writing Postcoloniality and Feminism* (Bloomington, IN, 1989).

[50] Hutchinson, *Nuer Dilemmas*, p. 39.

Nuer women and men referred to being 'in flux' or between cultures of 'modernity' and 'their parents', the actual shaping, experiences and practice of their (gender) identities reveal a re-working, re-shaping and development of the same. Many men and women voiced uncertainty about both their (gender) identities as well as their belonging. Statements along the line of 'I am Nuer, but somehow I am different. War and life in Kakuma has changed me and now I feel part but also apart of the Nuer here in Lɛr' were heard repeatedly from those who had spent time in Kakuma, displacement camps around Khartoum, in Ethiopia, Uganda, or had migrated to the USA or Australia.

Recognising their transformative dimension, I problematise (gender) identities as a matter of becoming rather than being a question of not 'who we are' or 'where we came from' but rather 'what we might become'.[51] Linking identity with the future provides a counter-representation of identity as constantly linked to our past. Identity, says Hall, belongs to the future as much as to the past:

> Cultural identities come from somewhere, have histories. But, like everything which is historical, they undergo constant transformation. Far from being eternally fixed in some essentialised past, they are subject to the continuous 'play of history, culture and power'. (quoted in Ang, 2000 p.1)

These interconnections make (gender) identities fluid and flexible rather than squarely defined by a particular place and isolated in a space. Liisa Malkki points out the transformative, relational and situational nature of identity: 'Identity is always mobile and processual, partly self-construction, partly categorization by others, partly self-condition, a status, a label, a weapon, a shield, a fund of memories ... a creolized aggregate.'[52] The dilemmas and transformations of gender ideas, identities and practice in the lives of the Nuer over time and space correspond to Hall's definition of identity as 'a kind of unsettled space ... between a number of intersecting discourses'.[53]

Coping with settling-in after return involved a (re)negotiation of gender and generational relations. As many pointed out, the moral panic caused by the behaviour of returnee women and youth were signs of the contestations of gender ideas, norms, identities and practices that return of the displaced prompted in their relations with those who had stayed behind. The narratives presented in this book point to gendered discourses and imaginings that people (women and men, boys and girls) used with reference to home and return. For Nyakuol, Kuok and Nyariek, the emplacement and community creation process affected (re)negotiations around marriage and access to resources and rights at personal and community

[51] Stuart Hall, 'Introduction: Who Needs Identity?', in S. Hall and P. du Gay (eds), *Questions of Cultural Identity*, (London, 1996).
[52] Liisa H. Malkki, 'National Geographic: The Rooting of Peoples and the Territorialization of National Identity among Scholars and Refugees', *Cultural Anthropology*, 1992, Vol. 7, p. 37.
[53] Hall, 'Old and New Identities, Old and New Ethnicities', in A.D. King (ed.) *Culture, Globalization and the World System* (Basingstoke, 1991).

level. Life stories are not only expressed through words, they are also conveyed through bodies, or, in Judith Butler's words,[54] the gendered performance. I thus examined how gender identities and subjectivities were re-configured according to the context (in Kakuma and in Lɛr). This book explores those gender values, concepts, practices and institutions that contemporary Nuer women and men, old and young, refugees, returnees and stayees, perceived as changing and were in the process of collectively redefining during post-war community formation.

I take an all-encompassing view of the transformative power of wartime migration and displacement on gender relations set against general changes of the social fabric. As Turshen and Twagiramariya show, forced migration may lead to the destruction of male-dominated structures of society, but, despite its devastating consequences on individuals, families and societies, forced displacement can open up opportunities for creating new forms of gender relations and social norms.[55] Despite calls to integrate gender within forced displacement studies, research on women has continued to dominate the field. But how is the conflict-induced mobility (of agro-pastoralist Nuer) gendered and generational and experienced differently by women and men, young and old? How are women and men's diverse and inter-generational experiences during war, in displacement and of emplacement after return affecting relations of power? This book extends the existing literature on forced displacement by developing an analytical framework situated in gender as a relational and inter-generational construct affecting both women and men.

NUER WOMEN AND MEN'S GENDERED ENCOUNTERS WITH DISPLACEMENT, EMPLACEMENT AND 'MODERNITIES'

Following the changes in gender relations prompted by colonialism, state formation and Christianity as examined by Hutchinson, this book shows how gender ideas, identities and practices have been challenged by the recent war, especially by southern Sudanese inter- and intra-community violence. Wars and displacement have had an ambiguous effect on gender relations, giving rise to both weakened and reinforced femininities and masculinities. As Nuer women and men pointed out, gender asymmetries and women's subordination have been reinforced in some spheres, but women-led autonomous households have emerged and women have taken up new informal sector economic activities to ensure family survival. Women's access to employment in refugee camps combined with international aid to refugees has further undermined the material bases of male authority.

These challenges have been reinforced by gender-mainstreaming prog-

---

[54] Judith Butler, *Bodies that matter: On the discursive limits of 'sex'* (Routledge, New York:, 1993).
[55] Meredeth Turshen and Clotilde Twagiramariya, *What Women do in Wartime: Gender and Conflict in Africa* (London, 1998).

rammes run by international organisations in Kakuma and by greater education opportunities for women and girls in the camp. Women's access to protection programmes offered by UNHCR and NGOs, and resettlement possibilities for women and girls at risk of (male) gender violence, has prompted men to perceive women's empowerment in Kakuma as a challenge to male power and position. Refugee women and men often expressed their concerns about the emergence of particular 'modern' femininities and masculinities forged in Kakuma that challenge the gender structures of power by undermining the basis and logic of men being in charge of women and children. At the same time, younger and older women expressed their concerns about an emerging reinforcement of new sources of male privilege. In complex and in flux post-war situations and the nation-formation period, it is impossible to reach definitive conclusions regarding directionality of change in gender relations. For example, the experiences of Western Upper Nile Nuer communities reveal signs of reinforcement of some aspects of female subordination as well as emerging new opportunities for women's empowerment.

In flux gender relations and displacement-induced transformations are also related to Nuer women and men's encounters with different kinds of modernities in Kakuma and post-war South Sudan. Conversations with men and women in Kakuma and Nuerland revolved around the political and social future of South Sudan, development and prospects for lasting peace. Women and men, young and old, were concerned with rapid social changes taking place in Nuer communities as a result of war, life in refugee camps and changing socio-economic conditions in southern Sudan. *Cieng mi pai ben* ('a new mode of life/custom has arrived') was a common observation of the older generation as they witnessed changes in gender relations and livelihoods taking place in Kakuma and in Lɛr. Many perceived life in Kakuma as 'modern' and 'civilised' in comparison to Nuerland. This encounter with modernity was of a particular kind, forged by the global humanitarianism of the UN and a refugee regime committed to gender equality. This manifested itself in the experiences with the international norms, values and rights espoused by the humanitarian community in Kakuma combined with other encounters with modernity – global communications, education, gender equality programming and transnational and diasporic connections to the west. I further develop this argument in Chapter 3.

In post-war southern Sudan, the encounter with modernity was two-fold. On the one hand, the Nuer women and men located it in the onset of state formation and the slow emergence of South Sudanese autonomy, and possible independence. This was combined with the influence of global capitalism and its impact on inter- and intra-community conflicts. Global capitalism continues, as it has done for decades, to drive conflict in oil- and water-rich Sudan (see Chapter 2). Globalisation and international capitalism are highly visible in post-war southern Sudan, where there are numerous multi-national oil companies. Roads, administrative buildings and modern technological connections are linking hitherto unconnected places in remote areas to the global capitalist enterprise, thus forging a particular modernity in Nuerland (see Chapter 4).

Older women and men perceived the arrival of modernity through transformations reflected in new social customs, behaviours and norms. *Cieng mi pai ben* was often located in the emergence of *wa nhiam* (development/progress) which came with education, Christianity and the infrastructure brought by oil companies and the international humanitarian community. It was also expressed in cultural norms introduced by returnees – including changing dress codes, 'moral panic' around mini-skirts and perceptions of the place of women in the community. Many who had stayed behind were aghast at this 'moral decay' and the perceived threat to culture.

My explorations of changes in gender relations in Kakuma and Lɛr are part of the emerging modernities resulting from the encounter between Nuer communities and global humanitarian and development enterprises. I locate this debate in the slowly growing literature on the effects of modernities on gender relations in Africa, and in particular on ideals, production and practice of masculinities and femininities, marriage, gender division of labour and gender rights.[56]

The dynamic ways and the dynamism that both returnee women and men employ in negotiating and shaping their gender identities and relations in Kakuma and in Nuerland reveal their agency. Despite more limited choices for women upon return to Nuerland, women (and some returnee men) continue to contest male privilege and the emerging forms of male hegemony. This book reveals that women's empowerment and emergence of alternative masculinities (pro-gender equality) are not linear processes but rather contingent on the cultural milieu in which they occur. The emerging gender relations are thus in flux. 'In flux' denotes the fluidity and transiting of gender identities and relations that occurs in the movement between places in which these identities are shaped.

The war-induced displacement setting chosen as a framework for the book allows us to better understand the lived gender experiences as well as (re)negotiation of gender and generational relations. By employing feminist analysis which centres gender, age, as well as other axes of difference, this study breaks away from men and women's independent experiences of displacement and mobility. It underscores the relational nature of gender and age and improves our understanding of the continuities and discontinuities of gender practices under rapid social change. It also emphasises the particular resistance of gender hegemonies despite challenges to the material basis of women's subordination.[57] My findings suggest that gender asymmetries are constraining for both women and men and, further, also fluid and contingent on places in which they occur. Yet despite changing sources of power, new gender hegemonies continue

---

[56] See Dorothy Hodgson, *Gendered Modernities: Ethnographic Perspectives of Modernity/Modernities, Gender and Ethnography* (New York, 2001); Lisa A. Lindsay and Stephan F. Miescher, *Men and Masculinities in Modern Africa* (Portsmouth, NH, 2003).

[57] Naila Kabeer, *Reversed Realities: Gender Hierarchies in Development Thought* (London, 1994); Kandiyoti, 'Bargaining with Patriarchy'.

to emerge. Although some women who enjoy access to resources and education as the new basis of power do manage to negotiate greater freedoms, those lacking these privileges suffer additional subordination. In particular, this book contributes to the understanding of challenges posed by forced displacement for young women and men and how their gendered desires and aspirations are altered during displacement and post-return emplacement.

TRANSFORMING GENDERED SELF THROUGH SEASONS

To reflect some of the Nuer meanings of daily life, including war, displacement and livelihood strategies, I use the metaphor of ecological seasons as understood and lived by the Nuer communities. As elder women and men often told me, despite changes that have taken place in the lives of the agro-pastoralist Nuer communities, they continue to be closely linked to their environment, landscape and cattle. In the past, ecological constraints influenced their social relations in an environment with a distinctive rhythm of backwards and forwards movement from villages to cattle camps – a response to the climatic dichotomy of rains and drought. This continues to be the case for those Nuer women and men who are still reliant on cattle herding and agriculture, especially those who stayed behind in villages. The elder women and men whom I encountered in Kenya and in Nuerland explained that the year (*ruon*) has two main seasons, *tot* (rain) and *mai* (drought). There are also two transitional periods between *tot* and *mai*, *rwil* (movement from camp to village) and *jiom* (wind). These observations reflected a historical relevance of the past, as noted by Evans-Pritchard in 1940. Throughout my stay in Nuerland, women and men, both young and old, used these terms to identify changes in ecological conditions as well as their changing ways of life throughout the year.

Chapter 2 – *jiom* – describes the emergence of 'the south' within Sudan and the causes of the second civil war. Based on the narratives of those women and men who stayed behind and those who were displaced during the conflicts, I sketch out the different nature of the most recent war and the ensuing south–south violence that had dramatic gender and generational consequences for the southern Sudanese population. The second part of the chapter, through the perspectives of 'lost boys' and 'invisible girls' of southern Sudan, considers the effects of recent wars and violence in southern Sudan on gender and generational relations. I conceptualise war as a social condition rather than simply a destructive force, and ask how conditions of war present challenges and opportunities for gender relations.[58] I explore the socio-cultural effects of war and violence, focusing on the gendered and generational experiences of mobility during wartime and displacement to Kakuma. Through exam-

---

[58] See Stephen Lubkemann, *Culture in Chaos: An Anthropology of the Social Condition in War* (Chicago, IL, 2008).

ining diverse trajectories of displacement, I explore the multiple experiences of living in war-zones, determined by gender, age and social status. This chapter reveals the contradictory effects of war on gender relations, which sustain, foster or subvert specific ethnicised, racialised and communalised femininities and masculinities, producing multiple femininities and identities. It also seeks to identify who gains and who loses from community militarisation and how gender practices and norms embedded in gender divisions within labour and marriage are shifting.

Chapter 3 – *mai* – explores experiences of gendered lives in Kakuma camp in the context of the production of 'modernity' through global UN humanitarianism, gendered modernity and its implications for gender relations. *Mai* corresponds to the dry season from mid-September to mid-March, when Nuer move from villages to cattle camps. I use the metaphor of *mai* to represent life in a refugee camp, to which the Nuer moved in search of protection, security and education due to conflict in Sudan. Kakuma's ecological conditions are comparable to those of Nuerland. The impact of changed livelihoods, education, and gender and human rights projects are analysed through the construction, negotiation and practice of gender identities, division of labour and marriage. I also show how new discourses of gender equality and women's rights and the emerging diverse forms of femininities and masculinities are contested and challenged by talk of 'our culture'. Kakuma as a (different) space not a *cieng nuära* (Nuer community village or home, or set of norms) opened up possibilities for the (re)negotiation of gender and generational norms and practices. At the same time, however, this gendered modernity was a temporal opportunity, undermining some of the gender and generational asymmetries among the Nuer communities.

Chapter 4 – *rwil* – follows the lives of Nyakuol, Nyariek and other Nuer refugees settling in Lɛr. Running from the middle of March till the middle of June, *rwil* is the season of moving from cattle camp (*wec*) to *cieng* to clear and plant fields. I use it as a metaphor of movement from the refugee camp to Nuerland. It develops the concept of gendered emplacement in its relation to movement and place as experienced by those who had been displaced and those who had stayed behind. I then set out the context of diasporic returns taking place in Lɛr and in South Sudan. Through the narratives of the displaced and the stayees the picture of irreversibility of displacement emerges. This points to the core of social change within the context of wartime displacement and emplacement. The chapter shows how Nuer women and men, young and old, struggle to uphold a sense of self and of community within the new and radically changed post-war homes in South Sudan. These negotiations of home, identity and community cut across gender, age and other differences and dynamically shape the self within the ever-changing new realities.

Chapter 5 examines how gendered imaginations, experiences and notions of home, return and emplacement are produced differently when gender, age, socio-economic and marital status and length of exile are taken into account. I also consider the different processes of settling in and emplacement through gendered access to land and livelihoods, especially in the context of particular modernities creeping into Nuerland. What are the general effects of gendered emplacement on the reordering of gender relations? How does the emergence of autonomous women households, women's access to paid employment and changes in livelihood strategies challenge, contest or conform to prevailing ideas about gender division of labour? Tensions between returnees and those who had stayed behind illuminate some of the contestations around the changing notions of gender relations.

Chapter 6 – *tot*– represents the rainy season, which lasts from about mid-March to mid-September. During this period, cattle and youth return from cattle camps and life concentrates on the village. New marriages are formed and crops are planted. This chapter focuses on the social and gender aspects of settling in and emplacement. I examine how masculinities and femininities are socially intertwined with the notions of community and home and how settling in and place-making become part of the (re)negotiation of gender identities practiced in Kakuma. I then show how emplacement for the young involves initiation of a marriage process, discussing how notions of marriage and conjugal relations are being transformed. This chapter demonstrates how gendered processes of settling-in play out on subjectivities and in opening up or constraining the expanded freedoms and autonomy gained by youth in Kakuma. The perceived 'transgression' of gender norms is contested and confronted by those who had stayed behind. These inter-generational and gender confrontations reveal the tensions and transitions of the social and gender basis of Nuer communities.

The final chapter starts with a comment offered by an elderly woman, Nyabieli, who reflects on the social changes that disrupted and altered *cieng nuära* in the course of the civil wars. She comments on the role of returnees (or visitors – *jaal* – as they are referred to by those who stayed behind during the conflicts). Her insights put into historical perspective the evolving gender relations among the Nuer community of Western Upper Nile since the onset of the 1983 conflict and point to some of the contestations and negotiations of the current transformations in gender relations. The chapter concludes with insights on gendered and generational displacement and their significance for feminist and anthropological theory, the anthropology of globalisation and the implications for migration and mobility theories. Lastly, I open up the question of the current nation-formation in South Sudan and its promise of a home based on gender justice for Nyakuol, Nyariek, Kuok, their families and friends.

2

Jiom – Season of Fighting and Running: Conflict, Mobility, Gender

'WHICH WARS DO YOU WANT ME TO TALK ABOUT?':
NARRATIVES OF WARS

On a hot afternoon in March 2007, I was sitting in a *luak* (cattle byre) watching Nyariek's mother grinding sorghum and cooking *walwal* (sorghum porridge). Nyariek, a 16-year-old girl whom I'd met in Kakuma, had recently returned to southern Sudan. When I bumped into her in Lɛr she invited me to visit her mother, whom she had not seen since leaving for Kenya in 2001. After travelling by an old mini-bus and walking for three hours through dusty savannah, we reached Maper, Nyariek's birth-place. Inside the *luak* I listened to women narrate stories of war and displacement. 'Which war do you want me to talk about?' asked Nyariek's mother, who had stayed in Maper throughout the conflicts:

> They were all here; they came like wind [*jiom*]. We suffered a lot here because of oil. First the Arabs came and this was the war of the government [*koor kume*]. Then the Dinka started fighting the Nuer and people had to run from one place to another. Then the Nuer started fighting each other. These conflicts were different because of [the use of] guns. The mothers stayed with children behind in the bush. Many men were killed and others ran away. Women were killed, and if you were lucky, you were taken as a wife by the enemy. Houses were burnt and cows and goats were all taken away. There was a lot of suffering and running.

Stories of war, violence, running and survival were a common narrative of many southern Sudanese I met in Egypt, and thereafter in Kenya and southern Sudan. The wind that came from behind the *luak*, as predicted by the most influential Nuer prophet Ngundɛng,[1] brought the turmoil of the second civil war to the Sudanese, and to the Nuer in particular, causing trau-

[1] Ngundɛng Bong is generally considered to be the first and most influential Nuer prophet. Seized by the divinity Deng, he combined the ideas of divinity and the spiritual behaviour of Aiwel, Deng and Nuer earth masters *(kuar muon)*, and by his activities he gave a new meaning to the concept of *guk kuoth* (the vessel of divinity). Born in the late 1830s into a family of Gaaleak earth masters living among the Jikany Nuer in Eastern Upper Nile, he is believed to have prophesised the second civil war, and especially the violence among the southerners (see Edward E. Evans-Pritchard, *Nuer Religion*; Douglas Johnson, *Nuer Prophets: A History of Prophecy from the Upper Nile in the Nineteenth and Twentieth Centuries* (Oxford, 1994).

matic changes in their lives. Although the first civil war devastated much of southern Sudan, including the communities of eastern Nuer bordering Ethiopia, severe flooding in the Western Upper Nile region spared the western Nuer from the disastrous consequences of the conflict experienced elsewhere. It was the second civil war, together with the discovery of oil in the Western Upper Nile region, the desire of the Khartoum government to control the latter and the subsequent nine years of inter- and intra-ethnic fighting (1991–2000) that took place among the Nuer (and Dinka) that decimated many Western Upper Nile communities and resulted in a collapse of local social and livelihood systems. The impact of inter- and intra-ethnic violence that resulted from the John Garang-Riek Machar split in 1991 marked a turning point for Nuer–Dinka relations and concepts of ethnicity and (gender) identity. Ethnicised violence followed across borders, and in 1996, fighting took place between Dinka and Nuer in Kakuma.

What are the implications of such violent conflicts for gender identities and relations of power? How do women and men, young and old, cope with and within violent conflicts? Wars historically have been symbolised as the 'touchstone of manliness', expressed through male aggression, brutality and violence, an image often perpetrated in literature, films, songs and tales.[2] A.M. White argues that men's roles as protectors of women are accentuated and that combat is seen as the ultimate test of masculinity. In much literature, women and girls have been misleadingly portrayed as victims, peacemakers and/or mothers of the nation providing support for heroic male combatants. Male agency dominates the discourse of war, while women and girls have been rendered silent and invisible.[3] Yet, such simplistic interpretations leave complex female and male roles in war, and consequent changes in gender relations, unexplained and untheorised. The narratives of the Nuer women and men I encountered in Kenya and southern Sudan suggest that war and conflict not only open up different possibilities for disempowering some women and empowering some men, but also creating opportunities to reverse some gender and generational imbalances. As the example of Nuer women in the next section shows, women play an important role in fostering militarised masculine identities, even though their own position is often weakened in the process.[4]

[2]   A.M. White, 'All the Men are Fighting for Freedom, All the Women are Mourning their Men, but some of us carried Guns: A Raced-Gendered Analysis of Fanon's Psychological Perspectives on War', *Signs*, 2007, Vol. 32, pp. 958–84.
[3]   Myriam Denov and Christine Gervais, 'Negotiating (In)security: Agency, Resistance and Resourcefulness among Girls formerly Associated with Sierra Leone's Revolutionary United Front', *Signs*, 2007, Vol. 32, pp. 885–910.
[4]   Although there is emerging literature on the multidimensional female roles in conflicts, there are relatively few studies that consider the ways in which women and girls negotiate their security and wellbeing in an unstable war environment. The few exceptions include contributions by Denov and Gervais, 'Negotiating (In) security'; Carolyn Nordstrom, *Girls and Warzones: Troubling* Questions (Uppsala, 1997); Mats Utas, 'Agency of Victims: Young Women in the Liberation Civil War', in A. Hohwana and F. De Boeck (eds), *Makers and Breakers: Children and Youth in Postcolonial Africa* (Trenton, NJ, 2005), who emphasise the importance of recognising agency among war-affected and girls and women.

WAR COSTS: MASS DISPLACEMENT AND DIVERSE MOBILITY

In the case of Sudan, the struggle for dominant, truthful discourse about the root causes of the conflict is coloured by religious, ethnic, cultural, economic and geopolitical overtones. Members of the Sudanese government, the rebel movement, dissident groups, and others continue to debate the principal causes of the conflict, while some international community commentaries continue to perpetuate the misguided image of 'Muslims against Christians' imaginaries. My analyses of the gendered and generational consequences of the second civil war and the inter- and intra-community conflicts are predominantly based on secondary sources, including key literature on the conflict in southern Sudan.[5] They are supported by primary material collected through life stories in Kakuma and southern Sudan.

The destruction of homelands

The cost of the most recent wars fell heavily on the civilian population, not only because they were denied protection, but also because of socio-economic collapse. The effects of the recent conflicts are so immense that it is impossible to discuss them all in this chapter. I will highlight only those consequences most central to this book. The southern Sudanese region has horrendous rates of maternal and child mortality rates (one in five newborns in southern Sudan fails to reach the age of five),[6] rampant insecurity, one of the lowest education rates

---

[5]   For example, Arop Madut-Arop, *Sudan's Painful Road to Peace. A Full Story of the Founding and Development of SPLM/SPLA* (BookSurge, 2006); Burr, Millard and Robert O. Collins, *Requiem for Sudan: War, Droughts, and Disaster Relief on the Nile* (Boulder, CO, 1995); D. Johnson, 'Twentieth-century civil wars', in John Ryle et al. (eds), *The Sudan Handbook* (Woodbridge; James Currey 2011); Harir and T. Tvedt (eds), *Short-Cut to Decay: The Case of the Sudan* (Uppsala: The Scandinavian Institute of African Studies, 1994); S. Hutchinson, 'Death, Memory and the Politics of Legitimation: Nuer Experiences of the Continuing Second Civil War', in R. Webner (ed.), *Memory and the Postcolony: African Anthropology and the Critique of Power* (London, 1998) pp. 58–71; S. Hutchinson. 'Peace and Puzzlement: Grass-roots Peace Initiatives between the Nuer and Dinka of South Sudan', in Günther Schlee and Elizabeth Watson (eds), *Changing Identification and Alliances in North-east Africa*, Vol. II (New York and Oxford: Berghahn Books, 2009), pp. 49–72; S. Hutchinson, 'Gendered Violence and the Militarization of Nuer and Dinka Ethnic Identities', University of Wisconsin-Madison, Cultural Pluralism Research Circle, 2000; S. Hutchinson, *Nuer Dilemmas: Coping with Money, War and the State* (Berkeley, CA, 1996); S. Hutchinson, 'Nuer Ethnicity Militarized', *Anthropology Today,* 2000, Vol. 16, pp. 6–13; Francis M. Deng, *War of Visions: Conflict of Identity in the Sudan* (Washington DC, 1995); Douglas Johnson, *The Root Causes of Sudan's Civil Wars* (Oxford, 2006); Jane Kani Edwards, *Sudanese Women Refugees: Transformations and Future Imaginings* (New York, 2007). There is also a vast grey literature related to the conflict that can be consulted via the Sudan Open Archive (sudanarchive.net).
[6]   In 2008, a census was carried out by the Southern Sudan Centre for Census, Statistics and Evaluation (SSCCSE, 'Key Indicators for Southern Sudan', Southern Sudan Centre for Census, Statistics and Evaluations, Juba 2011). Statistics provided are based on this census.

in the world,[7] high abortion rates due to rape and sexual violence, high levels of severe malnutrition and chronic depletion of assets through the loss of cattle and land.[8] With men driven into exile, recruited into rebel forces or killed, one of the consequences of the recent conflicts is a high number of single mothers, widows and orphans. As a result of war and famine, South Sudan has the lowest proportion of adults than any other country (16% are under five years old and 72% under thirty years old).[9]

During the wars, and as a result of recurring drought, southern Sudan was subject to chronic food shortages, suffering dramatic famines in 1984, 1988 and 1998. Based on his doctoral fieldwork in southern Sudan, Luka Biong Deng notes that southern Sudan was not prone to famines during previous conflicts.[10] Unofficial estimates, although never substantiated, suggest that roughly quarter of a million people died as a result of hunger and war in 1988 alone. As Alex de Waal argues, the famine became a political issue under international pressure. It was government-orchestrated through the deployment of the military, organised militia raids and army commanders and local government officials preventing relief assistance from reaching the affected populations.[11] Outraged by the mass starvation, the international community intervened in 1989 under the umbrella of Operation Lifeline Sudan (OLS), which brought international NGOs back to Sudan. Larry Minear, in his review of OLS, argues that the international community was committed to preventing another disaster from happening.[12] However, another famine struck in 1988, with Bahr al-Ghazal being most affected. While there are no confirmed figures of how many people died as a result, the UN estimated that of 27 million people, some 2.6 million were at risk of starvation, of whom 2.4 were located in southern

---

[7] According to the SSCCSE key indicators for southern Sudan (2011: 9), the southern Sudanese net enrolment ratio in primary school increased from 20% in 2004 to 48% in 2009. Female-to-male enrolment is the lowest in the world (35%). Only one out of every five children of school age is in class and around three times more boys than girls are in school. Only 2% complete primary school education. According to 2004 estimates, only five hundred girls finish primary school each year compared to two thousand boys. Southern Sudan is has an adult literacy rate of 27%, an adult female illiteracy rate of 84% and a youth literacy rate of 40%, with only 28% of young women being literate.

[8] See Amani El Jack, 'Gendered Implications: Development Induced Displacement in the Sudan', in P. Vandergeest, P. Idahosa and P. Bose (eds), *Development's Displacements: Ecologies, Economies and Cultures at Risk*, (Vancouver, 2007); Madut Jok, *Militarization, Gender and Reproductive Health in South Sudan* (New York, 1998); Luka Biong Deng, 'Confronting Civil War: A Comparative Study of Household Assets Management in Southern Sudan during the 1990s', *IDS Discussion Paper* 381 (Brighton, 2002).

[9] SSCCSE (2011), p. 3.

[10] Luka Biong Deng, 'Are Non-Poor Households always less Vulnerable? The Case of Households exposed to protracted Civil War in Southern Sudan', *Disasters*, 2008, Vol. 32, pp. 377–98.

[11] Alex de Waal, *Famine Crimes: Politics and the Disaster Relief Industry in Africa* (Oxford and Bloomington, IN, 1997).

[12] Larry Minear (ed.), *Humanitarianism under Siege: A Critical Review of Operation Lifeline Sudan* (Trenton, NJ, 1991).

Sudan.[13] Activists and analysts argued that the fault lay primarily with 'Sudanese government and militias and opposition forces that precipitated the famine and deliberately diverted or looted food from the starving or blocked relief deliveries'.[14]

The international aid that poured into Sudan through the OLS base in the Kenyan border town of Lokichoggio, as well as by plane, assisted war-stricken communities throughout the south and north. Some argued that food distribution had a negative impact on local agro-pastoralist communities who had stopped growing their own food due to insecurity and the availability of free food. Queuing for food became a permanent feature in local communities. During my stay in the region, I often observed airplane drops or food delivered by WFP or international and local NGOs. The willingness to collect free grain, rice and oil was criticised by many elderly women and men: 'Nuer [*nei ti naath*] have become lazy now. They do not know how to produce their own food any longer. This international aid made us into beggars.' However, numerous studies on the impact of food assistance in Sudan have not confirmed that it created dependency.[15] I will return to the discussion of changes in livelihoods in Chapter 4.

The wars saw the complete destruction of the fragile NGO-sponsored infrastructure established in southern Sudan in the 1972–1983 inter-war period. Bombardment of civilian targets, especially urban areas, by the Khartoum government destroyed most health facilities, schools and government buildings. Lack of basic infrastructure was one of the reasons often mentioned by refugees in Kakuma for delaying their return. Most importantly, people's survival methods had become more individualistic and household-oriented. Kinship networks underwent transformation and became more individualised, while people's ability to maintain their cultural and community-practices in regulating abuse of power declined dramatically (see Jok 2005: 151; Marriage 2006).

Changing conflict: the south–south war of the 'educated' (men)

The Khartoum–SPLA war changed its dynamic in late August of 1991, when the SPLA split, tearing apart southern communities.[16] The Khar-

---

[13] Human Rights Watch, *Famine in Sudan 1998: The Human Rights Causes* (New York, 1998).

[14] Ibid., p. 4.

[15] See S. Bailey and S. Harragin, 'Food assistance, reintegration and dependency in Southern Sudan'. Overseas Development Institute: London (2009); M. Duffield, J.M. Jok, D. Keen, G. Loane, F. O'Reilly, J. Ryle, P. Winter, 'Sudan: Unintended Consequences of Humanitarian Assistance – Field Evaluation Study', University of Dublin, Trinity College: April 2000; SRRA Database and Monitoring Unit, SRRA Annual Assessment Report, November 1998; Human Rights Watch 'Famine in Sudan 1998: The Human Rights Causes', HRW: New York. 1999 http://www.hrw.org/reports/1999/sudan/SUDAWEB2.htm#P374_19682 (accessed February 2014); S. Harragin, and C. Chol, The Southern Sudan Vulnerability Study, Nairobi: Save the Children (UK) 1999; SPLM Protecting Rights and Strengthening Resilience of the Civilian Population in Bahr el Ghazal Region OLS: 31 May 1999.

[16] See Øystein Rolandsen, *Guerrilla Government. Political Changes in the Southern Sudan during the 1990s* (Uppsala, 2005); Richard A. Lobban, Robert S. Kramer and

toum government had until then been unsuccessful in securing control over the oil-rich areas of Western Upper Nile and thus gaining a decisive military advantage. The event that changed the course of the war and the experience of displacement for the western Nuer was the split between SPLA commanders. This launched a new war: 'the war of the educated [elite]'.[17] In the Upper Nile town of Nasir, Riek Machar Teny Dhurgon,[18] a Nuer zonal commander of Western Upper Nile, together with former Nuer *Anyanya II* member Gordon Kong Cuol and Shilluk commander Lam Akol, staged a coup against John Garang and formed what became known as the Nasir faction of the SPLA.[19] They objected to John Garang's 'dictatorial' leadership and demanded independence for southern Sudan.[20] This was a departure from Garang's policy of seeking regional autonomy within a united Sudan. Initial conflicts between opposed national visions of southern Sudan's future quickly gave way to a drive for self-preservation. Machar and Garang reached for the ethnic card, with Machar protesting against alleged Dinka dominance of the SPLM/A.[21] Critics argued that Garang and the SPLA's Dinka leadership were favouring Dinka interests to the detriment of other southern communities. A number of authors agree that the coup leaders used ethnicity, development inequalities and unequal access to power to mask their personal interests and ambitions, thereby fuelling the inter-ethnic violence that continued until 1999.[22] This aspect was also confirmed by many of the research participants.

By 1992, the SPLA split had led to a new phase in the civil war between the two factions, resulting in an expanding confrontation and a 'regional subculture of ethnicised violence'.[23] This affected rural Nuer and Dinka communities, whose homelands turned into battlefields.[24] The SPLA-Mainstream or Torit faction was predominantly backed by Dinka

---

[(cont.)] Carolyn Fluehr-Lobban, *Historical Dictionary of the Sudan* (Lanham, MD, 2002) pp. liv–lxxiv, for a detailed discussion of the transformations within SPLA.

[17] Jok Madut Jok and Sharon E. Hutchinson, 'Sudan's Prolonged Second Civil War and the Militarization of Nuer and Dinka Ethnic Identities', *African Studies Review*, 1999, Vol. 42, pp. 125–45.

[18] Machar was educated first in missionary schools in Ler and later gained a university degree in Khartoum. Like John Garang, he received a scholarship to study abroad, first at Scotland's Strathclyde University, followed by a doctorate from Bradford Polytechnic. The Garang–Machar conflict is often referred to as war between 'two doctors'(Hutchinson, 'Gendered Violence and the Militarization of Nuer and Dinka Ethnic Identities' (University of Wisconsin-Madison, 2000), p. 6). Riek Machar is considered by many Nuer as the chosen one Nundeng predicted would bring peace and liberation to the Nuer.

[19] The SPLA Nasir or United faction changed its name several times due to defections and new alliances, becoming the South Sudan Independence Movement (SSIM) in 1994.

[20] Prunier cited in Rolandsen (2005).

[21] The Twic Dinka from Kongor district near Bor, the group from which John Garang originated, were seen as having particular control of the movement.

[22] See, for example, Peter A. Nyaba, *The Politics of Liberation in South Sudan: An Insider's View* (Kampala, 1997).

[23] Hutchinson, 'Nuer Ethnicity Militarized', *Anthropology Today*, 2000, Vol. 6, pp. 6–13.

[24] Ibid., p. 6.

(and Equatorians), while the SPLA-United or Nasir attracted mainly Nuer supporters. As Jok Madut Jok and Sharon E. Hutchinson argue, the Dinka and the Nuer provided most of the guerilla recruits.[25] The south–south violence that ensued and continued for nearly a decade destroyed thousands of Dinka and Nuer communities throughout Western Upper Nile, Bahr al-Ghazal and Jonglei Provinces. According to Jok and Hutchinson, several months of fierce fighting resulted in some 70% of the Bor Dinka being displaced in the southern Upper Nile region and hundreds of civilians being killed in the Bor massacre.[26]

War along the Nuer–Dinka frontier, as Douglas Johnson notes, had a direct impact on security among the Nuer, as inter-community fighting broke out between the central Nuer communities (Lou and Gaawar, and then between the Lou and Jikany).[27] The most devastating inter-community violence took place in Western Upper Nile. Throughout the 1990s, the Khartoum government exploited southern divisions, manipulating grievances and tensions between different guerrilla groups and using divide-and-rule tactics as part of a long-term strategy of waging proxy wars against the SPLA. The Human Rights Watch report of 2003, *Sudan, Oil, and Human Rights*, details the inter-fighting between western Nuer communities of Leek, Dok and Bul Nuer that led to massive human rights abuses and resulted in much of the displacement and depopulation in the region.

Although historically Dinka and Nuer communities were engaged in conflicts, the basis of their confrontation was economic.[28] Seasonal cattle raiding and competition over grazing land set Dinka and Nuer and different Nuer *cieng* against each other. However, these confrontations were different in scope and weaponry, combatants using spears and showing restraint by fighting according to community codes derived from the widespread fear of *nueer* (pollution). While stealing cattle and the occasional kidnapping of women and children were widely practiced, the intentional killing of women and children was strictly forbidden.

The older Nuer women and men argued that the new type of war that emerged after the 1991 split was 'different from the normal cattle wars between us'. The elderly in Lɛr and nearby villages described it as 'the war of the educated children [*koor gaan duël goära*]'.[29] A chief in Lɛr, Kuong Mabiel, explained how:

[25] Madut Jok and Hutchinson, 'Sudan's Prolonged Civil War', p. 126.
[26] Ibid., p. 128. The Bor massacre is considered by many Sudanese as a turning point in the ethnic confrontation. The attack of the Nuer-led forces, with the active participation of civilians under the leadership of one of the local chiefs, left thousands of Bor Dinka residents dead, with the rest seeking refuge, many fleeing to Kakuma. The Dinka–Nuer tensions continued across the borders, with fierce fighting between the different groups in Kakuma in 1996.
[27] Douglas Johnson, *The Root Causes of Sudan's Civil Wars*, p. 117.
[28] See Edward E. Evans-Pritchard, *The Nuer*; Sharon E. Hutchinson, *Nuer Dilemmas*.
[29] This metaphor refers to Garang and Machar. As they both had university degrees, they were perceived as the educated elite. Machar did not have the Nuer sign of manhood, *gaar* (six parallel marks on the forehead), and hence was often perceived in the eyes of the elders as a boy or child.

> In the past we would fight the Dinka, or other Nuer communities [*cieng*] over cattle or girls, but women were never killed. Now, it is the war of the gun and the educated, Garang and Machar, who are fighting for their own wealth and power. This was not *our* war; we do not understand the reasons for this war. We have nothing against the Dinka. We used to be one [*Jieng e nei ti naath raan kel*]. We can only fight them when they steal our cows.

These views were shared by the older Nuer women and men, who referred to the new dimension of the inter- and intra-ethnic conflict that swept through their lands as the worst experience of their lives. They all pointed to the personal greed and quest for power of the leaders as sources of the inter-community fighting. An elderly woman chief from Padeh commented:

> Brothers started killing each other, and this was because they wanted to have power and position. [Our] Children were killing women and old men, their own mothers and fathers, because they had guns and they thought that Divinity [*kuoth*] does not see it. These children got educated and they think they know better [than us, the illiterate]. This was the worst fighting we ever experienced, when you see your own people killing themselves. Their brains were wasted for nothing.

To escape the killings and forced recruitment by different Nuer factions, many young Nuer men became refugees in Kakuma. Mayang, a 27-year-old Bul Nuer from Mayom, was forced to join the Bul Nuer militia under the command of Paulino Matip. When he was wounded in 1997, he was sent home to recover. He took this opportunity to escape to Kakuma:

> I did not want to be a soldier any more. I did not see a sense in killing my own brothers, raping women and girls, and burning my homeland's property. This was not my war any longer, and I was not going to lose my life and kill my own people in the name of the political power struggles between Garang and Machar. They send their children and wives out [abroad] to education and safety, whereas they make us kill our sisters and brothers in the name of power. This is not what I believe in. This is the reason why I deserted. This war is against the Arabs, not against other Nuer, or against other southerners. We, as southerners, have to stand together, to fight our common enemy.

The number of deaths of Dinka and Nuer in the ensuing south–south violence exceeded the number of southerners killed in combat by the Sudanese army.[30] The collaboration of Riek Machar with the Khartoum government has been discussed extensively.[31] This, in turn, led to signing of a controversial political charter by Machar and Kerubino Bol with al-Bashir in 1996. In 1997, Machar and others created a militia, the Southern Sudan Defence Forces (SSDF), which was allied with the government. Machar was made chairman of the Southern States Co-ordination Council in Khartoum and promised a referendum on the future

[30] Madut Jok and Hutchinson, 'Sudan's Prolonged Second Civil War'.
[31] For example, Madut Arop, *Sudan's Painful Road to Peace. A Full Story of the Founding and Development of SPLM/SPLA* (Booksurge, 2006); M.W. Daly and Ahmad Sikainga, *Civil War in the Sudan* (London, 1993); Hutchinson, *Nuer Dilemmas*; Douglas Johnson, *The Root Causes of Sudan's Civil Wars*, 'Twentieth Century Civil Wars'.

of the unity of Sudan. Alienated from his old friends and supporters, he eventually split from Khartoum in 1999 and reconciled with the SPLA-Mainstream led by Garang on 8 January 2002.[32] In the meantime, the 1998 Dinka and Nuer Peace Workshop (held in Lokichoggio, Kenya) and the 1999 Wunlit Nuer-Dinka Peace conference were convened by communities to search for local reconciliation and to address some of the costs of the inter-ethnic violence.[33]

By late 1992, the economic livelihood system based on agro-pastoralism and fishing was destroyed in Western Upper Nile.[34] Most inhabitants of the oil-rich areas in Unity state, especially around Abiemnhom, were displaced. Francis Deng notes that Dinka and Nuer counter-insurgency attacks contributed to a higher frequency and degree of displacement among the non-poor households in Bahr al-Ghazal region than the Arab-sponsored militia raids (2008: 382). Similar displacement patterns among the Nuer residents of Western Upper Nile revealed that economics and prospects of enrichment through looting of property were key factors in triggering and sustaining the occurrence of militia attacks. They reported that during Arab attacks 'no household, no woman or child was spared'. Nuer militia attacks, however, usually targeted specific households, since 'the commanders were fighting each other, and they were eager to get their cows'.

Locating Nuer mobility: migration and displacement

The conflict that erupted in 1983 left around five million people internally displaced and an estimated 500,000-700,000 seeking refuge in neighbouring countries.[35] The Western Upper Nile region experienced most displacement during the 1990s conflicts over oil, with an estimated 70,500 Nuer civilians leaving the area between June 1998 and December 1999.[36]

The current migration and displacement of the Nuer population must be seen in the context of the wider mobility agro-pastoralist Nilotes. Seasonal migration with cattle or subsequently for work or trade has been an enduring feature of Nuer lives. In addition, the experiences of the eighteenth-century expansion of the Nuer saw migratory journeys from the Western Upper Nile towards the east, resulting in the absorption of thousands of Dinka and Anyuak communities. Although migration has long been an integral feature of the majority of agro-pastoralist

---

[32] Dianne Shandy, *Nuer–American Passages: Globalizing Sudanese Migration* (Florida, 2007), p. 37.
[33] See James Schechter, 'Lost Boys: Governing Sudanese Refugees in a UNHCR Camp', PhD thesis, University of Colorado, 2004, p. 71.
[34] J. Harker 'Human Security in Sudan: The Report of a Canadian Assessment Mission', January 2000; J. Rone "Sudan, Oil and Human Rights", Human Rights Watch: November 2002.
[35] In Kenya, over 70,000 Sudanese refugees resided in refugee camps in Kakuma and in Nairobi; in Uganda 212,000 were self-settled; in Ethiopia 96,000 were mainly in camps; in Egypt 30,000 lived in towns; and 45,000, 36,000 and over 200,000 were displaced to the Democratic Republic of Congo, Central African Republic and Chad, respectively (ICG, *God, Oil and Country*).
[36] Hutchinson, *Nuer Ethnicity Militarized*, p. 7.

Nilotic populations, this recent massive dispersal is unprecedented in its often forced nature, scale and direction. The option of returning to a previous place of residence was closed to many for years, sometimes decades. The massive displacement post-1983 opened up new migratory routes for Nuer communities as well as other southern Sudanese. Those living near border areas usually crossed over to Ethiopia, Kenya, Uganda, or the Central African Republic, settling either locally or in UN- or host government-administered refugee camps. Others migrated towards Khartoum and settled in squatter areas around the capital, where they were subjected to continuous harassment, displacement and abuse from the government and the local population.[37] In addition to emerging southern Sudanese (including Nuer) diasporas in nearby African countries,[38] the resettling of refugees in Western countries resulted in the creation of substantial Nuer communities in Canada, Australia and the USA.[39]

A 60-something woman chief of Padeh, a payam in Lɛr, recounted the story of her family:

> When the fighting with the Arabs started, our village was bombed. But we managed and we stayed in the village. But then Gadet[40] came and took all our cows. During the war, most of the children went to Khartoum. One of the daughters was taken [as a wife] by the Bul. She has not come back yet. My husband was killed by the soldiers in front of me. I stayed in the village because someone had to take care of the people. One of my sons went to Ethiopia, but I am not sure where he is now.

Nyamead, now in her late sixties, was one of the few who stayed behind after the 1998 destruction of Lɛr:

> All people from this area ran away, some went to Nyuong [south of Lɛr], others to Eastern Nuer, some to Khartoum. We remained [the] only two women here. During the war, Antonovs [Russian-made military planes used by the government of Sudan] used to bomb us. We would dig a hole and stay there during the day. At night we would go next to the primary school and hide there. There were no people here, only wild animals but they did nothing to us... *Why did you stay here?* I was very annoyed, my first child [son] died and my daughter died the same day. I was already a widow and an old woman. I asked myself: what type of life will I live? I decided to stay here and die.

As these narratives show, displacement experiences varied for women (and men). The majority of the Western Upper Nile population was

[37] See Munzoul Assal, 'Rights and Decisions to Return: Internally Displaced Persons in Post-War Sudan', in K. Grabska and L. Mehta (eds), *Forced Displacement: Why Rights Matter?* (London, 2008), pp. 139–58; Hutchinson, *Nuer Dilemmas*.

[38] There is a growing body of literature on the Sudanese diaspora, including refugees in Egypt who settled in Cairo and Alexandria (see bibliography).

[39] See Shandy, *Nuer-American Passages*.

[40] Bul Nuer, inhabitants of the Bentiu area and the Dok Nuer, residing in Lɛr county, experienced some of the most fierce inter-community fighting in the late 1990s and early 2000. Some Bul Nuer were supported by the Khartoum government and used as a proxy to destabilise the western Nuer communities. However, there were some Bul Nuer fighting for the SPLA and non-Bul Nuer in Matip's militia. Peter Gatdet kept changing sides (see Douglas Johnson, 'The Nuer Civil Wars').

displaced, with some migrating long distances and others searching for temporary refuge nearby. Nuer women and men narrated how their families, households and communities were separated due to constant insecurity, multi-directional violence, abrupt displacement and terror campaigns to clear oilfields for the economic benefit of Khartoum, multinationals and local warlords. Like that of Nyamead, most stories that I collected were told in a fragmented manner, with members of the same household having gone through a variety of experiences during the conflicts, some dispersing, others staying behind, joining the SPLA or counter-insurgent groups and/or becoming their victims. During the inter-ethnic fighting, the majority of the western Nuer who migrated moved to Khartoum, it being the closest and most accessible destination. When the Dinka–Nuer violence subsided and the Nuer–Nuer fighting intensified, many Dok Nuer moved south into Dinka lands. Almost all the people I met had relatives in Khartoum, Juba, East Africa and the west. Some even had family in China.

Although it is often argued that war-time migration (as opposed to economic migration) is characterised as forced, involuntary and unplanned,[41] the experiences of many southern Sudanese who became refugees in Kakuma or were displaced internally give a different picture. Strategising where, how and when to move was part of the dispersal process. Although some of the aspects of migration could not be planned due to increasing insecurity and escalating fighting, those who moved far away from their places of origin usually had some degree of control over their movement (see the next section). Access to mobility, however, was not equal and open to all. Displacement was highly gendered, with those in privileged positions having greater access to more secure places, and boys and men being more mobile as they searched for protection, livelihood and education. Hence, there were differences in people's and household members' experiences during the wars as well as barriers to sharing these experiences.

Mobility, diversity and gender: 'lost boys', 'invisible girls' and 'the world of women'

Most of the people whom I met had been displaced several times, with some migrating first to Khartoum, then making their way to refugee camps in Ethiopia, and later to Kenya or Uganda. Their narratives were filled with metaphors of running, constant movement from one place to another, hunger, starvation, death and a will to survive. Some travelled by foot, others by boat, truck, donkey and plane. The journeys took from days to months, depending on access, the resources at the household's disposal and distance to the destination. Some families followed husbands who had joined the SPLA, settling with them either around the military camps or in the refugee camps in Ethiopia. Others took the

---

[41] Egon Kunz, 'Exile and Resettlement: Refugee Theory', *International Migration Review*, 1981, Vol. 15, pp. 42–51; Anthony Richmond, 'Sociological Theories of International Migration: The Case of Refugees', *Current Sociology*, 1988, Vol. 36, pp. 7–25.

decision to separate, with men going into the bush, leaving some of their wives and the children behind. Later on, higher-ranking soldiers who reached refugee camps in Ethiopia and Kenya arranged for their families to join them, sometimes leaving one wife behind to look after property. There were also those who managed to reach refuge through their connections to international humanitarian and missionary organisations delivering aid during the war. Many bribed pilots of humanitarian planes to fly their family members to Kenya. Others, like the family of my research companion in Kakuma, Nyakuoth, came to Kenya through their church.[42] Hence, access to refugee camps in Kenya was partially considered a privilege open to influential SPLA officers, church members and humanitarian aid workers. Those without connections would often sell their remaining property (cows) and move towards Khartoum, a closer and thus more accessible location.

Differing access to migration was apparent in the demographic composition of the refugee population in Kakuma. According to official UNHCR statistics, there was a great imbalance in the percentage of women and girls to boys and men, being especially pronounced in the ratio of girls of marriageable age to boys or young men.[43] This had a direct impact on changes in gender and generational relations in the camp. At the same time, there were high numbers of elder women with children whose husbands had stayed in southern Sudan as they were fighting in the war, or had returned just after the signing of the peace agreement in order to secure positions in the southern Sudanese government. Many were widows of either high-ranking SPLA officers who had been able to take their families to a safe refuge outside the country. It should be noted that Kakuma camp was famous as a place for high-ranking SPLA officers. In fact, many of them sent their families to the camp for protection and education, visiting them when on leave.

Becoming 'lost boys': war as suffering, war as opportunity
I met Kim when I first arrived in southern Sudan in January 2007 in Rubkona. Kim was working as a field co-ordinator with a UN agency in Western Upper Nile. He was part of the 'lost boys' group who had left Sudan in 1988. He came back to southern Sudan in 2005:

> I was one of the SPLA child soldiers. The SPLA commanders came to the house of my parents and they requested that my father gives one boy to the army. My father had two wives, and my mother was the second wife. I was the first-born of my mother but I was not the oldest son.
> I was maybe eight or nine years old then. It was not supposed to be me who was going to be sent to the army. But because my father knew that I was smart and strong he was convinced that I was the only one who would survive this difficult journey to Ethiopia. That's why he convinced my mother to give me to the SPLA. My mother was crying and threatened him with divorce. But at the end she had to accept.

[42] Nyakuoth's father was a pastor in the Presbyterian church. When fighting intensified in Lɛr, he arranged for his family to be taken to Kenya through church connections.
[43] Country Operations Plan for Kenya, UNHCR Kenya (2006).

The journey to Ethiopia was very difficult. Many of the children lost their lives on the way. Once we arrived in Ethiopia we were in the Bilpam camp. In the morning we went to school, at one o'clock we would finish classes and prepare food for ourselves and then in the afternoon we had to go and do military training. Then we would be sent for military training every six months. Once the children reached the age of 12 they would be sent to combat. [...]

When the Mengistu regime fell in Ethiopia, you have heard of the crossing of the Gillo river, when so many of the Sudanese children were killed. I was about 11 years old then. The ones who were shooting at us, and I saw this with my own eyes, were women who were in the Ethiopian army [EPRDF army]. They had big guns and machine guns and they just shot everyone. They did not pay attention that we were children. I was thinking, how could they do that, they are women and have children themselves? But you know, women are more full of revenge than men. They do not forget.

The way to Kakuma through Ethiopia was very difficult. We were escorted by the teachers, who were given guns and they were in charge of our protection. ICRC gave us food on the way. We went first to Pochalla and stayed there nine months. Then we proceeded to Kapoeta, and then to Narus and from there to Lokichoggio. We finally arrived in Kakuma. We were some 16,000 boys who left from Ethiopia and only 14,000 made it to Kakuma. Among those, there were maybe some 2,000 Nuer. The majority were Dinka. Some of the boys then went back to Sudan, although it was not easy to cross the border because the Kenyan government was controlling it. Many of the lost boys then got resettled mainly to America.

Most of the young men in the camp like Kim and his friends were part of the group dubbed the 'lost boys'. They had left southern Sudan in the 1980s after being recruited by the SPLA, taken from their parents often without their knowledge, and put in military training camps in Ethiopia as part of the Red Army, described below. Following Mengistu's fall in 1991, the new Ethiopian government, which was composed of rebel groups supported by al-Bashir's regime, was hostile to the SPLA leadership and its constituency housed in the UNHCR-supported and SPLA-managed camps throughout Western Ethiopia.[44] As a result of the hostility and insecurity in the border region of Gambella,[45] the SPLA had to evacuate their camps and 200-350,000 Sudanese were forced back into southern Sudan, including Kim and many other young men I later met in Kakuma.[46]

Kim and other boys under the guardianship of their teachers undertook a long journey on foot from Ethiopia to Kenya via Sudan. Many died on the way, while others became severely malnourished and barely made it across the border. Some 16,000 were assisted with food and medicine by the ICRC during their passage. They reached the Kenyan border in April 1992, several months after leaving Ethiopia. The UNHCR set up an emergency camp first in Lokichoggio, the border town. A few months later it

[44] See Schechter, 'Lost Boys'.
[45] In addition to the threat that the Provisional Government of Ethiopia would allow Sudan's government to launch attacks from inside Ethiopia, refugees faced insecurity created by combat between Ethiopian Nuer and Anyuak militias in the Gambella area, where the bulk of SPLA bases were located, and marauding bands of armed men (Johnson 2006:88). The Sudanese air force initiated a bombing campaign against returnees and in 1992 launched a cross-border attack on Pochalla, where large displaced persons' camps were set up (HRW 1994).
[46] See Madut Jok and Hutchinson, 'Sudan's Prolonged Second Civil War'.

was moved to Kakuma for security reasons. The term 'lost boys' derives from the tale of Peter Pan and was given to this group by international aid workers in the 1990s when humanitarian agencies learned about their horrific conditions. It was later picked up by the media, US Christian organisations and the US government to justify the resettlement of 3,800 'orphan' boys in the USA.[47]

A larger group of young boys and men in Kakuma arrived in early 2000, and after, but the trajectories of their journeys and displacement were very different to those who came in 1992. However, as they had also experienced military training at a young age, they put themselves in the same category of 'lost boys'. Some came to Kakuma as a result of being wounded in Sudan, others to pursue education. The wounded were transported to the ICRC hospital in Lokichoggio and subsequently went to the camp in order to escape military life. Many young male soldiers in the SPLA or other rebel groups were sent to the camp by their commanders to further their education. As young men and boys reported on numerous occasions: 'We have a mission here; it is education; once the mission is complete, we will go back.'

Many of these young men had undergone multiple journeys and displacements. Tito, Bol and Gatmai, a group of young male friends from Lεr, escaped first to Khartoum to avoid military recruitment and to search for work and education. Later, they made their way to refugee camps in Ethiopia in hope of accessing education and food. As poverty and insecurity for the Sudanese intensified after Mengistu's fall in 1991, they went to Kenya, settling first in Nairobi and then moving to Kakuma. One of the three friends I met after their return to Lεr also had a short stint in Uganda while hoping to access education.

For these young men, war was a double-edged sword, marked by great suffering, sacrifice, brutality and violence, but it also created an opportunity to access education and improve family livelihoods. A 22-year-old Nuer in Kakuma told me:

> If we were not soldiers we would not have gotten the chance to be here. Because we were soldiers we managed to come to Kakuma. It was my father who was told to select two or three boys to be soldiers. One lost his life in the war as a soldier. Our father hid two of us and tried to get some ways for us to study.
>
> In Sudan we did not know anything, we knew nothing about Sudan. We only knew our village. But now, we have known the Sudan, Africa and the world at large. So it is a great advantage for us. If there was no civil war in Sudan we would not be able to study here. The civil war has given us a great advantage. So nowadays, as we go back, we already know that this is our land and we have to work for it. We do not expect white people to come from abroad and work for us, what are we? It is our land and our grand grandfathers lost their lives to prepare us for life. We have to work and make peace in our land. The war has given a great advantage to us, or to myself. Because without the war maybe now I could lose my life in a war [in local fighting over cattle or girls] or I would be keeping cattle. But now when I go back I will not be keeping cattle again. What I will be doing as I go back it will be official.

[47] The USA resettled the 'lost boys' as refugees on the grounds that they would be persecuted in their native Sudan. Halted after 9/11 for security reasons, the programme that brought the 'lost boys' to the USA restarted in 2004.

The USA resettlement programme encouraged young boys to migrate. As Dianne Shandy argues, 'the experience of Nuer refugee migrants demonstrates the ways in which actions of individuals were undertaken on behalf of family groups'.[48] She shows how through pooling of family resources, Nuer refugees were able to access third-country resettlement. When the rumour of resettlement to the USA spread in refugee camps and across the border to Sudan, many families decided to send their children to the camps. A number of young men in Kakuma reported that their families sold cattle or bribed church or humanitarian organisations in order to arrange the transfer of their children to the camps. There were also rumours, narrated to me by eyewitnesses, of the SPLA commanders sending their own sons and relatives to Kakuma as 'lost boys'. In 2006, the USA started receiving requests from the resettled 'lost boys', many now US citizens, to bring in their families from Sudan, or from Kakuma. In the words of one of the US officials, this is when the USA faced a dilemma.[49] The boys had been resettled as orphans, but some still had mothers, fathers and siblings in Sudan, Ethiopia or Kakuma, and had often had direct contact with them even before resettlement and were currently supporting them through remittances.[50]

As education became more valued, many boys decided to undertake migratory journeys in search of knowledge and access to schools. Families primarily sent sons to the refugee camps for education. In numerous cases, brothers and cousins would migrate to Kakuma and form boy-run households, while their sisters, mothers and fathers stayed behind in Sudan. By the late 1990s, Kakuma had become well known in Sudan as a place offering free education, and was often referred to by international humanitarians as a 'boarding school'. Some would even argue that Kakuma was a school (and a training camp) for SPLA soldiers.

The world of women and 'invisible girls'

As a result of war, it is estimated that women now outnumber men in South Sudan. There are no official statistics on the number of widows and orphans, but this gender imbalance has been acknowledged by the Government of Southern Sudan (GoSS), which created a post of Minister for Widows and Orphans Affairs. During my stay in the region, the minister was touring southern Sudan to estimate the number of war widows and orphans.[51] For widows of SPLA soldiers, GoSS provides jobs or reimburses rents. During my travels around the Greater Upper Nile region, I came across many villages inhabited only by women, chil-

[48] Shandy, 'Transnational Linkages between Refugees in Africa and in the Diaspora', *Forced Migration Review*, 2003, Vol. 16, pp. 7–9.
[49] Personal conversation (2006) with the US representative of the Bureau of Population, Refugees, and Migration. It is the US agency responsible for the refugee resettlement programme. I was told that at present the US government is keeping on hold the family reunification claims.
[50] Katarzyna Grabska, 'Lost Boys, Invisible Girls: Stories of Marriage across Borders', *Gender, Place and Culture*, 2010.
[51] See Mary Ann Fitzgerald, *Throwing the Stick Forward: The Impact of War on Southern Sudanese Women* (Nairobi, 2002).

dren and a few elderly men. Many women were widows or had been left behind to look after property. Those without family connections to the SPLA, churches or international organisations had much less chance of reaching distant destinations such as Kakuma. When I asked an elderly woman in Maper about the whereabouts of the missing men, she explained:

> All men have gone. Boys were taken to the army, men were killed during the war, went to fight in the bush, or went off to the north. Others went for refuge in other countries. We, the women, are the ones who stayed behind. We had to take care of the children, the property and the cattle, when the men were running.

The gender and generational imbalance in Kakuma, southern Sudan and in the resettlement countries[52] has been influenced by gendered access to migration (and mobility) among the Nuer. It has also been determined by the differentiated responsibilities of women and men in the household, with women staying at home to protect homesteads and men going to the battlefields.

Migration and displacement were affected by and affected Nuer gender identities, the division of labour and gender ideologies. Boys and young men were more mobile, with easier access to refuge than girls and women. According to Nuer gender ideologies, women and girls are more closely associated with the homestead, as this is their domain of work and protection. As sources of valuable bridewealth, the chastity and purity of girls is to be protected, as girls who are 'spoilt' (*keaagh*) lose value and command a lower number of cattle.[53] Although younger girls join their brothers in the migration during cattle grazing periods, migration for education and labour is exclusively reserved for male relatives.

When I inquired about the reasons for the lack of girls in Kakuma, a young man explained to me:

> In our culture, girls are not allowed to move on their own. They have to stay with the family. The boys are free to go and explore. Also, girls are not supposed to go to school because it is believed that they would become prostitutes and the benefit of a girl for her parents will be lost. The boys are the ones who get education. Girls do not have brains for it. They are there to serve us, the men, they are there to give birth to children and for the parents to get wealth [bridewealth payments in form of cattle] from them. As a Nuer, you cannot allow your daughter to go around by herself. Also, the conditions of the journey during the war were so difficult that the girls would have never survived them. It is only the boys, because they are strong, who were able to make it.

[52] The gender imbalance was also visible in the Sudanese communities resettled in the USA, Australia and Canada. In the USA, for example, in the period between 1990–1997, among the 4,306 resettled Sudanese, there were three adult males to one adult female (Shandy, *Nuer–American Passages*, p. 64). Only 89 'lost girls' compared to roughly 3,500 'lost boys' resettled in the USA in 2001 (Charles London, 'The Forgotten Children of Sudan', (Refugees International, 2003)). Hence, as Shandy argues, the 'selection of refugees for resettlement in the Unites States is gendered' (p. 64).
[53] Evans-Pritchard, *Nuer Religion*; Hutchinson, *Nuer Dilemmas*; interviews with Nuer men and women.

Nuer women and men offered further explanations of the high demographic imbalance in the camps. Access to refugee camps was mainly
through military recruitment, with the SPLA predominantly targeting
boys.[54] Migration to the camps was seen as a strategy of investment
in sons, education not being considered appropriate for girls. Only
a limited number of girls managed to make their way to the refugee
camps, mostly through coming with their families. In most cases, their
fathers or brothers were either in the military, had high political positions, or were active in a church. Others were sent by their parents to
support married female relatives who had migrated to the camps with
their husbands.

To summarise, although circumscribed by the conditions of war and
violence, southern Sudanese boys and male youth nonetheless had
greater room for manoeuvre with regard to war-time migration. Through
their modest strategic and tactic agency, they were trying to get out of
what Hendrik Vigh, in his study of youth soldiers in Guinea Bissau, refers
to as a lost generation 'locked' into a position of social confinement.[55]
Unlike the Guinean youth, who had fewer options for escaping the
violence, the southern Sudanese had some leeway, not only in deciding
whether to leave, but also where to go. Many found support through
kin members, family and friends in accessing education in Nairobi and
Kampala. Being a youth meant, as elsewhere in Africa, escaping socially
confining structures and experimenting with other paths to adulthood,
including migration and military training.

Their actions also show that despite war conditions, they were
pursuing longer-term life projects. Mats Utas draws on a term coined by
Vigh to describe this mode of social interaction as 'social navigation' –
'the way in which agents guide their lives through troublesome social
and political circumstances'.[56] Under the severe and brutal circumstances of war, military recruitment provided an opportunity not only
to re-configure masculine identities but also, for some, access to education and autonomy. Boys enjoyed greater scope to decide how, where
and whether to migrate while balancing their personal and communal
risks, costs and benefits. For Nuer and southern Sudanese girls (and
women), the gendered notions of femininity and their position in the
household and community at large made them more invisible and less
mobile. However, they were not simply passive victims of war, but
managed, as will be shown, to survive, resist and negotiate their position in the conflict zones.

---

[54] While the camp officials in Kakuma were well aware of this fact, the issue was
not publicly discussed.
[55] Hendrik E. Vigh, 'Social Death and Violent Life Chances', in C. Christiansen, M.
Utas and H.E. Vigh (eds), *Navigating Youth, Generating Adulthood: Social becoming
in an African Context* (Uppsala, 2006), p. 46.
[56] Mats Utas, 'Building a Future? The Reintegration and Remarginalisation
of Youth in Liberia', in P. Richards (ed.), *No Peace, No War: An Anthropology of
Contemporary Armed Conflicts* (Oxford, 2005), p. 408; Vigh, *Navigating Terrains of
War: Youth and Soldiering in Guinea-Bissau* (New York, 2007).

WOMEN AND MEN: WAR AND VIOLENCE

The ethnicisation of Dinka–Nuer warfare: violence on women's bodies

While women and children were targets of military action by the northern Sudanese state and its Arab militias until 1991, Nuer and Dinka fighters did not intentionally target and kill women, children or the elderly. However, subsequent south–south warfare was often characterised by the abandonment of codes of fighting both had previously honoured. Women and children became the primary victims of 'the war of the educated'.[57] The burning of households and crops, previously prohibited in Nuer/Dinka community confrontations, became part of war tactics in the south–south conflicts.

As Hutchinson shows, the 1990s south–south violence led to 'a rapid polarization and militarization of Nuer/Dinka ethnic identities' and 'a reformulation of the relationship between gender and ethnicity in Nuer eyes'.[58] Historically, Nuer ethnicity was based on the performative concept where women and children could acquire the ethnic/community identity of their husbands through marriage and the transfer of bride-wealth. As the Nuer women and men argue, 'girls and women belong to everyone, except in bed'. Hence, any Dinka girl or woman, and consequently a child, could become a Nuer through marriage. The south–south violence, however, led to the rejection of this fluid notion of ethnicity, as Hutchinson asserts, 'in favour of a more "primordialist" concept rooted in procreative metaphors of shared blood'.[59] This was confirmed by my respondents, who argued that 'now you can only be Nuer through blood' (i.e. if you were born a Nuer). Women and children could no longer acquire different ethnic identity through marriage and cattle. Hence, the ethnic identities of Nuer became more rigid, with blood taking precedence over bridewealth. As a result, Dinka and Nuer women and children became military targets as their ethnicity was now perceived as fixed. This also

---

[57] The elders I interviewed explained that the intentional killing of women used to be considered a cowardly act, an affront against *kuoth nhial*, which would bring disaster and misfortune to the community. In the past, in order to redress such acts, Evans-Pritchard and Hutchinson show how acts of homicide among the Nuer (and Dinka) were subject to a series of ethics and spiritual taboos that required an identification of the slayer and purification of his polluted blood through the payment of blood-wealth cattle compensation to the family of the deceased. The purification was completed by a blood release (*bier*) from the slayer's finger or forearm by the earth priest (*kuaar muon*) (Evans-Pritchard, *Nuer Religion*, p. 293). The purification of *nueer*, the pollution of blood through homicide, was considered necessary to avoid divine anger. The Nuer believe that without performing this procedure the slayer and his family would die, especially if they ever shared food with the family of the deceased. During the first civil war, with the influx of guns, this tradition started to change, as it became impossible due to the ambiguous nature of the bullet to identify the particular slayer. Hutchinson, in 'Nuer Ethnicity Militarized', discusses the changing nature of the taboo and the resulting change in Nuer ethnic identities.
[58] Hutchinson, 'Nuer Ethnicity Militarized', p. 7.
[59] Ibid., p. 8.

had implications for child custody disputes. In Kakuma, I witnessed a case around a child born to a Dinka woman married to a Nuer man. In Kakuma, she became pregnant by her Dinka lover. The Dinka community argued that the child belonged to the biological father, a direct contradiction of the paternity rules of both Dinka and Nuer.[60] In the end, the Dinka requested a DNA test, which was supported by a UNHCR protection officer, in order to establish custody rights.

This hardening of identities is common in ethnic-based conflicts across the globe, as women, no longer immune from inter-community fighting, are transformed into boundary-makers in ethno-nationalist identity struggles.[61] Ethnicity appears in part to be created, maintained and socialised through male control of gender identities, as women's fundamental human rights and dignity are caught up in male power struggles.

The indiscriminate killing of civilian women and children and wilful destruction of property by Dinka and Nuer military groups marked a new turning point in the south–north conflict and in the inter- and intra-community fighting. The Bul Nuer militia of Matip and the SPLA forces of Peter Gadet (also Bul Nuer, he kept changing sides) raided back and forth across the homelands of the Dok. In 1998, they destroyed the booming market centre at Lɛr, which was Machar's hometown and a hub for international humanitarian relief.[62] They kidnapped, raped and killed women and children, often in front of their husbands, brothers and fathers. Majok, a young man who escaped forced recruitment by the SPLA and stayed throughout the war in Lɛr, told me:

> When the Bridage [as the respondent referred to Paulino Matip's splinter group] came in 1998, I ran to the bush and hid there. Then I saw a group of seven, maybe ten, soldiers brought [sic] a young woman, my neighbour. They raped her, one after another, beating her in the process. I was in the bush and saw this all in front of me. I was too scared to stop them. When they finished, they just left her there, in a puddle of blood. She survived, but then she started losing weight. She complained to the chiefs, but nothing happened. Many women and girls were raped during the war. Most of them were then divorced by their husbands, or married by old men, who did not mind that they were already used [*keaagh*].

Through such acts, the militia men not only destroyed the ethnic identity rooted in women's bodies, but also humiliated Nuer men, who were powerless to protect their women and children. Rape, as in other contem-

---

[60] Both Dinka and Nuer consider paternity rights based on who paid for the cattle. Even if a child was born out of wedlock, the official husband who paid cattle for the wife is entitled to the child. However, the biological father can claim rights to the child provided he pays cattle compensation (*ruok*) for the child to the official husband.

[61] See, for example, Judy El-Bushra, 'Transforming Conflict: Some Thoughts on a Gendered Understanding of Conflict Processes', in S. Jacobs, R. Jacobsen and J. Marchbank (eds), *States of Conflict: Gender Violence and Resistance* (London, 2000), pp. 66–87; Nira Yuval-Davis, *Gender and Nation* (London, 1997); Dubravka Zarkov (ed.), *Gender, Violent Conflict and Development* (New Delhi, 2008).

[62] See Harker 'Human Security in Sudan: The Report of a Canadian Assessment Mission'; G. Gagnon and J. Ryle 'Report of an Investigation into Oil Development, Conflict and Displacement in Western Upper Nile' 2001; Rone 2003.

porary conflicts in former Yugoslavia, the Great Lakes, Liberia and Sierra Leone, was used both as a weapon to exterminate other groups,[63] as Majok's narrative suggests, and as a tool to subdue and emasculate rival men in order to undermine their morale and fighting spirit.

Nuer women and men mentioned grave suffering and profound trauma as a result of war.[64] The suffering was so great that at funerals women would not shed tears. 'Our tears have dried out. We cried too much during the time of wars, we lost so many children, we have seen so much death. We have no more tears left,' explained a middle-aged woman at a funeral of a dignitary in Lεr. Violence, death, loss and displacement were narrated in interrupted manner by refugees in Kakuma, as well as by those who had stayed behind in southern Sudan. There were unuttered words and prolonged silences. Many women often talked about rapes, violence, torture, hunger, running and fear endured during the wars. Nyadak, now in her late twenties, stayed in Lεr while her mother went for treatment to Kakuma. She recalled her experiences:

> You were never sure who would come at night to take you, your children, or your food. It could be the Arabs, or the Brigades, or the SPLA soldiers. If you made a mistake of giving all food to one group, the other would accuse you of being a wife of the enemy and they would either make you into their wife [rape] or kill you on the spot.

Caught up in the web of politicised and greed-driven conflicts between adult men, women, children and elders were all exposed to inter- and intra-ethnic violence that came from every corner, often from those who supposedly were their protectors. When telling their stories filled with struggle, death and suffering, these women often laughed, since laughter, as they told me, was the only way to cope with tremendous loss and pain. On other occasions, when asked about the war and their journeys through displacement, they would become quiet, or utter a few dismissive words: 'What is there to tell? It was war, and now it is over'. It was during these moments of silence, interrupted narratives and quiet nodding of heads that I also found a way of understanding their unbearable, indescribable and painful experiences. Studying violence, its gendered nature and its painful aftermath became for me a study of unspoken words, sighs and silences.

Militarised masculinities: From *gaar*, *mut* and *ric* to military training, gun and battalion

> I lived with an AK-47
> By my side
> Slept with one eye open wide
> Run

---

[63] Jacobs et al., *States of Conflict: Gender Violence and Resistance*; Zarkov, *Gender, Violent Conflict and Development*.
[64] The spread of indiscriminate violence is linked to Machar's relaxation of Nuer homicide codes in 1986. See Hutchinson in Webner, 'Death, Memory and the Politics of Legitimation: Nuer Experiences of the Continuing Second Civil War'.

Duck
Play dead
Hide
I've seen my people die like flies

(Emmanuel Jal, 'Forced to Sin'; Nuer 'Lost Boy' turned rap singer)

Nuer gender identities, and particularly masculinities, as Hutchinson argues, have been transformed as a result of colonisation, modern government, education and Christianity.[65] This shows how, historically, their gender and generational relations have been in continual motion. During colonial times, with the development of government chiefs, markets, courts and the introduction of churches, there were significant shifts in power relations within the communities and households. Young men usurped the elder generation as the rules of access to government positions and hence social position changed. This was also at the expense of the position of women, who found themselves in a more difficult situation to negotiate their power within marriage and the wider community. It is important to underscore the continuous process of social change with the specific context of second civil war-time displacement.

The recent wars, the south-south violence in particular, further affected the reconfiguration of Nuer masculinities and resulted in the emergence of 'hyper-masculinities' and the weakening of men's position as household protectors and providers. I use the term 'hyper-masculinities' to delineate the emergence of a particular type of masculinity that is legitimised through violence (usually physical and often armed) over others (especially women). As in other places riven by conflict,[66] Nuer everyday life has been militarised through the spread of guns, forced recruitment, indiscriminate violence and the spread of nationalist ideologies. The new, post-1983 concept of manhood (*wur* – man) was no longer based on *gaar* (initiation marks on the forehead) received in a group of age-mates (*ric*) and the master of *mut* (spear) but, rather, on the experience of liberation struggle, shared military life and possession of a gun (*mac*). The bond with modern weapons has become a new marker of manhood and a livelihood option for Nuer youth.[67]

The militarisation of southern Sudanese communities was widespread. Almost all young and middle-aged men whom I met in Kakuma and later in southern Sudan had at some point in their lives undergone military training and taken part in the liberation struggle, either in the ranks of the SPLA or the SSIM, or a splinter militia group. In the late 1980s, in need of recruits, Garang decided to create youth cadres who would be trained

---

[65] Hutchinson, *Nuer Dilemmas*.
[66] See Paul Richards, *No Peace, No War: An Anthropology of Contemporary Armed Conflicts* (Oxford, 2005); Utas, 'Sweet Battlefields: Youth and the Liberian Civil War', PhD thesis, Uppsala University, 2003; Vigh, 'Social Death and Violent Life Chances'.
[67] See also Cherry Leonardi, '"Liberation" or Capture: Youth in between "Hakuma", and "Home" during Civil War and its Aftermath in Southern Sudan', *African Affairs*, 2008, Vol. 106, pp. 391–412, on this issue among other youth in Sudan.

in military camps in Ethiopia. According to Human Rights Watch estimates, there were between 17,000 and 40,000 young recruits trained in
Ethiopia.[68] Garang referred to them as the 'Red Army', the 'army without
fear', or as 'Seeds of Sudan': a young generation made to believe they
were the future of an independent southern Sudan.[69] In this way, as with
many other communist-inspired movements, the SPLA became a major
factor in the modernisation project of southern Sudanese communities.
Military experience, education, outlawing scarification (see below) and
propagation of collective southern Sudanese identity became important
tools in constructing new personal and community identities.[70]

Kuok, whom I introduced in Chapter 1, was one of the many young
recruits I met in Kakuma, and later in southern Sudan. He was a shy,
softly-spoken youth of twenty-seven. His parents died from *kala azar*
(visceral leishmaniasis) when he and his siblings were very young.
Joining the SPLA was a means to manage his social marginalisation:

> We were by ourselves. The uncle took our sister to his house, but we, the boys,
> had to manage [by] ourselves. We stayed in Lɛr, in the town, surviving by
> ourselves. No one wanted to take us in. It was time of the war and many people
> were suffering. My life was very hard. One day I made a decision to go to Ethiopia.
> I heard from the SPLA soldiers that there was education in the [training] camps.
> With some other boys, we went to the SPLA barracks in Piliny, near Lɛr, and we
> told them that we wanted to join. I was hoping that I would get education and
> that I could help myself and my siblings later on.
>
> There were many children in the recruitment place. Most of them were
> recruited through the chiefs. SPLA commanders would come to the chiefs and
> tell them that they needed children, boys, to be sent to education in Ethiopia.
> Some children chose to go because they were in difficult situation, maybe they
> were orphans or the family situation was difficult. Others were selected by their
> family; usually disturbing, trouble-making children were sent to education, as
> education was not that valued then. Then there were others who were forced [by
> the SPLA soldiers].
>
> They were maybe 1,500 or more boys, some very small children who could
> not even walk [being too young to walk long distances]. We all walked together,
> through rivers and deserts and then reached Ethiopia.

Gatchang, in his early thirties, related a different experience of how he
and his brother were recruited:

> In 1983, my older brother, Gatkoi, decided that he wanted to join the SPLA. My
> father was opposed to this idea, but Gatkoi insisted. He wanted to wear a uniform
> and be a real Nuer man. I was still very small then.
>
> Before joining, he told my father that he wanted to be marked, but my father
> refused. Later I learned that it was our mother who wanted him to be marked
> because she wanted to have a son who was a '*wur pany*' [real man]. Gatkoi insisted
> that he wanted to get marks so others would recognise that he was a Nuer. In
> the end, my father agreed and my brother got his marks. Normally, '*gaar*' initia-
> tion is done in a group, '*ric*' [an age-set]. However, because it was the dry season
> there were no other boys to be marked then and my brother was the only one who

---

[68] HRW, *Civilian Devastation: Abuses by All Parties in the War in Southern Sudan*
(New York, 1994).
[69] See Dave Eggers, *What is the What?* (San Francisco, 2006), p. 300.
[70] See Carol Berger, 'The SPLA and Lost Boys', PhD thesis, University of Oxford,
2010, who specifically addresses this dimension.

received '*gaar*'. He then went and joined SPLA, got his uniform and a gun. He was sent to Ethiopia for training and came back after four years in 1987.

In that year, I, together with my uncle Rock, who was about two years older than me, were also taken by the soldiers to join the school, as we were told, in Ethiopia. Many children did not want to go. However, the soldiers would come to the house and would take all the boys above the age of seven with them, whether the families were in agreement or not. We were then sent to capture other children.

I remember that the soldiers told me to go to one of the cattle camps near Thonyor [a small village near Lɛr] and find some boys. I was running after a small boy who was trying to escape. Finally, I caught him and I was about to take him, when the boy started crying. He was crying very much and calling his father and his mother. He was very small. At that moment, I thought about my own parents and my heart became very, very sad. I felt very bad and I let the boy go and told him to run fast so others will not catch him. Many of the parents did not have any idea where the children were going and whether they would ever come back.

The stories represent experiences of thousands of other young boys who constituted the backbone of the SPLA recruitment strategy. While some children were taken forcibly by soldiers, other parents decided to send their sons to the army not only to support 'the national struggle'[71] but also to avoid death and starvation. Kim's narrative presented earlier in the chapter points to the fact that military enlistment became one of the family responsibilities that sons were supposed to fulfil. Their embeddedness in the household economy and roles as future protectors and providers for elderly parents underlined their willingness and obligation to join the army. Other men and boys, including Kuok, Gatchang and his brother, joined in willingly, as they saw it as an opportunity not only to access education, but also to gain their manhood, a livelihood, a position in the community and/or contest their social marginalisation.

In his analysis of the impact of war on Dinka communities in Northern Bahr al-Ghazal, Jok suggests that the condition of living under permanent conflict and political violence is one where 'fighting and defending one's family and property is a major preoccupation'.[72] The young recruits such as Kim and Kuok argued that family responsibility was the primary motivation for joining military groups and resorting to the use of guns. Family responsibility is a relatively unexplored proposition in the literature on youth militarisation. Anthropological explanations of youth violence focus rather on tensions inherent in gerontocratic societies.[73] More recent literature on conflicts in West Africa traces the socioeconomic nature of the youth crisis and how marginalised and

---

[71] January 2009 conversation with the father of Emmanuel Jal, now a famous rap musician, who originates from Lɛr. A former high-ranking SPLA officer, he ridiculed the notion of his son ever having been 'lost', explaining that he sent Emmanuel to the army because he wanted him to win fame as a liberator of the southerners. Emmanuel portrays the lives of the young recruits in his music, especially in his album entitled 'Warchild', released in 2008.

[72] Madut Jok, 'War, Changing Ethics and the Position of Youth in South Sudan', in J. Abbink and I. van Kessel (eds) *Vanguards or Vandals: Youth, Politics and Conflict in Africa* (Leiden, 2005), p. 177.

[73] See Eisei Kurimoto and Simon Simonse (eds), *Conflict, Age and Power in North East Africa* (London, 1994).

politicised youth become easily manipulated by political and economic interests.[74]

In southern Sudan, the common representation of the Red Army focuses on the forcible recruitment of the youth and their lack of agency. They are often described as a 'lost generation', pawns in the hands of adult combatants. Others such as Willis see 'chronic generational tensions' as the underlying roots of southern Sudanese youth militarisation.[75] The stories of Kim, Kuok, Gatkoi and Gatchang, however, show a much more complex picture of recruitment strategies, motivation and ways of coping with militarisation experienced by male youth. Intergenerational tensions were, rather, a consequence of youth militarisation, as will be shown in subsequent chapters.

Gatchang and Gatkoi's narratives also point also to their own agency in subverting, manipulating and taking advantage of their recruitment to achieve their more personal goals of autonomy and manhood. The circumstances under which young boys and men were recruited or voluntarily joined the army show that it was a combination of the overwhelming conditions of insecurity, war and lack of prospects for livelihood – together with family obligations and a new route to manhood and personal independence – that drove male youth into military life. Although there was tremendous pressure exerted during SPLA recruitment campaigns, the testimonies of Kuok and Gatchang reveal actual decision-making and the strategies used to avoid or use recruitment to achieve their own goals. This, I would argue, demonstrates youth agency. Despite being constrained by the overwhelming conditions of war, violence, starvation and political and community/household imperatives, some boys and youth were able to achieve some, albeit limited, degree of choice and to manipulate to some extent the circumstances, including migration in search of education and refuge in order to gain greater autonomy from the government and from their families.

These narratives point to another transformation in gender relations caused by war: the route to manhood. I met Wanten for the first time in January 2007, when I arrived in Bentiu. Lightly built and relatively short for a Nuer man, his face is handsome and has no marks or dots. Wanten was always smartly dressed in slacks, polished and pointed shoes, a pressed shirt, a Kenyan beaded belt and a small New Sudan flag pin in his collar. Born in 1980 near Rubkona in Western Nuerland, in 1987 he was forcibly recruited by the SPLA, who came to his parents and demanded a son for education in Ethiopia. He was taken to Funyido (also pronounced and spelled 'Punyido') camp in Ethiopia where he underwent a nine-month training course, living in military barracks.

---

[74] See, for example, Peter M. Kagwanja, '"Power to Uhuru": Youth Identity and Generational Politics in Kenya's 2002 Elections', *African Affairs*, 2006, Vol. 105, pp. 51–75; David Keen, *Conflict and Collusion in Sierra Leone* (Oxford, 2005).
[75] Justin Willis, 'Who put the "Y" in the BYDA? Youth in Sudan's Civil Wars', in B. Trudell (ed.), *Africa's Young Majority* (Edinburgh, 2002).

We would go to school in the morning with our AK-47 next to us, and then in the afternoon we would be trained. This lasted for nine months. Then, those who were bigger would be recruited to fight. Others would wait for their turn in the camp, going through the training every day. We were all armed.

We were all boys of different ages from Dinka and Nuer groups. There were no other children around. The conditions in the camp were bad. There was not enough food, we were often starving, there was nothing there. We were all thinking a lot about our families. We missed them very much. They knew nothing about what was happening to us, they knew nothing about where we were. Some of the boys would go crazy; they would sometimes start shooting around. Their minds would go crazy because they were traumatised, they were missing their parents, they were starving. Many of these boys died in the camp, others shoot themselves. We were all children with guns. We all kept thinking...

As a boy or a man you are not supposed to share your thoughts and feelings with others. So we did not talk about fear and loneliness. We kept it to ourselves. These thoughts were just going through our minds.

In the camps, our commanders and trainers were all Dinka and Nuer. They were all Sudanese. They used to tell us: 'We are training you to fight the enemy so that you can chase the enemy from our land. You are the future leaders of Sudan. You will take over our place as we are the old people who will go.' This is what we were told and this is what we believed. We did not think much about the usefulness of the fighting as we were children and we followed what we were told. I was scared at times but then I had to overcome my fears.

I fought for the first time in Pochalla. This was the first time I was shooting at the enemy. At the beginning, I was scared and I was shivering so that I could not even shoot. After five minutes or so I overcame my fears and started shooting. Then it became easier. Some of the boys were given drugs so that they would kill without fear. I never took the drugs because I knew there might be some side effects. After the battle, we did not share our fears and frustrations. You cannot talk about it. You have to be strong as a Nuer boy and man. You cannot show your weakness.

This narrative points to the transformation of both the route to manhood and concepts of masculinity. The initiation for boys through *gaar* has been progressively challenged and opposed by educated and baptised youth and by the architects of the national liberation project of South Sudan. SPLA leaders promoted non-ethnic differentiation in the army ranks,[76] prohibiting scarification and telling them that military training was initiation into manhood as the army battalion had replaced the age-set. In 1987, Machar, at that time the SPLA zonal commander of the Western Upper Nile, issued a decree outlawing Nuer scarification.[77] Life in the training camps, as the story of Wanten shows, was portrayed as a way for children to become 'responsible people' (*wic*) able to take care of themselves, which in Nuer and Dinka culture was a sign of adulthood. One of the young men in Kakuma told me:

As long as you were recruited as a soldier, you had to be a soldier. I was able to fight and kill people. This meant that I was a responsible person to myself. And the way I was trained, I had more experience than a child who was not trained. There was no other person who could take care of me. I became a responsible person.

[76] See Hutchinson, *Nuer Dilemmas*, pp. 270–98.
[77] Although fewer youth were scarified, especially those in urban areas, *gaar* continued among some displaced Nuer in Khartoum and among more isolated rural communities. It was completely outlawed in Kakuma.

Wanten's narrative also reveals how the gun has helped reconfigure Nuer concepts of masculinity. Many of the elderly men and women whom I met in southern Sudan talked about the past spear-fighting between the communities as the 'real wars' where the masculinity of the Nuer and Dinka was tested. An elderly woman from Lɛr who stayed in Sudan throughout the wars explained the difference between guns and spears:

> In the past, if you as a girl wanted to test whether your boyfriend was a real Nuer man [*wur nuära pany*], you would ask him to bring you a Dinka cow. But now these boys who run with guns are not real men, they are cowards who kill women and children, and steal property to enrich themselves. It is easy to kill with a gun; you do not have to be responsible [*wic*] to do it. The gun shoots by itself, whereas the spear requires you to think and dodge.

The new masculine identities of the gun-toting youth contributed to inter-generational conflict. The elders often felt that they were no longer able to control the youth, who had acquired power due to access to guns and resort to extreme violence and disregard of community obligations.

Wanten's experiences of first encounters with the gun and fighting demonstrate how the SPLA, like other armed forces, employed an ideal of hyper-masculinity in its military training in order to encourage aggressiveness, fearlessness and competitiveness. A growing sense of entitlement to the domestic and sexual services of women was also strongly promoted. Gatkoi, Wanten and other young men recalled the glorification of the power of the gun after their recruitment. Guns also marked fearlessness and opened up a range of new possibilities, not only in liberating communities, but also in exercising power over others by looting their property, raping their wives and taking their daughters for free. Prior to the 1991 split, the gun was a symbol of powerful, non-ethnicised and communal (military) masculinity. These ideas were clearly expressed in one of the SPLA graduation songs:

> Even your father, give him a bullet!
> Even your mother, give her a bullet!
> Your gun is your food, your gun is your wife.
> (Tape played by some of the respondents)

The result was a socially isolated community of male youth, armed and brutally trained not only to kill, but also to torture and loot. This new type of masculinity that emerged might be coined as 'hyper-masculinity', denoting the exaggeration of male stereotypical behaviour, particularly by its emphasis on strength, aggression and domination over women and over one's elders. The reliance on the gun for survival continues to create major problems for the disarmament of local militia and civilian groups in southern Sudan.[78]

Yet, the story of Wanten also reveals the traumatic experiences of boys who grew up in isolation from their parents, relatives and kin and

[78] See Matthew B. Arnold and Chris Alden, 'This Gun is our Food: Demilitarising the White Army Militias of South Sudan', *Norwegian Institute of International Affairs*, 2007.

were forced to be part of a nationalistic project of the leaders of the South Sudan Liberation Movement. Their fears, lack of food, unbearable living conditions and separation from their loved ones were manipulated by the commanders to create cadres of fearless, aggressive fighters with nothing to lose.

The new masculine identities propagated by the commanders in the camps were further reinforced through Garang's propaganda messages broadcast to southern Sudan, the military training camps in Ethiopia and refugee camps in Kakuma. My Nuer and other southern Sudanese friends and acquaintances often played these taped exhortations at home, at work and in market cafes.[79]

For other men, those who lost property due to wars, whose wives and children were either stolen, raped or killed, the decline in their ability to secure livelihoods and provide protection for their families, homestead and cattle sparked, argues Hutchinson, a 'crisis of masculinity' that manifested itself in rising domestic violence and sexual abuse against women.[80] Her observation is confirmed by women and men in Kakuma and Nuerland who complained about the loss of men's *buom* (strength, power) to provide for the family. The complaint of NyaChakuoth, an elderly female returnee from Kakuma, was typical:

> Look at them, they are not men any longer. They cannot protect us. They are the first ones to run to the bush when the rebels came. When my husband was beaten by the Bul militia, he cried like a child and told them straightaway where our food supplies were. We lost all our food. He was really useless.

The spread of violence against women that took place, especially after the 1991 SPLA split, can be seen partially as a result of the emasculation of men. I would support Henrietta Moore's arguments about the 'thwarting' or emasculation of particular gender identities. She explains that 'thwarting can be understood as the inability to sustain or properly take up a gendered subject position, resulting in a crisis, real or imagined, of self-representation and/or social evaluation'.[81] In the case of Nuer male youth and men, thwarting is linked to their marginalisation and impoverishment due to war and to their inability to receive expected rewards or recognition from assuming their *wutni nuäri* position (Nuer masculinity). This results in their emasculation. As they see themselves as unable to provide protection and secure livelihoods for their families and protect their women from being kidnapped, raped or killed (see above), they resort to violence. They direct it towards other women, and also their own women, resulting in an increase in domestic violence. The perpetuation of this violence continues, as we shall see, in refugee camps and after return.

---

[79] Carol Berger in her PhD study of the Red Army recruits provides insightful analysis of the changing notions of manhood among the Dinka as a result of the nationalist politics of Garang, 'The SPLA and Lost Boys'.

[80] Hutchinson, 'Nuer Ethnicity Militarized'. See also Madut Jok and Hutchinson, 'Sudan's Prolonged Second Civil War' for the impact on Dinka men.

[81] Henrietta Moore, *A Passion for Difference*, p. 66.

2.1 Returnee boy in military uniform, Lεr, 2007 (© Katarzyna Grabska)

2.2 Military parade in Lɛr, southern Sudan, January 2007 (© Katarzyna Grabska)

Femininities and agency reconfigured: Violated women, 'luggage women' and daughters of the AK-47

Women's positions and roles during the civil war were more varied and complex than that suggested by the standard portrayal of victims of violence in the literature. In this instance, they took up arms alongside their male relatives in the war against their Arab enemies, often joining the SPLA as combatants or supporters.[82] They carried the wounded and luggage and provided food and other domestic services. Although Garang's rhetoric stated that women's primary responsibility was to preserve the future generations and stay out of the frontlines, some girls were recruited. According to the Nuer women and men who went to Ethiopia, the SPLA created a female battalion, *Ketiba Benet*, in 1986. Three hundred girls were trained in the Ethiopian camps alongside the Red Army male recruits.[83] The battalion fought only once. 'Too many women and girls died and [the] SPLA realised it is better to keep them in the barracks to help us, the men', commented a refugee who had been a young recruit. A few of the Nuer women refugees in Kakuma went first with their husbands to Ethiopia, where they were subsequently trained as soldiers. The vast majority lived around the military barracks in the

[82] Fitzgerald, *Throwing the Stick Forward*. These were new roles for women, especially for the Nuer, who in the past did not take part in the military struggle.
[83] HSBA, 'No Standing, Few Prospects: How Peace is Failing South Sudanese Female Combatants and WAAFG', The Sudan Human Security Baseline Assessment Brief No. 8, September 2008, p. 2; Judith McCallum and Alfred Okech, 'Small Arms and Light Weapons Control and Community Security in Southern Sudan: The Links between Gender Identity and Disarmament', *Regional Security, Gender Identity, and CPA Implementation in Sudan*, Africa Peace Forum and Project Ploughshares (Ontario, 2008), p. 47.

training camps and supported the male soldiers through the provision of domestic and sexual services. Some of the militia groups also recruited women. Based on the pre-registration of women combatants carried out under the disarmament plan of the UN Mission in Sudan (UNMIS), there were some 3,600 women combatants in 2005.[84] Photograph 2.2 shows women soldiers in a parade in Lɛr in 2007.

The post-1991 inter-and intra-community violence further under-mined the social position of women. Women's bodies and their blood became vehicles of male confrontation and the nationalist struggle. During previous inter-community feuds, women did not take part in the fighting, but protected wounded fighters. As elders' narratives suggest, they were perceived as protectors and saviours who would accompany brothers, fathers and husbands to local battles, and if their men were injured they would cover their bodies and shelter them from the enemy's attack. If a fighter, even from the enemy's side, ran inside a house, he was considered to have reached a place of sanctuary and could not be targeted by the opposing side. After the rules of non-targeting of women in inter-community feuds were abandoned and women became the targets of the ethnicised violence, their protective abilities were taken away. Elderly Nuer women and men commented on the changed tactics and social position of women. Joy, a widow in her late forties, explained that:

> In the past, we, women, relied on the men to protect us. The men would go to fight the Arabs, and women would migrate to a safe place and stay behind preparing food and water for the soldiers. The men were the ones fighting the enemy and women relied on the men for protection. But then things changed. The Arabs started stealing women and children, and then the Nuer started fighting Dinka and each other. It was very bad to see the fighting between your own people. At the same time, you cannot escape because you belong there.

Women became not only targets of gender violence and ethnic anni-hilation, they were also less able to reach safe havens. Hutchinson suggests that the primodialist turn in Nuer ethnicity was prompted by the northern military strategies of 'divide and rule'.[85] It also reflects the global trend towards women and children becoming the victims of milita-rised violence. The gendered nature of violence in the government–SPLA war and, more significantly, in the south–south conflict, contributed to the displacement and reformulation of gender identities. Amani El Jack analyses the effects of the oil-induced displacement on the lives of Suda-nese refugee women in Uganda.[86] She notes the gender-based violence that these women endured during the various conflicts, with many suffering numerous rapes at the hands of Arab soldiers, SPLA troops and other southern rebels. As my findings suggest, this in turn undermined the position of women in the community, leaving them more vulnerable than men. Often trapped in Sudan, they were less mobile.

[84] HSBA, 'No Standing, Few Prospects', p. 5.
[85] Hutchinson 'Nuer Ethnicity Militarized'.
[86] Amani El Jack, 'Gendered Implications'.

The militarisation of southern Sudanese society spread across communities and households beyond the military ranks and into the realms of women.[87] In Kakuma and southern Sudan, women and children recounted stories of owning guns, using them to defend themselves and to wreak revenge on enemies.[88] Young children would carry guns larger than themselves to protect herds in the cattle camps. Women and girls used weapons as a means of protection, to exert power over others and to exercise some autonomy. A 16-year-old girl from Akobo boasted to me about her mastery of the gun and that she preferred this to education: '[I]t is easier to be rich when you have a gun. You can just shoot and you get what you want. With school is too much trouble'. When I expressed my surprise, Nyadak added: 'when I go back to Sudan I will be a killer ... because I have to kill all the Arabs and revenge my family'. This reveals how women were not merely passive victims of military conflict but actively participated in instigating and perpetuating violence. They also saw themselves not only as family members to be protected but also as those who were in charge of protecting others.

This illustrates the different views that women hold about their own position within the family and community. Despite camp education about gender equality and numerous encouragements for girls to pursue schooling, Nyadak dropped out and was married to a man from Central Nuerland, with whom she had a daughter. I saw her one day in the camp cooking for her husband. She was very subdued and initially did not want to talk to me. Finally, she smiled and told me: 'Remember what I told you about the gun? If my husband abuses me, I will also kill him! War made me not afraid of men!'. Hence, such war experiences for women marked a transformation in their self-esteem. Despite traumatic experiences, women were (becoming) militant in claiming their rights and respect. These narratives also point to the profound militarisation of the community, the household and personal relationships. They also show how femininities were transformed as a result of ethnicised violence. This militarisation penetrated all segments of society, even reflecting itself in Nuer naming practices: for example, NyaKlang means 'daughter of the AK-47'.

Women also actively contributed to the war effort as perpetrators of violence. Their well-known powers to influence male kin through shaming were widely exercised during the conflict. Machar acknowledged the power of Nuer women to shame their male relatives through songs that had a substantial influence on the recruitment of soldiers into the SPLA.[89] The story of Gatkoi shows the influence of mothers on their sons to join the army. During my stay in Western Upper Nile, I

---

[87] The Small Arms Survey estimates that there are between 1.9 and 3.2 million small arms in Sudan, with two-thirds in the hands of civilians, 20 per cent owned by the Khartoum government, with the remainder split between the SPLA and other southern militias (2007: 2).

[88] Women started using guns in their domestic disputes. In Kakuma, I heard of two cases of women who, while quarrelling with their co-wives, shot them with guns belonging to their husbands.

[89] Hutchinson, *Nuer Dilemmas*, p. 157.

often heard women praising the heroic war efforts of their sons, brothers and husbands through songs and stories. It was only when the soldiers started to die in battle and many sons did not come home that women and girls changed the content of their songs and refused the courtship of soldiers ('I would not marry a ghost'[90]).

Women's songs did more than just encourage men to join the fighting ranks. They also incited other women to violence, particularly during the Dinka and Nuer inter- and intra-fighting. Jok and Hutchinson both talk about the role of women in fuelling inter-community violence, encouraging male relatives to raid cattle and revenge deaths.[91] During his flight from Ethiopia, Kim, the 'lost boy' from Lɛr, saw women not only encouraging other men to fight but also shooting enemy children.

During the war, women took on more community responsibilities and leadership roles. In Lɛr, I met two elderly women who had stayed in Sudan throughout the conflicts and been nominated as community chiefs in charge of food distribution and provision of services for orphans, widows and people with disabilities. Their role was to pass messages and concerns of women to male paramount chiefs, the SPLA military command and counter-insurgency groups. When inter-community violence spiralled out of control, women took on peace-making roles. Women in exile became particularly active in pro-peace campaigning. Many of these initiatives took place in Kakuma. Some women warned their husbands that they would not cook, have sex or 'produce children for the South' if they did not stop fighting.[92] Others used nakedness to shame their male relatives. In 2002, a group of southern Sudanese women marched naked on the streets of Nairobi to protest the ongoing inter-community fighting in southern Sudan.[93]

Several women's diaspora groups organised themselves across ethnic divides to demand peace. The Sudanese Women's Voice for Peace, the New Sudan Women's Federation and the New Sudan Women's Association achieved international prominence, drawing attention to the forgotten conflict. Some leading women peacemakers were eventually included in the Machakos peace negotiations, but their role in drafting the peace agreement was minimal. Anne Itto, a former minister and now an MP in the southern Sudan national assembly, complains that there was no mention of the suffering or the role of women in the war in the final version of the peace agreement.[94] Many Nuer women in Kakuma and in Sudan expressed their dissatisfaction: 'It was not our peace, it is the peace of the men, of soldiers. Our [women's] suffering and dead children were not recognised'. Not until the drafting of the southern Sudanese interim constitution was there specific mention of gender issues.

---

[90] Ibid., p. 159.
[91] Hutchinson, 'Nuer Ethnicity Militarized'; Madut Jok, 'Militarization and Gender Violence in South Sudan', *Journal of Asian and African Studies*, Vol. 34, pp. 427–42.
[92] Anne Itto, 'Guests at the Table? The Role of Women in Peace Processes', Conciliation Resources, 2006, p. 2.
[93] Ibid.
[94] Ibid., pp. 2–4.

Changes in rights discourse and the institution of marriage

Discourse of rights associated with the social position of women and men also underwent transformation during the war. While men were expected to maintain the war front, women's primary duty was keeping up the reproductive front. Throughout the conflict, military and community leaders urged women to continue have children as their contribution to the struggle. 'We were losing many people, many soldiers in the war against the Arabs, and many children were dying due to bad conditions. Women had to give birth more often, this was their duty,' the commissioner of Lɛr explained.

As a result, women often had large families whom they needed to support single-handedly as their husbands were either in refugee camps or fighting in the bush.[95] A mother of five told me:

> You see, during the war we had to give birth to many children, the Sudanese woman is tired now. She has to work so hard. Now that the war is over we do not want so many children, maybe two or three; they go to school and get education and this is how they will make us famous. Not through guns and struggle.

Jok's studies among the Dinka show that, during the war, weaning taboos were not respected and women had to shorten gaps between pregnancies.[96] Since men were in the bush, women reported being transferred between different men, sometimes family members, other times unrelated men, in order to conceive.[97] When abducted by the enemy, they were often taken as wives by powerful commanders and had to fulfil their reproductive responsibility.

Marriage and sexual services are often used by women and girls in conflict zones as means of survival. Some females use their gendered position as women to access greater security and wellbeing. In Sierra Leone, as Utas and Denov and Gervais show, girls negotiated their insecurity through marriages to powerful commanders, who not only provided them with greater access to food but also minimised the risk of sexual violence from others.[98] In southern Sudan, many women who stayed behind talked about 'protection and convenience marriages' to local commanders and soldiers in the absence of their own husbands. Nyajuc, who stayed in Lɛr during the war, told me:

[95] Many women had between 10 to14 children, often losing more than half due to disease and conflict.

[96] Several taboos persist among the Nuer and Dinka with regards to weaning periods. Women during those times are regarded as 'polluting' and are not allowed to drink milk or engage in sexual intercourse. Children are weaned at the age of two or three, when he or she is able to walk and is no longer perceived as *riem* (blood), but instead acquires a status of a *gat* (child). During the war, the nursing period was often reduced to one year or less. See Madut Jok, *Militarization, Gender and Reproductive Health in South Sudan*.

[97] A study of female combatants by Geneva Call points out that some travelled to the frontlines in order to get pregnant by their husbands (2008: 3).

[98] Myriam Denov and Christine Gervais, 'Negotiating (In)security'; Utas 'Agency of Victims'.

> We had to give birth to children, our husbands were in the bush, so what were we supposed to do? It was better to go to the barracks – at least there you not only get a child but sometimes also some food, or maybe the man will protect you from other rebels.

This reflects both agency and resourcefulness through the use of their gender and bodies in the search for protection, power, status and survival.

Women's reproductive contributions to the liberation struggle are, however, not acknowledged in public discourse in post-war southern Sudan. During the SPLM campaign in Lɛr, the regional representative praised the role women played during the war, thanking them for their services for the heroic soldiers, but their reproductive contribution was downplayed or was often ignored, even though it had tremendous consequences for their health and position in society. 'Due to war, women do not give birth to children any more. There were too many children, too many women taken by force then,' commented the Women Union's representative in Lɛr. 'First the men came and made you into their wives,[99] and now the husbands show up and divorce us,' complained another widow who was taken by the Bul militia during the war.[100] I will return to these issues in Chapter 6. For now, it suffices to say that as a result of war and violence men acquired greater rights over women's reproductive capabilities, confirming Hutchinson's point that 'women's status as independent agents in men's eyes has declined in the context of militarised glorification of the raw power of the gun'.[101]

In addition to the changing reproductive rights discourses, war also affected the marriage institution. First, the marriageable age for girls and boys lowered significantly. Girls in southern Sudan had formerly married at a much younger age than boys. A girl was considered to be of marriageable age as soon as 'she had breasts and had had her first menstruation'. Before the civil wars, young men would have to attain maturity, which usually happened in their late twenties or early thirties, to be allowed by their fathers to marry. This had to do with the ability of a man to provide for the household and to fulfil his socially determined roles of a responsible man and father.

During the war, many girls were married much earlier, sometimes even before they had started menstruating, as parents were worried about losing potential bridewealth due to fighting and the imminent threat of death. In addition, many parents complained that their daughters were 'forced' (raped) or taken away by soldiers 'for free', without any bridewealth being paid. Parents also insisted that sons marry earlier (many men got married in their late teens), as they were afraid that they would be killed in the war, recruited or migrate in search of jobs, education or refuge. Early reproduction was thought to be necessary in order to sustain the household, *cieng* and community existence. As the number of available young men declined and their wealth perished, girls were often

---

[99] The word 'rape' does not exist in Nuer. The concept of rape is expressed through the metaphor of 'becoming somebody's wife, or being taken by force'.
[100] See also HSBA, 'No Standing, Few Prospects'.
[101] Hutchinson, 'Nuer Ethnicity Militarized'.

married to commanders who had cattle or to old men who remained in the villages. Due to very early marriages, lack of food, constant flight, stress and trauma, many young women were unable to conceive or take a pregnancy to full term. Many were thus divorced or abandoned by their husbands and the husband's family, leaving them with little security.

THE WIND AND THE CHANGE

The wind that brought the second civil war to the south, particularly Nuerland, left communities devastated and dispersed and altered gender identities, institutions and ideologies. It affected women and men differently, not only in terms of their access to migration and refuge, but also by altering their social (gender) identities, rights and position in the community. Lene Hansen and Louise Olsson have argued that 'security is gendered through the political mobilisation of masculine and feminine identities that are linked to practices of militarism and citizenship'.[102] Because of their physical and sexual vulnerability, women and girls experience violence and insecurity differently from men. The changing nature of conflict and violence among the southern Sudanese that emerged after the SPLA split directly affected the production, sustenance and fostering of specific ethnicised and militarised femininities and masculinities. The new warfare, the proliferation of guns and the abandoning of ethics resulted in women (and children) shifting from 'military assets' to 'military targets'.[103] Militarisation contributed to the re-configuration of gender identities with the emergence of hyper-masculinities among some men, the emasculation of others, while reconfiguring and often undermining the position of women. Even so, women and girls managed to exercise their modest agency in order to cope with wartime violence and brutality.

As Jennifer Hyndman and Malathi de Alwis note, 'membership in a particular nation shapes one's political, economic, and social locations at least as much as one's gender identity, and in ways specifically articulated *through* gender differences'.[104] In recent decades there has been extensive analysis of links between gender and nation, contextualising these relations within post-colonial societies. Gender has been identified as the key factor in the construction and reproduction of ethno-nationalist ideologies.[105] Gender identities are inter-connected and mutually constitutive. Women are often positioned as care-givers, home-makers, and bearers of tradition and national culture, while men are portrayed as protectors of the family, the nation, and their properties. War and conflict

[102] Lene Hansen and Louise Olsson, 'Gender and Security', *Security Dialogue*, 2004, Vol. 35, p. 406.
[103] Madut Jok and Hutchinson, 'Sudan's Prolonged Second Civil War'.
[104] Jennifer Hyndman and Malathi de Alwis, 'Beyond Gender: Toward a Feminist Analysis of Humanitarianism and Development in Sri Lanka', *Women's Studies Quarterly*, 2003, Vols 3-4, pp. 212–26.
[105] Cynthia Enloe, *Bananas, Beaches and Bases: Making Feminist Senses of International Politics* (Berkeley, CA, 1989); Kumari Jayawardena, *Feminism and Nationalism in the Third World* (New York, 1986).

further alter, contest and re-shape concepts of masculinities and femininities. The process of militarisation is both determined by and determines how gender relations are practiced and negotiated and how masculinities and femininities are defined.[106]

Both Nuer women and men played key roles in the militarisation of society and gender identities. As Jacklyn Cock argues, 'militarisation is a society process that involves the mobilisation of resources for war on political, economic and ideological levels'.[107] Gender identities are accentuated, exaggerated and essentialised in the context of war and conflict, with men being perceived as the protectors of women and the nation, while women are portrayed as dependable, vulnerable, inactive and passive, needing their men to protect them and their home. As the case of the Nuer women and men suggests, actual experiences of women and men are much more complex, revealing the agency of both women and men and their ability to navigate through the war zones.

There are contradictions around changes in gender relations resulting from violent conflicts. My findings add new perspectives to the literature on the gender effects of wars, which often focus on the victim–perpetrator debate. In Nuerland, militarisation led to a reconfiguration of gender identities, rights and institutions. Inter- and intra-community violence resulted in the reconfiguration of the relationship between ethnicity and gender. Nuer (and Dinka) women became boundary-makers of new ethnic identities shaped by men, often through violence inflicted on women's bodies. Women's roles in the war, however, were more fluid and multidimensional, with some actively engaged as perpetrators and supporters of violence. Thus, women's and girls' roles in conflict zones go beyond being victims of violence, involving instead a myriad of positions as perpetrators, actors, porters, commanders, domestic and sex slaves, spies and human shields.[108] Nuer women have been able to exercise some limited agency to contribute to war efforts, and to resist and survive in the conflict zones despite having borne the brunt of the violence.

These new forms of Nuer masculinities and femininities combined with new forms of Nuer mobility and differentiated access to migration and refuge for boys, girls, women and men went through new transformations in refugee camps. Fragmented and dispersed households and communities experienced different changes in gender identities, ideologies and institutions. Changes in Nuer cultural institutions and the weakening of established coping mechanisms have affected women's and men's ability to regulate power and gender relations, often leaving women in more disadvantaged positions. Even though findings demonstrate that war and conflict have mixed consequences for gender relations, women's exercise of agency due to their position as women and their vulnerability to physical and sexual abuse has been much more constrained than that of boys and men.

[106] See selected bibliography.
[107] J. Cock, 'Women and the Military: Implications for Demilitarisation in the 1990s in South Africa', *Gender and Security*, 1994, Vol. 8, pp. 152–69, p. 153.
[108] See Denov and Gervais, 'Negotiating (In)security', p. 886.

3

Mai – Season of Displacement: Becoming 'Modern' in Kakuma

What was life like in Kakuma? Was it life? There was debate about this. On the one hand, we were alive, which meant that we were living a life, that we were eating and could enjoy friendships and learning and could love. But we were nowhere. No matter the meaning of the word, the place was not a place. It was a kind of purgatory...

(Valentino Achak Deng cited in Eggers, 2006: 373)

On arrival at Kakuma refugee camp – located in the dry savannah rangeland of Turkana nomads – one encounters football fields with crowds of multi-national refugee youth. Across the road are the high fences and barbed wire of the UNHCR compound, with its prison-like lights and security guards. 'Welcome to Kakuma Refugee Camp!' reads the sign on the gate to the NGO compound. Everywhere there are slogans meant to educate the residents: 'Women rights are Human Rights'; 'Ten days of activism against gender-violence'; 'Women are good decision-makers'. There are constant announcements of workshops and many refugees were too busy to talk to me as they 'have workshops'. Lony, a 'lost boy', described his experience after arriving in Kakuma in 1992:

When Mengistu fell and the Sudanese were expelled from Ethiopia, we arrived in Kakuma. This is where we found the real refugee life. We were put into a camp managed by UNHCR. They put all the minors under the responsibility of Radda Barnen [Swedish Save the Children], gave us food and opened a school. We were divided into groups within our communities. We first lived in Zone One, together with others [ethnic groups]. But in 1996, when the fighting between the Dinka started burning our [Nuer] homes, we ran to UNHCR. They segregated us into different zones, and Nuer got their own Zone Five.

I began to live a different life [from military life in Ethiopia]: church, school and sport. I was also a youth leader in the community and in the church from 1997. I was the deputy youth leader in the whole camp. I got a big responsibility then: catechist, altar boy, youth leader, and I was now engaged and could not do any wrong things. I became now another model in the community. The UN also taught us about other things, like 'women and children rights'. I am modern, civilised. Because of the UN, school and church, Nuer in Kakuma became different. We are somehow 'modern' like you, civilised and pro-women.

3.1 Women's rights campaign in Kakuma refugee camp, 2006
(© Katarzyna Grabska)

3.2 Signpost – NGO compound, Kakuma, 2006
(© Katarzyna Grabska)

'MODERNITY', GLOBAL HUMANITARIANISM, GENDER AND GENERATIONS

For refugees waiting in limbo for years, sometimes decades, the experience of displacement and life in refugee camps is life-changing. Encounters between the population traumatised by war and displacement and the global humanitarian enterprise within Kakuma entailed engagement with the complex, overlapping cultural processes and material structures of a particular modernity. Kakuma was not the first encounter with modernity for the Nuer. Colonialism, missionary proselytising, government, markets, infrastructure, guns, modern armies and oil companies brought, as in other parts of Africa, enlightenment-inspired notions of individuality, progress, order, rationality and civilisation. In the camp, refugees' experience of modernity has been different. It is the rarely recognised and discussed encounter between the 'localised and de-territorialised refugee' and global UN humanitarianism which, combined with diasporic connections created through resettlement programmes, has opened new possibilities for change, so-called development, progress and empowerment.

The displaced Nuer population, like other groups in the camp in Kakuma, experience modernity of a particular form. It is dislocated, gendered, ambivalently chosen and experienced through a profound contemporary form of a hierarchical set of relations defined by the encounter between the UN system and refugees. Because refugees are (presumably) temporarily outside the 'national order of things', they are unable to claim their citizenship rights and protection from their governments and are subjected to a refugee regime, which includes national and international institutions, law, policy and practice that have been put in place to address 'issues of refugees'.[1] Its diverse actors include the UN, host governments, implementing agencies and donors.

I analyse this particular form of modernity at three levels. First, modernity in Kakuma is structural, imposed through the implementation of a refugee regime and the design, residence pattern, population make-up and creation of space. This is reinforced by camp management structures set up by the humanitarian organisations introducing education and health services and ideas around human rights and gender equality. This particular experience of Kakuma as a modern place was linked to specific experiences of settling-in after returning to southern Sudan. Second, modernity has unfolded as a result of access to global communication and technology and through resettlement in Europe, the Americas and Australia. It is manifested not only by the use of modern technologies and western clothing, but also in the ideas that the Nuer communities hold about themselves and their social world. Third, modernity in Kakuma is gendered and generational; it is experienced differently by women and men, the young and the elderly. Modernity represents not only struc-

---

[1]   Nick Van Hear, 'Editorial Introduction', *Journal of Refugee Studies*, 1998, Vol. 11, pp. 341–9, p. 342.

tures and infrastructure, but also ideas and identities that constitute part of social imaginings. In this way, gendered experiences of modernity resulted in what James Ferguson has called 'a form of consciousness' rather than an objective condition of exposure to market forces among the displaced.[2]

The chapter is located within the debates on globalisation and modernity, looking at the disunity within unity and local re-interpretations and creation of multiple forms of modernities.[3] I seek to extend debates on what constitutes the nature of this encounter. Much of the literature on African modernities situates seemingly traditional cultural practices – witchcraft, ethnicity, and 'autochthony' – as recent responses to a globalising capitalism and emergence of the rationalising modern nation-state.[4] I wish to understand how modernisation for the contemporary Nuer women and men has been created through the imposition of and encounters with global humanitarianism. In particular, I am interested in the connections between this modernity and gender relations and identities.

KAKUMA AND ARRIVAL OF A NEW CUSTOM: *CIENG MI PAI BEN*

As Nuer men and women told me, Kakuma is a place marked by suffering and hardship but also by the arrival of a modern mode of life. Nyakuol, introduced in Chapter 1, described changes in the camp: 'Kakuma, there are schools, "UN", churches, "women rights" (*cung man*). Our children go forward/progress (*wa nhiam*). Now Nuer girls and boys are knowledgeable and educated. In Kakuma, a new Nuer custom/mode of value has arrived (*cieng mi pai ben)'*. The English words 'modern' and 'civilised' were often used by young refugees to distinguish their new identities and modes of behaviour from those who had stayed behind in Nuerland. Other English expressions such as 'women's rights', 'human rights' or 'development' were widely used by Nuer speakers.

The Nuer metaphor often used by my respondents to describe these new identities was *'nei ti cike ker'*. This signifies people who have awoken and have seen light, which many, like Lony, associated with literacy, Christianity, awareness of human rights and gender equality. It was interpreted as a distinction that produced new aspirations and identities among women and men and impacted conjugal relations. Young girls who attended school participated in community activities and learnt English were referred to as 'knowledgeable and educated' (*nyiiri nuäri ti*

---

[2] James Ferguson, *Expectations of Modernity: Myths and Meanings of Modern Life on the Zambian Copperbelt* (Berkeley, CA, 1999).
[3] Ibid. See also C. Breckenridge, S. Pollock, H. Brabha and D. Chakrabaty (eds), *Cosmopolitanisms* (Durham, NC, 2002); Aihwa Ong, *Flexible Citizenship: The Cultural Logics of Transnationality* (Durham, NC, 1999).
[4] For example, Jean and John Comaroff, *Modernity and its Malcontents: Ritual and Power in Postcolonial Africa* (Chicago, IL, 1993); Peter Geschiere, *The Witchcraft of Modernity: Politics and the Occult in Postcolonial Africa* (Charlottesville, VA, 1997).

ngac ke ngoani). The camp was a site of forging modern gender identities, which were often described by refugees, and confirmed by humanitarian workers, as 'educated civilised pro-women men' and 'new empowered women'. I explore these experiences of *nei ti cike ker* in the encounter with the modernising structures of a refugee regime committed to gender mainstreaming.

The camp as a space of modernity

Located at the crossroads of Kenyan and South Sudanese pastoralist routes, Kakuma Refugee Camp represents a meeting point of different worlds.[5] For some, it is a site of UN humanitarianism and a place of refuge, while for others it opens up possibilities to access education and business. For the majority, it is a temporary waiting place. Located 127 kilometres south of the Kenya–Sudan border and 120 kilometres north of the district capital, Lodwar, it has a dry and hot climate.

Following the collapse in 1990 of the military dictatorship of Siad Barre in Somalia and the demise of the Ethiopian dictator Mengistu Haile Mariam, Kenya witnessed an unprecedented influx of populations seeking refuge. As Kenyan refugee policy shifted to confining refugees in camps away from urban economic centres, the Kakuma camp received its first Sudanese refugees in 1992.[6] By 2006, it had become the second largest refugee camp in Kenya[7] and one of the world's largest. When I first arrived in April 2006, the refugee population, reported to be 92,000, comprised nine different nationalities: Sudanese (75%), Somalis (around 21%), Ethiopians (3%) and Rwandese, Burundian, Congolese, Eritreans and Ugandans (1%). [8] Registered camp residents included those who settled in cities, despite the Kenyan policy of refugee encampment. High numbers of Sudanese, Ethiopians and Somalis reside in Nairobi, Kitale and Eldoret, some returning to the camp during the headcount exercises carried out regularly by UNHCR. That September, I witnessed an increased traffic of *matatus* (minibuses) bringing refugees to Kakuma and then carrying them back to the cities with food rations. Refugees continued to return to the camp to maintain their refugee status in Kenya as this guaranteed their legality and access to services in the camp,

[5]   Prior to the influx of refugees, Kakuma was an insignificant village in Turkana district with a population of around eight thousand primarily pastoralist Turkana. See James Schechter, 'Lost Boys', p. 44.
[6]   See Marc-Antoine de Montclos and Peter Mwangi Kagwanja, 'Refugee Camps or Cities? The Socio-Economic Dynamics of the Dadaab and Kakuma Camps in Northern Kenya', *Journal of Refugee* Studies, 2000, Vol. 13, pp. 205–22, pp. 205. The first camp opened in Lokichoggio in 1991, but following the influx of Sudanese refugees, it was transferred to Kakuma in 1992.
[7]   In 2006, Kakuma was hosting around 40% of the total refugee population in Kenya, with 60% in Dadaab Camp, located near the Somali border in north-eastern Kenya. Due to ongoing civil war in Somalia, the Dadaab camp now shelters almost 250,000, mostly Somalis.
[8]   UNHCR Kenya, Country Operations Plan for Kenya, 2006. During my follow-up visit to Kakuma in September 2007, the camp population was 75,000. Due to Sudanese repatriation and the influx of more Somalis, by August 2008, it had dropped to about 51,000, of whom some 13,000 were Sudanese.

access to education in Kenyan schools as well as medical services.

Its multi-ethnic character means that populations from different groups live among each other in ways far different from the interactions in places of origin. In 2006, thirty-four Sudanese ethnic groups were represented in the camp, with Dinka and Nuer dominating. The heterogeneous character of the camp was also a result of the presence of the local Turkana communities who, until the early 2000s, used to live within the camp among refugees. Due to increased insecurity, escalating economic interdependence and tensions between the Turkana communities and refugees – a situation common in host/refugee relations – the Kenyan authorities ordered the Turkanas to leave the camp. Nevertheless, they continue economic activities: many, including children, work as servants for refugee households while others sell water, firewood and alcohol. Some women offer sexual services to the predominantly male refugee population.

Since the signing of the CPA in January 2005, there has been organised repatriation of southern Sudanese assisted by UNHCR, the International Organisation for Migration (IOM) and the host country governments. Many have returned by their own means. By the end of 2012, some 334,000[9] Sudanese refugees had returned to southern Sudan from Uganda, Ethiopia, the Central African Republic, the Democratic Republic of Congo and Kenya, with UNHCR's facilitation. Due to the post-independence fighting and especially the more recent conflicts that erupted in December 2013, many South Sudanese became displaced yet again, with large numbers heading for Kakuma.

The forging of ethnic and inter-cultural identity within the camp was partially through its layout. The population was managed through the design of the camp divided into sections, zones and groups (see map 2). Refugees were accommodated according to their nationality and, after 1996 clashes between Dinka and Nuer groups, also on the basis of ethnicity. Kakuma I was six zones; Zones 1 to 4 and 6 were predominantly southern Sudanese; while Zone 5 was occupied by a mixture of nationalities. Kakuma II and III were predominantly inhabited by Somalis, while Kakuma IV was occupied by mixed nationalities. As a result, different concepts of modernity were being forged, despite the multi-national and multi-ethnic make-up of the camp population. Although previously *thok duël* or *cieng* through the father's name was a sufficient source of local identity, in the camp people started identifying themselves as 'African', 'Sudanese', 'Nuer', 'Dinka' and so on. When asked about their origin, most refugees replied, 'I am an African, I am Sudanese, from South Sudan. But I am also Nuer, from Bentiu'. Hence, not only was the space and place of interaction and residence produced through the layout of the camp, so was the particular way of being modern, which was expressed in terms of being 'ethnic'.

However, interactions between different nationalities and ethnicities

---

[9]   These estimates are based on figures of those who left the camps, rather than those who arrived in southern Sudan. As my data suggests, many South Sudanese remained in exile instead, often moving to cities or other host countries.

in the camp were present in daily life, including schools, hospital and clinics, markets, workshops and training sessions run by humanitarian organisations. Young people, especially those at school, built inter-cultural friendships. For example, Nyakuoth had strong friendships with Dinka boys and Ethiopian and Somali girls. There were also – despite disapproval from relatives – some marriages across national and ethnic boundaries.

Structured modernity

The modernising effect of humanitarian policies is rarely mentioned in the literature on refugee camps. The Kenyan government is a signatory to the 1951 UN Refugee Convention and the 1969 OAU Convention on the Specific Aspects of Refugee Problems in Africa. Since the arrival of four hundred thousand Somali refugees and thousands of Sudanese in 1991–2, daily management and assistance to refugees has been delegated to the United Nations High Comissioner for Refugees (UNHCR). This UN agency is responsible for the overall co-ordination and protection of refugees in Kakuma, with assistance being provided through its partner organisations. The dislocated form of modernity produced in Kakuma is partially a result of the type of refugee system put in place.

Although Kakuma is theoretically in Kenyan territory, in practice the camp's legal regime is multifaceted. The Kenyan government is conspicuously absent from regulating daily activities in the camp.[10] International (human rights) law operates at the level of the UN and NGOs through refugee status determination, protection, assistance and resettlement policies. Kenyan laws regulate the criminal behaviour of refugees, including cases of rape and murder, which are handled by Kenyan mobile courts. Nation- and ethnic-specific administrative systems and customary laws are regulated by refugees through their local governing structures and courts, which handle common crimes and civil issues such as divorces, elopements and forced marriages. Laws have thus produced dislocated modernity. As a result, Kakuma is neither Kenya nor Sudan, but somewhere in-between, an extra-territorial space. This has had consequences for Kakuma as a particular place in (re)negotiation of social, and in particular gender, relations among the Nuer.

The refugee regime in Kakuma, as in the typical refugee camp situation described by Voutira and Harrell-Bond,[11] is mostly top-down, based on a specific division of labour and highly hierarchical structures of power between refugees, NGOs, the UNHCR and the local population. Fences, wires, procedures and permits often separate these groups. The

[10] The District Officer represents the Kenyan local administration in Kakuma. The Kenyan police have a post just outside the camp. In the camp, each of the refugee nationalities and ethnic groups has its own administration. Local security groups, courts and committees dealing with water, food, health, education, repatriation and women's issues.
[11] Eftihia Voutira and Barbara E. Harrell-Bond, 'In Search of the Locus of Trust: The Social World of the Refugee Camp', in E.V. Daniel and J.C. Knudsen (eds), *Mistrusting Refugees* (Berkeley, CA, 1995).

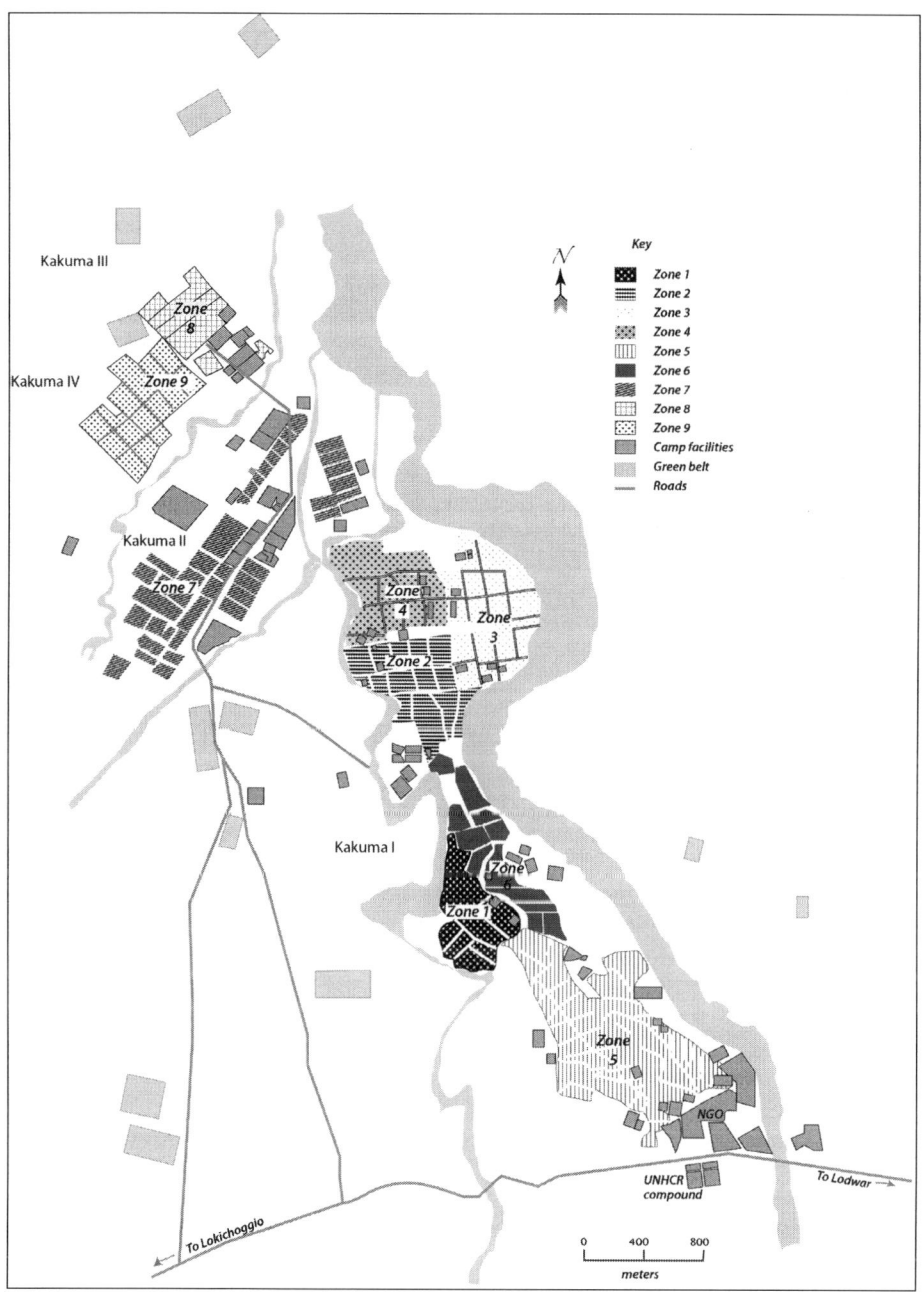

Key
- Zone 1
- Zone 2
- Zone 3
- Zone 4
- Zone 5
- Zone 6
- Zone 7
- Zone 8
- Zone 9
- Camp facilities
- Green belt
- Roads

Kakuma III

Zone 8

Kakuma IV   Zone 9

Kakuma II

Zone 7

Zone 4   Zone 3

Zone 2

Kakuma I

Zone 6

Zone 1

Zone 5

NGO

UNHCR compound   To Lodwar →

To Lokichoggio

0   400   800

meters

Map 3.1 Kakuma Refugee Camp. UNHCR 2006

UNHCR, being in charge of overall management and protection of refugees, has a superior position. There are tensions between it and NGOs,
whose employees often feel exploited. Some told me of their resentment
at having to 'do the daily work' for which the UNHCR then takes credit.

Relations between the UNHCR and the refugees themselves are
also contentious, partly due to the structure of interactions. The UN
compound is located on the other side of the road from the refugee camp
and is protected by high fences, bright lights and armed guards. Early in
the morning, crowds of refugees gather in front of the gates, queuing for
days in the sun to register their claims. Once allowed into the compound,
they are put into fenced-off areas where they wait hours to be interviewed. Some UN and NGO employees use patronising language in referring to refugees: 'They are my refugees, I work for them, but sometimes
they are like children. They only want to be assisted,' commented a UN
employee. Such attitudes indicate and exacerbate the power dynamics
between 'us' (aid workers) and 'them' (refugees).

Aid workers often complained about the mischievous behaviour of refugees, who make up stories of rape and abuse to qualify for resettlement,
or register multiple times with different names to access larger rations.
A UNHCR officer accused them of being liars: 'Look at them, when they
go to meetings they come dressed very nicely and then they say they are
suffering [from] poverty. Others come to say they were raped, but they
don't even cry'.[12] During my stay, the UNHCR was preoccupied with
'detecting fraud' and conducting biometric verification of 'real refugees'.
All refugees had to re-register, be fingerprinted and issued with new identity cards. A UN employee explained that this was in order to identify the
'recyclers' – refugees who registered several times in order to gain higher
rations. 'We are also trying to bring down the population of the camp. We
need to know who is really in the camp; those who are outside will be de-activated,' commented another UNHCR officer. De-activating 'recyclers' and
'bogus refugees' was a task that preoccupied most of her time. Due to time
pressures, there was no consideration of the reasons for people's residence
outside the camp: 'If they have gone outside the camp that means they do
not need our assistance. They will be de-activated,' she argued. However,
numerous refugees complained that due to limited education and livelihood opportunities, many people moved to the cities but still needed
protection and a refugee status in Kenya, without which they are 'illegal'.
'The UNHCR is cheating us. They are supposed to protect us, but instead
they see us as cheaters and they de-activate us,' complained a young man
studying in Nairobi. 'This puts many people at risk'.

Although the UNHCR and NGOs have set up numerous refugee
committees meant to enable refugees to participate in programme design
and implementation, their participation rarely goes beyond consultation
or information-sharing. I participated in several meetings between the

---

[12] See Gaim Kibreab, 'Pulling the Wool over the Eyes of the Strangers: Refugees
Deceit and Trickery in Institutionalized Settings', *Journal of Refugee Studies*, 2004,
Vol. 17, pp. 1–26; Barbara Harrell-Bond, 'Response to Kibreab', *Journal of Refugee
Studies*, 2004, Vol. 17, pp. 27–8, on 'refugee cheating' as a survival strategy.

Sudanese refugee repatriation advisory committee and UNHCR and NGO representatives. Humanitarian workers mostly announced their plans and passed information to refugees, rather than hearing their input. The refugee chair of the committee complained:

> Although they [the UN] call us to come to meetings, they do not give us chance to talk. And when we tell them how the repatriation process should go, they say that they have budgetary constraints and that the programme was already decided by Geneva and nothing can be changed now. They [the UN] do not see us [refugees] as equal; they call us volunteers and make us do their work to mobilise communities [to repatriate].

This demonstrates that despite the UNHCR's commitment to a rights-based and participatory approach, the implementation of the policy continues to treat refugees as recipients and beneficiaries rather than partners with rights and entitlements.[13]

Refugee relations with NGOs are marked by power dynamics. Although the NGO compound is at the entrance to the camp, refugees need special permits or appointments to enter. Despite being located in a semi-desert with extreme water shortages, the NGO compound has irrigated trees offering shade from the blazing sun and a swimming pool (and a gym) for the use of humanitarian staff (see Photo 3.2). By contrast, refugees were entitled to a daily ration of a mere two litres, taps often ran dry and refugees had to wait hours to receive their entitlement. Those who could afford to do so bought water from the Turkana.

Tensions were also visible among refugees. Those who worked for NGOs and the UNHCR often expressed their superiority to the rest of the camp population. Perceived as having access to powerful decision-makers, some refugees exploited their position. 'These refugees working for the Lutheran World Federation (LWF) are corrupt. When my husband abused me and I complained to the refugee worker, he told me that for the case to go to the UN I needed to give him *kidikidoko* [KiSwahili: a small bribe],' a married woman complained. I repeatedly heard of incidents of refugee workers extorting money or sexual services from other refugees in order to gain access to the UN compound or to register claims for resettlement.[14] The UNHCR was also investigating several allegations of fraud and misconduct against refugee workers.

The camp's top-down structure exacerbated tensions between different ethnic groups. Nuer community and other smaller groups felt that Dinka groups, and SPLA representatives in particular, dominated the Sudanese administration. A chairman of the Nuer community complained:

> The UN always gives more power to the Dinka to administer the Sudanese in the camp. They always try to dominate others, the same in Sudan. This is why,

[13] See Harrell-Bond, *Imposing Aid* (Oxford, 1986); Jennifer Hyndman, *Managing Displacement: Refugees and the Politics of Humanitarianism* (Minneapolis, MN, 2000).
[14] See Bram J. Jansen, 'Between Vulnerability and Assertiveness: Negotiating Resettlement in Kakuma Refugee Camp, Kenya', *African Affairs*, 2008, Vol. 107, on resettlement policies and negotiations of vulnerability and assertiveness among refugees.

in 1996, when clashes between the Nuer and the Dinka erupted in Kakuma, the UN had to separate us into different zones [residence] and create separate local administrative structures for each tribe.

Conflicts often result in fighting in Kakuma, mirroring the tensions in southern Sudan.

Refugees are not only managed by rules, fences, regulations and the intimidating presence of international organisations. They are also finger-printed, subjected to regular headcounts and unable to challenge restrictions of rights. According to Kenyan policy, refugees are not allowed to own land and carry out agricultural activities. UNHCR and NGO incentive-based employment programmes offer only limited income-generating opportunities. Kenyan restrictions denying refugees the right to employment without a work permit meant that at the time of my fieldwork some 1,200 worked on an incentive basis rather than for a salary.[15] Camp residents were also denied movement and access to free education outside the camp. The encampment policy, often described as warehousing, the restriction of refugee rights and the language of power used by humanitarian workers resemble the organisation of labour camps rather than spaces of protection. This particular form of modernity in the camp is characterised by lack of choice and democracy. The imposition of humanitarian management structures on refugees combined with the Kenyan government's refugee policies has created a system constraining rights, freedoms and choice. Refugee become objects to be 'managed', 'controlled' and 'silenced' without much possibility of 'opting out' of the system.

The UNHCR and its partner organisations do provide a range of educational, training, health and income-generating services, these services are criticised by refugees for their inferior quality and neglect of agriculture and self-reliance. However, they are still considered major pull-factors that continue to bring Sudanese across the border.[16] While debating the decision to repatriate, a number of Nuer refugees bemoaned of the lack of infrastructure in their villages. Nyakuol commented:

> Although life here in Kakuma is hard, at least you have school and hospital. But when we go back, we will not be able to educate our children. Sudan is still [behind]; there are no hospitals and when you get sick, you cannot get help.

For many refugees, especially South Sudanese and Somalis, educational, health, training and income-generating services were of better quality than those available in their own war-torn societies.

---

[15] Guglielmo Verdirame, 'Human Rights and Refugees: The Case of Kenya', *Journal of Refugee Studies*, 1999, Vol. 12, pp. 54–77, p. 66. Refugees often complain about being exploited and being paid much less than their Kenyan colleagues for doing the same work, receiving a mere $25–35 per month. As Douglas Johnson points out, this is a hold-over from Operation Lifeline Sudan (OLS), where aid agencies would not pay Sudan Relief and Rehabilitation Association (SRRA) or Relief Association of South Sudan (RASS) counterparts a salary, but would give them 'incentives' in tea, sugar, soap, wellington boots, etc. (private communication).
[16] This point was confirmed by Nuer and other southern Sudanese research participants, and by LWF, IRC and UNHCR employees.

Raan, a young Nuer man, expressed the view of many young people: 'Education is the biggest incentive to stay here. Otherwise, this place is a prison. But we persevere, because we want to gain education, knowledge and be more "civilised"'. Here, modernity is being forged through the Kenyan education system.[17] By 2006, there were seven pre-schools, twenty-four primary, four secondary schools and the Training College for Teachers in Kakuma. In the 2006 academic year, there were over 21,000 primary enrolments and 2,981 secondary students.[18] However, access to education is highly gendered. In the lower grades there is gender parity, but by fourth grade girls start dropping out due to domestic obligations, marriage and the prejudice against female education prevalent in many of the refugee communities. Girls represent a mere 11% of those attending secondary school.

On morning strolls through the Nuer zone I rarely saw anyone in the dusty alleys. Children and youths were in school, younger men at training courses or work, while women and older men were busy with community activities, collecting food rations, queuing for water, exchanging food items in the market, cooking, or checking on the arrival of financial transfers from relatives abroad. Clearly, the management and infrastructure of Kakuma refugee camp was not only designed to deliver aid efficiently, but also to keep refugees in check, who busied themselves with daily activities while waiting, often in limbo or for decades, for a permanent solution to their precarious condition.

The proliferation of rules and laws imposed by international institutions as well as the Kenyan government marked a change in the traditional governing structures for the predominantly agro-pastoralist Nuer and other ethnic groups. In the name of efficiency, aid provision structures are designed to control and silence refugee populations. Through the particular modernity created by global UN humanitarianism, refugees in Kakuma have been subjected to international processes, policies and discourses on human rights norms and standards that have dramatically changed their lives and social relations.

Other encounters with modernity in daily life in Kakuma

In addition to being a site of UN-sponsored modernity, Kakuma offered other experiences of *nei ti cike ker* – the market, church, global communications and infrastructure. Markets offer imported goods from across the continent, as well as communication and technology, thus turning arid Kakuma into a booming, multi-cultural, vibrant environment rather than an isolated rural settlement. The presence of refugees and the international humanitarian agencies triggered an influx of business, job

[17] Education in Kakuma is based on the Kenyan curriculum and provided in English, free of charge, up to secondary level. Access to universities is enabled through distance-learning programmes run through the National Council of Churches of Kenya (NCCK).
[18] LWF Kakuma, 'Gender Report 2005–2006, Kakuma Refugee Camp', Field Report; UNHCR–Kenya 'Country Operations Plan for Kenya', education statistics, 2006.

and trading opportunities attracting Kenyans from other parts of the district and the country. As Marc Antoine de Montclos and Peter Mwangi Kagwanja rightly point out, Kakuma emerged as 'an urban enclave in a sparsely populated and economically underdeveloped part of Kenya'.[19] From a village settlement of five thousand inhabitants in 1990, within a decade Kakuma had become a town of forty thousand. As a site of intense of international attention, Kakuma's cosmopolitanism was thriving. Planes, buses, and four-wheel drive vehicles continue to regularly disgorge foreign dignitaries, donors, ambassadors, international humanitarian staff, journalists, missionaries, researchers and activists. The Internet, websites[20] and research publications connect Kakuma with the world.

Kakuma is classified as a 'care-and-maintenance' camp, with the population relying on humanitarian assistance provided by the UNHCR, the WFP, the government and other partners. This includes the distribution of water, food, and firewood. The Kenyan government has deliberately sited refugee camps in semi-arid areas unsuited for cultivation, which constrains refugees' ability to grow food, making them reliant on humanitarian handouts and, as with other camps, creating a dependency that undermines their social identity and further marginalises them. For the agro-pastoralist Nuer and Dinka, this policy has also meant a change in their livelihoods, means of exchange and social identities. These predominantly cattle-keeping populations have had to turn to paid employment. 'In Kakuma, the cows were not around and we had no cows to talk about. I knew only that in the Nuer tradition we marry with cows, and use cows for sacrifices. Money was what we talked about,' Kuok explained. As a result of limited income-generating opportunities available in the camp, or working as traders, restaurant-owners or service-providers,[21] the cattle-keeping Nuer have become reliant on money to subsist.

As with changes wrought in Nuerland by the arrival of missionaries in the early twentieth century, the significant presence of missionaries in Kakuma brought new ideas of civilised and modern life. In the Nuer zone alone, there were eleven different churches providing ecumenical educational and support services. Refugees' houses are decorated with symbols and pictures of Christ. Youth and women particularly constantly refer to God and the Bible, emphasising that through the church they have found a 'new light'. 'This is a real God, not like these small gods of our ancestors. We are now more civilised [through Christianity]', commented one young Nuer man, a former soldier. Lony, a 'lost boy', first encountered God and church in the training camps in Ethiopia:

> But then, I was too small to understand. Only when I came to Kakuma, and later in 1994, when I was baptised and was nominated to be an assistant catechist,

---

[19] de Montclos and Kagwanja, 'Refugee Camps or Cities?', p. 206.
[20] See, for example, http://kakuma.wordpress.com/
[21] Ethiopian and Somali refugees run most businesses. They trade goods brought from across the continent, run Internet cafes, restaurants and computer training centres and provide hairdressing, tailoring, mini-bus and money transfer services. At the time of my fieldwork, the Sudanese market was dormant, with only a few stalls offering basic vegetables and grains.

> I discovered a new life. I became different, civilised somehow, and educated. I became a modern person who believed in big God, not in small gods.

Most young people as well as older women in Kakuma have been baptised. Nuer men referr to the church as being 'for women and children'. Some older men were baptised in Sudan and through their connections to church gained access to the camp, for example, to participate in Bible schools in Kenya. The majority did not join the church. 'We are old and we have our gods. We let the women go to church [*duel kuoth*] and we will follow them later', Tot said. Conversions were an important gendered marker of difference between the younger and older generations.

The connection to the world outside the camp was no longer a distant possibility, as many relatives and friends migrated to neighbouring countries or joined programmes and resettled in the west. The daily flow of remittances to the camp and visits of resettled 'lost boys' in search of wives have become integral to a wider transnational and diasporic network of families and communities.[22] Being in the camp offers opportunities for diasporic connections via phone, email and radio[23] and television exposure to western, mostly American, consumerism. Some Nuer 'lost boys' often mentioned that they 'have friends everywhere' and that 'the world is like a global village now', one connected through email and the Internet.

Worldliness was also expressed through the informal naming of different sections of the camp after major world events. For example, the areas known for alcohol production and video and computer game stalls were called Baghdad and Hong Kong. 'We call it Baghdad because when you go there, you drink so much, and then everybody fights, it is like total collapse. Like the war [and Saddam Hussain's collapse] in Baghdad', explained a Nuer young man. In this way, a connection between the local refugee and the global modern world is also being forged.

Gender mainstreaming and workshops
The encounter of localised refugees with the global UN humanitarianism produced a gendered form of modernity due to the UN's attachment to gender equality in assistance and protection programming. Implemented by the UNHCR and its partners, the policy used rights- and community-based approaches and age, gender and diversity mainstreaming (AGDM), aiming to 'enhance the protection of women and girls who are displaced, returnee and stateless and to ensure that they are able to enjoy their rights on an equal basis with men and boys'.[24] The policy was partially a result of numerous studies focusing on the vulnerability of refugee women to sexual and gender-based violence (SGBV) and the

[22] See Katarzyna Grabska, 'Lost Boys, Invisible Girls: Stories of Marriage across Borders', *Gender, Place and Culture*, 2010, Vol. 17, pp. 479–97.
[23] For the role of remittances and modern technology in maintaining transnationally nomadic lifestyles, see Cindy Horst, *Transnational Nomads: How Somalis Cope with Refugee Life in the Dadaab Refugee Camps of Kenya* (New York, 2006).
[24] UNHCR Kenya, *Handbook for the Protection of Women and Girls* (Geneva, 2008), p. 21.

statistics of refugee populations expressed in terms of 'the majority being women and children'.[25]

Since the 1970s, the UNHCR and other humanitarian organisations have attempted to recognise the special needs of refugee women. Initially concerned with protection due to insecurity in the camps, including rapes and sexual exploitation, the policy evolved into a transformative endeavour. The most recent version states:

> UNHCR has the responsibility to promote gender equality and work towards the elimination of violence against women and girls of concern as integral parts of our protection mandate.[26]

The outcome of the policy is supposed to lead to greater gender equality of the sexes while raising the status of women through their 'empowerment'.

Kakuma was one of the first camps where gender programming was implemented. However, as the head of the UNHCR in Kakuma commented to me in 2006, 'ten years after the start of the programme, the women are still suffering and there is little gender equality in the camp'. AGDM was implemented through a multi-dimensional programme of awareness-raising, empowerment, assistance and protection. Awareness-raising and training on human rights and gender issues are mainly implemented via billboards, campaigns and workshops. Talking a walk through the camp, one could not help noticing billboards warning against domestic violence, rape and discrimination against women: 'Women are Good Decision-Makers', 'Women's Rights are Human Rights', 'Real Men Educate Their Women'. This last slogan was misleading, encouraging education for women, but at the same time emphasising the men's ownership over them. These gender-awareness campaigns crossed borders with the returning refugees, with similar posters and billboards now seen throughout Juba.

The importance of forging global ideas of citizenship, human rights and gender equality through workshops became apparent on my first day in Kakuma. While looking for Sudanese planning to repatriate, I was pointed in the direction of workshops organised for potential returnees. Around thirty young people (among them eight girls) were participating in a human rights and gender training course for Nuer returnees organised by the Lutheran World Federation (LWF) repatriation unit. Nyamai, a tall, well-dressed 16-year old, was chosen to translate for those who did not speak English. She was outspoken and not afraid to speak out in front of men. She was also among the few Nuer girls attending secondary school, thus representing a 'new generation' or 'an educated and knowledgeable' girl (*nyial ti ngac ke ngoan*). Paul, in his twenties, explained: 'These workshops are good; they teach us how to be modern. We have now understood that women and men are equal. Our generation is pro-women'.

I participated in many workshops during my stay in Kakuma – the UNHCR and NGOs wanted to prepare and educate Sudanese for their

---

[25] Susan F. Martin, *Refugee Women* (Maryland, VA, 2004).
[26] UNHCR Kenya, *Handbook for the Protection of Women and Girls*, p. 23.

return to Sudan. 'Through these workshops, we can educate them [refugees] and make them a bit more civilised, modern. They will be ready to go back to their countries and re-build them', the head of LWF training services told me. The 'civilising' mission of these workshops was also confirmed by the UNHCR social services officer. There were umpteen workshops on water, sanitation, the CPA, civil and citizenship rights, human rights, gender and peace-building. They struck me as part of an accelerated modernity project of creating a gendered Sudanese citizen. Most refugees were constantly attending workshops designed not only to teach about women's rights, but also to 'sensitize them [boys and men] and create space for women's and girls' empowerment'.[27] Women were expected to participate in the workshops, but although some came, their participation was limited due to their lack of fluency in English. Research participants often proudly showed their certificates of attendance and used 'gender-correct' language to impress me with their new status of *nei ti cike ker*. Special assistance programmes targeting girls and women were provided to 'support their empowerment in the economic and public decision-making domain, by training in mobilisation, leadership and organizational skills, women's and girls' rights, by capacity building for entrepreneurship, and by micro-credit support'.[28] Every woman and girl I interviewed in Kakuma had attended at least one of the numerous courses offered, mainly tailoring, cooking, sewing, knitting and nursing. Some schoolgirls managed to get beyond the essentialised female and domesticated courses, learning how to use computers or repair electrical appliances instead. As a key activity to facilitate women's empowerment, the UNHCR and NGOs strengthened women's community-based organisations and promoted women's leadership.

The main element of AGDM (and becoming *raan ca ker* – an awoken person) was the provision of education for girls under the following slogan: 'If you educate a boy, you educate an individual; if you educate a girl, you educate a nation'. Girls received scholarships and assistance, including school uniforms and supplies provided by the UNHCR and NGOs. The Jesuit Refugee Service (JRS) supported girls at risk of domestic abuse or forced marriage with scholarships to attend Kenyan boarding schools. The LWF, charged with overseeing education in the camp, nevertheless, reported problems with girls' attendance. In order to address high rates of early dropouts due to the burden of domestic duties, early marriages and pregnancies, the UNHCR and the LWF built a dedicated girls' boarding school, an initiative supported by UNHCR Goodwill Ambassador Angelina Jolie and named after her. It finally opened in 2005, but only four classes were operational at the time of my fieldwork. To gain entry to the school, girls had to take exams and justify their vulnerable position in the community. Some places were reserved for victims of gender violence, mainly girls who were at risk of rape, domestic exploitation or abduction for marriage.

[27] Ibid., p. 25.
[28] Ibid,, p. 28.

The main focus of the UNHCR's gendered protection was combating sexual and gender based violence against women and girls that was common in refugee settings.[29] Apart from gender-dedicated NGO and UNHCR units monitoring the security in the camp, there were also designated protection areas for violated or at-risk women. They included Safe Havens and Protection Areas run by the JRS and UNHCR. In cases of greater danger to women and girls' security, the UNHCR either transferred them to another camp or recommended them for resettlement. A UNHCR officer explained the rationale of AGDM:

> Men are the perpetrators of gender violence here. We want them to respect women's rights, and girls and women have to be empowered. They have to know that they are equal to men, and have the same rights. If we educated them and give them income-generating possibilities, they will be empowered.

Hence, the goal of these policies was to alter gender relations by achieving gender equality, creating new (gender) identities and eliminating gender-based violence, discrimination and injustice. This particular gendered modernity had direct consequences on the negotiation and practice of gender identities in the camp.

PEOPLE WHO HAVE AWOKEN: GENDERED AND GENERATIONAL IDENTITIES

The camp, as a gendered place, was a site of renegotiation of gender relations, including identities and ideologies. But to what extent were they reversing the previous gender imbalances? Were they in fact emancipating women while correcting some of the male biases embedded in the gender ideologies of southern Sudanese and the Nuer communities? Before I attempt to answer these questions, I will first discuss the demographic gendering of the camp.

The transformations in gender relations were influenced by age and gender imbalances. Of the 92,000 refugees in Kakuma, 59% of the refugee population were men. Approximately 50% of the population was under the age of eighteen. Of the camp's Sudanese population, 60% were men, those under eighteen represented 49% of the total population and 31% were between eighteen and thirty years old. Only one in five Sudanese camp residents was older than thirty. A significant part of the youth were unaccompanied and almost entirely male minors, being the initial group of 'lost boys' who arrived in Kenya in 1992. One in four Sudanese refugees between the ages of five and eighteen was female, while among the Nuer there were three times more young men than young women.

---

[29] Jennifer Hyndman, 'Managing Difference: Gender and Culture in Humanitarian Emergencies', *Gender, Place and Culture*, 1998, Vol. 5, pp. 241–60; Cawo Abdi, 'Refugees, Gender Based Violence and Resistance: A Case Study of Somali Women in Kenyan Camps', in E. Tastsoglou and A. Dobrowolsky (eds), *Gender, Migration and Citizenship: Making Local, National and Transnational Connections* (London, 2006); UNHCR Kenya, 'Statistics of the Kakuma Camp Population', 2007.

The length of displacement and the point in a person's lifecycle when displacement took place were important determinants of gendered experiences in Kakuma. Those who had spent their childhood and youth in refugee camps had had different upbringings to those who had recently arrived from Sudan and spent their formative years in conflict zones. The former were exposed to education, gender equality and human rights programming and grew up in a multi-cultural environment. The latter brought with them already formed identities and due to their lack of English their exposure to the education in Kakuma was more limited.[30] Although there are no specific statistics on the age/gender/length composition of the population, life stories and in-depth qualitative interviews that I collected in Kakuma and Sudan revealed that older men and many young men who had arrived as 'lost boys' in the camp in 1991–2 had left for Sudan or the USA between 1997 and 2006. By 2006, the majority of young men over the age of eighteen had arrived since the early 2000s. By contrast, the majority of female and male youth younger than eighteen, as well as most women, have been in the camp since the mid-1990s. This gendered and generational composition of the camp was significant in terms of the changes in gender relations.

'Modern educated pro-women men' versus '*kuong-yong* and domino' men

Sharon E. Hutchinson (1996) notes the emergence of 'bull-boys' (unscarified young men) as a result of the spread of education and Christianity in eastern Nuerland in the 1980s. In the narratives of the western Nuer 'lost boys' in Kakuma, their first exposure to modernity was through education and Christianisation in the Ethiopian SPLA training camps. In their life stories presented in the previous chapter, Kim, Kuok and Wanten talked about their first encounters with school and the church. For them, the experiences in Kakuma were a continuation of this transformation, marking a new route to adulthood and manhood. Thus, the (re)negotiation and forging of new gender identities and relations was part of the ongoing process of change instigated by forced displacement.

A 'lost boy' in his twenties explained how war-induced displacement was advantageous:

> Without this displacement there would not be Kakuma and we would not have the chance to come here and gain education. Now, Kakuma has changed us, it has changed our Nuer culture. *Entedi, kon dholi ti ngac ke ngoani* [young men/boys who are knowledgeable, educated and have deeper insights into the way the world works]. We know about women's rights and that girls and boys are equal. We are different.

Young men often described Kakuma as a chance of accessing a different status – of *dholi ti ngac ke ngoani. Ti ngac ke ngoani* was associated with

---

[30] Educational, training and community activities were in English, including communication with the UNHCR and NGOs.

3.3 'New' young men,
Kakuma, 2006
(© Katarzyna Grabska)

education (the power of the pen), knowledge of the world beyond the village and awareness of gender equality issues. Young boys, girls, women and men, especially those who had spent most of their lives in refugee camps in Ethiopia or Kenya, praised Kakuma as a chance that opened up their minds and created new opportunities. There was a general concern about the place of the *nei ti naath* in the wider world. 'The world of 2006, of today, has changed. We, Nuer, have to do other things now,' asserted Majang, referring to the need of education and vocational profession. The youth recognised the new circumstances of their world and saw themselves not only as part of their village, but also as part of South Sudan, Africa and the world at large.

Both older and younger people's narratives about 'the way things changed in Kakuma' were filled with references to the past. Women and men referred often to 'the old days of *cieng nuära*' (Nuer culture) as signifying stability and order and 'proper' Nuer masculinity. They noted that the 'old values' still defined *wur nuära pany* – the ability to talk in public, make decisions and distinguish between good and evil. The way to attain them was, however, different. In their comments on the changing routes to manhood, the elderly talked with nostalgia of the no longer valued rituals. Tot, an elder from Akobo, commented that 'to be a mature man now is to go to school, to be able to talk well and to have experience in town. It is also a question of age'. Initiation through *gaar* was being replaced by other signs of manhood and maturity in Kakuma. The power of the pen replaced the wartime power of the gun and, together with baptism, had eliminated *gaar*. While conversing with a group of young men about the process of manhood in Kakuma, one said: 'I refused to be initiated. Now peace is coming and there is no more initiation by marking'. Paul, in his twenties, explained to me in English that this 'means he is now civilising. He has changed from the tradition to the world of today. Cultured modern people do not have marks'. Although tradition was associated in narratives of young and old with *gaar*, the 'world of today', the modern world signified new routes to manhood.

However, as Tot's friends – also elders – stressed: 'Nuer men are now modernised through education and church, but they still need to respect, Nuer culture. We, the elders, are still the guardians of the culture'. It was through the reference to 'our culture' that the elders attempted to maintain their moral authority and seniority over the youth, often faltering and challenged as a result of life in Kakuma.

The strong presence of the church in Kakuma (and in southern Sudan) had also important implications for (re)defining masculinities and gender relations. Despite the official proclamation that 'women and men are equal in front of God', church structures are intrinsically patriarchal. There was a certain contradiction between the UN's and global humanitarian ideas about gender equality with the church's vision of society. Some of the pro-women young men who were devoted Christians often spoke of their entrenched inequality, quoting the Bible and pointing out that as Eve was made out of Adam's rib, women are naturally inferior to men and should serve them. This rhetoric was skilfully used by younger and older people, including some women, to re-affirm and deepen patriarchal gender relations.

Young men also related changes in the concept of age-sets that are no longer based on group scarification. Wanten, a 'lost boy' separated from his family, explained how:

> When we arrived in Kakuma, this is when we were put in houses with other boys. They were not from our community and we learned how to share lives with those from other tribes. We divided domestic tasks among ourselves, such as cooking, fetching water and collecting.

Being housemates or classmates marked a new concept of *ric*. A common narrative of becoming lost boys was part of the journey to manhood through a shared group experience. Kuok explained that:

> When I was recruited in Lɛr by SPLA, there were many young boys in my group. We did not know each other. But throughout the journey on foot and by barges to Ethiopia, there was a lot of danger, fighting, killing. Children were dying of starvation. We had to learn how to help each other. In our group, we were five. Matok was the one who saved us when we were crossing the river to Ethiopia. We did not know how to swim and he grabbed a piece of tree, and this is how we survived. Later, in Kakuma, we lived together and assisted each other. Now, some of us are in America, one is in Nairobi and some went back to Sudan.
>
> At the beginning we were very disturbing [trouble-makers] as children and as students. We did not obey teachers' authority because we were used to the authority of the gun. But then, through church, school, sports and social clubs we began to live a different life.

'New' men boasted of their abilities to resolve conflict and bring peace through dialogue, negating the old rules of Nuer warrior men being ready end conflicts through fighting.[31]

[31] See similar transformation of 'warrior' masculinities of the Masaai (Hodgson, 2004).

Access to education became a new route to adulthood and another characteristic of a 'real Nuer man'. In the past, parents had been reluctant to send their sons to predominantly missionary-provided education since it meant 'giving your son away to white people'. The least favoured son would be sent to a missionary school, either by choice or as a result of pressure from the priests. The elders told me that they feared that the child would come back 'different from the rest of us in the village'. 'The educated men were called then foreigners [*turuk*]. They knew the life of town [*rek*], not the life of village [*cieng*],' explained Tot. *Turuks'* access to government jobs and collaboration with *kume* (government) created a rift in *cieng* structures. As Hutchinson shows, elders felt threatened by these 'new fashioned *dholi*' (boys).[32] The attitude to education only began to change after the first civil war, and became desirable during the second war. The same is true of changes in manhood among the Maasai in Tanzania.[33] Parents saw the potential benefits of education: their children might access a government income and a position in the community, which would enhance their own wellbeing. In Kakuma, educated boys had a superior masculinity, and so parents sent their sons to the camp specifically to access education.

New Nuer men had also mastered gender-talk. Wanten told me that 'we are like you now [western]. We recognise that women and men are equal and that women have rights. Women are behind our successes'. They also claimed that they only want to have one wife and a few children 'because as a responsible man you have to do family planning. You have to be able to afford to feed your family and educate all your children'. Others stressed: 'God only allows you to marry one wife. Also, economically, this makes more sense'. Through gender sensitisation, reproductive health and family planning workshops and the spread of Christian doctrine among the youth in the camp, young men were thus adopting modern concepts of family.

Whether this new gendered language was a lived and practiced masculine identity – rather than an image adopted for the benefit of western foreigners, including myself – was not always clear. For example, almost all the young men I talked to in Kakuma claimed that they would have only one wife, and that she would be an educated woman over the age of eighteen. However, many of those whom I met later in Nuerland had married young uneducated girls and kept them at home, despite claiming that their wives were sent to school. Also, by the time I left Lɛr, several were looking for a second wife. These young men skilfully deployed the western image of a respectable man in order to gain acceptance, minimise their marginalisation as refugees and access benefits such as education sponsorships. I also found it easier to associate with young men who held views closer to my feminist stance rather than those who mistreated and disrespected girls and women. While the rhetoric

---

[32] Sharon E. Hutchinson, *Nuer Dilemmas: Coping with Money, War and the State* (Berkeley, CA, 1996).
[33] Dorothy L. Hodgson, *Once Intrepid Warriors: Gender, Ethnicity, and the Cultural Politics of Maasai Development* (Bloomington, IN, 2004).

remained 'pro-women', in daily life the young men continued to behave differently.

At the same time, young men often referred to Kakuma as a space where they were able to gain relative freedom from the community rules and expectations of 'respectable good Nuer behaviour'. As Paul commented, 'Here we are able to do things that are not considered man's job, like cooking, washing clothes, fetching water, bringing firewood and food rations. Our mothers and sisters are not with us, so we have to do the domestic work'. Although they were not enthusiastic about these domestic tasks, men often fulfilled them due to the lack of female relatives in the camp without being harassed and ridiculed by others. However, once they went back to Sudan, they were under community pressure to conform to local masculinity ideals. The new modern masculinity was not only strategically chosen but also limited.

New Nuer masculinity was also strongly intertwined with the development and reconstruction of southern Sudan. Here, Paul explained that 'We have to get educated in Kakuma in order to go back and rebuild our country and community.' His friend, a former soldier and now a secondary school student in Kakuma added: 'To be a man is to help your country'. To be a man was no longer restricted to being a Nuer man. Rather, the source of identity was the greater nation, Sudan, or southern Sudan. This was partly a result of nationalist sloganising and the experience of the liberation struggle propagated by the SPLA. Dignitaries from southern Sudan who came to encourage repatriation referred to young men as 'agents of change', 'future leaders of Sudan'. To be educated was not only to assist oneself and his family and community, it was also an obligation to 'do something for the country' and a collective mission to bring peace and development. As one young man said, 'if you are educated, you have to drop the gun now. This is a war of development and you have a duty as a man to do something for your country'. For the Nuer youth, the experience of modernity, intertwined with the shifting concepts of masculinity, was not a moment (being in the camp), but – as with the Zambians studied by Ferguson and the Manjacos in Guinea Bissau researched by Eric Gable – a meaning, a way of imaging the world, and being able to collectively contribute to its change.[34]

While some of the hyper-masculine youth were turning into *dholi ti ngac ke ngoani*, others found themselves emasculated. Married men and elders who came to the camp as adults often complained about their inability to provide for their families due to the conditions in Kakuma. Garjul, a father of four in his mid-thirties, succinctly described the new dependency:

> In our Nuer tradition, a Nuer man cannot be assisted [given a cow] twice. If you are given assistance all the time, you are seen as a weak man, and lose respect. UN is our father here. It provides us with food, shelter, and water and protects us. It has made us, Nuer men [*wutni nuäri*], into children [*gaat*]. It is not possible to be a leader and elder [*kuäär kä diet*] in Kakuma, even if you were a soldier.

[34] Ferguson, *Expectations of Modernity*; Eric Gable, 'The Funeral and Modernity in Manjaco', *Cultural Anthropology*, 2006, Vol. 21, pp. 381–415.

This metaphor of the dependency on the UN as a provider for the household was seen non-masculine and reflected the weakened position of men. Robbed of the title of *guar* (father) in the household, some men felt that the material basis of their superior position with respect to their wives and children had been undermined. By describing the new conditions in exile as *enteme kon gaat* (literally, we are now children), older men indicated their perceived emasculation and disempowerment. They expressed their bitterness and helplessness:

> There are no jobs, no way to perform our traditional roles. We lose respect at home and in the community. Look, our wives run now to UNHCR since this is their new husband. The UN gives them food, shelter and when they say that we beat them, the UN takes our wives and children away from us and sends them to migration [resettlement]. Boys are leaders now [*dholi kuääri entäme*].

Men felt challenged in their positions not only because of the UN as a 'new father' but also by the growing power of young, educated men and women. As with the new young leaders among Burundian refugees in Tanzania studied by Simon Turner,[35] in Kakuma most leadership roles in local courts, refugee administration and international agencies are held by younger men. I was surprised to learn that the Nuer court had twelve members, including three women, all of whom were under thirty, some of them single. In Nuerland, only senior elder men in their late forties or fifties who are married with children and have gained the status of respectable men are elected court members. According to UNHCR gender programming, women were supposed to be included in all community leadership structures and their participation was required in official meetings.[36] As the international organisations preferred to deal with those who were literate and able to communicate in English, this eliminated almost all elders and senior men. The Nuer community chairman complained: 'Now, women and [male] youth run the community affairs'. Hence, the creation of new and shifting of old dimensions of power challenged the material basis of men's superiority, making older men insecure in their (gender) positions.

Men's narratives also reflected their concerns about losing control over their wives and children. Tot, an elder with two wives, lacked qualifications and was unable to provide for both his families. His 'idleness' bothered his wives because they had to struggle to find food for the children. Tot lamented:

> My older wife told me that I was useless, that I was staying home and doing nothing while she had to take a job as a cleaner in the hospital to support the family. She finally quarrelled with me and ran to protection [the UNHCR]. She told the UN that I was beating her. They took her and the children away from me. Now, they might even go for resettlement. I feel I have no control [over them] because of 'women's rights' [*cung man*].

[35] Simon Turner, 'The Barriers of Innocence: Humanitarian Intervention and Political Imagination in a Refugee Camp for Burundians in Tanzania', PhD Dissertation, Roskilde University, 2001.
[36] See AGDM guidelines in UNHCR Kenya, 'Statistics of the Kakuma Camp Population'; also Nuer constitution in Kakuma.

3.4 Nuer court elders in Kakuma, 2006
(© Katarzyna Grabska)

Some men felt that human rights rhetoric was employed in the camp to chastise men. 'In the camp, women are practicing their human rights [*cung naath*]. When you are unable to provide for them, they go to other men and have many husbands', explained Majang, a Nuer counsellor working for JRS. He added:

> In Sudan, it was forbidden for the lady to go to another man. Here they go with other men, and if the husband talks strong to the wife she goes to UNHCR for protection and says: 'now he will experience the meaning of human rights'. Also, here people interact with other cultures, they see how other nationalities are living and practicing [their gender relations] and the women think they are free to do it.

The lack of control over women's sexuality concerned many men. They located it in their inability to provide for their wives, and partially as a result of women rights. I often heard men complaining about women's control over food rations. Majang told me:

> Before, we could control the woman through the access to food, but now, since she can go to the UN directly, the woman has more power in the family and you might feel that you are not a man.

As a result of women having their own ration cards and not having to rely on men for food, the source of men's control over the household was further undermined. The ration card eroded much of the material basis of women's subordination.

Bol, an Anglican church elder, talked about the social pressure of carrying out masculine responsibilities and the inability to do so in the camp:

Since women can go away now because of the UN, the other people will see you as a weak man. The man worries that if other people see the family not taken care of, with dirty clothes, malnourished children, with nothing to eat – this will be perceived as a problem for the man. The man might fear that the community will insult him and will see him as unable to provide for the family. He will not be respected in the community. This pressure comes from all the people, women and men. This pressure can be very big for men, because the man is seen as the responsible person who should provide for his family and ensure its wellbeing. For the man, it is very shameful if he cannot provide for the family.

Hence, maintaining masculinity was also linked to the opinion of others. Men also felt that international law undermined their rights over their children. Bol fondly reminisced about a past when paternal rights were stable:

In our culture, once you married a woman with cows, the children and the woman belong to you. But here, when there is a quarrel in the family, the woman runs for protection [to the UN] and the UN takes the children away from you.

Feeling helpless, men often reacted to loss of status by drinking, gambling or domestic violence.

Women vocally expressed disapproval and disappointment with the 'new emasculated men'. A mother lambasted them:

Look at them, they are useless, our men. They are no longer men. Men in Sudan are strong, they have muscular bodies and they bring you food and protect you. Here, these men are skinny; they sit around playing cards and dominoes and do nothing, and waste our food on *nyalonglong* [local alcohol]. We call them drunkards [*kuong-yong*] and 'domino men'.

Some men in Kakuma strongly felt that the camp conditions and the gender programming challenged their masculinity. As Cornwall and Lindisfarne observed, 'masculinity appears as an essence or commodity, which can be measured, possessed, or lost'.[37] In Kakuma, militarised (hyper-masculinities) and emasculated masculinities were being re-shaped and transformed to 'educated civilised Christian future leaders of Sudan'. Similarly to socio-economic change in rural and urban East Africa,[38] human rights and humanitarian logic disempowered men such as the elders. The felt emasculation of men revealed the material basis of these men's power and authority over women. They perceived the newly gained position and bargaining power of women in Kakuma as a direct threat to their prestige and status.

Educated and empowered girls and women versus women at risk

Just as masculinities were modernised so to were Nuer wartime femininities. Nyamai, a 16-year girl, was one of the few Nuer schoolgirls in the camp. She left Nuerland in 1997 together with her mother and siblings

[37] Andrea Cornwall and Nancy Lindisfarne, *Dislocating Masculinity: Comparative Ethnographies* (London, 1996).
[38] Margrethe Silberschmidt, 'Disempowerment of Men in Rural and Urban East Africa: Implications for Male Identity and Sexual Behavior', *World Development*, 2001, Vol. 29, pp. 657–671.

when the bombings intensified. Her father, who was among the teachers escorting 'lost boys' from Ethiopia to Kakuma, arrived in the camp in 1991. Through his connections with the SPLA he arranged for his family to join him. An educated man, he sent all his six children to school and having worked for UNICEF in Sudan since 2001, he could afford better education for his children. Some were in Nairobi and Nyamai was in a Kenyan boarding secondary school. In the camp, Nyamai was a girl youth leader in the camp and participated in drama clubs, played volleyball with boys, went to the Catholic Church and represented girls at workshops and public events. Ambitious, and not afraid to speak out in front of men, she was one of the new generation of girls in Kakuma:

> The difference between girls in Kakuma and in Sudan is that girls here are allowed to go to school and they are educated. But there, girls are not allowed, because the family only looks into the wealth that they will get from marrying the girl. There, when the girl grows up, they immediately find her husband. Here, the girls are given a right to choose. They are allowed to play sports, move freely, are allowed to attend choir competitions and church events. Here, parents realised that it is good for girls to do these things. But in Sudan, from what I hear, if you interact with boys, you are seen as a prostitute. Here, the NGOs are making this change. They are encouraging girls to participate and become leaders. Also, it depends on the parents. Those parents who have been here long, they see the benefit of education and exposure for girls. So they let us do these things. But those men who came from Sudan recently, they do not accept human rights and they think that they can make women and girls work for them here. But they realise that we are different and they go back to Sudan.

As Nyamai's account illustrates, education, awareness-raising, mixed-gender sport and cultural activities, workshops and the promotion of girls' participation as leaders were ways to redress discrimination and socialise girls into role models that went beyond marriage. Parental readiness to give new opportunities to girls made a difference. For those either born in Kakuma or who had spent much of their childhood in displacement, these new ideas of empowerment and gender equity were becoming a reality. UN and NGO staff often commented that girls were the ones 'who were coming up'. Although girls were still expected to perform the bulk of domestic chores and many complained about being overworked, some mothers encouraged their sons to take on cooking, washing, fetching water and cleaning as they thought it was good for them.

Schools were a crucible forging new role models for girls and women (see Photo 3.5). Girls' narratives in Kakuma were influenced by these ideals and reflected new possibilities for girls and women. During my visit to the Angelina Jolie boarding school, a group of girls shared their dreams of becoming pilots, doctors, engineers and parliamentarians. They strongly believed, or wanted to believe, that 'male' professions were now attainable. Nyamai also had plans:

> When I finish education, I will become a lawyer. I will go back to Sudan and make people aware of the rights of girls and women. Girls are the ones who are the most discriminated in the community. They have the least rights. But to be a respected woman, I will still need to get married and have children.

Although girls still referred to marriage and children as routes to womanhood, they also saw other possibilities beyond being wives and mothers. Their aspirations revealed their awareness of the need for change of the gender imbalances that kept them in subordinate positions.

In several of the workshops, I noticed girls, especially those who spent most of their lives in the camps, speaking up, taking on leadership roles and voicing their views. Girls were redressing their weak positions in the community thanks to the freedoms and opportunities that the UN gender-based programming offered. Nyawal, a 15-year old, commented:

> The constitution in [southern] Sudan says that there is equality between men and women, boys and girls, and the rights of women have to be respected. It says that women shall have rights as they are all human beings and they are equal in front of God.

As a result of civic education, gender training and Christian doctrine in Kakuma, girls were becoming aware of their rights as well as the politics of southern Sudan. They walked freely, often by themselves, through the camp, socialised and shared food with boys and wore trousers, thereby subverting gender division of space by transgressing public spaces reserved for men. In wearing trousers, girls were asserting themselves as modern and progressive. Using the rhetoric of rights, girls were skilfully negotiating and expanding their limited space in Kakuma, and using their agency in resisting the hegemonic discourse of *cieng nuära*, the muting of girls' voices.

Changing negotiations around marriage also revealed girls' greater agency. Nyakuoth often struggled with community pressure to marry:

> There are only few girls here in Kakuma. But there are many men. We [girls] have a lot of choice. They all want to marry you, and especially the lost boys who went to America. They come back to marry girls from Kakuma, because they want educated wives. Sometimes there are two or three of them who try to engage you, and then there is fighting in the community.

This fierce competition among suitors raised the profile of girls and increased their and their parents' bargaining power in negotiating bridewealth. Pressure also came from male relatives in the camp, who saw the material advantages of Nyakuoth's marriage, it being a solution to their difficult financial situation. In Kakuma, due to the lack of cattle, marriage payments were mainly in cash. Due to the dire situation in the camp, where resources were scarce, marriage was seen as a way of improving one's wellbeing, even if it was just a temporary solution. Parents expressed their preferences for girls to be married to 'lost boys', as they were able to pay higher bridewealth due to their jobs in resettlement countries and were better placed to provide financial support to the family of the bride. Some girls often did not feel that they could oppose parental decisions. As Nyaklang, a girl engaged against her will to a man resettled in the USA told me: 'You cannot go against your father, otherwise they will say that you are a dog, you will not be seen as a human being. As a girl, you have a duty to assist your family [through marriage and bridewealth].'

3.5 Female role models in the Angelina Jolie boarding school for girls, Kakuma, 2006
(© Katarzyna Grabska)

Some girls, like 17-year old Nyagajak, who was engaged to a US-based
Nuer, saw marriage to a 'lost boy' as a chance to access a better life:

> I am happy to be married, to be finally a woman in my home. I will have a title
> and will be respected in society, especially because my husband is in the US. He
> will assist me with clothes and nice things and then I can move to Nairobi. You
> see this watch, [she pointed to a gold, shining wristband] it was an engagement
> present from him. America 'lost boys' are better [as husbands], they have jobs
> and can provide for you.

Those who were engaged and were already receiving support from
their future husbands walked around the camp wearing smart clothes,
expensive jewellery and negotiating with rival suitors by mobile phone.
Some perceived their position as women/wives (*ciek*) having been
enhanced through marriage to 'educated and somewhat civilised' men,
as they often referred to the 'lost boys'. Others were engaged to 'lost boys'
and benefiting from their support while continuing a relationship with
a *luum* (boyfriend) in the camp.[39] Not only have girls become a highly
desired commodity, they are able to better negotiate their own choices.
Girls' narratives, their behaviour and the frequent fighting over brides
clearly signalled changes in their power in negotiating marriage.

Some girls in the camp escaped domestic violence, family pressure and
arranged marriages by eloping with their boyfriends or 'running' to the
UN or NGOs.[40] Stories also circulated about girls who committed suicide

[39] Conversations with research participants and witnessing cases in the LWF
gender unit.
[40] Interviews with LWF gender unit supervisor, UNHCR protection officer and
JRS counsellor.

to protest community pressure. I witnessed several cases of arranged marriages where girls sought UNHCR or NGO protection from families allegedly forcing them to marry 'lost boys'. These types of cases were the majority that the LWF gender unit, UNHCR protection section and Dinka and Nuer courts dealt with. During one court session I learned of the case of a 15-year-old girl and a 'lost boy' in his late twenties. The girl went to and NGO and reported that she was being forced to get married, but it transpired she had been having two relationships – one with her fiancé in the USA, which her parents perceived as an official engagement as he had paid initial bridewealth, and another with a man in Kakuma. Matters came to a head when the future husband arrived in the camp. The issue was discussed between the UN and NGO representatives and the families of the betrothed. It was decided that due to the age of the girl, the marriage could not proceed. Through the policy of protecting girls from under-age and forced marriage, humanitarian workers were strengthening the position of girls within the households. Girls used 'running for protection [to the UN]' not only as a threat to humiliate the family, but also to exercise their agency by manipulating UN policy.

In addition to attending school, church and workshops, other hallmarks of 'being civilised' as expressed by girls and male youth was through dress, possession of mobile phones, cooking practices, bodily hygiene, 'knowing something' and listening to different music and dance (from *buul*[41] to disco). All were expressions of the embodied modern identity. As in other cases of the encounter with modernity discussed in the literature on its embodiment among Chinese and Thai migrant women,[42] their bodies were marked by both modernity and difference – with newly fledged gestures, dress codes, desires and dreams representing the new Nuer girl, boy, woman and man.

Some women, and older and younger men, frowned upon these manifestations of freedom. Commenting on the behaviour of Kakuma girls, Kong, a youth who had spent four years in the camp, stated that 'they have gone mad; they are walking loose (*wa loorä*). The school has turned them into prostitutes, they roam around and think they are men'. Newly won freedoms and possibilities for girls threatened gender power relations among the Nuer, and the southern Sudanese in general. The metaphor of 'wa loorä' aptly describes the fear, especially by men, of losing control over their daughters, sisters and potential wives. Despite being able to wear jeans, mini-skirts and tight tops, to listen to rap music, have boyfriends, attend school, have more scope to negotiate marriages and speak up in public, girls in Kakuma were aware these were temporary freedoms. Many feared going 'home' to southern Sudan, as they were aware of the lack of freedoms and marginalised position of girls. Nyamai told me: 'Once we go there, we will be forced to marry a local *wur nuära* [a metaphor of a

[41] In cattle camps, girls and boys go to *buul*. They gather around a fire, dance and court each other to the sound of a drum and singing.
[42] Mary Beth Mills, *Thai Women in the Global Labour Force: Consuming Desires, Contested Selves* (New Brunswick, New Jersey: Rutgers University Press, 2002); Aihwa Ong, *Flexible Citizenship*.

scarified illiterate man]. You can forget about education. In Kakuma, we have some freedom and the UN, at least'. This was a feeling that was also shared by some women. In the absence of their husbands and relatives, women felt relatively free from social obligations. Hence, Kakuma as an extra-territorial space, physically distant from the control of relatives and community, opened up possibilities for transgressing some of the gender norms, opening up spaces – albeit fleetingly – for greater autonomy.

Women in the camp were busy with workshops, training courses, women support groups, community meetings and earning money. Those like Nyakuol, widow of an SPLA commander, were considered role models. They spoke in public meetings and men and women regarded them as a *kuäär*. Chatting with a group of women leaders, Nyalada, the chairwoman, explained:

> To be a woman now is more than just giving birth and taking care of home. Yes, these are [still] important. But here in Kakuma, we, the women, have access to education and training. If you are educated, you can also contribute to the family through your work. There is also the UN and 'women's rights'. We are more respected in the community. We are leaders now. Because of much work, Kakuma woman is very tired!

The production of new routes to womanhood was partially due to the UN gender-mainstreaming strategy of empowerment, which created new opportunities for women through access to skills, resources, income-generation and leadership.[43] Also, like Nyakuol and Nyalada, most women in the camp were either widows or single mothers. In the absence of their husbands and older male relatives, they were forced to take on more household, responsibilities, while the limited employment prospects for men made women's financial contributions significant for family survival.

Some women, especially those who had been in the camp for a long time, took advantage of these new possibilities. 'If you have a job and can earn money, the man will respect you more. He will be afraid that if he abuses you, you will just go and leave him [alone]. If you have a job, you can always support yourself and your children', explained a young wife. Access to jobs and income were important components in negotiating greater security and autonomy from their husbands in the 'conjugal bargain'.[44] This view reveals how gender power asymmetries within the Nuer household are based on the material contribution that men and women make. Household and family appear to be not havens of harmony and co-operation, but rather 'site[s] of subordination and domination, of sexual hierarchies of many kinds, and of conflicts of interests between its members, especially between husbands and wives',[45] but also between daughters and parents. Access to an independent income affords women an enhanced negotiating position within the household.

[43] UNHCR, *Handbook for the Protection of Women and Girls*, p. 28.
[44] Ann Whitehead, 'I'm Hungry, Mum: The Politics of Domestic Budgeting', in K. Young, C. Wolkowitz and R. McCullagh (eds), *Of Marriage and the Market: Women's Insubordination Internationally and its Lessons* (London, 1981).
[45] Ibid., p. 92.

UN procedures to fingerprint women and issue them with individual ration cards has also allowed women and girls greater say in household matters. To be able to be repatriated to Sudan, each potential returnee had to register in person. Nyakuoth, who wanted to continue her education in Kenya, expressed her approval: 'This finger is my power. They [her family] cannot force me to go back if I do not want'. Decision-making was shifting from the communal – vested in the male household head – to the individual. This was particularly apparent with regard to repatriation decisions. Many households separated, as some members decided to remain in Kenya.

As in other refugee situations, ration cards gave women direct control over household resources and, as mentioned earlier, led to men feeling emasculated.[46] Nyadak, married to an Anglican pastor, spoke for most women:

> It is better for us women to have access to food rations. We know what to do with it. If it is the man who collects it, he will sell it for alcohol. Women are more responsible because they take care of the family. Now, we can control it better and men have to ask us if they want to sell part of the ration.

UN policies to protect women at risk antagonised many men. They complained that women were abusing the system and 'running to the UN', even in the most trivial cases. By using the feminised image of vulnerability, women were able to manoeuvre greater autonomy. The UN ration card and the UN's gender equality policy brought changes at the household level, with women improving their position in the 'patriarchal bargain'.[47] They also contributed to grinding down structures of social power in the household and undermining the material basis of gender asymmetry.

Yet, pro-women policies often had unanticipated effects and actually ended up marginalising women. Women were often added rather than fully incorporated into UN and NGO programmes and administrative structures in order to meet the gender balance requirement and not from a desire to obtain gender equality. Angelina, in her mid-thirties, laughed as she described her experience of workshops:

> These workshops are a funny thing. We, as women, are often called to participate. But then, these trainers, usually men, forget that we are illiterate and we do not speak English. They speak all in English, even if they are Nuer, and we, the women, we sit there like stupid, silent, not understanding anything. During the breaks, when men enjoy tea, we sit in the classroom trying to write down all the difficult terms. But we do not know what we are writing. This is useless.

[46] Agnes Callamard, in her study of Mozambican refugees in Malawi, argues that access to flour gave women greater household bargaining power, 'Flour is Power: The Gendered Division of Labour in Lisongwe Camp', in W. Giles, H. Moussa and P. Van Esterik (eds), Development and Diaspora: *Gender and the Refugee Experience* (Dundas, Ontario, 1996), pp. 176–98.

[47] Deniz Kandiyoti, 'Gender, Power and Contestation: Rethinking Bargaining with Patriarchy', in C. Jackson and R. Pearson (eds), *Feminist Visions of Development: Gender Analysis and Policy* (London, 1998).

Like elder men, whose seniority and position in the community were undermined due to their lack of English and education, some women felt marginalised for the same reasons. They realised that they were tokens, not participants, and that the display of the hierarchical power of the humanitarian regime through the use of English and need for qualifications widened the divide not only between aid workers and refugees, but also between the (mostly illiterate) women and older men and educated youth.

Kakuma was a world of relative freedom for women and men able to transgress gender norms, unlike (South) Sudan, which was perceived as a place of entrenched real Nuer gender norms and ideologies. Since the Nuer kinship and family system constructs women as 'less able to act as subjects than male subjects are able so to do',[48] girls had less scope to manoeuvre. Although gender policies in the camp intended to empower and enhance the position of women and girls, the result was not always as intended. Girls who had access to education and leadership coaching and had spent prolonged time in the camps gained stronger positions in the community. Some women enhanced their bargaining power by taking advantage of the essentialised identities as 'women refugees' imposed on them, while others suffered disempowerment. Thus, the process of re-shaping and negotiation of new identities was intertwined with other categories of difference, including age, wealth and seniority, and resulted in the production of multiple, often competing, forms of gender identities.

CONTESTING GENDER POWER, IDEOLOGY AND 'OUR CULTURE'

'Our culture': past and present gender orders

As a place of gendered modernity, the camp was an arena of contesting gender power and ideology. Conversations repeatedly referred to previous times and *cieng nuära*. When narrating their lives or gossiping about the present, women and men cited *cieng nuära* to state their moral position, and to show the supremacy of the past values. Having spent over fifteen years in Kakuma, Bol reflected:

> In our Nuer culture [*Ke cieng nuära*], we used to marry with cows. Women and men knew their roles in the community. Marriages were stable, men had cattle, were the heads of family and protected the home. They were respected by their women and children. Women gave birth to children, cared for them and stayed peacefully, without quarrels, with their husbands and other co-wives. Children respected the elders, who had the authority in the community affairs. Now, in Kakuma, there is no respect, things are different. Girls run loose [*wa loorä*], parents cannot control their children, women run to the UN and men are drunkards and sit around idly without anything to do. In Sudan, we marry with cows and the lives are good. Here, the money corrupts everything.

[48] Ann Whitehead, 'Women and Men; Kinship and Property: Some General Issues (1)', in R. Hirschon (ed.), *Women and Property, Women as Property* (Kent, 1984), p. 180.

Sarah, a widow in her late fifties, left Sudan in 1988. She first went to Ethiopia so her children could go to school. When war broke out in Ethiopia in 1991, they fled to Kenya, via Sudan, arriving in Kakuma in June 1992. She reminisced:

> *Ke cieng nuära*, when a man and a woman got married, a good woman meant that there was no quarrel in the marriage. Woman obeyed and served her husband. To show respect, she did not talk in front of other men and served the food on her knees. If they produce good children, then the family grew nicely together.
>
> *Ke Kakuma*, we do not see anything good here. We cannot cultivate our farms and we cannot have cows. We cannot take care of our own lives, we just have to wait for the distribution centre. Another thing is that the woman can be left by herself with her four children and the husband has gone somewhere else. Or he is a drunkard and sits idly. She is left without anything. Because there are so many children in the camp, she also has to take care of others. And these children have their own minds now, they do not respect mothers and elder women any more. But there are also those women who have gone mad. They take on lovers in the absence of their husbands and this causes another problem. This is not like the past.

These commentaries about the past in *cieng nuära* and Kakuma signify how things used to be done and how they should be done. *Cieng nuära* was equated with stability, morality and an order located in women's obedience and respect of seniority and gender. For elders, life in Kakuma undermined this certainty and stability, representing moral decay and the loss of Nuer community and family values. Their narratives reflect worries about changing patterns of intimate relations between wives and husbands, and also relations between parents and children and between generations.

Although older women and men complained about these changes, women were more vocal about the failure of men to fulfil their end of the conjugal bargain. These complaints were also common among younger recently arrived men.

The older generation made references to *cieng nuära* to show the structures of authority that once governed the Nuer as well as the duties of good wives, mothers, husbands and children. These narratives reveal their own fear of the rapid social changes that were taking place in their communities due to war and lives in refugee camps. They also indicate the worries about 'losing control' and position at home and in the community. This reflects similar concerns of older and younger people in Ado-Odo town described by Andrea Cornwall in the wake of their experiences with modernity. In their complaints about 'wayward women' and 'useless men' of the present, Ado-Odo residents sought to express their concerns about their authority, livelihoods and reputation being undermined.[49] For the older Nuer in Kakuma, it was not only their lifestyles that were changed due to the encounters with particular modernity. They pointed to 'loose girls', 'women running mad' and 'disrespectful youth' as

---

[49] Andrea Cornwall, 'Wayward Women and Useless Men: Contest and Change in Gender Relations in Ado-Odo, SW Nigeria', in D.L. Hodgson and S. McCurdy (eds), *'Wicked' Women and the Reconfiguration of Gender in Africa* (Portsmouth, 2001), p. 69.

threatening their own position in the communities. These commentaries spoke also about control, agency and autonomy and pointed to female agency as a main source of concern.

Reinterpreting 'our culture': gender ideas challenged

For younger men who had arrived from Sudan more recently, references to 'tradition' and 'our culture' were usually made to illustrate a specific gender order. When I came back from southern Sudan to Nairobi, I heard that a girl I had helped with a scholarship to attend a secondary school in Nairobi had been beaten by her cousin and, as a result, run away from her family. When I finally managed to contact her, she told me how her cousin accused her of being a prostitute and having 'boyfriends' just because she was spending time with male school friends who were neither Nuer nor from her *cieng*. When she confronted her cousin, arguing that her life was hers to live, he resorted to violence and beat her until she bled. When I discussed this with her uncle, he commented:

> You do not understand our culture. In our culture, men beat women and girls when they make mistakes. This is the reason Kong [the cousin] was beating her. [...] In our culture, girls do not have boyfriends; they do not spend time with boys, this is forbidden. They are seen as prostitutes, otherwise.

Kong himself was adamant about his cousin's 'unacceptable behaviour':

> We don't want this Kenyan culture. If she wants to live like a Kenyan, let her go. She will not be part of the family. We will reject her. She is trying to be a man; she thinks that if she is educated she is a man and that her life is in her hand. She is a Nuer, she is still just a girl.

Another male cousin who also grew up in Kenya told me, in English, about the changes that this adolescent girl was trying to implement:

> You were trying to do something that is not acceptable in our culture. You were living the way you learned how to live in Kenya, in a multicultural environment that is open. But we, the Nuer, are not ready for these changes that you were trying to bring to our culture. I had to do the same. I used to be a basketball player and wore dreads. But your mother and other women in the family advised me strongly that I had to drop this attitude and start behaving like a Nuer in order to be respected. Our culture will not accept mixing with other clans,[50] or even tribes [ethnic groups]. They are not ready for this. You will have to drop this if you want to be part of the family.

After a long discussion with girl's mother and cousins, I was able to convince them to let her continue with schooling. However, her cousin and elder brother decided to ostracise her from the family. 'She is no longer considered as part of our family. If you want to take care of her, then she will be under your responsibility,' Kong told me. The girl's mother understood her daughter's intention to pursue her education

---

[50] Some respondents incorrectly used the word 'clan' in English when referring to their lineage, *cieng*. The respondent is saying that girls were not allowed to mix with other *cieng* (secondary segments) and clan (*thok duël*) members.

but was in a difficult situation, facing strong opposition coming from the male relatives. Eventually, the girl resumed her education and graduated in January 2010. When I talked to her on the phone in May 2010, she mentioned that she wanted to study further in order to get a good job. 'Now that I have defied my family and went against them, especially the men, I need to get a good profession to be able to live my life independently of them,' she insisted. 'I want to study international relations so I can be an ambassador one day and show the men in Sudan that women are worth more than just being wives'. In her case, as with some of the other girls whom I befriended, experiences in the camp, access to education and ideas about gender equality shaped a new femininity concept. Transforming femininities emphasised women's ambitions for greater freedoms and autonomies, not only financial but also in terms of own choice. Yak, the girl's brother who also grew up in the camp, condemned his male relatives:

> These traditional Nuer men who arrived from Sudan recently, they do not know anything about the life here. They do not understand that the lives of girls are different here. They have rights, according to human rights, and that they should not be beaten. They were also educated and have different minds from the girls in the cattle camp in *cieng nuära*. Here, in Kakuma, girls and boys are equal and we do the same work. But these people who arrived recently still live in the past. What they have done to [my sister] is not right.

The LWF gender unit supervisor confirmed the challenge that 'reforming' the behaviour of recently arrived men presented:

> The biggest problem is with Sudanese men .... They are the keepers of the culture. [Through our pro-women programmes], we managed to educate some of them, but then they leave for Sudan and new ones arrive here. The ones who are coming now from Sudan are the real perpetrators; they are the guardians of the culture. They cause all the problems and violence in the camp.

These narratives reveal contestations around norms and values located in women's subordination, girls' proper behaviour and men as guardians of gender norms and order. They also point to the challenges Kakuma has brought to the order and stability enshrined in 'our culture' discourse. Kakuma girls' experiments with stretching their freedoms are especially challenging for male newcomers. These tensions manifest themselves not only in inter-generational conflict, but also in inter-gender conflict, as men of all ages feel challenged and threatened by the Kenyan culture being adopted by young women and men who have spent most of their lives outside Sudan. They feel especially challenged by girls' ability to express themselves and contest some existing hegemonic social structures. As a result, they often reinterpret the notions of tradition and *cieng nuära* to legitimise their dominance over women and girls. Previously, the social control of sexuality and place for girls was strictly exercised by any male relative or clansman.

Those young men recently arrived from southern Sudan took upon themselves the role of 'guardians of culture and tradition', one which they often reinterpreted. Prior to the wars in 1983, notions of gender ethnicity among the Nuer were much more flexible. For example, inter-ethnic marriages between Dinka and Nuer were not uncommon and women were not defined as markers of culture. However, as the narrative of the cousins of the girl whom I helped demonstrate, mixing with other ethnic groups is now condemned. This illustrates how gender norms of ethnic identity are being redefined, equating women to markers of culture, of whom men are the guardians.

Much feminist literature on nationalism focuses on the role of gender in the construction and reproduction of ethnic-national ideologies.[51] Findings from wars in southern Sudan and displacement in Kakuma confirm that during social and political upheaval women often become the 'iconic representations' of cultural and/or ethnic-national identity.[52] These narratives also reveal men's fears of 'losing Nuerness' as a result of mixing with 'other cultures' and any challenges to the male-defined gender order. Through recourse to 'our culture', these men attempt to rectify their perceived loss of position in the gender bargain. Their responses were partially a result of the conditions in the camp, the education of girls', women and girls' awareness of their rights and the expanding freedoms arising from gender programming. The strict inter-pretations used by some men of what it means to be a Nuer shows how identities gain importance in confrontation with others, or when a group feels threatened.

Resorting to violence to punish unacceptable female behaviour was commonplace in Kakuma. There was a significant increase in wife beating between 2000 and 2005. Rising numbers of women and chil-dren were accommodated in the JRS Safe Haven and in the UNHCR Protection Area. In 2003, JRS admitted twenty-five women for security reasons, reported twenty-eight new cases in 2004 and in 2005 accom-modated additional thirty women and their families. At the time of my stay in Kakuma, both protection areas were at full capacity, with JRS hosting thirteen women with children (forty people in all) and the UNHCR having fifteen houses filled with women and their children.[53] During the LWF gender unit's weekly meetings, I listened to reports of numerous cases of domestic violence. In my conversations with women and girls, I often heard complaints about domestic violence. Beatings were perpetrated by fathers, husbands and other male relatives, but women also beat their daughters and younger children. Women and men often attributed this high level of violence to the difficult socio-

---

[51] See, for example, Cynthia Enloe 'Feminism, Nationalism and Militarism: Wari-ness without Paralysis?', in C.R. Sutton (ed.), *Feminism, Nationalism and Milita-rism* (Washington DC, 1995), pp. 13–34; Sylvia Walby, 'Post-Post-Modernism? Theorizing Social Complexity', in M. Barrett and A. Phillips (eds), *Destabilizing Theory: Contemporary Feminist Debates* (Cambridge, 1992).

[52] Samita Sen, 'Motherhood and Mothercraft: Gender and Nationalism in Bengal', *Gender and History*, 1993, Vol. 5, pp. 231–43.

[53] LWF Kakuma, 'Gender Report 2005–2006'; JRS Kakuma, 'Gender Cases in the JRS Safe-Havens, Statistics 2003–2006', 2006; UNHCR Kenya, 'Country Opera-tions Plan for Kenya'; interviews with NGO and UN staff.

economic situation in Kakuma. Comments made by Sarah, an elderly woman, were typical:

> Men have nothing to do, they go idle, drink and then rape girls. Fathers fear they are not men as they cannot work. They drink and then beat their wives and children. Women are frustrated because they have not enough food at home, so they beat their daughters. There is a lot of crying in Kakuma.

This thwarting of masculinities revealed itself in men imposing their dominance over women (and children) through violence.

Family and home was thus a place of control and gender power. A young boy in Kakuma explained the male-dominated model of the Nuer family to me as follows:

> Even if the wife is better educated, you the man, you are still in control of the family. People cannot be the same in sharing power and control. Because when you marry a girl she comes to your house as your wife. You as a man you are in control over the family life. [...] You must be the person who controls the family decisions since you paid bride-price for the girl.

The idea of finite power that cannot be shared and has to be vested in the hands of men and elders was pervasive. Even some Nuer men educated in Kenya often took the position of being guardians of culture and gender traditions and imposed their dominance over girls, and women, through physical violence, gossip and public shaming. Despite their acquired proficiency in gender equality jargon, when it comes to rights for their sisters and female cousins they feel their own power and position is threatened. During a workshop on gender issues for prospective returnees, men debated the idea of an educated wife. They all agreed that men would never accept an educated wife, especially those who were still in Sudan. 'This is against their culture for a wife to control the family. Other men would laugh at you,' said 18-year-old Eliah. Fear of losing their position among their peers was closely related to the behaviour of others. They resorted to chastising women in order not to lose face. Hence, freedoms for girls, such as interactions with boys at school, in public places, in the church or while playing sports, were acceptable in the camp but condemned outside. Thus, emancipation and greater gender equality were linked to a particular space and strategic, not universal.

Although people of all ages recognised that there were changes in the *cieng nuära* due to displacement and encounters with gendered modernity in Kakuma, change was not an easy thing. During a gender awareness workshop, I asked participants to identify customs they would like to change. Women and men pointed to forced marriages, lack of freedom of movement for girls, wife inheritance and girls' inability to choose their husbands. In other conversations, women often complained about the physical violence that men exerted over them, and that bride-wealth limited their autonomy within the household. However, they also recognised the challenge of changing some of these customs. A young, educated man at the workshop summarised the paradox succinctly:

The fact that we all say that things can be changed in our culture might be because we would like to change them. However, in fact change is very difficult, because we were taught by our ancestors that traditions are written in stone and are there to protect our society and community and they are the things that make us. Hence, if we say that we would like to change them – we might be cheating ourselves.

For some, then, cultural chance was a threatening prospect, as it undermined their dominant position. War, displacement and experiences in Kakuma have created a structural challenge to the gender ideology and power in Nuer and South Sudanese societies. These changes pull and push in different directions, constantly being (re)negotiated and practiced. Displacement has led to opportunities (albeit contested ones) for girls and women (and younger generations) to reconfigure some gender asymmetries, but men (and some women), especially those who grew up in Sudan, strongly resist the idea of more freedom for girls and women.

Kakuma's significance for the (re)negotiation and practice of gender relations can be interpreted through the relativity theory Sahlins proposed to understand the Nuer. Sahlins argues that Nuer actions are relative and situational rather than universal imperatives depending on whom it concerns.[54] In Kakuma, relativity has extended to the place. Hence, practicing different gender relations in the camp was possible because it was not a Nuer space – it was a *jääl*'s space, not *cieng nuära*. In *cieng nuära*, the Nuer women and men have to adapt to village life. Using 'our culture' and tradition reveals conflicts and contestations around changing gender ideas and allocations of rights and duties. In this way, (reinterpreted) culture, as a contested and strategic concept, is used to express not only nostalgia for the past lost order manifested in *cieng nuära*, but also dismay about the moral corruption currently afflicting gender order. Nuerland was often idealised by the older generation and some younger men as a place of stability and morality, with a set of rules and specific gender relations. Returning to Sudan was equated with a return to stability and normality, where previous and thus 'proper' gender and generational relations would be re-established and 'there will be respect (*luth*) again'.

ASPIRATIONS AND CONTRADICTIONS

Notions of being and becoming modern, and aspirations to become modern, are a palpable and potent ideology throughout most, if not all, of Africa. Young people are particularly likely to appropriate notions of development, modernity and progress, reworking them and at the same time reassessing their future through them, trying to make sense of their current, dire condition. Refugee camps, as temporary spaces of extra-territorial protection, are also spaces where particular forms of modernity are forged. The structural, imposed, dislocated and gendered modernity in Kakuma was a result of the highly hierarchical refugee

[54] Marshall Sahlins, *Tribesmen* (New Jersey, 1968).

regime, its attachment to gender equality, as well as other encounters with modernity in the camp. Refugees are subject to dramatic changes in their livelihoods: a reliance on food aid, the lack of control over resources and modes of life and the results of education and training programmes. These changes continue to have direct impact on the negotiation and everyday practice of social and gender relations among refugees.

'It is only at the point of breakdown that every order reveals its systematic contradictions'.[55] For the Nuer women and men, the wars and the displacement that followed represented that point of breakdown. Displacement and experiences of particular gendered modernities in Kakuma led to political, economic and social relations that dramatically unsettled previously taken-for-granted gender arrangements. Although modern-minded young men mastered gender- and pro-women talk, and girls and women gained better access to education and autonomous income-generation, the UN's attempts to emancipate women did not necessarily lead to greater gender equality. Some of the material basis of men's dominance over women and seniority-based power relations were challenged. Girls' and women's transgressions of *cieng nuära* gender norms reveal female agency in contesting the prevailing hegemonic gender structures. Yet these contestations often met with a violent response by those – particularly older men and those recently arrived from (South) Sudan – who felt their authority, livelihoods and power were at stake.

To some extent, Kakuma represented an extra-territorial space where some gender and social relations could be transformed, questioned and re-negotiated. This is similar to other displacement situations. In the case of Tamil and Muslim women in post-conflict zones in north-east Sri Lanka, Darini Rajasingham-Senanayake describes the opportunities and the relative freedoms that present themselves to the internally displaced, especially the younger generation who distance themselves from caste and gender hierarchies, acquire responsibilities, engage with the authorities and discover new 'spaces of economic agency'.[56] In Kakuma, although different behaviour was tolerated, it was controlled through the violence of emasculated men. The new behaviour of young men, and especially girls and young women, was perceived as threatening the moral order. As a result, gender ideology became more articulated and redefined in terms of girls' subordination and gender power differences/asymmetries widened.

A refugee camp as a space is not only about suffering, poverty and the violation of human rights. Like Kakuma, it is a space of expanded possibilities of, in the words of the Nuer, 'coming up', 'becoming modern and civilised', 'being someone' and 'being a better person'. Through their encounter with a particular UN global humanitarianism 'modernity',

[55] See Deniz Kandiyoti, 'Bargaining with Patriarchy', *Gender and Society*, 1988, Vol. 2, pp. 285–6.
[56] Navnita Chadha Behera and Meenakshi Thapan (eds), *Gender, Conflict and Migration*, Vol. 3, Refugee Watch Online, 2008, p. 178.

the Nuer concept of themselves has undergone questioning and transformation. Through access to education and an awareness of gender equality and human rights, new gender identities of *nei ti cike ker* are being imagined and forged. Attempts by Kakuma youth at worldliness through education and talk, diasporic connections, dress codes and new body language sought to minimise their marginality as refugees. They also reflect claims for equal rights of membership in an unequal global society. Yet at the same time, the global humanitarian regime itself is based on highly hierarchical relations and its attachment to gender equality produces a particular encounter with modernity for localised refugees. Making 'the other' closer to 'western modern us' is promoted through the exposure to human rights and western standards of modernity. I argue that youth, both female and male, in the kind of societies that Clifford Geertz called 'out of the way places' often become 'modern' or 'awoken', if only in their aspirations, their fashions, fantasies, desires and their social 'imaginaries' of themselves.[57] Nuer youth – male and female – imagine themselves capable of worldliness, while some young men assert an abiding commitment to locality and their roots through the discourse of 'our culture'.

Although some change in gender ideology was possible in Kakuma, in *cieng nuära*, as the Nuer argued, 'we have to practice the culture of the grandfathers'. 'Home' was idealised through the discourse of 'our culture' and had profound consequences for repatriation aspirations and decisions. Return to Nuerland was, however, viewed differently by genders and generations, as they are differently positioned in the new system of gender relations.

---

[57] Clifford Geertz, *The Interpretation of Cultures: Selected Essays* (New York, 1973).

4

Rwil:
Season of 'Returns'

At Home

At home is where we belong
At home is where we make our own choices and decisions
At home is where we are chosen to be leaders
Leaders of our own people
At home is where we talk
Talk about our people's affairs
Yes east or west home is the best
(Dau, young refugee man, Kakuma)

'As any displaced and dispossessed person can testify, there is no such thing as a genuine, uncomplicated return to one's home' – Edward Said, *Out of Place: A Memoir* (New York, 1999)

NYAKUOL AND KUOK

Shortly after my arrival in Lɛr in early January 2007, I visited Nyakuol, the widow I had met in Kakuma. There, she had been a leader of the women's support group in the southern Sudanese Nuer community and spoke out openly against under-age pregnancies and girls' lack of access to education. After 15 years searching for refuge due to the civil war in southern Sudan, in December 2006 she and her four children repatriated to Lɛr with the assistance of the UNHCR. Her oldest daughter resettled with a cousin in the USA, while the oldest son chose to stay in Kakuma to complete his secondary education. Nyakuol commented: 'I wanted to come back to see my family and because my friends were leaving [Kakuma] and I was alone. I wanted to have a permanent place. Kakuma was not home, we were there only because of war'.

Nyakuol's elder sister, Nyapiny, who returned from Khartoum in 2005, gave her temporary shelter. She lived on a small plot next to the landing strip. Before the conflicts, her family had been influential and prosperous, with large herds of cattle and plots of land. When the war broke out their cattle were killed and the land was taken by the government. Nyakuol's parents died and her siblings were dispersed. Three sisters and a brother went to Khartoum, while the eldest brother moved to Juba. Nyapiny, like all her sisters, she was a widow, having lost her husband in 2002, while

4.1 Repatriation flight of Nuer refugees from Kakuma to Bentiu, December 2006
(© Katarzyna Grabska)

four of her six children died during the inter-Nuer conflict. In 2001, she sent her daughter and her son to Nyakuol in Kakuma.

In April, I met up with Kuok, who had recently come back to Lɛr on his own rather than through the UNHCR repatriation. 'This is just in case if I do not like the life here in Sudan, I can always go back to Kakuma. But once you have gone with the UN and give back your refugee card, you cannot go back to Kenya,' he explained. 'The overland journey was dangerous, especially on the border with Kenya and Uganda, where there was shooting. The SPLA escort accompanied our convoy that carried wives and children of high-ranking soldiers who were going to visit their husbands in Juba.'

When Kuok arrived in Juba, the southern Sudanese capital, he felt lost, knowing nobody. Through tracing his ethnic and *cieng* connections, he finally found a half-brother working in the same city. Back in Lɛr after a 20-year absence, Kuok was searching for his relatives. Although his parents were dead, as were his brother and a younger sister, his elder sister and her family were still in Lɛr. He also found some of his uncles and learned that many others had died during the war. This is what Kouk had to say about the difficulties of returning:

> '*Beben cieng*' is more of a process that takes time. Some of the returnees from Kakuma get frustrated after a short time and they decide to go back [to Kenya]. This is because they are not settled, they go from place to place, they do not

have a house; it is difficult to get a job. There is discrimination against the East African returnees by those who stayed here. When you go to Bentiu, everything is in Arabic and you cannot find a job if you do not speak the language. When you speak English, they do not know what you are saying.

For the people, security is the most important. They need to know that their area is secure and that they can feel safe at home. Also, they need to know that they can establish themselves, find their relatives, get a piece of land, build a house and be settled. [...] Here, the peace is still [not stable]. We are not sure whether it will really last. There are some people who talk about unity with the Arabs and this will create a lot of problems. People still do not trust.

What do 'home', 'homecoming' and 'settling-in' mean in the context of refugee return? How do notions of 'home' and 'emplacement' differ when gender, age, class and marital status are taken into account? The existing literature on forced displacement is somewhat silent on these questions. In this chapter, my concern is predominantly with the gendered and generational notions of and experiences of 'home' and settling-in.

MOVEMENT, PLACE AND GENDERED EMPLACEMENT

The context for analysing the gendered and gendering processes of home-coming and settling-in of Nuer refugees is what the forced migration literature calls 'the return and repatriation of displaced populations'. These terms are based on sedentarist assumptions about the relation between people, place and culture. Laura Hammond notes that these processes are meant to replant people back in their culture linked to the place of origin. In this section, I set out the analytical context of the relation of return and repatriation to a place, home and the processes of emplacement.

Hammond offers a poignant critique of the humanitarian discourse of repatriation:

> Terms to be found in the discourse of repatriation include: reintegration, rehabil-itation, reconstruction, rebuilding, readjustment, readap*tation, reacculturation, reassimilation, reinsertion, reintroduction, recovery*, and *re-establishment* (Gmelch 1980; Allen and Morsink 1994; Allen 1996). Among the most problematic terms of the repatriation canon are the words return and returnee, which imply that by re-entering one's native country a person is necessarily returning to something familiar. These terms are riddled with value judgments that reflect a segmentary, sedentary idea of how people ought to live, what their relation to the homeland should be, and ultimately how they go about constructing their lives once the period of exile ends. The implication of these terms is that returnees should seek to move back in time, to recapture a quality of life that they are assumed to have enjoyed before becoming refugees or that those who remained behind currently enjoy. ... [Moreover,] because post-repatriation life, or 'home' in the discourse of repatriation, is rooted in the country of origin it is considered by outsiders to be necessarily better that the life in exile.[1]

This cuts to the heart of the policy of repatriation organisations. The UNHCR identifies local integration, resettlement or repatriation as

[1]   Laura Hammond, 'Examining the Discourse of Repatriation: Towards a More Proactive Theory of Return Migration', in R. Black and K. Koser (eds) (Oxford, 1999), *The End of the Refugee Cycle? Refugee Repatriation and Reconstruction*, p. 230.

durable solutions for refugees, with the latter being the preferred solution. As other authors have noted, these discourses are rooted in the notion of 'territorialised national identity'.[2] By implication, displacement and war-time migration mean losing one's place and rooted identity, culture and social relations. Return, however, is necessarily equated with re-entering one's own culture, identity and community linked to a specific place. As Hammond points out, for policymakers and practitioners, putting people 'back into their place' (equated with birthplace) is the ultimate 'cure' for the 'refugee problem'. She adds that this is connected to the assumption that once in their own place, people will re-establish economic self-sufficiency, re-construct social networks, become full participants in community/society and remain citizens with access to rights.[3]

The notion that return is a natural and optimal solution has been questioned by many. Studies by Marita Eastmond, Joakim Ojendal, Richard Black and Khalid Koser, Lynellyn D. Long and Ellen Oxfeld and Laura Hammond,[4] for example, have shown that prolonged, devastating wars, ongoing conflicts, insecurity and lack of infrastructure might not only make it impossible but also impractical for some to return. As Black and Koser note, '[The] implicit assumption that at the end of the conflict, a return to a "place" called "home" is both possible and desirable ... can be questioned in both its aspects: return "home" may be impossible'.[5] Those who have developed strong ties and established their lives in countries of exile might not want to give up opportunities that these places offer. The social and economic investments made over the years in exile make some refuse return to their place of origin. Also, shifts in social and gender relations and new possibilities of greater gender equality in countries of resettlement might make some women (and men) reluctant to lose newly gained status and freedom. Economic opportunities and greater possibilities of actual enjoyment of rights in countries of exile might also discourage return.[6]

---

[2] Liisa Malkki, *Purity and Exile: Memory, and National Cosmology among Hutu Refugees in Tanzania* (Chicago, IL, 1995); Laura Hammond, *This Place will become Home: Refugee Repatriation to Ethiopian* (Ithaca, NY, 2004); Oliver Bakewell, 'Repatriation and Self-Settled Refugees in Zambia: Bringing Solutions to the Wrong Problems', *Journal of Refugee Studies*, 2000, Vol. 13.
[3] Hammond, 'Examining the Discourse of Repatriation', p. 23.
[4] Marita Eastmond, 'Transnational Returns and Reconstruction in Post-war Bosnia and Herzegovina', *International Migration*, 2006, 44, Issue 3, pp. 141–66, Marita Eastmond and Joakim Ojendal, 'Revisiting a "Repatriation Success": The Case of Cambodia', in Black and Koser (eds), *The End of the Refugee Cycle?; op. cit*; Lynellyn D. Long and Ellen Oxfeld (eds), *Coming Home? Refugees, Migrants, and those who Stayed Behind* (Philadelphia, NJ, 2004); Hammond, *This Place will become Home.*
[5] Black and Koser, *The End of the Refugee Cycle*, p. 7.
[6] See, for example, Gaim Kibreab, 'Access to Economic and Social Rights in First Countries of Asylum and Repatriation: A Case Study of Eritrean Refugees in Sudan', in K. Grabska and L. Mehta (eds) *Forced Displacement: Why Rights Matter?* (London, 2008); Lucia A. McSpadden, 'Contemplating Repatriation to Eritrea', in Long and Oxfeld (eds) *Coming Home*, pp. 34–49.

As Hammond, Liisa Malkki, David Turton and others have argued, for nomadic or agro-pastoralist populations such as the Nuer communities, displacement as well as return rarely reflect their life-worlds and life-paths.[7] Nuer social identities and livelihoods are both localised and mobile (*yodth* – migration), linked to cattle migration and coupled with labour and trade. The recent conflict-induced migration, although undertaken under extreme conditions of insecurity, and often marked by rupture of social and economic networks, was frequently referred to by women and men as 'movement'. 'They went/ran to Ethiopia, Khartoum, Kenya [*cako wa Kenya*]' was a phrase that women and men used to describe their war-time mobility. These various movements were accompanied by 'spatial practices' to produce and maintain a 'precarious sense of place' in contested and new environments.[8] In Kakuma, Nuer local courts and the creation of a local Nuer administration to address the issues of the Nuer community were ways to establish and maintain continuity to a place. So were the references to *cieng nuära* and the insistence on observing some of the gender norms and practices, including the marriage process, which was closely scrutinised, usually by male elders. The question that follows is how these women and men experience return to their *cieng* after forced displacement?

These issues are located at the centre of academic debates about 'place', 'home' and 'identity'. Preoccupied with the impact of globalisation's, anthropologists have been laying down the groundwork for a theory of place.[9] There has also been much debate on the concept of 'place' as a field-site,[10] and human geographers have drawn distinctions between the concepts of location and place. For example, Edward Casey provides a phenomenological definition of space and place.[11] He argues against the notion of space as a neutral, infinite and empty environment, and place as space inscribed with culture. According to him, place provides a way for space and time to come together. Hence, identity and being is directly linked to place.

I follow the definition of return and repatriation proposed by Hammond, which accommodates the continuum of movement and displacement. She defines return as varying both qualitatively and in terms of its duration; it should be understood as a process by which a returnee establishes the social, political, and economic ties that define him/her in a meaningful way – as a member of a community with primary ties to country or region

[7]   Hammond, *This Place will Become Home*; Malkki, 'Refugees and Exile: From 'Refugee Studies' to the Natural Order of Things', *Annual Review of Anthropology*, 1995, Vol. 24, pp. 495–523; David Turton, 'The Meaning of Place in a World of Movement: Lessons from Long-Term Field Research in Southern Ethiopia', *Journal of Refugee Studies*, 2005, Vol. 18, pp. 258–80.

[8]   Turton, 'The Meaning of Place in a World of Movement', p. 265.

[9]   See, for example, Eric Hirsch and Michael O'Hanlon, *The Anthropology of Landscape* (Oxford, 1995) and Arjun Appadurai, *Modernity at Large: Cultural Dimensions of Globalization* (Minneapolis, MN, 1996).

[10]   See, for example, James Clifford, *Routes: Travel and Translation in the Late Twentieth Century* (Cambridge, 1997) and Steven Feld and Keith H. Basso (eds), *Senses of Place* (Santa Fe, NM, 1996).

[11]   Edward S. Casey, *The Fate of Place: A Philosophical History* (Berkeley, CA, 1997).

(but not necessarily the village or city) of origin, rather than to the location of exile. Hammond describes the process of integration as involving the creation of a new code of citizenship, whereby power and legitimacy are redefined both by pressure from above (by political leaders) as well as negotiation from below (within the community).[12] She also links it to the place-making projects theorised by Turton, who argues that 'how people experience place, and how it becomes inextricably bound up with their social and personal identities ... is a product of social activity'.[13] Hence, place is produced through spatial practices and representations, with human beings as active agents in their construction. This notion is especially useful to understanding the activities and place-making projects that the displaced Nuer undertook after return to their *cieng* in Nuerland, and to how their description of these places as sites of security, stability and authenticity contrasts with their seemingly temporary relocation to Kakuma.

Place-making projects in the context of returnees' settling-in have been defined as 'emplacement'. Hammond, in her study of Ethiopian returnees' experiences in Ada-Bai along the north-western Ethiopian border, demonstrates how emplacement involves 'the interworking of place, identity and practice in such a way as to generate a relationship of belonging between person and place'.[14] Hammond and Malathi de Alwis show how returnees and refugees have been successful in transforming such abstract, and hence often threatening, spaces into familiar places or territories through material and representational practices that endow them with value and belonging.[15] Such analyses demonstrate the fluidity and dynamism of place and provide insights to unpack the economic, social and political practices that Nuer women and men employed in Lεr in order to transform the (often unfamiliar) place to 'something like home'.

I build my definition of emplacement around the concept of Arjan Appadurai's 'locality production'[16] and extend it to include the re-negotiation and creation of new sets of social norms, including gender relations. I argue that displacement might result not only in loss but may also create an opportunity to construct new social norms in the context of interactions and integration processes between returnees and those who had stayed behind. Hence, such an approach might provide an avenue for problematising return as part of a process for those moving as well as those who had stayed behind. This has been little explored in literature on forced migration.

[12] Hammond, *This Place will Become Home*, p. 188.
[13] Turton, 'The Meaning of Place in a World of Movement', p. 275.
[14] Hammond, *This Place will Become Home*, p. 83.
[15] Ibid. Cf. Yi-Fu Tuan, *Space and Place: The Perspective of an Experience* (Minneapolis, 1977) p. 215, quoted in Malathi de Alwis, 'The "Purity" of Displacement and the Reterritorialization of Longing: Muslim IDPs in North-Western Sri Lanka', in W. Giles and J. Hyndman (eds) (Berkeley, CA, 2004) *Sites of Violence: Gender and Conflict Zones*, pp. 213–32.
[16] Appadurai, *Modernity at Large*, p. 178–9, defines locality as a 'phenomenological quality', or 'dimension' of social life, as distinct from 'neighbourhood', which he defines as an 'actually existing' social form in which locality is 'realized'.

Nuer women and men described emplacement as *nyuuri piny*, which literally means sitting on the ground/earth. It is a metaphor for a process of settling-in and becoming part of a community. Emplacement in Lɛr was performed through a myriad of activities such as accessing land, building a house, farming, finding a job, cooking, reconnecting with and visiting friends and relatives and taking part in community events. In addition, emplacement was linked to the practice, negotiation and (re) production of gender relations, including starting a marriage process. It also entailed being and becoming (again) a Nuer and losing the status of *jaäl*, as often suggested by returnee women and men. This entailed (re) learning the dominant social norms, including gender and generations, and acquiring gender identities of *cieng nuära*, as determined mainly by those who had stayed behind.

Returnee women were often referred to as 'loose' and 'shameless', as they transgressed the social spaces between women and men. This congruent identity links the personal experiences of place and *cieng* to wider gendered social and communal obligations, rights and networks of mutual support. Emplacement of the Nuer involved both material and moral aspects of practice. It was often a dialectic between gendered practices and representations by returnees and those who had stayed behind that turned an unfamiliar or changed place into a familiar safe home. In this way, I link it to the concept of hybridity of place, home and oneself. Yet, I use the term 'hybridity' to denote the complex mixing of experiences and social norms that result from diasporisation and relate to new forms of identity. Thus, hybridity of place, home and oneself underline the fluidity of these concepts in order to dispel the certainties of fixed location. Even so, I echo Floya Anthias' view that 'issues of exclusion, political mobilization on the basis of collective identity, and narrations of belonging and otherness cannot be addressed adequately unless they are located within other constructions of difference and identity, particularly around gender and class'.[17] In Lɛr, places were both experienced and emplaced differently by old and young, women and men.

For the southern Sudanese dispersed throughout Sudan, Africa and around the world, transformations during the wars might have altered the meaning of home and the desire to return. It is thus imperative to examine refugees' conceptualisations and meanings of repatriation, as well as expectations and imaginings of home.

DIASPORIC RETURNS, PLACE AND 'HOME'

The experience of emplacement for the Nuer communities and individuals in my study was in the context of repatriation from Kakuma. It was part of a wider diasporic patchwork of homecomings of populations

[17] Floya Anthias, 'New Hybridities, Old Concepts: The Limits of "Culture"', *Ethnic and Racial Studies*, 2001, Vol. 24, pp. 619–41, p. 620.

displaced to a variety of places, to a place, a home, that went through transformations during the wars. I describe each of these aspects below.

Repatriation from Kakuma within the patchwork of returns

On an exploratory visit to the Malakal, the capital of Upper Nile state, in April 2006, I witnessed the arrival of a repatriation plane with refugees from Kakuma. Some sixty nicely dressed women, young men and children disembarked. Girls and women were neatly coiffured and young men wore rapper-style t-shirts, elegant trousers and earrings. They were welcomed by the UNHCR and its partner organisations and then taken to a way-station – temporary accommodation – where they were given food. Shortly after that, they were to be transported to their final destination. The reception of the returnees was not well coordinated. However, as the way-station was still under construction, people were accommodated in a large tent surrounded by mud. That night, it rained heavily and all their belongings and food were soaked through. The UNHCR was unable to transport people to their final destination; returnees had to make their own arrangements instead. Ruan, a young returnee, whom I met later again in Rubkona, shared his experience with me:

> It was really tough, we have not been to Sudan in a long time, and they took us to a place that was not our place. I used to be a youth leader in Kakuma, so I organised people and told them to sell their food rations. For the money we received, we rented a truck that took us to the river from where we embarked on a boat. After a five-day-long river journey, we arrived in Rubkona. We were all exhausted and many of us still needed to travel more to reach our villages.

When I first arrived in Kakuma, the official repatriation to Sudan organised by the UNHCR and supported by the Tri-Partite Agreement (2006) between the governments of Kenya and Sudan and the UNHCR was underway. Trucks decorated with UNHCR and New Sudan flags, loaded with luggage and filled with South Sudanese, mainly young men, left for the border with Sudan each week. The Nuer (and Dinka) populations were largely transported by air, as their homes were far from the border, with small 50–seaters carrying returnees to their old/new homeland. I followed several repatriation convoys and witnessed the preparation for flights in Kakuma and their reception in southern Sudan. As I mentioned earlier, Nyakuol, as well as another two hundred and fifty Nuer who arrived in Western Upper Nile between November and December 2006, were repatriated through the UNHCR. Others, like Kuok and large numbers of the 'lost boys', decided to go by themselves or with the support of Sudanese churches, the SPLA or local organisations.

The UNHCR's repatriation programme was part of a regional operation. According to UNHCR statistics, by January 2010, around 331,000 refugees from the region had been repatriated to Sudan, including 174,000 assisted by the UNHCR. During my stay in Kakuma, repatriation was slow – in 2006 only 1,800 individuals repatriated. It picked up during 2007 and 2008, with some 15,000 returning to Sudan through the UNHCR. By the beginning of 2010, of the 5,000 Sudanese registered in

Kakuma in 2005, only 8,000 remained. Some 47,000 either returned to Sudan by themselves, or moved, like many of the research participants, to other towns in Kenya or Uganda. At that time, it was estimated that roughly 25,000 South Sudanese refugees still remain in Kenya, mostly living in urban centres. The returns from Sudan's neighbouring countries are coupled with returns from the north of Sudan. As the UNHCR emphasises, this 'remains a sensitive issue, and means of regularizing the presence of South Sudanese who remain in the north have yet to be found'.[18]

Since independence in 2011, new violence has affected various parts of the south. By the end of August 2011, the humanitarian community estimated that more than 3,070 people had been killed in inter-communal and militia-related violence and 304,400 had been displaced both internally and across the borders.[19] In the inter-ethnic violence between the Lou Nuer and the Murle groups in Jonglei area, it is estimated that around 1,000 people were killed and 60,000 were displaced between December 2011 and January 2012. In addition, conflicts in the north in Blue Nile and South Kordofan areas continue to result in an influx of north Sudanese refugees into South Sudan. In December 2013, tensions within the GoSS led to a major rebellion and civil war in South Sudan, with ethnic undertones. The areas of Bentiu and Rubkona were burnt and the entire population displaced. The ongoing fighting displaced over a million people within South Sudan and across borders. These new internal and cross-border displacements have added to the complexities of the settling-in of the returning populations.

Those who decided to remain in Kenya delayed their move to southern Sudan due to perceived insecurity, livelihoods options and infrastructure in that region. For example, Nyakuoth's mother and her four children moved to Nairobi, where she enrolled them in schools. 'I am not ready to go to Sudan yet. First, I want to make sure that my children finish school. I am worried that there is no chance for them in Sudan due to lack of schools,' she explained. Some people initially registered for return, but then changed their minds before departure, a practice that frustrated humanitarian personnel.

While refugees worried about the prospect of establishing viable livelihoods in southern Sudan, much of the UN and other humanitarian agencies' repatriation discourse was focused on numbers. According to the UNHCR, while repatriation also involves the successful 'reintegration' of returnees, in official reports success was mainly measured in terms of the number who crossed the border. In its 2012 evaluation report, the UNHCR notes:

> The UNHCR has achieved a major success in southern Sudan in supporting the voluntary repatriation of more than 135,334 refugees between late 2005 and May 2008. This represents a significant achievement, involving Tripartite agreements with five neighboring countries, at one time, the simultaneous operation of four repatriations corridors. Despite security problems resulting from the activities of the Lord Resistance Army (LRA) and other armed groups, the widespread

[18] UNHCR, 'UNHCR Global Appeal 2012–2013 South Sudan', Geneva, 2012.
[19] Ibid.

presence of mines and UXOs, and significant logistical challenges, the organised return process has taken place in conditions of safety and dignity. The operation, moreover, has resulted in the closure of refugee camps in the Central African Republic (CAR), Democratic Republic of Congo (DRC) and Ethiopia.[20]

The information, mobilisation and registration campaign was already underway when I was in Kakuma. Information was disseminated through leaflets, meetings and films. Camp residents were informed about the situation in southern Sudan and the UNHCR propagated the idea of home. Humanitarian workers and refugee volunteers wore T-shirts with pro-return slogans such as 'Let's go home', 'Sudan: There is nowhere better than home'. The latter was suggestive of Dorothy's 'there is no place like home' in the *Wizard of Oz*. One could read this metaphor as Kakuma being Oz, a more comfortable yet less beloved place, and the refugees as Dorothy in search of a 'beloved home' and the UNHCR as Oz as being able to fulfil Dorothy's dreams.

This image of 'real home' was reinforced by UNHCR- and NGO-sponsored visits by senior southern Sudanese politicians who shared their views on the situation in southern Sudan and urged their return. A commissioner from Eastern Equatoria addressed a crowd of mainly young male refugees:

> Your country is very important and you should come back to rebuild it. You have to decide, but if you come home you will be somebody. Don't ask to go to Australia, America, you will be nobody there, you will be a slave. We need teachers, doctors. All ministers and governors will come from you.

Other officials compared returning to southern Sudan with gaining control over their lives:

> We have been refugees for too long. We have to relieve ourselves from this agony. This thing has been engrained in our blood for too long. Let us rebuild our country ourselves.

One commissioner compared southern Sudan to a cow:

> Who will take care of the cow [if you are not there]? There is no one there to take care of the cow and the cow will be eaten by a hyena. It is time to go and take care of the [abandoned] cow.

'Return to Sudan' was interpreted as a process of becoming an adult and acquiring wider community responsibilities.

Those interested in repatriation were not only mobilised, registered and informed. They were also medically screened, sensitised and trained in mine-awareness, gender and human rights, hygiene, sanitation and civic rights. Although repatriation was supposed to be voluntary,[21] it was

[20] UNHCR, 'Evaluation of UNHCR's Returnee Reintegration Programme in Southern Sudan', Geneva, 2008, p. 6.
[21] UNHCR-sponsored repatriation is based on principles of 'voluntary' return in safety and dignity. In Kakuma, voluntariness was ensured through individual registration of those interested in returning and who signed a Voluntary Repatriation Form (VolRep). The two principles were supposed to be fulfilled by providing

also encouraged through the gradual limiting of services provided to refugees in the camp. The UNHCR and NGOs were closing schools and health clinics and reducing food rations. A young man reflected a common view: 'We are going to Sudan not because we really want to, it is because of the budget cuts in the camp. You cannot survive here any longer. The life has become too hard'. This was also one of the reasons why Nyakuol and Kuok decided to repatriate to Nuerland. Those who had family members working in Sudan or in resettlement countries and sent them regular remittances moved, like Nyakuoth's mother, to Nairobi or elsewhere.

When I arrived in Bentiu in December 2006, displaced populations were on the move, heading to towns and villages, looking for relatives, friends, land, livelihood opportunities and possibilities to create a 'home'. Buses transporting repatriates from the north, mainly Khartoum, arrived in Rubkona and Lɛr on a daily basis. They brought with them beds, mattresses, fashionable clothing, household items and the legacy of years of absence and experiences of a different life. Convoys organised by the International Organization for Migration (IOM) and the GoSS brought displaced Nuer from IDP camps in Khartoum, while UNHCR planes transported refugees from Ethiopia, Uganda and Kenya. Those who had made their own arrangements arrived arriving by road, river and air.

The rapidly changing landscape of Lɛr was also a sign of returning populations and the process of physical emplacement. With the changing image of the village, new *duëel* and *luääk* appeared every day: the market bustled, the bus station was crowded and prayers were offered for the newly arrived during Sunday services. In June 2007, the local branch of the South Sudan Relief and Rehabilitation Commission (SSRRC)[22] estimated that 4,700 returnees were residing in Lɛr, this number being two-thirds of the total population. Most had come from Khartoum and other areas in Sudan and around 15% from Ethiopia, Uganda and Kenya.

Through the patchwork of returns from different directions, with diverse cultural baggage and with different experiences, the fragmented lives of Nuer households were being pieced together. A mother of a friend from Kakuma who had remained in Lɛr during the wars while her sons dispersed in different directions shared worries felt by many:

> I do not recognise my sons, they have changed. One went to Khartoum, and another to Kenya. Now, they do not talk and participate in family discussions. They are just quiet when we talk. Kim [who was in Kenya] goes out of the house and wants to spend time by himself, just staring into empty space. This is not what we [the Nuer] do. [My sons] have different habits and I do not know how to relate to them. They feel like strangers to me.

(cont.) detailed information to the communities about the conditions in southern Sudan, including security, infrastructure, economic and social stability. Return in dignity was implemented by providing returnees with basic assistance, including plastic sheeting, iron sheets, jerry cans, agricultural tools and seeds and equivalent to three months' grain rations.

[22] During the war, the relief wing of the SPLM/A was the SRRA (Sudan Relief and Rehabilitation Association), which later changed its name to SSRRC. Now officially a branch of GoSS, the SSRRC co-ordinates relief, rehabilitation and assistance to southern Sudanese and monitors returnees.

Nyapiny lost her husband during an attack on Lɛr in 2002, after which she was taken by the Bul Nuer rebels to the north where was forced to become a 'wife' of one of the commanders. She finally managed to escape and came back to Lɛr in 2005. That same year, Nyakuol's brother, Bol, returned from Khartoum after fifteen years of displacement and settled in a nearby village. NyaSunday, his 17-year old daughter had also been with Nyakuol in Kakuma. Bol had not seen his daughter in twelve years. The two of them had to learn anew how to be a family. A few months after Nyakuol arrived, her half-sister arrived with her family, after twenty-five years of displacement in Khartoum.

For many returnees, family (re)unification was often uncomfortable. Isaac, who had spent twenty years as a 'lost boy' in Ethiopia and Uganda, told me: 'I prefer to spend time with my friends from Uganda, instead of my brothers. We have more in common, the life in Ethiopia [military camps] and in Uganda [as refugees]. My brothers stayed here and I do not know them and their lives'. As with other returnees, for example, in Vietnam,[23] my Nuer friends from Kakuma and others who were displaced to Uganda often talked about 'feeling strange' with their families, who they barely knew after years of separation.

The complexities of returning to southern Sudan were later recognised by repatriation organisations. The UNHCR Sudan repatriation evaluation report took a critical stand on the concept of reintegration in southern Sudan, noting that, '[it] does not fully capture the situation in question'. The report stresses that throughout Sudan's independence, the region has been a site of a regionalised civil conflict, and that:

> ties of kinship and reciprocity interconnect those that stayed and those that left. In this context, reintegration is not 'reconstruction' in the sense of putting back together a condition that existed in the past; everything has changed. It is useful to see return and reintegration in South Sudan as part of a new and emerging situation.[24]

Indeed, emplacement was creating 'a new and emerging situation'. It was a creative, ongoing process of constructing new space, reconciling cultural differences and creating new homes, and often requiring adaptation, mutual understanding, the (re)negotiation of norms and gender relations and a (re)production of social norms and relations. It was first experienced at personal and second at household/family level. Emplacement also occurred in the context of a place, home, a site of return which had changed due to war(s). Almost all described *cieng nuära* as being in flux.

Nuerland: Returnees' encounters

In Kakuma, Yak, a young married man from Bentiu, told me: 'when I think about Sudan, and my village, I remember rivers, forest, fields, fresh fish and cattle. It was very green, not like Kakuma that is like a desert. The life was good there, but this was before the wars. Now, I do not even

[23] Lynellyn D. Long and Ellen Oxfeld (eds), *Coming Home?*
[24] UNHCR, 'Evaluation of UNHCR's Returnee Reintegration Programme', p. 11.

know if I find my parents'. Those recently arrived in the camp, or those displaced as adults, often reminisced about their 'lost home', bringing memories of land, landscapes, animals, activities, community and their past. However, these narratives were often filled with uncertainty about what was awaiting them 'back home'. Before leaving Kakuma, Nyakuol expressed her fears:

> We, the widows, we recall what happened there and we think about it. ... we think about Sudan and we have in our minds all the problems of going back for the widows. We are caught up between two worlds [Kakuma and Sudan], and none of them is good for us. Even now, people are talking about peace in Sudan, but we do not believe this.

Some women and men talked about the pain of witnessing brutal killings of relatives, and the flight and insecurity that changed idealised memories of home. Others, especially young people born and brought up in camps, had few recollections, often basing their images of home on an amalgam of stories heard from elders and new meanings of home being propagated by international organisations. 'Home' was emerging as a territorial locus of citizenship rights, freedom and stability.

When I asked about their first impressions of southern Sudan, returnees from Kakuma all expressed their surprise, often disappointment and, sometimes, sadness. Yak, who left his wife in Kakuma and went to Nuerland to complete their marriage, commented:

> When the plane landed in Rubkona, I was very surprised to see the place.[25] It was so dusty, desert-like, not what I remembered from before. There were also mosques everywhere, and *'gallabas'* [Arabs] trading in the market. This did not feel like home.

Others, like Wanten, realised on arrival in Nuerland that home no longer existed. Wanten felt 'lost' all over again:

> I could not go to my village, to my home. All my relatives were killed during the war and there was no more *cieng*. The village does not exist any longer. I decided to settle in town instead.

After his twenty-year absence, Kuok could not remember much:

> I do not know this place. I have to first find some relatives, who will point me to my people. I do not recognise it; it has changed. It is also different from Juba, where I arrived first.

Western Upper Nile or Unity state was still relatively remote and rural. It lacked the bustling circus of UN peacekeepers, the four-wheel drives of humanitarian and development agencies, donor governments, Kenyan, Ugandan and Chinese businessmen and the increasing number of cars driven by southern Sudanese military, government officials and emerging local businessmen seen in the streets of Juba. Yet, its land-

---

[25] Rubkona is twinned with Bentiu and is the capital of Unity state and the administrative headquarters of the oil industry.

scape, livelihoods and infrastructure also underwent significant changes during the wars. Due to its geographical proximity to the north and the presence of large oil reserves, the area was dominated by people from the north. Many northern traders established their businesses in Rubkona and Bentiu and spread further south to villages in the Dok areas. Even the market in Lɛr had over a dozen stalls run by northerners trading in spices, grain and household items and selling fried beans, fried fish and coffee.

Due to its proximity to the north, easy road access and presence of northern troops, Rubkona was dominated by Arab traders to a far greater extent than Bentiu or Lɛr. Walking through the market, one could see Arab men dressed in white *jallabiyas* (long white robes) and Arab women in *tobs* (full-body scarf-wraps). There were also numerous mosques, whereas churches dominated Bentiu's landscape. For the many Nuer returnees with traumatic memories of war-time Arabisation and Islamisation, Rubkona was a shock. Although daily relations between the northerners and the Nuer communities were marked by mutual dependency, underlying tensions were constantly apparent. I witnessed racist accidents, fights and exchanges of insults and heard of women having been raped by northern Sudanese soldiers.

Physical space had changed dramatically as a result of war and arrival of modernity. Major towns in the north of the region were dominated by northerners and Arab culture. The topography of Bentiu was being transformed by the emergence of government administrative structures, including the offices of the governor, state parliament and high court. Although GoSS administrative structures were being slowly set up in Unity state, the ongoing military presence was overwhelming. The Sudanese Armed Forces (SAF) – the northern forces – had barracks in Rubkona near the UN compound in which I initially stayed after my arrival in Nuerland. Bentiu also hosted a large contingent of SPLA forces. Throughout Unity state, there were SAF and SPLA stations in different market villages along the road connecting Rubkona/Bentiu and Adok, a port on the Nile. The militarisation of life in the state capital and throughout the region was visible by the presence of soldiers and guns. I witnessed the glorification of the military during a celebration of the first anniversary of the north–south peace agreement. The stadium in Bentiu was filled with military officials and local dignitaries who, for hours, watched a parade of Russian and Chinese made tanks, artillery, SAF and SPLA battalions and police units. They were followed by local chiefs, youth and women's groups and children dressed in military uniforms all praising the war efforts.

Unlike Juba, the international humanitarian presence contributing to development was limited in Western Upper Nile. The UN had a small compound based in Rubkona for representatives of UNDP, the Office for the Co-ordination of Humanitarian Affairs (OCHA), the WFP, IOM and UNICEF. Their work was limited to food distribution, receiving refugees and internally displaced returnees and information-gathering. There were also a few NGOs, including Action Against Hunger, which ran livelihoods support programmes and feeding centres, Médecins ans Frontières

(MSF), which was in charge of clinics and a malnutrition feeding centre in Bentiu, and Care International, whose role was to support medical and agricultural self-sufficiency programmes. The military character of the capital was intensified by the presence of United Nations Mission in Sudan (UNMIS) with a contingent of Indian peacekeepers.

Apart from the presence of these international organisations, local Nuer communities and individuals were globally connected through the presence of international oil companies, including those owned by China and Malaysia. The main road from Rubkona towards the north was peppered with vast oil fields around Heglig, while the road heading south towards Lɛr and Adok was dominated by large, fenced-off oil fields around Tharjath. The companies had their own airstrips and were connected to global space through satellite, internet, TV, mobile phones, electricity and Chinese and western food. By contrast, the nearby Nuer communities had no access to running water, electricity or health services. Some young Nuer men were employed by oil companies as security guards or in other menial capacities, although their interactions and relations were marked by subjugation and exploitation, being paid cents while the oil companies were making billions.

During the war, oil companies, including the Canadian company Talisman, contributed to displacement from Western Upper Nile. In the post-war environment, oil businesses were supposed to contribute to development. This mainly manifested itself in newly constructed roads, local government offices, schools and hospitals in Rubkona/Bentiu, Lɛr and other county capitals. Their presence however, had disastrous consequences for the daily life of the Nuer. While I was there, there were several floods in different parts of Western Upper Nile that destroyed Nuer hamlets, food storage and cattle. I accompanied NGO staff on a mission to the northern part of Unity State to assess the situation in thirty-four villages where inhabitants had lost livestock and food supplies and were succumbing to cholera and malaria. Many roads connecting the oil fields to distribution centres in the north were built without taking into account local ecological conditions. A chief from Padeh, a small village in Dok area, explained that most of the roads were cut through dykes and seasonal rivers, blocking the natural run-off during the rainy season and causing flooding. I heard complaints from villagers about the uncompensated clearing of Nuer lands by the oil companies and the fatal poisoning of children and cattle by chemical waste. Similar observations were reported by international and local NGOs.[26]

Lɛr, the Adok county capital, located roughly one hundred kilometres south of Bentiu, was far less urbanised and Arabised than Bentiu and Rubkona. A dirt road built by one of the Chinese oil companies links Bentiu with Lɛr and passes through the lush lands of the Jagey and Dok people,

---

[26] *Sudan Tribune*, 'South Sudan Villagers, Environment suffer from Oil Boom', 5 March 2008; European Coalition on Oil in Sudan (ECOS), 'Briefing Note: Instruments to address South Sudan's Petroleum Legacy Issues', Utrecht, 2011; Bonn International Center for Conversion (BICC), 'Oil Investment and Conflict in Upper Nile State, South Sudan', Brief 48, 2013.

a land with scattered huts, cattle camps, occasional market villages and military outposts. Completely destroyed and burnt during the attacks of the Bul Nuer militia in 1998, and again in 2001, by 2006, Lɛr had only a couple of concrete structures left, including the MSF-Holland hospital, a Presbyterian church and a primary school. Upon her arrival, Nyakuol was confused:

> When we finally arrived in Lɛr, I did not recognise the place, my home. I remembered that my sister lived around the airstrip, but there used to be many huts, many people. Because of war and fighting, there are few people left, and all trees are gone. It took me a long time to find my sister's place.

Homesteads made out of mud and grass-thatched *duël*,[27] and occasionally *luääk*, were spread along both sides of the road and ended at the river. The name Lɛr comes from a *neem* tree introduced by missionaries in the mid-twentieth century. Prior to the wars, it had been densely vegetated, with trees offering welcome shelter from the midday sun. During the wars most neem and mango trees had been cut down by soldiers.

Lɛr's centre was located around the main square, which was used as a football and parade ground. The commissioner's compound was located to the right of the road and the bus station. The old market contained a few stalls (shacks selling coffee and beans) and the dilapidated building of the administrative headquarters. During my stay, a Chinese oil company financed the construction of a new brick-built headquarters.

Lɛr's southern limits were marked by the primary school (which was being renovated by a Sudanese NGO through oil money), the auction place for cattle and the main market. The market was located in an area that was regularly flooded during the rainy season. From June through to September, residents had to walk through deep mud to buy their supplies. Lɛr's market was not as busy as those in Rubkona and Bentiu, as it had fewer northern traders selling a smaller range of goods for higher prices. During my ten months in Lɛr, the market began to grow, with new stalls opening up to sell beans, water pipes (*shisha*) and coffee.

Those who had stayed behind during the wars commented how the place – how home – had changed. Ruai, a young married man, described some of the differences:

> When I look at the situation now, there is a great change in the Unity state. There are roads, and there is food. People are not suffering from hunger. But Unity state was the state most destroyed during the war. We have oil so we are targeted by the government [the Khartoum government]. You see the oil fields, they were not here before. Oil companies took over our land.

The school, the hospital, the Presbyterian and Catholic churches, the government and SPLA administrative offices and the Chinese oil trucks were the few signs of development and modernity in Lɛr. The road that was constructed during my stay – linking Rubkona/Bentiu, via Lɛr, with

[27] Only a few houses – those of dignitaries, military commanders and prosperous traders – had zinc roofs.

Adok, a port on the White Nile – opened up another connection to modernity. It allowed traders from Uganda and Kenya to transport their goods on barges from Juba to Adok and further northwards by mini-buses and trucks. One of the main concerns in Lɛr was the price of beer. Prior to the construction of the road, it was transported from the north at great cost. Now it came flooding in from Uganda and Kenya, reaping vast profits for local Nuer businessmen. From my house near the main square, I often saw young boys using bicycles to transport cases of Heineken to the county headquarters and the military barracks. Roads and beer were signs of development that many of the local politicians praised.

There were also other connections between the global and the local in Lɛr. A hub of humanitarian operations during the wars, Lɛr remained a base for a few international organisations – including the IRC, MSF-Holland, Save The Children and Across. UNICEF, Care International and the WFP ran occasional assistance programmes in Lɛr out of Rubkona.[28] The town's landing strip was used by the WFP, MSF and government planes to transfer food, supplies and international personnel. Their planes often had to make several passes to scare away children and cattle before they were able to land.

An older English-speaking returnee Nuer man who had been away from Lɛr for thirty years and come back for a short visit expressed, like other returnees, surprise at how things had changed:

> War has changed the Nuer traditional values and customs in a negative way. Respect for the elderly has been eroded, and rude and aggressive behaviours are entering the Nuer culture. In our country in the past, not even orphans and handicapped would beg for money on the street. Asking for money was only in the family – if you were a very close relative, others would ask you if you had enough. But asking for money on the street was considered as shameful. Now all are asking for money continuously, they especially asked the white people. It is the UN and the war which have ruined our culture in this way.

These views were also shared by those who had stayed behind. However, elder women and men often blamed militarised young men for the change in Nuer social norms. PanMadeng, an elder in the Presbyterian Church who had remained in Lɛr commented:

> [Due to their experiences in the bush], they [young men] became arrogant. They have guns and think that they do not have to respect others. This war has created many changes here. [Because of it], there is no more respect [pöc] between children and parents, the young and the old, women and men.

War and the presence of international aid organisations have weakened the social networks of support in which families and *cieng* members had effective mechanisms to cope with economic and environmental shocks by sharing resources and assisting each other. Before the wars, the Nuer relied heavily on cultivation, fishing and cattle-herding. In the 1970s and 1980s, These agro-pastoralist livelihoods were coupled with emerging trade and labour migration to the

---

[28] There were also some small, local, community-based organisations and NGOs.

north. Although alternative food sources were becoming available in the emerging markets across Western Upper Nile, the penetration of the state and trade were rather limited. Cultivation, fishing and hunting made communities generally self-sufficient. Famines caused by wars and droughts and subsequent international aid created considerable reliance on free food distribution, which in turn contributed to changes in livelihood and social support networks. The continuous supply of WFP food aid in the post-war period, for example, further deepened reliance on food and undermined self-sufficiency. Although some people returned to growing their own food, there were also those who preferred to collect or buy it.

The landscapes, infrastructure and livelihoods of those who did not move had undergone changes due to wars, oil exploration, the opening up of Western Upper Nile to the rest of the region and the increased commercial and trading networks. While returnees had changed, so too had stayees and their 'homes'.

WE CANNOT BE THE SAME NUER AS OUR PARENTS:
THE IRREVERSIBILITY OF DISPLACEMENT, HOME AND BEING
IN FLUX

Dau, an educated Dinka man in his early forties from the Nuer-inhabited areas of Western Upper Nile, fled to Khartoum in 1983 and through contacts with Catholic missionaries gained a university education. After his return twenty years later to his place of birth, he was perplexed:

> Our families are not used to this [village] life and this culture any more. We, the ones who are in our forties now, are the generation which is in-between our culture and the modern life. [Due to war] we have gone to towns and are living the life of towns, whereas our fathers are still living the traditional Dinka culture back in their villages.
>
> ... I am in fact very confused whether what we are doing is right. I am not sure whether the culture of town and of modern life that we have adopted and have taught our children is the right culture. Yes, we are going through so-called development, but this means we are going away from what our grandfathers used to do and how they used to live their lives. When I go to visit my parents, for me it is difficult to accept some of their traditional cultures, for example, slaughtering of animals and believing in different gods.
>
> ... Also, there are certain things that I do that they cannot understand and they see me more as a foreigner. I come from there and I belong to that land, but my life has been very different and I live my life differently. They do not know how I live my life and they see that I am different now. I am Dinka from Pariang, but I am also a foreigner in my fathers' land. For my children it is even more difficult, because they are so far away culturally from that life. They do not know anything about the Dinka traditions and they will not be able to relate to that life. I feel that our Dinka culture is being lost.
>
> We are going through very abrupt changes now. The war, displacement, oil, the coming of Christianity and the fact that people have gone to different places and now are coming back with different cultures means that our traditional Dinka cultures are going through a change. Many of the cultures have already changed, and the change now is much more abrupt. It is accelerated. I feel that the real culture will die with our fathers. Because once they are not here, we who

have gone through a transition already will not be able to maintain the Dinka [or Nuer] culture.

Yes, we still marry with cows and the cows are still important for us. But the meaning of money is also changing now. Also, the way we want to live our lives is different now. We want things, we have broader views on life, we have access to information, we have seen many places. We cannot be the same Dinka as our parents.

Dau's narrative mentions some of the returnees' dilemmas of being in flux between the old and the new, the culture of grandfathers and modernity, also felt by many Nuer. He points to the intergenerational difference in experience of war, displacement and return. Another important realisation is that not only those who moved changed due to their exposure to other cultures, education, modern life in a town and through conversions to Christianity. The coming of development and modernity at home, as Dau points out, threatens the culture of the grandfathers, i.e. social and cultural customs that have distinguished Dinka, or Nuer, from other groups. Thus, the rift between those who had moved and those who had stayed behind, the younger and the older, becomes more profound.

The coming together of Nyakuol and her dispersed family members reflects other household dilemmas that resulted from being separated by war. Nyakuol's niece, NyaSunday, who was with her in Kakuma and finished seven grades of primary school, found it difficult to communicate with her father, Bol, after return. NyaSunday was often frustrated:

These people do not understand that we, the ones who were in Kakuma, are different. My father insists that I get married because he is in need of cattle. But I want to continue with my education, I am not a cattle-camp Nuer girl [nyal nuära]. I have changed, I am modern town girl and I want to finish my school before I get married. Our lives were too different during these years. We do not understand each other.

Kuok often complained about his family members who had stayed behind in Lɛr during war:

I do not understand these people here and they do not understand me. When I wash my clothes or want to cook for myself, they tell me that I am doing woman's work. I saw one of my cousins beating his wife. When I advised him not to do it, he now is upset with me and does not want to talk to me. When I come to his house, he says, 'just talk to my wife'. In Kakuma, we have learned the goodness of education and that women and men are equal. But here, the people are still. They treat women as their property.

Also, if you did not take part in the struggle, you are seen as a coward. People say that you are arrogant [because of] education and they do not consider you. Only those who were in the military get jobs now. The power of the gun is more than the power of the pen. You can be kuäar (a leader) if you have military rank. People [who had stayed behind] have changed.

These experiences and narratives show that displacement as a process is irreversible and that home is not static. Its impact on social relations, gender relations in particular, was discussed by women and men seeking to reconcile old modes of livelihoods with new ways learned far away from 'home'. For those who were displaced as children and grew up in refugee camps in Ethiopia, Kenya and elsewhere, relocating to southern Sudan was part of their ongoing migratory trajectory. They experienced and adapted to life in different practices often marked by changes in gender identities and ideologies (see Chapter 3). The move to southern Sudan was one filled with anxiety. Although they were supposedly going home, southern Sudan was a place that they barely remembered, let alone being familiar with its lifestyles. For them, it required learning the place anew, an issue to which I return in the next two chapters.

Thus, the idea of refugee return has to be qualified and considered in relation to those who had stayed behind. In the context of displacement, often multiple displacements to multiple and diverse destinations, individuals' experiences are different, and there are barriers to sharing them. For example, there are substantial differences in the cultural, societal and educational upbringing and war-time experiences of those who had stayed behind or fled to Khartoum to those who had migrated to East Africa. One of them was language. I witnessed this at a meeting with the director of social development of the local government in Bentiu. In a room crowded with his staff, visitors and women serving tea, our conversation was simultaneously translated into four languages. The director, a Dinka educated in Arabic, spoke neither English nor Nuer. His assistant, a returnee from Uganda, spoke English, Nuer and some Dinka. My translator, a returnee from Kakuma, spoke Nuer and English. The discussion went on for a long time, as it needed to multiple translations in order for all to understand each other.

Dress was another visible point of difference between those who had stayed behind and those who had gone to East Africa. The former were more conservatively attired, often influenced by Arab fashions, while men who had been away often wore rapper-type clothes and the girls short skirts or tight trousers and blouses. Returnees from East Africa were perceived as being less respectful towards elders but at the same time having more awareness of the rights and position of women and girls. Young returnee men from Kakuma complained about feeling discriminated against, looked down on by the government and stayees. Kuok and his friends talked about the challenges of findings jobs in government offices and institutions (including schools), as they felt that those who were educated in Arabic in Khartoum or had stayed behind and took part in the military struggle were favoured by the Khartoum-educated and military-dominated administration in Bentiu.

Kuok told me that 'when you come back home you have to adapt, because otherwise you will be seen as a stranger, as a foreigner'. Feeling different and often estranged from family members who had stayed behind or had gone to Khartoum, Kakuma returnees often complained about their loneliness. They felt like aliens in the land of their grandfathers and grandmothers. An educated, middle-aged Nuer man working for an international NGO in Lɛr explained this succinctly:

> There is a problem with the integration of these people [returnees]. They come back but nobody knows them. They are not given jobs with the government because they are not known and their behaviours is not known. The community has to assess them first, they have to know what is in their minds and what they will be teaching the people here. Also, their behaviour is completely different from those who stayed here. [...] They have changed and their culture is different from the Nuer culture. When you come back here you should do like the other people are doing: if they are cultivating the land you should cultivate the land, if they are building the house, you should build the house. Do not be different from them.

Dak, a married man returning from fifteen years in Khartoum found a way of coping with his return: 'When you come home, it does not matter whether you are educated or not, you cannot go against the culture. When you come home, you are Nuer and you have to act as Nuer'. Here, 'act[ing] like a Nuer' involved an adaptation process, especially for those who had been displaced for most of their lives. For educated male returnees in their mid-thirties who had come back from Khartoum after two decades of displacement, adaptation was a two-way process. 'The two sides have to learn how to live together,' he added. As these narratives reveal, the return home and subsequent emplacement are rarely to an empty place. The negotiation and (re)integration process, an integral part of settling-in, involved points of tension and cultural clashes between those who were exposed to different cultures during their displacement and those who had stayed in the area and witnessed war. For those who came from Khartoum, where there were no gender and human rights work-shops, the adaptation process was easier. In fact, at times, the cultural ideas about proper gender relations clashed between those who had been to Khartoum and those who were displaced to Kakuma. Thus, emplace-ment is a creative adaptation, a process of cultural and social (personal) transformation.

Forced displacement is an extreme event and disjunction. The social change that might accompany such a disruption, however, emerges as a process that is fragmented, happening at different points and in different arenas, not always simultaneously. As the experiences of war and displacement show, change has not only taken place in sites and social arenas among those who had moved but also among those who had stayed behind. This temporal dimension of home plays a key role in regulating the power to put oneself and others in a place and to invest a place with significance.[29] Thus, 'the myth of home'[30] as static and territorialised needs to be empirically investigated rather than assumed. In this way, a process of emplacement is made up of a myriad of things and events, sometimes contradictory, as different sections of the population, including members of the same households, have gone through different experiences during the wars. Homecoming is a way of experiencing fragmented (family and community) lives put

[29] Feld and Basso, *Senses of Place*, p. 8.
[30] See Roger Zetter 'Reconceptualizing the myth of return: continuity and tran-sition amongst the Greek-Cypriot refugees of 1974', *Journal of Refugee Studies*, 12 (1), 1–22 (1999).

together. As Peter Loizos shows in the case of return to Cyprus, home-coming might be more accurately described as a loss rather than a gain.[31]

[31] Peter Loizos, 'Displacement Shock and Recovery in Cyprus', *Forced Migration Review*, No. 33, 2009, pp. 40–2.

5

Season of Settling-in: Land and Livelihoods

NYAKUOL: BECOMING MEN

When I saw Nyakuol in Lɛr, she told me that Nyapiny, her sister, had given her a hut. She had settled temporarily, having to wait for a survey until the GoSS gave her land. Nyakuol's family of seven and Nyapiny's of three shared two small huts. The suitcases Nyakuol had brought from Kenya were piled up in the corner. Her return 'home' was difficult:

> When we arrived here, there was not much support. The UNHCR took us by plane to Bentiu and then transported us by bus to Lɛr. We were maybe fifty heading for Lɛr. They gave us some food, sorghum, rice, oil and dried beans. That was supposed to last for three months. But when you come home, you have to make gifts to your family and relatives. There are many guests who come to greet you. The food was eaten within a month. Now, the cultivation period is over and we have no food.
>
> At the beginning I was very happy to be back. I was with my family whom I have not seen for over ten years. Now, many of them are also returning to Lɛr. My twin sister who is in Khartoum, I have not seen her since 1983. I wanted to come home to be with my family. But now things are getting difficult. I am very unsettled.
>
> Our life here is hard because we have no money. Now, in Sudan, if you have no money [yiou], you cannot get food. Everything here is about money. Our land is gone and the cows are dead. I have to rely on my family [for support]. I want to first settle down [nyiuuri piny] – to have a permanent land and house – and then I need a job. In Kakuma, I used to work with IRC [International Rescue Committee] as a midwife, and I was a leader of women there. I have all my certificates from courses that I took in Kakuma so this might help me to get a job. I am a widow and I have to rely on myself to provide for the family. No one else is going to help me. I decided to settle far from my husband's family and now I need to manage. I am worried that my children will not be able to go to school. Here, there are no good schools [duël gora].

A few months after Nyakuol returned to Lɛr, she had, with the help of relatives, built a house, started a business in the market, sent her children to school and started cultivating land. Her neighbours formally recognised her house (*cieng* Nyakuol), which was a sign of her settling in. Kuok told me:

> Look at Nyakuol, she is like a man now. She can take care of her own '*cieng*', she even brings food home, and she has a business. She is also a *kuaär* among

the women. She has the strength of a man. Women are becoming the real *wur* in southern Sudan now.

In what ways are returnee women becoming 'the real men', socially, politically and economically? What were, and remain, their gendered strategies and experiences of emplacement in the aftermath of return migration? In what ways have their survival and settling-in strategies shaken the gender power ideology that previously defined Nuer communities? How are returnee men finding their place within the post-war home, and how are their relations of power, privilege and status are being (re)defined in relation with those men and women who had stayed behind? These questions are at the core of the current debates in Nuer and other southern Sudanese communities in the context of community (re)creation and state formation in post-war South Sudan. They point to the key social transformations in forced displacement and refugee return. Through their actions, women and men contest, reconfigure, or reinforce gender identities and unequal power relations within their households and communities.

For those born in exile, home or place of origin takes on an imaginative form, at times constructed through narratives of and interactions with others.[1] Thus, return is often to a place of which migrant women and men have little or no knowledge or direct experience. Although much of the migration and development discourse has focused on the economic dimension of migration, the need to study transformative social processes involving those who had stayed behind has also been acknowledged.[2] In order to fully understand the processes of socioeconomic change in the context of migration and displacement, it is critical to consider gender and inter-generational relationships.[3]

What does the statement 'a real man' signify in the context of the gendered emplacement of Nuer returnee women in South Sudan? As Sharon Hutchinson indicates, the concept of 'real men' was rarely used among the western Nuer people until the 1990s.[4] For the eastern Jikany Nuer, *wut pany* (real man) was intrinsically linked to the concept of manhood and masculinities. The superior masculinity centered around the virtues of being 'majestic', 'virtuous' and 'glorious'.[5] Women and men I encountered in Kenya and in southern Sudan used the term 'a real man' in reference to someone who is able to take care of his household, to make decisions and is respected by the community. In what follows, I analyse the metaphor of women becoming men in the context

---

[1]   See Chapter 4.
[2]   See, for example, N. Nyberg-Sørensen, N. van Hear and P. Engberg-Pedersen, 'The Migration-Development Nexus: Evidence and Policy Options; State of the Art Overview', *International Migration*, 2002, Vol. 40, pp. 3–71; UNDP, *Human Development Report: Overcoming Barriers: Human Mobility and Development* (New York, 2009).
[3]   See, for example, P. Essed, G. Frerks and J. Schrijvers (eds), *Refugees and the Transformation of Societies: Agency, Policies, Ethics and Politics* (Oxford, 2005).
[4]   Sharon E. Hutchinson, *Nuer Dilemmas*, p. 289.
[5]   Ibid.

of their emplacement strategies in southern Sudan, realised through (re)building livelihoods and gendered experiences of access to land and political rights.

IMAGINED AND LIVED 'HOMES' AND RETURN

Cieng as home, as village

Of particular interest in my analysis is the depiction of 'home', since '*wane cieng*' (let's go home) was one of the most common references that refugees made to their movement from refugee camps to Nuerland. In anthropological discourse, the concept of 'home' has been defined as a place where people live, a physical place, to which they return either permanently or for visits, or a place to which they of dream of returning but are often unable to as a result of the prevailing conditions that forced them to leave in the first place. In western conceptualisations, geographers have referred to 'home' as the 'exemplar of place'[6] and the 'territorial core'.[7] Yi-Fu Tuan, however, attributes the characteristics of intimacy and wellbeing to home.[8] Others have personalised home by adding themselves to this notion.[9] In western depictions, home emerges as a gendered feminised place.[10] The construction of home as a women's place resulted in both place in general and home in particular being produced as sites of nurture, stability, reliability and authenticity. As Wenona Giles puts it, 'the idea of home is a contradictory phenomenon: while it may confine women, it may also represent escape and freedom. For some it is a locus of resistance and struggle'.[11] In recent years, with much focus on global displacement and migration, the challenges of homecomings have been the focus of many discussions. Many of these reflections have been produced by authors who themselves experienced displacement, including Edward Said.[12]

For the Nuer women and men, the meaning of home is strongly interlinked with social relations and land. There are two distinct words, *cieng* and *duël*, that generally refer to home. The word *cieng*, as Edward E. Evans-Pritchard tells us:

[6]   Gillian Rose, *Feminism and Geography: The Limits of Geographical Knowledge* (Minneapolis, 1993), p. 53, quoted in Malathi de Alwis, 'The "Purity" of Displacement and the Reterritorialization of Longing', p. 215.
[7]   Douglas J. Porteous, 'Home: The Territorial Core', *Geographical Review*, 1976, Vol. 66, pp. 383–90.
[8]   Yi-Fu Tuan, *Space and Place: The Perspective of an Experience* (Minneapolis, MN 1977).
[9]   Gaston Bachelard, *The Poetics of Space*, (Beacon Press, 1969).
[10] Gillian Rose, *Feminism and Geography: The Limits of Geographical Knowledge* (Minneapolis, MN, 1993).
[11] Wenona Giles, 'Public and Private Constructions of Gendered Violence in Ethnic National Conflict', in D. Indra (ed.) *Engendering Forced Migration* (Oxford, 1999), pp. 83–93, p. 85.
[12] Edward Said, *Out of Place: a Memoir* (New York, 1999).

has the general sense of 'home', [and] may be employed to describe a residential group of any size, from single homestead to large tribal division. It is usually coupled with the name of a lineage when it refers to local groups of any size.[13]

Cieng, therefore, refers to a village, a community, 'a corporate group with a feeling of solidarity' characterised by strong kin and clan ties.[14] Refugee women and men in Kakuma also stressed that *cieng* is linked to land and the right to land. Land is usually passed through inheritance from father to son, while women acquire a right to land through their husbands.

The second word used to describe a home, *duël* (or *dhor*), generally refers to a grass thatched mud hut – a residence of household members. The English word 'home' – associated with the division between domestic and private as opposed to public and communal spheres and domesticity and femininity – does not have the same meanings in Nuer language. Like other pastoralist communities,[15] for Nuer women and men, the distinction between private and public does not take place within a home sphere. As the research participants often pointed out, *duël* as a residence of a household is neither a private nor a personal place. It is, rather, a place where the daily activities of the household members take place, involving co-operation and conflict between men and women, and children, with specifically designated social obligations and rights related to one's social position within the household and the community. It is also a place of meetings, production and reproduction, open to visitors, where family and community issues are discussed.

Women and men repeatedly referred to their strong attachment and sense of belonging to a specific *cieng*. In the 1930s, Evans-Pritchard commented that 'the Nuer have a great affection for their homes and, in spite of their wandering habits (moving with the cattle during dry season for grazing or migrating for trade), men born and bred in a village are likely to return to it even if they live elsewhere for some years'.[16] Paul, who spent seven years in Kakuma, expressed his strong attachment to home:

> When I think of home, I remember *cienq* is where you belong to. You have lost your grand-grandparents, your grandfather and your grandmother, you have left your parents there. Also you have a freedom, you have a responsibility and a right. You are free to cut a tree and no one is going to accuse you that you are destroying the environment. But here in Kakuma, you cannot cut this tree. Soon you will be jailed. You have no freedom here. [...] You have responsibility for everything at home. I cannot term Kakuma as home but it is a temporary home.

Other research has identified the cultural trauma associated with recent displacement, pointing to the deep attachment to place that many

---

[13] Edward E. Evans-Pritchard, *Kinship and Marriage among the Nuer* (Oxford, 1951), p. 3.
[14] Ibid., p. 1.
[15] See Dorothy L. Hodgson's studies of the Massai in *Once Intrepid Warriors: Gender, Ethnicity, and the Cultural Politics of Maasai Development* (Bloomington, IN, 2004) and Henrietta Moore's study of the Endo in Kenya in *Space, Text, and Gender: An Anthropological Study of the Marakwet of Kenya* (New York, 1996).
[16] Evans-Pritchard, *Kinship and Marriage*, p. 1.

agro-pastoralist people, women in particular, feel, and the shame that accompanies the compulsion to move: 'To a Dinka, his country with all of its deprivations and troubles is the best in the world. Until recently going to foreign lands was not only rarity, but a shame'.[17] As I show below, like a Dinka man, the connection to home remained an important one for the Nuer women and men, even if they did not decide to settle permanently in their village. *Cieng*, however, became also reinterpreted through a practice of (re)establishing social connections. As some were unable or unwilling to find their relatives, they decided to establish new kinds of fictive kin ties that replaced *cieng* based on *maar* (kinship).

The rest of this chapter demonstrates how, due to changing circumstances resulting from wars and years of displacement to diverse places, the Nuer women and men came to define a *cieng* not only as a geographical location with ancestors, but also as a conceptual and physical space wherein social, economic and political activities intersect.[18] While some settled in familiar places, where they had once lived or where they left their relatives and resources behind, others undertook homemaking projects in unfamiliar places. Both groups, however, underwent a process of creating rather than re-constructing a sense of identity and community in dialectical relations and practices with each other, and with those who were displaced and those who stayed behind. These ties included (re)establishing relations with long-lost relatives, (re)casting relations with distant kin, and creating kin relations based on common experiences during displacement rather than only on blood. As with Russians returning to the Russian motherland from ex-Soviet republics, this homecoming and place-making required 'both physical and cultural reconstruction by migrants upon return'.[19]

Imagined 'homes' and 'real homes': land, rights and the state

Sarah, an elderly woman who had been in Kakuma since 1992, associated home with a good life, (memories of) friends and family and her duties in the house:

> When we think about *cieng*, we think about *home*. Not about Kakuma. We think about the place where we were born. I think about my own home, not the whole Sudan, my home in Bentiu. Things there were very good for me. All the lives for young and old people are good. We think about how we decorated our houses, how we smear them, and the food that the husband brought from the river.

The Nuer women and men in Kakuma, both young and old, referred to *cieng* as having a territorial dimension, a place linked to specific environmental, landscape and livelihood characteristics as well as a place of

[17] Luka Biong Deng cited in Rogaia Mustafa Abusharaf, *Wanderings: Sudanese Migrants and Exiles in North America* (Ithaca, NY, 2002), p. 54.
[18] Laura Hammond, *This Place will become Home: Refugee Repatriation to Ethiopian* (Ithaca, NY, 2004), p. 10.
[19] Hilary Pilkington and Moya Flynn, 'From 'Refugee' to 'Repatriate': Russian Repatriation Discourse in the Making', in R. Black and K. Koser (eds), *The End of the Refugee Cycle: Refugee Repatriation and Reconstruction* (Oxford, 1999), pp. 171–97, p. 196.

birth and belonging. As with images of home in other exiles' narratives,[20] home and homeland are idealised in order to cope with the suffering they experience in displacement. Nuer women and men referred to images of green fields, cattle, fish and rivers and idyllic village life. While Kakuma, like other refugee camps, was perceived as a temporary place, Sudan was seen as a 'permanent place'. One of the South Sudanese politicians visiting the camp expressed this as follows:

> Camp is not a permanent place, when you get home you will build a place that is permanent. All of you will have a piece of land of your own. You can secure a place in one of the towns.

This narrative demonstrates the importance of the rights to access and use of land, vital in order to create a permanent place, even if it involves mobile locations for pastoralist communities.

The decision to return home was thus influenced by the possibility of accessing land and resources. These were some of the first elements of the settling-in. Before her departure, Nyakuol told me:

> The biggest problem is that women in Nuer cannot own land. As a single woman without any assistance, it is not easy to cultivate the land. Another problem is that if you are a widow and you are rich, others can come and take away your land and your property. The relatives of the husband could come and take away everything, cows, the grain that you have.

In the narratives of Nuer refugees in Kakuma, home does not only take imaginative and social relations forms but is also linked to territory. Refugees in Kakuma often talked about Sudan as their homeland and country. The idea of home was strongly intertwined with land and access to rights and freedoms. The construction of (South) Sudan as a national homeland had started during the war, and was further propagated by international organisations and South Sudanese politicians in Kakuma. In addition to NGO civic education programmes for returnees, slogans like 'Sudan is home' printed on t-shirts were worn by NGO and refugee staff in the camp, which formulated and strengthened the idea of 'being Sudanese'. This was visible in the expanding notions of personal identity of the Nuer and other Sudanese. A widow commented: 'I am Dok, this is where I was born and this is where I was married. But I am a Nuer, and I am also a Sudanese. Sudan is my home'. South Sudanese politicians visiting the camp emphasised the need for the southern Sudanese to return in order to gain control over politics in Sudan: 'Let us be the majority at home. The northerners are still the majority in the south. You need to come back to make Sudan our place'.

The nationalistic discourse of the need for southerners to return to southern Sudan was linked to the CPA's provision for a 2011 referendum to determine whether southern Sudan should remain with Sudan or become independent. The GoSS was running campaigns in refugee and

---

[20] See, for example, Said, *Out of Place*; Giles, 'Public and Private Constructions of Gendered Violence'.

IDP camps to encourage southerners to go back, as they wanted to secure a majority of the vote. Associating *cieng* with a country entails expansion in the Nuer view of the world and their place in the greater context of social and kinship/ethnic relations. Hence, *cieng* no longer meant a single community and household but became associated with a greater community of diverse ethnic groups linked to each other by virtue of shared borders, shared identities and common suffering at the hands of the northern Sudanese, the 'Arabs'.

The duties and expectations of returning refugees had strong masculine undertones. Young men were expected to contribute to the development and (re)building of Sudan by sharing the skills and resources that they had gained during life in exile. These convictions were often expressed by the young men in Kakuma and in Lɛr. To them, homemaking meant state-creation and nation-building and a larger development of infrastructure and services in southern Sudan, including the provision of education, medical services and defending the country against its enemies. The role of women was expressed in the gendered views similar to those found in other war-torn societies entangled in the gendered visions and rhetoric of the nation. During a campaign meeting organised by the SPLM in Lɛr, the local secretary general referred to women as 'mothers of the nation' and praised their role in supporting men, bringing up children and building the domestic sphere of southern Sudan. Once again, women became bearers of the collective identity and duty to give birth to the nation.

NYUURI PINY: GENDERED SETTLING-IN

Social networks
The processes of emplacement and place-making projects that returning Nuer women and men were engaged in were affected by and affected gender relations. Here I come back to the metaphor widely used by Nuer women and men to describe the activities and changing subjectivities of returnee women (and men). Prior to the war, gender relations among the Nuer polygamous communities were characterised by hierarchical relations, with women occupying generally subordinate positions within the household and the community. Yet, these power relations changed throughout the life-cycle. Girls of marriageable age occupied strong positions within the household as they were wooed by prospective husbands, although their social position and power to negotiate within the household declined after marriage. As their age and the number of their born and surviving children increased, married women gained in status and enjoyed a stronger social position within the household than that of their male age-mates.

The metaphor describing women as 'social men' has partial origins in the social position of infertile women who, through their parents' cattle, were able to take a wife and establish their own households. They were also doing 'men's work': cultivating, building *luak* and owning cattle and land. They were perceived in the community as 'social men' and given the same degree of respect and scope for engagement in community affairs. Similarly, women who were married, had several children and had obtained their own land and house could also be considered as 'social men'. In this understanding, their 'social men status' was linked to their economic autonomy, perceived more as their husbands' brothers than as their wives.

'Imagined homes' took on a lived meaning through the experience and practice of settling-in. When my neighbour Nyabol, a married woman in her forties, came back to Lɛr in December 2006, after ten years in Khartoum, she found her son was also there. She had not seen him since 1998, when he left Khartoum for Ethiopia and subsequently Kakuma:

> When I came, I settled at my sister's house. My husband was with another wife in the village, and since I have been living in town for a long time, I could not imagine going back to the village. I decided to settle in Lɛr, which is more of a town than village. My sister, who was living in Lɛr, helped me out. She accommodated me, gave me food and welcomed me. In Nuer tradition, anybody can help you, even a person who is not related to you. No one can reject a visitor [*jäal*], and this is how we, the returnees, are called here.
> It is very difficult for me to settle here. First I need to get land and then a house. Once I will be sitting with all my things in my *duël*, I can say that I am settled in my home [*nyuuri piny ke ciengda*]. When I have my property, people will then recognise me: 'This is the home of Nyabol' [*Eno cieng Nyabol*]. For now, I am still a visitor, staying with my sister, and not many people know me here. I feel like a stranger and they call me '*khartoumi*'. Once I have my own land and house, I will stop being a returnee. I will be citizen of Lɛr [*raan Lɛr*]. But this takes time.

Nuer hospitality provided important social support for the initial settling-in of returnees.[21] Although often creating burdens for relatives who had stayed behind, those who found relatives had an easier time making a new start. Nuer returnee women and men in Lɛr quickly realised that homecoming and settling-in is a long-term process; establishing oneself in a place, acquiring land, building a *duël* and creating a space in the community is done gradually. Some decided to settle in a place different from their place of origin or birth, mostly in urban areas or small towns , a result of lifestyle changes during displacement, and in order to better access paid employment. Those coming from Khartoum, Kenya, Uganda and Ethiopia mostly settled in Bentiu, Rubkona, Lɛr or other towns. Becoming *raan* South *Sudani* or *raan* Bentiu, Rubkona or Lɛr, which in the literal translation meant becoming a person or a man from these places, was on the mind of almost all returnees. *Raan* was, however, often translated and used to mean 'citizen'. Returnees often emphasised that access to rights and obligations embedded in citizenship through nationality, or by belonging to a specific place, was an important aspect in ensuring a belonging beyond *thok duël* or *cieng*. It meant the politicisation of belonging and identity linked to the creation of a nation state.

---

[21] Sharon E. Hutchinson, *Nuer Dilemmas*, p. 161.

Homecoming could not be considered complete without a ceremony of animal sacrifice. As Hutchinson shows, until the 1990s, Nuer lifestyles and identity remained intertwined with cattle, and the meaning of cattle remains inscribed in many ceremonies, including homecoming.[22] All returnee men and women whom I met in Nuerland had to partake in a homecoming ceremony. This was supposed to be performed by the immediate family and clan members immediately upon the return of displaced relatives. However, as in some cases, returning women and men were not able to find their immediate relatives, they either looked to more distant family members or were welcomed by government officials. In some cases, it took months or even years before the ceremony could be carried out. The importance of the ceremony was more for those who had stayed behind than for the returnees themselves. When Nyabol, and later Liep, her son, arrived in Lɛr, they invited me to their ceremony. Nyabol's husband, who had stayed behind during the conflict, slaughtered an ox and their long-lost son, Liep, jumped over the carcase.[23] In order to leave behind the misfortunes they had suffered while away they had to wash themselves with the blood of the bull. Only by doing so can a person be considered by the relatives who had stayed behind to have fully 'come home'. Yet, for the returnees, the process of homecoming was much longer and entailed several other elements of settling-in. Liep confirmed this:

> Now, I am at home. But this is for my relatives. For me I still need to settle in; there are many things I need to do: I need a house, I need a job, I need to marry.

Those who had spent decades in refugee camps in East Africa, many of whom had converted to Christianity, rejected the ritual, arguing that their new faith did not allow pagan rites. This often led to conflicts with those who had stayed behind. 'Look at these *jäal*, they have become people of the town [*rek*], they have lost our culture,' lamented some of the elder women and men. In some cases, I was invited instead to church prayers organised to welcome returnees, although the sacrifice of an animal usually followed.

To better understand the experiences of returnees, I decided to carry out a small-scale qualitative survey of returnees' socioeconomic experiences of settling-in. In July and August 2007, after eight months in Lɛr, I interviewed thirty returnee women and men (twenty from Kakuma and ten from Khartoum). My aim was not to carry out a broad statistical analysis, but rather to gain a more in-depth understanding of the priorities and phases of the emplacement experience. Bringing separated household members back together was the most important aspect of settling-in expressed by all respondents. Access to land and building a house were the second most important factors in *nyuuri piny*, followed by access to jobs and livelihoods. One young man who had spent twenty years away, first in Ethiopia and then in Uganda, explained:

---

[22] Ibid.
[23] In some cases, families too poor to afford an ox slaughtered a goat. Local authorities welcomed returnee convoys with the same ceremony.

> This is my home. This is where I belong, but I also have to bring all my family home. When they are all home, this is when we can say we have come home. For now, we are scattered. But I am also keeping my house in Uganda. I spent there many years and this is where my friends are from. I will keep my house there just in case something happens in Sudan.

In a society based on strong communal and kinship ties, families live closely and rely on kin relations in their everyday life. Women and men often told me:

> We, the Nuer, we do not like to stay by ourselves. This is when we are lonely. We have to be with our family and relatives. This is when our hearts are happy [*ci locde te*].

Thus, bringing household members together was a priority for many returnees. During the first weeks and months after arrival their in Nuerland, most returnees tried to find relatives and re-establish their social networks. Those who were unable to find immediate family and kin – they might have perished or disappeared during the conflict – relied on more distant kin relations. Upon his arrival in Lɛr, Kuok found he had no direct relatives living there:

> My parents were long dead and my siblings were either dead or scattered around. I had no choice but [to] look for my uncles who lived in a different part of Unity state. They are not my real uncles, meaning brothers of my father or my mother, but I call them this way. Some of them were the cousins of my parents and some neighbours. At least, there was some connection [between me and them], even if not immediate blood. This is how you can create your *cieng*, also this will be useful when I have to marry. I have to have a *cieng* to be able to marry.

(Re)casting old kinship ties or (re)creating ties with distant family and kin members became a necessity for some returnees. At times, they could rely on the hospitality of their distant family members, which enabled them to start the settling-in process. (Re)creating a *cieng*, even in the absence of immediate kin members was an important process of emplacement. Forging community bonds was a pivotal step in establishing oneself as well as being able to create a household through marriage.

Some returnees, however, decided to create new community bonds rather than (re)create previous *maar* relations. When Nyakuol was searching for a place to build a house, she specifically looked for a piece of land that was in the vicinity of other friends from Kakuma:

> These people here [who had stayed behind or went to Khartoum] call us Kakuma people [*nei ti ti* Kakuma]. I decided to settle close to my friends from Kenya because they know me better than my relatives, who I had not seen in decades. We went through many things in Kakuma and we can assist each other better. Our families do not understand us. They went through different experiences. They think we have a lot of money and things because we were in Kenya. They do not know how hard it is to be a foreigner in some[one] else's land. I feel closer to Nyakwong and Nyajung, the other widows from Kakuma, because we have lived there together.

Relying on previous relationships from Kakuma, or Ethiopia, proved to be an important source of support and community building among the returnees. For example, a middle-age medical assistant who previously had worked in Kakuma and was now employed in the MSF-hospital supported several of the elderly women from Kakuma after their return to Lɛr. Based on their friendship and precious shared experiences of displacement, these women were able to find employment as cleaners in the hospital.

Such relations went beyond financial and emotional support. They often lead to creating fictive kinship ties. In 2007, Gatbel, a young man in his late twenties, who had resettled with his wife Angelina in Canada from Kakuma, came to Lɛr. Gatbel was one of the 'lost boys' and in Kakuma he had lived together with other boys in a household run by Nyatap. Nyatap was a middle-aged woman who was unable to have children. In 1990, she accompanied her soldier husband to Ethiopia, and then moved to Kakuma. After her husband was killed in the war and Nyatap stayed in the camp. She decided to take care of a group of fifteen young 'lost boys', to become their 'mother'. Despite not having any direct *maar* relationship, Gatbel treated her as his real mother. When he visited Lɛr finalise the marriage process to Angelina, he asked Nyatap to represent him at the negotiations. 'I will even have to give a cow; these 'lost boys' are my real children,' Nyatap told me. As a mother of the groom, she had to contribute to the bridewealth payment.

Several other returnee young men relied on their previous Ethiopian and Kakuma friends and companions to establish new, fictive kinship ties. Hence, the meaning of *cieng* as a 'corporate group with a feeling of solidarity' was being (re)interpreted to include new relations based on shared experiences rather than blood.[24]

When Gatleak, another 'lost boy', returned from Kakuma after twenty years away, he learned that his family was dead and all their property lost. He found Nyakuol, whom he knew from Kakuma, and she helped him during the first months. He commented: 'These people of [South Sudan] here they do not know you; we only know those who were with us in Kakuma. We help each other, because otherwise it is impossible to survive here'. Social and support networks developed in places of displacement were an effective support system. Not all were so fortunate, however. Some young male returnees searching for immediate family members complained that their relatives did not want to support them. Kuok once told me:

> I have asked my relatives for the cows from my sisters' marriages that are supposed to be my share. This would help me to settle in, because when I came I had no money and my parents were dead. But my uncle is dodging and he is pretending that there are no cows. He is cheating me, but there is nothing I can do. Sometimes it is difficult to get the property from your relatives. If they love you, they will share with you. If they are stingy, they will hide it and tell you that all cows died during the war. Since you were away, you cannot do anything. My friends from Kakuma help me out for now.

[24] Evans-Pritchard, *Kinship and Marriage among the Nuer*, p. 1.

Gatleak decided to take family members to court in order to claim his share of cattle. This was one of the issues that made some returnees rely on their Kakuma friends rather than their families while settling-in.

The meaning of community was also being (re)negotiated by the returnees. As a result, within Lɛr and Nuer Dok *ciengs*, new '*Kakumi*' and '*Khartoumi*' communities were emerging. This was visible in the language used by the officials in Lɛr. At a meeting organised by the local commissioner's office to discuss land allocation for the returnees, the administrators asked returnees to sit in groups according to their places of displacement. When I arrived at the meeting, my Kakuma friends waved to me and shouted: 'Nyapiliny, come here. The Kakuma people are here [*Nei ti ti Kakuma jene thin*]! You are our sister, you are with us'. The new sister- and brotherhoods based on displacement were becoming a new kinship mark for the returning populations. Establishing oneself within Lɛr was marked by (re)creating links and relations with family and clan members and/or forging fictive kinship ties based on war-time experiences.

Gendered access to land
As my survey revealed, access to land and building a house were the second most important factors in *nyuuri piny* followed by access to jobs and livelihoods. However, the experiences of accessing resources varied by gender, marital status and age. Nyajung, a mother in her thirties with six children who was married to an influential politician in the area had spent seven years in Kakuma. When she returned to Lɛr, it was relatively easy for her to re-establish herself, as her husband had a high government position in Bentiu and her family (who had stayed behind) had kept her land and resources intact:

> I got the land waiting for me, and my husband gave me money to construct a house. I can now welcome visitors in the house. People in the community now know me, and they come to visit me. I am integrated, because I can now exchange with others. I give and they can give.

Women whose husbands had stayed behind or came back to Nuerland before them were able to access land much more readily. In Nuer custom, land is owned and inherited by men and women acquire the right to temporary use based on their affiliation with male relatives. Unmarried girls and young women have access to land through their fathers, while married women settle on the land of their husbands. The situation is more problematic for widows, even though, in principle, they are entitled to the land of their deceased husbands. However, due to the loss of property, government appropriation of the land (in towns and market centres) and the general impoverishment of households during the wars, it is difficult for widows to execute their use rights. A female chief in Lɛr recounted numerous stories of returnee widows being chased away off their husbands' land by family members. These cases, however, rarely reached the local courts, as women's (formal) rights to hold land were limited by customary practice.

With the encroaching of *cieng kume* (government) into Nuer areas, the GoSS interim constitution stipulated that everyone, regardless of gender and age, has a right to own land.[25] Although this was at the time a southern Sudan-wide law, its application at community level, especially in villages, was not clear. As Lɛr was considered a town and the land was owned by the government, government laws applied. Several land surveys were carried out by local government to demarcate plots and divide them among communities, who had to pay for them. Those who had previously owned land in Lɛr were given priority. A parcel of 500m^2 cost about US$100. Only part of the land in Lɛr was surveyed in 2006 and the land largely sold to those resident in Lɛr at that time. Those who arrived after 2006 were unable to purchase land titles and had to wait for the next survey.

In June 2007, the Lɛr county land commission parcelled land outside Lɛr into fifty plots and announced they would be sold to returnees. However, more than three hundred returnee households from Khartoum arrived between April and June 2007, all needing land. Kakuma returnees were not even considered.

Thudan, displaced as a boy first to Ethiopia and then Kenya, was away for seventeen years. When he came back to Unity state in 2005 he obtained a good position with an NGO, and although not originally from Lɛr, he wanted to buy land in order to settle:

> It is easy to settle for young men. When you come by yourself, and you find your relatives, they will give you land. I got my land and my share of cattle in the home village in Nyal. But here, in Lɛr, I am new. I do not know anyone and I have to wait for survey to get a permanent home. For young men who come with education and get good jobs, it is easier to get settled. They can get a job and buy land. The most difficult, it is for widows, because they have to rely on themselves and they have to provide for the whole family. For them, according to *cieng nuära* it is not easy to get access to land. They have to beg from their male relatives.

Most survey respondents shared his views on the difficulties of settling-in and widows gaining access to land. Some widows complained about not being able to settle permanently. Nyakuol's sister, who had returned from Khartoum, lamented the fact that:

> We are considered as returnees here, we do not have a permanent home. Instead we have to keep moving from one place to another. We do not have our place, our home.

Nyakuol herself was in a similar situation. It took her five months to construct a temporary shelter on the small plot her brother had given her. In June 2007, Nyakuol moved in with her four children. She built a hut and a small kitchen, and was in the process of digging a latrine. She also decided to cultivate a small garden. 'Now, I feel that I have a home, it is still not permanent, but I am at least with my children under one roof and people can come to visit me. I am starting to settle-in,' she told me. As I have already mentioned, the ability to host and extend assis-

---

[25] GoSS, 'Interim Constitution', 2005, parts 2 and 12.

tance to others were important signs of being part of a community. To be emplaced was to be able to reciprocate others' hospitality and share in the daily practice of social relations that define a *cieng*, a community and oneself within it.

Among the returnees whom I knew in Lɛr, there were only a few who managed to settle permanently and acquire land title during my stay. Among the survey respondents, only two men had acquired land title. The majority built temporary shelters on non-surveyed land, often rented from relatives, and expressed the feeling of being unsettled. Disputes over land and cattle were commonly heard by the Lɛr county court, which I often attended. They usually involved returnees and those who had stayed behind, further estranging members of war-separated households. Nyajial, a woman chief in Lɛr, explained:

> These cases are on increase now. Many returnees, especially from Khartoum, are coming now and demanding their property. For us, it is difficult to find the cattle. For the land, we always advise them to go back to the village and share the land with their relatives.

The issue of land was hotly debated during a land workshop convened by an NGO in Lɛr. A number of women participants claimed their legal rights to land and complained about the discrepancies of the law's enforcement. An SPLA women's secretary in Lɛr noted that:

> The constitution says that we are all equal now, that women and men have the same right to own resources, including land. But these are just government laws. In community laws, women still have no rights. When we want to buy land, we have to register it in the names of our deceased husbands, or brothers, or fathers. Even the commissioner here does not practice what the government law says. He still follows the culture [customary practice].

Other women shared their stories of being chased away from land belonging to their husbands and fathers and not being able to claim their rights in court. Nyajung, who spent seven years in Kakuma, commented:

> In Kakuma, women and girls were given rights by the UN. If men abused them, they could go to the court and got their compensation. But here, there are no women rights. When your land is taken away from you, no one is going to hear your complaints.

Although the modernity project of creating a democratic South Sudan based on rule of law and equality of rights was being forged in theory, its implementation in daily community life was very different. The GoSS has included gender equality and commitment to the promotion of women rights in all spheres, often under pressure from donors and development agencies. However, for women in towns and villages, access to legal rights remains a distant option.

For those who were displaced internally within Sudan, it was relatively easier to come home, even if for a short visit, before making a decision to stay. Those who became refugees across international borders found these visits more difficult due to the physical distance between their places of exile and their home destination. Also, for those who were away for a short time (a few years) homecoming was usually easier due to access to their previous resources (land and cattle) and remaining family and kin members. One of Kuok's friends, Tito, was away for ten years and decided to settle in Lɛr upon his return from Kakuma in 2004:

> I had some education, was used to living in town, and could not imagine living with my parents in the village. I came to Lɛr, but I knew no one here and I had to struggle. Settling-in takes time, especially if you do not have resources and relatives to help you out. The government will not support you. Now, after three years of being here, I found a job, and I have a house. But I am still not completely settled.

Place-making in the aftermath of the wars and the encroaching modernity project of the state was implicitly questioning some of the established norms of resource ownership. While for men permanent settlement through access to land was guaranteed, not only through the customary practice but also by law, for women, access to land had to be negotiated through and was dependent on men. Although according to southern Sudanese law 'women were becoming men' in terms of their equal access to rights (including to land), in practice they remained women who, as in other post-war contexts, had to negotiate access to resources through their male relatives.[26]

'WHEN WOMEN BECOME MEN': ACCESSING LIVELIHOODS

Fears of 'return' and changing livelihood strategies in Nuerland
In Kakuma, women and men, young and old, worried about being able to make a living in Nuerland. Kuok initially delayed his return due to lack of a job. Although he had a good education, and was the only Nuer who graduated from the Teachers Training College in Kakuma, his prospects of finding employment without connections in southern Sudan were poor. Several young men who went back searched in vain for jobs with local government as teachers or with NGOs, despite having qualifications. Frustrated, some went back to Kakuma to look for further education and survival opportunities.

For women, especially widows, the main concern was access to income. Nyakong, a pastor's wife who spent a total of twenty years in refugee camps in Ethiopia and Kenya, explained:

> The problem is that we have come here [Kakuma] and have seen the goodness of education. But for us, the women who have not finished education, there are no possibilities. We are worried that if we go home and we have no education we might not get jobs. We want to get education first, abroad, for example, and then we can go.

---

[26] See Liisa L. North and Alan B. Simmons, *Journeys of Fear: Refugee Return and National Transformation in Guatemala* (Montreal, 1999); Gaim Kibreab, 'Rethinking Household Headship among Eritrean Refugees and Returnees', *Development and Change*, 2003, Vol. 34, pp. 311–37.

During a meeting with two commissioners who came to Kakuma to encourage repatriation, several women voiced their concerns about return. The politicians stressed that those who are educated should go back to southern Sudan to help rebuild it and that they will be able to find good jobs. One of the women responded: 'And what happens to us, the old women, who suffered so much during war and brought up all the children? We don't have education, when we go back, what will we do? Sweep commissioners' compounds?' The changing employment market in southern Sudan and emphasis on the need for a qualified workforce were sidelining the uneducated and illiterate, mainly women. This perpetuated their subordinate position by pushing them into under-valued 'female' jobs.

For the Nuer refugees in Kakuma, the idea of 'home', and going home to Nuerland, was linked to being free, independent and self-sufficient. The concepts of freedom and belonging were pervasive in their narratives of home. For both women and men, it was defined as access to livelihoods, education and health services, an important determinant of their decision to repatriate. They were also aware that cultivating land, fishing and herding cattle, done previously, might not be a viable livelihood strategy in southern Sudan. While some have forgotten or never learned how to cultivate land, others realised that in the changing economy, money (through paid employment) was becoming increasingly more important in household economic strategies.

There were also significant changes in livelihood strategies that took place at home. Nyajuc, a widow in her late seventies, stayed in Lɛr during the wars. She had given birth to twelve children, of whom only five had survived. Three of her children were displaced – in Ethiopia, Khartoum and Kenya – and one son joined the SPLA. Sitting under a mango tree, she told me about the livelihood changes over the past fifty years:

> When I was young, we relied on cultivation and cattle. Money had no value at that time, and our lives were about cattle. This was before the government. Then the white people came, the missionaries and the British, and with them a government. Men started migrating to Khartoum for labour, and traders from the north reached Lɛr. Some men became traders, like my husband. Money came to our lives, but for most of us land and cattle were still the main ways of making a living. Now, after the government war, lives of the Nuer have changed completely. People in this generation have learned they can use money to buy food. They don't cultivate, but buy food from the market. Also the UN gives them food. There are also government jobs, in the offices, or as teachers. Even soldiers and police receive money. The government gives education to children [boys], they can get a job and bring something to eat. For us, the old women and those who are not educated, we do not have much chance. We can only get some money from the government and make beer.

An elder from a nearby village of Piliny told me:

> The war has brought a lot of change to the Nuer. Now, to be a man is to be educated and to get a job. Everything is about money now. We do not know where the money comes from. We see the goodness of the money when we can use it and buy things, like the bed and the mosquito net and the food. Also, there is a change towards cattle. Before people never sold cows, but nowadays they sell

them because there is not enough food. The land has become like an old man and is not producing any longer. We, the old people, we do not produce, we only need food. And for this, we need money. Even my wife earns money now. She makes reed mats and sells them to the northern traders. This is how we get some small money. In the rainy season, we still cultivate. Our sons who are in Kenya and in America send us money sometimes so we can buy beds and chairs.

These narratives suggest a fundamental change in the livelihoods of the Nuer communities. Although most (especially those who had stayed behind) still relied on cattle herding and land cultivation, other ways of making a living were being introduced. Many stayee men ran small businesses in the market. Some younger educated men worked as salaried teachers, priests, county administrators, nurses and NGO employees. However, hardly any changes took place in relation to agricultural production. Women and men continued to cultivate mainly sorghum and maize, while some NGOs encouraged people to introduce new crops and vegetables (tomatoes, spinach, beans and potatoes). Cultivation remained exclusively manual, as cattle were reserved for bridewealth and sacrifice.

Elders' narratives also point to the emergence of money as a primary exchange mechanism in the wake of the post-2005 peace agreement, continuing the changes brought by colonisation and the emergence of government. Monetarisation led to the emergence of a banking system in Bentiu, when two banks, the Omdurman Bank run by northern Sudanese and the GoSS controlled-Nile Commercial Bank opened up. During my visits to the bank, I often saw soldiers, NGO and UN employees, as well as local government officials depositing salaries or arranging transfers from relatives abroad. Inexorably, Nuer cattle-keepers were becoming money-keepers. The influx of remittances from relatives resettled in the West not only brought an influx of cash but created another transnational connection for the local Nuer.

The narratives suggest two other important trends: paid office jobs were mainly open to educated men, and women resorted to other ways of making money. During an evening chat with Nyamuc, who had stayed in Lɛr during the conflict, she told me about family finances. Her husband works in a clinic in Rubkona, where he lived with his third wife and their two children. Nyamuc, his first wife, lives in Lɛr with their four children. Her husband divides his monthly salary between the two families and, in addition, supports his mother. Nyamuc receives US$150 per month and, as the money was not enough, she has to work. Like many other women (stayees as well as returnees) in Lɛr, she started a tea business in the market. A couple of chairs, a kettle, some charcoal, tea glasses, tea, coffee and sugar were her initial investment. Every morning, she left the house at seven a.m. and returned late at night. Her profit was roughly US$2 per day, enough to buy food for her children. Food was her main monthly expense, followed by soap, charcoal and other basic household items. Nyamuc complained about her co-wife in Rubkona:

> She is very lazy, she has only two children, but she doesn't work. She only sits at home and cooks for the children. She sleeps the whole day instead of helping the

husband. I think it is better when a wife and husband both work. The wife brings something home for the family and the husband does the same. It is easier. When there is no job it is bad, because there is no money and no food.

Nyamuc's narrative suggests a major shift in attitudes towards earning money and contributing to the household. In the past, women's work was limited to taking care of the children, cultivating land, milking cows and cooking. In the emerging money-dominated economy, women recognised that they needed to make their own financial contributions to improve the wellbeing of the household. Women who 'only' did the housework were perceived as lazy. In Lɛr, Rubkona and Bentiu, women's paid work was visible in the emergence of female-owned businesses such as tea/coffee-making, selling reed mats, cooking in local food stalls, and providing cooking and cleaning services to government offices. Although often frowned upon by men, and perceived as 'not real jobs', women's incomes both benefited their households and gave them enhanced financial security. 'If you have a job and own money, you can even leave your husband when he mistreats you. But if you have no [personal] money, you have to rely on him to bring food home,' Nyamuc stated. Thus, women's greater contribution to household income increases their bargaining position within it and strengthens their autonomy.

The results of my socioeconomic survey revealed that twenty-five respondents had largely relied on cultivation and cattle herding prior to displacement. Only a few had previously engaged in trade or migrated to the north in search of paid labour. They had, however, returned to a dramatically different post-war situation. Most of their property had been stolen, their cattle killed and their land expropriated by the government or relatives. To (re)establish oneself, a person needed resources that now included money.

Access to livelihoods
Establishing a viable livelihood was the third most important factor for settling-in for twenty-four respondents. The majority of both women and men described having a job as part of being fully settled. However, finding income was not easy, for both women and men returnees. For women it was especially hard to access money in order to secure livelihoods for their families. After her arrival in Lɛr, Nyakuol struggled at first:

> A life of a widow in [South] Sudan is not easy. I have decided to settle far away from my husband's relatives, because I do not want to be abused by them and I prefer my independence. But this means I am also alone and have to rely on myself. My brothers cannot help me too much, because they are also struggling. They gave me four head of cattle and two goats. I sold two cows and a goat and decided to start a business. But here, for a woman, it is not easy to run a business. All the traders in the market are men, and if you as a woman want to open a shop, you have to register it in the husband's name.

Four months later, Nyakuol opened a shop in the market after acquiring some land. According to local practice, she was not allowed to trade in the market but she was given permission to build a shop under her deceased husband's name. This she subsequently rented to two Darfuri men. From this income, she was able to construct a house and send her two eldest children to school in Bentiu. The rest of the money she used to hire (male) help to prepare her garden for cultivation. The contradictions between customary laws and practice that forbade women to trade and own property and national laws that ensured equal access to resources and rights and freedoms for women and men were often debated. Most women (both returnees and stayees) and some men (mostly returnees) lamented the fact that local authorities were unwilling to uphold the interim constitution.

Other returnee widows or single women employed various strategies to make money. Although still married, Nyakwony, Nyakuol's best friend, preferred to live away from her husband. Her husband, a well-paid NGO driver who lived in Bentiu, had seven wives of whom, Nyakwony was the oldest. She had spent most of her life in Khartoum and then in Kenya. She had some basic education and previous business experience, having run a small shop before leaving Lɛr in 1990. Arriving in Lɛr in 2006, she said: 'When you get old, it is better to stay away from your husband. It is fewer quarrels. My children are adults now, and they can help me out as well. One son is in Australia and a son-in-law is in America. They send some support'. Autonomy and self-reliance were important for her. Her daughter, who married a 'lost boy' in America, once brought a TV from Kenya. In Lɛr, however, there was no electricity and generators were restricted to NGOs, the representative of the local government – the Lɛr commissioner – and a few well-to-do traders. Nyakwony sold the TV to a trader wishing to open a café/bar in the market. She used the money to open a shop, which she rented to northern traders.

Using social capital acquired in Kakuma, another widow, Nyachan, found a job as a cook for an NGO. In Ethiopia and Kakuma she had worked with several NGOs: 'I have my diplomas and a bit of education, and experience with working with foreigners. I know how to cook, and this is the reason I got a job with an NGO. For us, the returnee women who know something, are a bit educated and have seen other cultures, it is easier to get jobs'. Most women employed by NGOs and the commissioner were returnees. Three of the older single women from Kakuma worked as cleaners in the MSF hospital in Lɛr, while another two got jobs with the commissioner's office as a cook and a cleaner respectively. Women got jobs perceived as 'female', which largely reflected their domestic responsibilities.

In general, both women and men claimed that it was much more difficult for women to find jobs. Kuok explained:

> There are not many paid jobs here. The ones that exist, like office jobs, teachers, nurses, or in the government, need educated people. The problem here in Sudan is that women are not educated, since they were not sent to school. The ones who are educated are men. This is the reason that women have to do menial jobs, like cleaning and serving food.

Of the fifteen women I interviewed, only one had finished primary education. Two had completed six classes of primary school. Among the fifteen men, all had completed at least five classes of primary education. Five had finished secondary school, of whom two had obtained university degrees. While their lack of education constrained women from entering the labour market, so did their domestic obligations. As Nyachan explained:

> There is a certain problem with jobs for women. The office jobs require you to be in the office the full day, and as a woman you have to take care of the children, you have to cook for them. A woman cannot be in the office the whole time.

Other sources of income for women came from beer-making and government pensions paid to widows and former combatants. Some women got jobs with the local police. Both the police and army also hired women, again mainly to do menial work, giving them possibilities of establishing independent incomes.

Nyayena, a young mother in her early twenties who had spent ten years in Khartoum and then seven in Kakuma, returned to Lɛr in 2007. She had problems as her husband had failed to complete bridewealth payment for her and had taken another wife. She was very upset and told me that he did not support her. Nyayena had finished a year of secondary school in Kenya and was hired as a midwife in the MSF hospital as soon as she arrived, making her the only woman in Lɛr with a professional job. 'As a woman, you need your own money, so you do not have to rely on your husband. I also do not want to rely on my father, and this is the reason that I think is good to have a job.' Like Nyayena, all the other returnee young women and girls from Kakuma valued paid employment, and talked about the need to have a job in order to establish greater autonomy. The majority of the stayee women relied on cultivation., with a few women running coffee/tea businesses in the market, selling reed mats or doing menial work. Their access to money was much more limited than that for returnee women.

For the latter, 'becoming men' – through access to autonomous income and livelihoods – was restricted to certain social categories. Usually, those who were better educated, wealthier and who already enjoyed a greater social status were able to more easily negotiate their social position. Thus, gender inequalities have to be considered within a wider set of socioeconomic and political differences.

Men's access to income was easier. All fifteen male survey participants had secured paid employment within two to twelve months of their arrival in Lɛr. Some returnees had found jobs before repatriating to southern Sudan, usually with NGOs, the UN or the GoSS, which helped them with the costs of repatriating. Others, like Kuok and his friends, struggled to find employment. Almost all of them complained about discrimination by local authorities. During one of our chats, Kuok expressed his frustrations about establishing a livelihood after return:

> We, those who were away from this land, we do not know how to cultivate and how to take care of cattle. When we come back, most of us have no property [cows and land], so it is difficult to get a living. When you come from East

Africa and you got some education, people here in Sudan will envy you. Those in powerful positions in the government are the ones who never left Sudan and thought in the bush. Some of them were also in Khartoum. They only give jobs to those who they know. We, the ones who were away from here for a long time, we are not known. People here feel threatened because we have some education and speak English. They think that we will take their jobs. This is the reason they do not want to give us jobs. The only places where you can get employment is with NGOs and the UN, but they do not have many vacancies and you have to know someone to get a job there.

Many young men returnees from Kakuma found employment as nurses or medical assistants with MSF, while others worked for international and local NGOs in Lɛr. None were employed in the commissioner's office. His staff had either never left Lɛr or had been with him in Khartoum. The men surveyed were all employed as teachers, nurses or UN/NGO staffers. Within two months of his arrival, Kuok was registered as a government teacher, and although he was a ghost teacher – there were no open posts – he received a monthly salary of US$200. In addition, he obtained two teaching positions with a local NGO.

The market was also changing. Once, it had been a male preserve with eateries and shops mainly owned and frequented by men. Now, coffee places, although exclusively visited by men, were run by women, especially those displaced to Khartoum. The Arab habits of eating *fuul* (fried beans) and drinking coffee were brought back by returnees from Khartoum. I was often the only woman drinking and eating in the market, although at the end of my stay, I noticed that several women who had come back from Khartoum smoked shishas (water pipes) and drank tea and coffee in public, stretching gender boundaries. Most eateries were owned by northern traders, as for the Nuer men it was a gendered taboo to enter the kitchen, which was perceived as a 'female' space by both women and men. In the 1980s Hutchinson reported the complete absence of Nuer male cooks, but there were now several men, mainly returnees from Khartoum, who had opened food stalls and cooked outdoors.[27] The gendered division of labour was slowly changing, especially outside the household space. Kuok pointed this out to me one day over a bowl of *fuul*:

> We, the men, cheat women. We cook outside the house, but when we come home we pretend that this is a female task. But in Kakuma most of us men cooked, since women were not around, and here you see some who continue to do it. But then they get challenged by women, who tell them that they are doing women's work.

Cultivation remained a complementary source of livelihood for both women and men. During the rainy season, the residents of Lɛr were busy preparing fields and gardens and cultivating crops. Most women returnees planted small gardens near their houses with maize, sorghum and some vegetables. I helped several returnee women with doing this. While planting seeds and exchanging jokes, an elderly woman who had spent five years in Kakuma, which is where I met her, told me: 'I feel that

[27] Hutchinson, 'Rising Divorce among the Nuer, 1936–1983', *Man*, 1990, Vol. 25, pp. 393–411.

I am settled. When you cultivate your land, you really know you are at home. You are free to produce your own food'.

Becoming autonomous: the changing gender division of labour

When I asked Kuong, the chief of chiefs in Lɛr, about the large number of divorce requests filed by women that I had noticed during my visits to local courts in Lɛr and Bentiu, this is the explanation that offered:

> Now women come to the court and ask for divorce. Before it was rare; the war has changed people. Many couples were separated during the war, and husbands feel that they lost everything. Men often went to the bush, to Khartoum or migrated to East Africa. Women either had stayed behind or left for refuge and stayed away from their husbands. When they come together, husbands drink because they have no jobs or no property, and women now demand that their husbands buy clothes and provide other things than only food. Women can also get their own money through small jobs or business, and they can even go away and stay by themselves. They do not need men too much to take care of them.

Indeed, access to alternative livelihoods and independent income marked a slow emergence of autonomous female-led households. Not only were returnee women, especially widows including Nyakuol, choosing to establish autonomous households away from their husbands' relatives, but so too were married women like Nyakwony. For those women who were by themselves in Kakuma, where they enjoyed access to some rights and greater recognition due to gender policies and access to autonomous livelihoods, return to Nuerland meant (re)unification with their husbands and families. This involved reconciliation and the (re)building of conjugal relations, and often subjugation to local expectations of 'a good wife' combined with limiting their space of decision-making and powers. Although no written records of divorce exist in Lɛr, from the marital survey that I carried out with fifty returnee and stayee women and men (see Chapter 6), as well as from the court cases that I attended in Lɛr and Bentiu, divorce was clearly on the rise. As with Hutchinson's findings among the Leek Nuer in 1980s, the willingness of chiefs to grant divorce was increasing.[28] Marriages were being dissolved even after the birth of numerous children. Although divorcee women were usually eager to re-marry, there were also some who decided to establish their own households. Thus the concept of being a woman, and of female entitlements and responsibilities, were being contested and (re)negotiated in post-war Nuerland.

To acknowledge the importance of gender equality issues, political parties and the southern Sudanese government created several posts responsible for gender equality issues. A wife of a local warlord and an influential politician in Lɛr was nominated the local SPLM Lɛr gender secretary. A stayee, she explained some of the reasons for changes in women's lives:

> Before, men did not allow women to work outside the home. But now, there are many women who are employed. The situation forced people to change. Women

[28] Hutchinson, 'Rising Divorce among the Nuer'.

have to do work because they have to feed their children. Many women became widows during the war, and now they have to manage by themselves. Working outside the house brings change. The change did not start by itself. If the woman is employed somewhere and she has income, she then realises that she has a right to take a part. Men ignore women as housewives. They say that this is the work women have to do, but they do not consider it. They will consider you [a woman] if you have income. Then they give you some rights and respect. There are areas, however, where women are still not equal, like land ownership. I know no lady who registered her land in her name. Also, some men feel threatened by the power of women who work outside. This is the reason they do not allow them to go outside to look for jobs, and they even want to control the dress of the women. But some women challenge it now, especially those who are a bit educated and have seen other places.

The emergence of autonomous female households was not only the result of women deciding to challenge distribution of power at home and free themselves from often abusive relationships. In most cases, women's access to autonomous income and the desire to get a job was dictated by the post-war situation in which they found themselves. The crisis created by war and changes in the livelihoods forced women to enter paid employment, especially those living in towns and market centres. Crises thus revealed contradictions in the material basis for women's subordination and opened up opportunities for women to improve their intra-household bargaining positions. As with Eritrean women returnees studied by Gaim Kibreab, Nuer returnee women often suffer greater challenges than men in settling-in, being more constrained in access to resources.[29] Through creative ways of accessing livelihoods they carve out for themselves a greater degree of autonomy and enhance their intra-household bargaining position and access to social power. Examples of successful returnee women were being replicated by local women, including my host. Conjugal relations based on exchange were thus being questioned and renegotiated.

In the absence of men, some women not only took on male responsibilities as household providers but also entered other roles traditionally perceived as being male. For example, Nyakuol and her sisters negotiated bridewealth payments with Gatbel's male relatives; he was marrying one of Nyapiny's daughters. In the absence of their husbands, brothers and father, the women sat down to settle the bridewealth, a task traditionally performed by male relatives of the groom and the bride. These women were not necessarily challenging the existing gender order, but rather taking on some of the male-inscribed tasks to continue the custom of marriage based on bridewealth.

Government policies and returnee experiences were also changing local attitudes towards women and their contributions to the household. Nyalada pointed out that:

> Before, women had no rights and were not allowed to talk in front of others in general meetings. Now, the situation is changing. The peace agreement gave women twenty-five per cent representation, and now women have to be in all government positions. Also, many people have some ideas. In the past, there

---

[29] Gaim Kibreab, 'Rethinking Household Headship'.

were no educated women. Now, there are people who went outside and saw that women have rights in other countries. They adapt the cultures of other countries. Now the minds of women are more open and they are serious about participation in public life and working.

Displacement and exposure to other cultures, as well as GoSS gender equality-policies, opened new possibilities for renegotiating gender relations. Access to money and autonomous livelihoods meant that the process of settling-in altered the gendered division of labour. Thus, independent widows who were struggling to establish their own households and support their families were at times perceived as 'social men'. Similarly, with the emergence of autonomous households, some of the returnee women were gaining the social position of men. A number of returnee women friends were shown respect in the community by being invited to participate in SPLM political campaigns and elections, to give speeches and to assume leadership positions in the community. Their political presence was a sign of an emerging and transformative citizenship code, one that had started during the war with the emergence of women as chiefs. Returnee women were carving out a new place for themselves, entering spaces previously reserved for men. Yet, as we have seen, although their social position was being slowly recognised in national laws, with gender equality as one of the principles and the guarantee of equal rights for women and men, in practice there was sometimes a reluctance to fully adhere. Access to land for example, remained problematic. Some of the returnee women, at times, were able to manoeuvre their womenly social positions to gain greater autonomy and rights within the community.

ARE WOMEN REALLY BECOMING MEN?

In Lɛr, returnees were pursuing specific strategies to make a place they once called home or a place that they chose to reside in into a home. While connected through war-time migratory experiences beyond the village to wider Nuer diasporic communities in Sudan, Africa, Europe, North America and Australia, their image of *cieng* expanded. Some maintained multiple homes and households in and outside of southern Sudan. However, accessing land, establishing a viable livelihood and being considered part of the community were the main constituents of being settled. It also entailed transfer of acquired identity from a *jäal* to a *raan*.

The daily strategies of returnee women in Lɛr demonstrate how locality production in the context of emplacement and homecoming generates debates about transformations of social, and gender in particular, relations in the independent South Sudan. By resorting to creative practices of building physical homes, accessing land, resources and seeking livelihoods, Nuer returnee women engage in shaping 'senses of place', turning a changed or unfamiliar place into a home.[30] In the context of interac-

---

[30] Steven Feld and Keith H. Basso, *Senses of Place,* (Santa Fe, NM, 1996).

tions and integration processes between returnees and those who had stayed behind, the post-war setting creates an opportunity to construct new social norms. What emerges is a contestation of pre-war gender and social orders, with some women seeking to reconfigure unequal gender relations. Meanwhile, the diverse war-time experiences and the coming together of dispersed communities sets in motion social transformations of the meaning of home, place and oneself as a 'real Nuer'. The social practices of the Nuer women underscore Floya Anthias' version of hybridity of these concepts and reveal emerging social (gender and class) hierarchies in post-war South Sudan.[31]

Filtering the notions of home and emplacement through the gender lens shows complexities, different strategies for and challenges to (re) establishing oneself in the process of return. The processes of return and settling-in are experienced differently by different women through their gendered survival strategies. Nadje Al-Ali's research among Bosnian refugee women demonstrates the need to avoid the homogenisation of women's experience.[32] I have shown how different women, depending on their marital status and access to resources, pursued a variety of emplacement strategies. I thus contest the undifferentiated category that conceals the complexity of women's (and men's) lives and the differences in their living situation. Settling-in for (some) returnee women might, at times, prove more difficult, especially in the gendered access to resources and re-establishment of their previous family networks.

The context of rapidly changing opportunities and pressures for returning women push them to use creative strategies to access land, livelihoods and political rights and to create a home for themselves and their families, often by establishing women-headed households. Opportunities for widening their autonomy and opening spaces for change are partially due to changing livelihood strategies, the emergence of money and paid jobs as the primary source of income. Experiences in exile and exposure to women's empowerment programmes, including education, training and gender equality awareness, contribute to envisaging a more equal gender order in post-war communities. While some women negotiate their access to land by invoking new national laws, others use their social status (as daughters, wives or widows of influential men) to access resources. One question that needs further investigation is what position women will occupy in the context of the state-building processes in South Sudan. How will the diverse claims and experiences of women be accommodated in the emerging South Sudanese nation?

It is important to note that while some women do enjoy the status of 'social men', albeit limited, others suffer further marginalisation. Widows without wider networks of family support, women with children

[31] Floya Anthias, 'New Hybridities, Old Concepts: The Limits of "Culture"', *Ethnic and Racial Studies*, 2001, Vol. 24, pp. 619–41.

[32] Nadje Al-Ali, 'Loss of Status or New Opportunities? Gender Relations and Transnational Ties among Bosnian Refugees', in U. Vuorella and D. Bryceson (eds), *The Transnational Family: New European Frontiers and Global Networks* (Oxford, 2002).

by Arab husbands, illiterate elder women and those coming without any financial or social capital and resources, find it more difficult to establish themselves and negotiate their social position. While gender remains an important determinant of hierarchies, access to power, livelihoods, resources and privilege are increasingly linked to the level of education, status and war-trajectories.

6

Tot – Gendered Emplacement:
Identities, Ideologies and Marriage

KUEM AND NYARIAL:
SUITS, TROUSERS, MINI-SKIRTS AND LEARNING TO WEAR A *TUAC*

On a May morning in 2007, the preparations for *tuoc*, the wedding dance
marking a stage in the Nuer marriage process were underway. This was
also the beginning of *tot*, the rainy season, which often saw marriages
being concluded. The bride's family was busy cooking and getting her
ready for the dance, while negotiations around bridewealth were taking
place in a *luak* (cattle byre). It was decided that half of the groom's cows
were to be transferred to the bride's family. The groom, Kuem, a Kukuma
refugee who now was in his late twenties and had a lucrative job, was
marrying Nyaluak, a beautiful near-16-year-old who had never left Lɛr.
The daughter of a high-ranking influential commander, and considered
'somehow educated' – Nyaluak had finished four grades of primary school
– she commanded a high bride-price. Her father demanded seventy head
of cattle, the highest bridewealth payment known in Lɛr, where thirty to
thirty-five was the norm.

Kuem, one of the many 'lost boys', was recruited by the SPLA in 1988
and taken to Ethiopia for military training. From 1991 to 2006 he was a
refugee in Kakuma, after which he went to Nairobi, where he finished
secondary school. He subsequently found a job with an NGO in Lɛr and
returned to his father's home for the first time in eighteen years. One of
Riek Machar's brothers[1], Kuem's father had stayed in Lɛr during the wars
to look after his family's property, while most of his children were either
killed or displaced throughout Sudan and East Africa. An influential local
guan kuoth,[2] he was introduced to me as a '*kuäar moun*'. Hence, due to his
family background and his 'advanced' education, Kuem was being asked
a premium price.

---

[1] Riek Machar was then the vice-president of southern and later South Sudan.
[2] Among the western Nuer the concept of '*guan kuoth*' is applied to a whole
range of persons possessing a kuoth (god spirit). Earth priests (*kuäar muon*) must
have a *kuäar muon* lineage (see Douglas Johnson, *Nuer Prophets: A History of
Prophecy from the Upper Nile in the Nineteenth and Twentieth Centuries* (Oxford,
1994). While Riek Machar's family is not part of a *kuäar muon* lineage, they often
lay claim to the *kuoth* Teny as a way, some argue, of strengthening Riek's political
credentials.

6.1 Returnee young men, 'Lost Boys' at a marriage ceremony in Lɛr, 2007
(© Katarzyna Grabska)

As half of the cattle were transferred, I heard singing and saw groups of women and men dancing. The men were carrying spears and sticks and singing in praise of the forthcoming marriage. Both the groom and his best friend wore elegant black suits and a *tuac* (leopard skin) tied around their waists (Photo 6.1). The horns of the large oxen earmarked for celebratory slaughter were decorated with ribbons and flowers. The meat was to be shared between the bride's family. Two smaller cows were gifts to her *cieng*. While some elements of *tuoc* were preserved, for example, negotiations and transfer of cattle, singing and sharing of food, new customs were also apparent. This was not just the presence of dignitaries with satellite phones and armed guards; fashion was also changing. The groom's party, all former 'lost boys' and returnees, wore elegant attire, resembling models from a fashion magazine. Yet, the girls had to remove *tuac* tied around the men's waists, signifying an opportunity for the flirting to begin. The groom had a spear in his hand, symbol of Nuer manhood, but looked perplexed and unsure what he was supposed to do with it. The bride and her friends were also dressed according to returnee fashion. Instead of traditional beads around their waists, they wore tight jeans, mini-skirts or trousers and had colourful hair extensions worn by some women in East Africa.

Among the men, I saw Jany, a returnee young man I'd met before. He had spent most of his life in Khartoum and in Kenya and had only recently arrived in Bentiu. When I inquired why he was carrying a stick, he explained:

> I have no idea. This is my first Sudanese wedding. I just came from Bentiu for the wedding because Kuem is one of my relatives, but also a friend from Kenya. I am just watching other people and trying to figure out what I should do. I was given this stick, because people told me that I have to have one. But I am not sure what I am supposed to do with it. This morning there was a lot of running – we went with the bull to the house of the girl and then were running up and down from one house to another. I am tired now. I am newly arrived here and I have to learn to be a Nuer, I have to learn all these traditions. This is part of making a home here.

Kuem saw me and shouted happily:

> Hey, Nyapiliny *khaway*, are you coming to my wedding today? I am getting married and will finally have my home. This is a real homecoming for me, I will be a Nuer!

In the afternoon, I went to the wedding dance (*tuoc*) on the outskirts of Lɛr, near the *luak* belonging to Nyaluak's father. During the dancing and flirting between the bride's and groom's relatives, young men with *gaar* and spears started fighting. I was told this was a common occurrence at Nuer weddings. The sudden arrival of armed soldiers, who dispersed the spear-carrying youth, was a novel addition to the wedding ceremony. Surrounded by a group of women singing and shouting wedding rhymes, the groom and his mates looked bored and lost. In his elegant suit, *tuac* and spear, Kenyan-educated Kuem felt confused. He later explained that: 'I felt really lost, like a lost boy, who is between different cultures'. He was trying to make sense of his diverse experiences and find his own identity. Marriage to a local girl and the establishment of his own household was supposed to give him a local identity – now he was going to be *wur nuära pany*, a 'real man', a responsible man in his community, no longer perceived as a lost person with many identities and dilemmas.

The multiple experiences and images of the wedding reflected many people's bewilderment and dilemmas, the struggle between holding on to a strong culture and tradition while trying to embrace *cieng mi pai ben* and a new lifestyle often brought by returnees. My neighbours, friends and passers-by were preoccupied with the transforming social relations, especially changes in the behaviour of the youth, contestations around behaviour considered appropriate for a *nyal ma goa* or a respectable woman' and for a *wur nuära pany*. In this chapter, I ask how homecoming and settling-in are experienced differently by young women and men and how return is intertwined with gender relations, identity and self? To what extent does homecoming challenge the previously gained greater freedoms in refugee camps? How are new gendered aspirations and ideas about being a woman or a man practiced in the context of family reunification with those who had stayed behind? With the social and cultural landscape of settling-in and emplacement for returning populations dominated by reminiscences of wars and militarisation of Nuer society, what are the consequences of these new gender identities and practices (through the marriage process) brought by the returnees?

GENDER IDENTITIES, IDEOLOGIES AND 'SELF' IN FLUX: THE EXPERIENCE OF 'HOMECOMING' AND SETTLING-IN

> People call us 'lost women', because we have been away from here for a long time and we don't know Nuer culture. We know nothing and we don't fit in here. We are really lost.

This is how Nyayena, a twenty-something-year-old mother who had spent most of her life in Khartoum, Kakuma and Nairobi, described home-coming to Lɛr. Her feeling of 'being lost' reflected that of Kuem, the young groom bewildered by his unfamiliarity with local marriage customs. Being 'lost' no longer related only to the experiences of young boys forcibly recruited by the SPLA in the 1980s but more widely connoted tensions around identity and self facing those who had grown up in displacement. It reflected the feeling of being detached from the local cultural practices. To quote Jany, one of Kuem's friends, in order to be 'known and settled', the process of *beben cieng* and *nyuuri piny* involved 'learning how to be a Nuer man and getting to know the Nuer culture'. Young returnee women and girls similarly referred to their challenges of settling-in. Hence, gendered emplacement involved the (re)creation of gendered community relations, identities and practices. At times, this meant the (re)negotiation of self, gender identities, aspirations and practices. These processes questioned some of the assumptions about gender ideologies and institutions, prob-lematised timeless discourses around *cieng nuära* and produced a state of gender and community relations in flux. I develop this point by focusing predominantly on the experiences of young men and women.

Landscape, place, home and gender identities

How are masculinities and femininities intertwined socially, and how do *beben cieng* and place-making become part of a redefinition of gender relations? Creating one's own *cieng* through marriage is a critical point for Nuer femininities and masculinities. Here, I elaborate on the meaning of *cieng*, and home.

A 23-year old single man from Bentiu who was a refugee in Kakuma described *cieng* as 'a place of living. If I get married, I will say that I have a home, "*cieng*". Home means also family, a unit.' Girls, however, referred to two ideas of *cieng* each representing different stages in their passage to adulthood. Nyayena told me that, for her, '"*Cieng*", home, is a place where I was born. This is when I was a girl in my father's home. Now, I am married, I am *ciek* [a woman] and I am in my own home, in my husband's *cieng*.' Through marriage, the transfer to her husband's house and subse-quent procreation, a girl (*nyal*) becomes a woman (*ciek*), gains rights to property in the house and ability to control domestic work and resources through her own cultivation.

Cieng is thus a gendered space and is experienced differently through the performance and realisation of masculinities and femininities. The underlying gender ideology embedded in the creation of *cieng* through marriage influences the different social identities of women and men, and girls and boys, within the home and household space. The visual and lived representation of this difference is practiced in separate spheres of life within the household, whereby men and boys usually sleep together with the animals in a *luak,* whereas women, girls and smaller children live in a *duël.* Their different spatial and social positions determine their responsibilities and status in the household and society at large, decision-making, access to resources and entitlements (*cung*).The formation of an 'own household' through marriage and procreation relates to the passage to full adulthood. Through shared division of responsibilities and procreation, men's and women's identities are socially intertwined and are likewise interwoven with *cieng.*

Cieng as a space of household is also a place of power relations embedded in gender and generational ideology. As Henrietta Moore points out, marriage 'links the formal system of social control and reproduction with the means by which command over resources and reproduction is achieved'.[3] Marriage and *cieng* are therefore not only sites of reproduction, but also of interpersonal relations. Deniz Kandiyoti identifies two ideal-typical types of male dominance: one found in the Middle East, South Asia and East Asia and another in sub-Saharan Africa.[4] Naila Kabeer describes these models as corporate and segmented households, respectively. Corporate patriarchal households 'are more likely to generate material pressures – and incentives', as Kabeer argues, 'for women to acquiesce, however reluctantly, in a centralized decision-making process. [...] Conversely, segmentation of the household economy and a more dispersed distribution of intra-household resources tend to be associated with greater access by women to resources within the household and to extra-household resources'.[5]

The Nuer form of household is similar to the segmented model, where women exercise relative autonomy in resisting male appropriation of their labour. Sharon Hutchinson discusses extensively the cattle-over-blood ideology, which defined and dominated relations of power and authority between the sexes and among various age groups, including dominance of senior over junior men.[6] Until the 1980s, this ideology was dominant and had powerful consequences for the division of rights and responsibilities at home and in the community. Men's privilege and women's subordination were (and continue to be) linked to cattle-based bridewealth payments and the locality (usually patrilocal)[7] where girls as married women entered the territory of the men and their families. By giving birth, women secured rights in property and long-term autonomy from their husbands. Through bridewealth, men gained entitlements

[3] Henrietta Moore, *Space, Text, and Gender An Anthropological Study of the Marakwet of Kenya* (New York, 1996), p. 65.
[4] Deniz Kandiyoti, 'Bargaining with Patriarchy', *Gender and Society*, 1988, Vol. 2, pp. 274–90.
[5] Naila Kabeer, *Reversed Realities: Gender Hierarchies in Development Thought* (London, 1994), p. 127.
[6] Sharon E. Hutchinson, *Nuer Dilemmas.*
[7] See McKinnon (2000) for further discussion.

over their wives' sexuality, productive and reproductive labour and secured paternity rights over their children. Only through their reproductive powers and some access to economic activity, are women able to exercise some autonomy. By having their own garden, women produce their own food in addition to providing labour for large plots owned by their husbands. Thus, women's overt resistance to male domination through economic autonomy decreases their vulnerability to male power.[8]

As Hutchinson shows, although the cattle-over-blood paradigm was still in place in the early 1980s, it was being rapidly undermined by the emergence of new categories such as cattle-of-money and money-of-work. In this way, the ability of the senior men to maintain power through control over cattle wealth was being reduced.[9] With the emergence of money and alternative ways of acquiring wealth through paid work, youth was gaining greater control over their lives in terms of decision-making. Wars and displacement brought new challenges to the gender ideology underlying Nuer household relations. Return to southern Sudan meant a confrontation between diverse rights discourses.

This confrontation was also an integral part of the gendered emplacement process, or, as Laura Hammond argues, 'the interworking of place, identity, and practice in such a way as to generate a relations of belonging between person and place'.[10] In particular, the processes of gendered emplacement were linked to the emerging landscape of community's self-conception. I follow Hammond's definition of 'landscape' to refer to 'the collection of meanings associated with the place that are produced through both interaction with that place in everyday practice and reflection on that place through imagination, visualization, narration, performance, and even policy formulation'.[11] I find Carolyn Nordstrom's citation of Michael Watts (1992) useful, whereby 'Landscapes are ways of seeing – seeing not only outward to culturally constructed realities, but inward to ideas and ideals of self and identity.'[12] In what follows, I analyse the gendered notions and experiences of landscapes and emphasise the diversity and the uniqueness of these experiences as perceived by returnee women and men. Gendered emplacement in this context is best understood as an ongoing process of creating and reconfiguring the web of social norms and relations that constitute a community and finding one's own place within a place.

Becoming *wur nuära pany*

Tut, a young returnee man from Kakuma, told me of the experiences of a young returnee man who had been absent from Lɛr for twenty years:

[8] Kandiyoti, 'Bargaining with Patriarchy', pp. 275–8.
[9] Hutchinson, *Nuer Dilemmas*, pp. 203–4.
[10] Laura Hammond, *This Place will become Home*, p. 83.
[11] Ibid., p. 82.
[12] Carolyn Nordstrom, *Girls and Warzones: Troubling Questions* (Uppsala, 1997) p. 179.

[He came] from Kakuma with his diplomas and wanted to marry a village girl. When he went to a *buul* [dance], he didn't know how to use a spear and how to dance. The village girls were making fun of him that he was really still *dhool* and that he should not be flirting with them. When he approached one of them and asked her to marry him, she rejected him because he did not have *gaar*. The man was so desperate that he got *gaar* in order to marry the girl. We, the returnee men, despite our years and education, are perceived as boys or as women here.

This narrative reflects the dilemmas of those young men returning to their *cieng* after years of absence whom stayees often referred to as *dholi* (boys). Due to their lack of *gaar* and their inability to use *mut* (a spear) and take part in *buul*, they were ridiculed by local girls and young men as not being fully men. Although this attitude was more common in rural areas, young returnee men often felt that their war-time migration and Kakuma routes to manhood were not fully recognised by stayees. Although their participation in military struggle was praised, especially by government and army officials, it was less impressive for prospective marriage partners. Education did not guarantee entrance to full adulthood, especially in the eyes of those residing in rural areas.

In the mid-1990s Jany's father, who was the son of a local politician, transferred his family from Khartoum to Kenya to access better education and security. Jany grew up in Nairobi and Kitale, attending Kenyan boarding schools and receiving a diploma in social development. He came back to Bentiu in 2006 and explained, in fluent English, that:

When I first came I did not understand these people. I never really lived here and I did not know *cieng nuära*, although I am a Nuer. But by being here and observing, I have learned slowly. As a returnee, you bring a different culture with you. In order to be accepted, you have to learn the culture and behaviour of those who are here. Otherwise, you will be lonely and isolated.

There are certain things that I still find weird, like, for example, the need to greet people every time you see them, even though you have greeted them a few minutes earlier. Also the dressing style. Here, men wear a t-shirt under their shirts. When I tell them that this is far too hot and that it is not practical, they see me as someone who is dressing badly. So you have to adapt if you want to have friends here. I am slowly forgetting Kenya and the culture of Kenya. It is becoming blurred now.

I haven't married yet, because I do not like the way people marry here. Also, I do not understand it. I can't marry someone whom I have seen on the street and whom I don't know. But this is what people do here. They see a girl on the street, they admire her appearance and then they ask her to marry them. If I do not know the girl and her behaviour, how can I marry her?

When you come back here, your father tells you how you should treat your wife. He tells you that you have to beat your wife and you should not even be talking to her, because she is really not there to be with you. She is there to produce children and to serve your family. When your father tells you these things repeatedly, you slowly change the attitude towards women. I have seen some of my friends who were also in Kenya and got educated; they are marrying local girls and then beating them, even when they are pregnant. When I asked one of them why he was beating his wife, he told me that she had made mistakes and that she needs to be punished. If you do not beat the wife, she will not respect you and not serve you well. This is also one of the reasons why I have not married yet.

I have to first learn this culture and then I can marry. I am still not full of this culture. In Kakuma, people were free and they did what they wanted to do. They were not controlled by their families and relatives, because they were not there. I have been slowly adapting to this culture. I have been slowly learning this place. But you have to behave the way the people are behaving here, because if you are different no one will respect you.

Jany's narrative illustrates the dilemmas of cultural adjustment for youth and the gendered and social aspects of emplacement, learning local social relations and (re)gaining a Nuer identity by meeting expectations associated with being a respectable Nuer man. For Kuem, wearing *tuac* and learning how to use a spear were steps towards becoming a real Nuer man during the wedding ceremony. Becoming *wur nuära pany* meant learning Nuer manners, dress codes, attitudes towards elders and women and how to treat their wives. The process of social emplacement also implied a change in gender ideologies, especially views on the treatment of women, from those learned in exile, in Kakuma, to those accepted and valued in *cieng nuära*, in Lɛr. The confrontation between 'modern' Nuer masculinities and the militarised and *cieng nuära* forms resulted in reshaping concepts of masculinity. Jany and other young men constructed their landscape through everyday reshaping and practice expressed through gendered selves.

Kim, one of the 'lost boys', got a job with the UN in Bentiu. He complained about post-return family pressures:

> As a Nuer, you cannot refuse to support [the family]. If you refuse, others will see you as a selfish person and they will abuse you and tell you 'you are bad'. You cannot lose the support of your community, and the pressure to assist all is huge. Everybody wants support but no one is willing to work. Also, when you give them something, no one tells you 'thank you'. Next day people come back and ask for more and you never see the result of your support. They just eat the money. It is not easy to balance the expectations of the community and one's own position. People here think that if you work for one of the UN agencies you have a lot of money. They do not understand that money is earned by working hard. They think it just comes like this. When they are lying on their beds and sleeping, I have to run around and sweat a lot in order to earn money. The people here have no concept of hard work. [...] Here in Nuerland, it is very difficult to be rich. If you have something, you have to share with all. Especially as the oldest son, you have a responsibility [to support family members]. The social pressure is very strong, and this is the reason that some Nuer do not come back. I have been here for over a year now, but it is very difficult to live here among the people.

One of Kim's friends from Kakuma, a 28-year old 'lost boy', added:

> When I came back home after 17 years of not seeing my parents, I experienced several culture clashes. First, they wanted to marry a wife for me. Second, when I chose a girl from Eastern Nuerland my family rejected her because she was from a different tribe. This was a shock to me, because in Kakuma we were all mixed, from all tribes and all nationalities. The third cultural clash was the support that my family expected from me. [It] was difficult to understand for the family that I am unable to support all but finally they accepted. We are different I have spent years outside and have learned different culture. Now it is difficult for me to be here. I am like a stranger. I have to learn my place again.

Settling-in involved movement from a multi-ethnic and multi-national place to one that was homogenous, albeit differentiated by diverse experiences due to war and displacement. It also required a re-evaluation of the Kakuma gender equality ideas to which young men had been exposed in Kenya. While the principle of exogamy in marriages was still maintained (marrying a fellow clan member was forbidden, as it was considered incestuous), marrying with other ethnic groups, tribes or *cieng* was not allowed by elders. This was a continuation of hardening of ethnic identities observed during the war and based on ethnicised violence. In Kakuma, due to limited potential marriage partners, inter-tribe or inter-*cieng* marriages were common, whereas in Lɛr, settling-in demanded following *cieng nuära* rules (although often redefined) to be accepted as a fully respectable member of society, because otherwise they were seen as 'bed children'.

The personal aspirations of returnee young men often clashed with those of their stay-put relatives. They were expected to take on the roles of elders and be responsible for family wellbeing, thus experiencing a shift from Kakuma's freedom from Nuer male social obligations to subjection to household responsibilities and controls in Nuerland. This was part of becoming a Nuer adult man. For young me, the process of emplacing oneself did not only indicate a passage to manhood but also challenged previously learned and practiced concepts of alternative masculinities. 'To become a real Nuer man' was linked to the (re)casting of identity politics and (re)interpreting old and new norms of the Nuer landscape of communal and personal identity.

Their modern, more self-oriented, views on life acquired in Kakuma were challenged by the communitarian basis of Nuer manhood. To pass the test of full manhood, returnee youth needed to meet the obligations of supporting the family. They often felt overwhelmed by these expectations and felt exploited, misunderstood and lonely. Although family networks act as a buffer against socioeconomic uncertainty, being a source of solidarity and security, they can also bring about inequalities by exercising pressure to conform to gender and generational household obligations. Amid the changes brought about in Kakuma and post-return economic hardship, family ties were being challenged by the strengthening of the returnees' individual choices that were incompatible with previous household norms. In other words, individual choices resulted from different war-time trajectories, whereby displaced individuals embrace multiple cultural reference, thus revealing strong, individual aspirations quite different to those who had stayed behind.

Being a respectable Nuer man also required constraining relations with girls. Wanten explained:

> [In Kakuma] we used to do a lot of things together. Here, it is more difficult to meet girls. If you want to do it, you have to do it in secret, so that her parents don't know. If they see you with her, they will think you want to marry her. Here, boys and girls are not supposed to be seen together in the same places unless they are related.

In Nuerland, gender segregation of spaces is much stricter than in Kakuma. This is particularly the case when young girls and men reach marriageable age, as they are not supposed to interact with each other.

For some returnee men, life in Lɛr was a challenge to the gender division of labour that they had practiced in Kakuma. Gatmai had spent ten years away seeking refuge and education in Khartoum, Ethiopia, Kenya and Uganda and now, aged twenty-eight, was faced with a post-return challenge:

> The people who stayed here see us as women, because we do not do the work of the men. We do not know how to build a house, we do not take care of the cattle, and we have no cattle, in fact. Also, we do not know how to do things that they [the men in the village] do. We do not know how to fight. We used to know how to fight with spears, but now we have forgotten it. They make fun of us and say that the work that we are doing here is not real work. That we are like women.

Those who left Sudan as very young children and grew up in exile tried to continue carrying out domestic tasks after return. They were seen as 'women' and often challenged by men as well as women. Nyalada, Kouk's aunt, who had stayed in Lɛr told him, 'This is our task and our responsibility. As a man, you cannot do it or otherwise people will think badly about us, the women.'

This is an example of how change is often resisted and how gender equality seen as an aberration of 'appropriate gender behaviour' and a transgression of gender spaces that is often challenged by women. It demonstrates the dilemmas of young returnee men trying to live new selves in a context where new (greater gender equality) is not valued. Here, the processes of social emplacement resulted in a confrontation of diverse gender ideologies, gender identities and norms. For returnees and stayees to construct a common and shared landscape of social relations and norms they needed to (re)evaluate their and competing diverse (gendered) values. While those men and women who were displaced to Kakuma learned about gender equality and women's rights, those who had stayed behind perceived such rhetoric as threatening to what they believed were the core social principles of *cieng nuära*. To become part of the community, and hence emplaced and settled in, some young men felt obliged to shed their Kakuma-acquired views.

For the stayees, women and men, gender equality and new labour gender divisions represented unfamiliar discourses. Some (stayee) women and girls actively maintained male prestige and dominance by not allowing men to perform female-inscribed duties. 'Being like a woman' meant loss of prestige for men. For their sisters and wives, especially those who had stayed behind, men taking over female domestic tasks threatened to diminish their own social standing. This corresponds with the observation put forward by Sherry Ortner and Harriet Whitehead that 'the sphere of social activity predominantly associated with males encompasses the spheres predominantly associated with females and is, for that reason, culturally accorded higher value'.[13] For some Nuer women and men, this is usually represented in the division of gendered spaces within the household, where the kitchen is reserved for women

[13] Sherry Ortner and Harriet Whitehead, *Sexual Meanings: The Cultural Construction of Gender and Sexuality* (Cambridge, 1981), p. 8.

and the courtyard men's meeting and decision-making place. Contestations over this gendered division of space between stayees and returnees meant (re)interpreting and forging the landscape of social norms and interactions that defined the community.

'Being different, isolated', 'feeling like a stranger' and 'not fitting culturally' were terms young men often used to describe their initial feeling of homecoming. However, through settling-in and learning the place, young men were slowly re-evaluating their views on manhood and masculinity, and partially conforming to the local social relations. A few decided to follow local customs and took part in local spear-fighting. Others, including Kuem, married local girls to gain prestige and local roots. Some adjusted the clothes they wore, and their manners and attitudes towards young women by showing dominance through beating them and imposing burdensome domestic chores. Kuok commented on the changed behaviour of some of his male friends from Kakuma:

> We, the Nuer, we cheat women. When we are away from home, we cook and do all the domestic work. But when the women are around, we make them do all the work and we say it is shameful for us as men to enter the kitchen.

Some men decided to conceal their ongoing domestic work to ridicule. Others, despite their initial vowed commitment to monogamous marriages and Kakuma gender-equality, decided to take second wives. In 2010, when I learned that Nyal, a 'lost boy' working for an NGO in Lɛr, had married for the second time, I inquired what happened to his gender equality beliefs. He told me: 'Oh that, I left it with LWF in Kakuma'.

Those men who were in Kakuma for only a short time defied the ideals of human rights and gender equality promoted by the international organisations. Most of them felt happy to be back in Nuerland. They gladly abandoned the 'female' domestic tasks which the lack of sisters and mothers had necessitated in the camp. Likewise, for older married men, settling-in and emplacement implied re-gaining their masculinity and manhood, which had been severely undermined by food aid in Kakuma. Dak, a father of two, described his experience of returning to Lɛr after an absence of six years:

> Before I went to Kakuma, I was a leader [*kuäar*]: I was a soldier, had my land and my wife and was able to assist them. In Kakuma, I became like a child, in need of constant assistance from the UN. When peace came to Sudan, I decided to come back, because I needed to [re]establish myself. In Kenya, you are in a foreign land and you have no rights. Here, you are at home, *nyuuri piny*. The process of establishing yourself takes along time, but you will be the one in charge of feeding your children. It is not only building your house, it is about your whole life. It is about control over your environment, becoming a real Nuer man again, independent and in control of your future.

Being in control over the household and resources, being self-sufficient and able to provide for a family were important steps in regaining manhood for those men who felt emasculated due to wars and displacement. In a sense, although experienced through continuous struggle and effort to piece together a livelihood, return was for most men marked by strengthening their former position. Dak's brother, Jal, also a returnee from Kakuma, like a few other returnees took a second (local) wife. This was a sign of prestige and 'being a real Nuer man', as he argued: 'When you have many wives and children, you are considered a strong man [*wur bume*]. We, the Nuer, need many wives to have many children [so that] we can be famous'. Again, part of 'being a real Nuer man' meant exercising power over women and their children. I witnessed several cases of returnee men becoming more abusive towards their wives, often beating them and forcing them to do more domestic work, thus re-creating their war- and displacement-thwarted masculinities.

What emerges from the different emplacement strategies and experiences of the returnee men is a certain degree of dissonance. They also show that the practice of gender identities and relations is contingent on a place, a locale. While new modern masculinities were valued and practiced (even if in a limited manner) in Kakuma, post-return emplacement in Lɛr required the (re)evaluation of these identities and norms. This finding reveals that changing gender relations and identities and women's empowerment are not linear processes. The different pressures that places poses for women and men show that the cultural milieu in which gender identities and relations are practiced and negotiated are relevant to how they are shaped. While a move towards greater gender equality is possible in one place, the move to a cultural setting characterised by significant gender discrepancies does not guarantee that more equal gender identities and relations will be immediately transplanted.

Becoming *nyal and ciek nuära*

Gladys, a 17-year old daughter of a local commander, spent fifteen years in Kenya and came back to Lɛr in April 2006. When I ran into her at a water pump, she recounted her initial feelings about life in Nuerland:

> When I arrived in Lɛr, I thought I would not survive here. Most of my life, I spent in Kenya and didn't know the life in the village. I didn't know how people were behaving and what I was supposed to do as a girl. I spent all my life in schools and had no idea about the responsibilities of a Nuer girl. At the beginning I refused to do anything, but then I realised that I could only survive if I learned the life of the village. I slowly learned how to carry water on my head; look at me, I am a professional now! I learned how to make traditional foods such as *walwal, kisra, akop*; how to grind sorghum on a stone and how to serve people. At first, I didn't even enjoy the local food, I didn't like the taste. I missed *chapatti*.[14] After a while I adjusted and now my life has become much better. The one problem that I had was lack of job. I had nothing to do apart from the work at home, because despite being an educated girl it is difficult to find work here. People don't want you to work outside the house. There is no freedom for girls here, and girls are valued only when they are married and bring bridewealth.

For long-displaced girls, coming home to Nuerland was a fundamental challenge. They had to learn to (re)negotiate their greater space and freedoms gained in displacement. The process of 'learning to be a *nyal nuära*'

---

[14] An Indian flatbread made in Kenya of corn rather than wheat.

required doing what the locals do and becoming acquainted with local customs, obligations and the responsibilities considered female in *cieng nuära*. Young women between the ages of fourteen and twenty who were born in exile or had spent most of their lives displaced found it hard to settle-in. Like Gladys and my other female friends from Kakuma, they were perceived and saw themselves as different: most were educated, single and more open in their behaviour and attitudes than those who had stayed behind. Within Nuer gender ideology, girls are conceptualised differently within the space of home and household, with specific obligations, limited freedoms and socialised subordination to male relatives. For displaced girls, homecoming meant confrontation with strict interpretations of what constitutes 'good, obedient and respectable' behaviour for Nuer girls and having to reshape Kakuma-acquired concepts of femininities.

Returnee girls' contestations of their social status were reflected in speech, dress codes, social interactions and particular mobilities. Returnee girls, especially those from East Africa, were visible on the dirt roads of Lɛr. Wearing tight trousers or mini-skirts and colourful hair extensions, they played sports with boys and young men, conversed freely with their male friends, moved around the village and often travelled far by themselves (see Photo 6.2). They also had little idea about such Nuer girls' duties as milking and grinding sorghum, having received pre-ground flour from the UN in Kakuma. Returnee girls also stood out as the only female students still in higher primary education, with most local girls having never enrolled or subsequently dropping out to marry. They were bringing new ideas of change, some of which were not appreciated. The behaviour of returnee girls and young women was usually frowned upon, especially by local women. My host, who had stayed most of her life in Lɛr, told me:

> Look at Nyariek, she thinks she is a man. She is not behaving like a good girl. She roams loose, wears bad clothes and talks with men. My daughter, Nyamuc, she is a good girl. She stays at home, does the [domestic] work, does not go out unless to fetch water or charcoal and does not socialise with boys. She shows *pöc*. These Kakuma girls are bad [*jiäke*]!

Comments about the inappropriate behaviour of Kakuma girls were commonplace in daily conversations. These girls were introducing a threatening foreign culture and, as 'loose' girls, bringing shame on their families. Returnee girls were ostracised and looked down on with disdain by the majority of stayees. In her study among northern Sudanese communities in Cairo, Anita Fábos used the concept of propriety, *adab*, to describe the moral stances and attitudes among Sudanese migrants.[15] For them to be a real Sudanese meant to subscribe to certain moral, ethical and aesthetic values, to have *adab*. In Lɛr, to have *pöc* was linked to acquisition of a good reputation through being shy, showing respect and not straying far from domestic space.

[15] Anita H. Fábos, *'Brothers' or Other? Propriety and Gender for Muslim Arab Sudanese in Egypt* (Oxford, 2008).

6.2 'New' Nuer young women, Lɛr, 2007 (© Katarzyna Grabska)

The moral panic described in Chapter 1 led to police banning mini-skirts and trousers. The Lɛr police commissioner outlawed them and called on women to behave 'morally'. Sermons in both Catholic and Presbyterian churches were punctuated by references to 'bad behaviour'. It was common to see local men and women disparagingly flicking returnee women's clothing. For those who had been displaced to Khartoum, dress styles were influenced by Arab standards.[16] Such women wore modest Arab garments (a long skirt and a shirt) with a full-length *tob* overdress, another sign of the conflicting norms under contestation in South Sudanese nation-building.

Dorothy Hodgson and Sherry McCurdy show how women and girls are labelled 'bad' or 'loose' because 'they disrupt the web of social relations that define and depend on them as daughters, sisters, wives, mothers, and lovers'.[17] As with the Tutsi and Ha women studied by Margaret Lovett in western Tanzania, Nuer girls and women 'learned that their subordination was a life-long condition'.[18] The labelling as 'good' of stayee girls who conform to respecting the authority of their fathers, then later their husbands and sons, and who did not visibly challenge prevailing gender norms, maintained existing gender hierarchies and created new inequalities. By contrast, returnee girls with their 'loose' manners were seen as 'bad'. Stayee girls demonstrated respect by carrying out domestic duties, not speaking back to men, agreeing to marriages arranged by their fathers

[16] Rogaia Abusharaf, *Transforming Displaced Women in Sudan* (Chicago, IL, 2009).
[17] Dorothy L. Hodgson and Sherry McCurdy, *'Wicked' Women and the Reconfiguration of Gender in Africa*, (Portsmouth, NH; Oxford; Cape Town, 2001), p. 6.
[18] Margaret Lovett 'She Thinks She's Like a Man': Marriage and (De)constructing Gender Identity in Colonial Buha, Western Tanzania, 1943–1960", in Hodgson and McCurdy (2001) p. 53.

(and mothers) and going out for no reason. Returnee girls like Nyariek go against the hegemonic configuration of gender, 'the norms of "appropriate" gender roles, relations, responsibilities, and behaviour'.[19] Passed on through internalisation and socialisation, bestowed through references to *cieng nuära* and tradition, these gendered norms become sources and thresholds of local moral and social orders. As in other communities, women and girls were seen as bearers of national or community culture.[20] When Nuer adolescent girls overstep these gendered boundaries, they threaten the community's moral foundations, a keen threat to those men and (mostly stayee) women who have much to lose from changing norms.

However, the constraints facing returnee adolescent girls were acknowledged by some male relatives and other returnee men. Amaring, a brother of NyaSunday, expressed his concerns:

> Girls here have no rights and no freedom. They are punished for wearing trousers and mini-skirts, not allowed to play sports and don't go to school. Their only right here is to get married and do domestic work. They are very tired, as they are overworked. It is hard for my sister and others like her who were in Kenya. They are not used to this.

This comment also points out to the generational differences in the experiences and aspirations of returnees and stayees.

Some of the stayee girls and women also expressed their grievances and emphasised the difficulties for younger generations to adjust to life in Lɛr. As a woman chief in Lɛr stressed, 'these girls from Kakuma suffer the most. In Kenya they had more opportunities and they were more respected. Here, they do the most work at home and have no voice'. Despite the professed dedication of the South Sudanese authorities to gender equality and equal legal rights, in the local courts, girls could not speak for themselves. During a court session in Lɛr I witnessed a male chief blocking a returnee girl from expressing her views in a divorce case: 'You are a girl, you have no right to talk here. It is your father who will decide. Girls have no brains'. This was one of the many salutary reminders for 'Kakuma girls', as they were often referred to, that in Nuerland their social status was different. Caught between different gender ideologies, yet being aware of their legal rights, required painful re-adjustment to an inferior gender status.

Nyakuol, for example, complained that:

> Here in Lɛr, life for women is different; there is no 'human rights'. When you disagree with your husband, he will just beat you, and even if you complain to the court or the police, they will laugh at you. Your neighbour, Nyamuc, complained about her cousin beating her, and the police wanted to put *her* in jail. These people here are still [backwards]. They have no idea how to treat women. They say they give us 25% [of representation], but in fact, they are the ones who always talk in meetings. There are no [or almost no] women in the Lɛr administration, and the

---

[19] Hodgson and McCurdy, *'Wicked' Women*, p. 6.
[20] See Nira Yuval-Davis, Gender and Nation (London, 1997) and J. Schrijvers, 'Fighters, Victims and Survivors: Constructions of Ethnicity, Gender and Refugeeness among Tamils in Sri Lanka', *Journal of Refugee Studies*, Vol. 12, no. 3, pp. 307–33, 1999.

ones that are there are wives of commanders and big people. When they give a woman a job, they just want you to do domestic work, like serving food, cooking, washing and sweeping [the] compound. The life for us women here is more difficult, because we learned in Kakuma that as humans we have rights and we are equal, but here the women are still behind. For the girls it is hard, because they were free in Kakuma to attend school, to participate in the community, but here they are just expected to cook and do the domestic chores.

This shows that women displaced to Kakuma are acutely aware of their subordination, experiencing return and settling-in as a loss of freedom and rights. They often reminisced about their lives in Kakuma, their schooling, the freedom to move around and interact with other girls and boys and the reduced domestic obligations, as they had them shared with their brothers and other male relatives. 'In Kakuma, our brothers used to cook and help us with domestic work. But here, they say that they are men, and they cannot go to the kitchen,' commented Gladys. Adolescent girls and young women also enjoyed greater freedoms in choosing boyfriends and husbands. *Beben cieng* to Nuerland meant entering stricter community and family obligations that undermined privileges and freedoms acquired in Kakuma. This points to the fact that social change is not a linear process, but is instead fluid, contradictory, complex and time- and space-dependent.

These processes are negotiated between differently positioned actors whose agendas do not always tally with gender or age. The characteristics of womanhood acquired in Kakuma were (re)negotiated during contact with women and men who had stayed behind or been displaced to Khartoum. Similar to the experiences of settling in by young returnee men, the process of adjustment and confrontation of different (gender) values held by returnee women and girls from those of stayees demonstrates that gender identities and relations are shaped and reshaped within a place. The production of gendered locality implied (re)negotiation, adaptation and contestation of gender norms, identities and self in the context of confronting a diversification of gender identities resulting from diverse experiences of war and displacement. The social, economic and political context of these negotiations was crucial in determining the durability of social change. Although 'running to the UN' was no longer available to them in Lɛr, women's small yet active contestation of norms set gender relations in flux. Thus, the formation of gendered communities in the process of emplacement offers an opportunity to (re)define the landscape of social and gender relations of *cieng nuära*. This was also visible in the changing practices of the marriage process.

SETTLING-IN AND MARRIAGE

By March, when the rains started arriving in Lɛr, and when cattle and youth returned from cattle camp, life concentrated around *cieng. Tot*, the rainy season, is a time for new marriages to be negotiated and for wedding dances. Marriage is on everybody's mind, with bridewealth negotiations taking place in *luak*, 'reserving' their future wives by paying some cows for them, or taking girls home to the husbands' households. Every night, I heard and saw dancing and singing crowds late into the night. I was repeatedly invited to celebrations as talk about marriages intensified among returnee young women and men. The latter were especially eager to build their own home. In the words of Evans-Pritchard, a (Nuer) man '[...] cannot have a home without a wife'.[21] This reflected the feelings of many young Kakuma men, who defined *nyuuri piny* as a long-term settling-in process. About this, Kuok said:

> You need to first find your relatives, then you need to have a job, build your own house, and then [you] need to have cows and need to marry. This is when you will be established and settled.

The majority of single men and women who participated in the socio-economic survey described in Chapter 5 identified the settling-in process with the initiation of marriage, full passage to adulthood and then establishing a household. Marriages and starting one's own household were linked to the (re)creation of social networks and forging of community bonds that were integral parts of making and finding one's place after return.

Hutchinson argues that marriage, for the Nuer, as in many societies, is 'less a state of being than an extended process subject to competing interpretations and manipulations'.[22] As mentioned earlier, it is a pivotal institution that determines gender ideology based on the cattle-over-blood complex and regulates male dominance over women. It is also an institution that controls kinship relations, the handling of resources and inter-generational power structures. The different stages of marriage and the transfer of cattle-based bridewealth payments progressively expand husbands' rights over their wives and children. They also maintain the kinship-based management and transfer of resources, with kin contributing to the bridewealth payments and so building *cieng* alliances.

Young Men: marriage, choice and brides

'You can only be a *"kuäar"* if you have a wife and children and you are responsible for them. This is when you will be respected and given a position in the community,' argued my male friends. For young returnee men unable to get married in Kakuma,[23] marriage was an important element of passage to manhood, forging community bonds and enabling them to find their own place within it. Most of those who arrived in Nuerland before 2006 were already married or in the process of doing so when I settled in Lεr. Those who arrived during my stay were 'running after

---

[21] Edward E. Evans-Pritchard, *Kinship and Marriage among the Nuer* (Oxford, 1951) pp. 92–3.
[22] Hutchinson, 'Rising Divorce among the Nuer', p. 393.
[23] These reasons included lack of resources – relatives and cattle – as well as high bridewealth, limited number of marriageable girls and high competition with those young men resettled in the west. See also Katarzyna Grabska, 'Lost Boys, Invisible Girls'.

cows' in order to initiate marriage. The metaphor of 'running after cows' represents the efforts of prospective grooms to accumulate bridewealth. Since cattle-based marriages remained the rule in Western Upper Nile, young men had to mobilise the support of family and kin (and other social networks) to secure bridewealth. Despite the increased monetisation of the Nuer economy, and some returnees having salaried jobs, cattle remained the primary method of payment. 'Marriage with money is not a marriage. Those who married with money in Khartoum, Kakuma and America will have to come here to marry with cows. Only when women have cows on their back, the marriage is legal,' said Kuong, Lɛr's chief.

Cattle-based bridewealth was the means of maintaining some of the norms that defined Nuer social identities vis-à-vis transforming post-war landscape of community's gender relations. Young men in formal employment often saved their monthly salaries and bought cattle in Lɛr. Cattle-of-money rather than cattle-of-blood was becoming dominant, a continuum of a change noticed by Hutchinson in the 1980s among the Western Leek Nuer.[24] The ritual significance of cattle acquired through bridewealth rather than money was diminishing. As one Lɛr elder put it, 'Cows are cows [*yang e yang*]. They have the same significance whether you got them through your work or through marriage'.

Marriage was being contracted by returnee young men for three main reasons. Some were finalising a process initiated in Kakuma; others were getting married under pressure in order to fulfil family obligations; and some were eager to establish their own homes. 'Running after cows' often resulted in conflicts with relatives who had stayed behind. As discussed in Chapter 5, returnees were in need of land and cattle in order to establish themselves, as many of them had lost everything during displacement. Their return home, however, put pressure on the war-impoverished households of stayees. Jial one of Kuok's friends in Ethiopia and Kenya, shared his sorrows:

> I was away for nineteen years and I had no contact with my family who stayed in Sudan. When I came back in 2006, I learned that my father was dead and that he used all the cows [for his second marriage]. There was no property left; the land was taken by the government. Now, I am sitting on my cousin's land; and even my brothers could not get married due to lack of cattle. I had to start from zero. I will only be able to marry once I get some cows through my job.

Those who came back to Lɛr and were unable to find relatives and retrieve property felt unsettled often referred to themselves as returnees, unable to start preparing for marriage.

Yak, who spent twelve years in Kakuma came to Bentiu through UNHCR repatriation after finishing secondary school. He had left his wife and eight month-old baby in Nairobi:

> The reason for coming here is to finish the marriage process. In Kakuma, Angelina and I had a relationship, and when her brothers found out that she was pregnant, they imprisoned me. I told the [Nuer] court [in Kakuma] that I wanted to marry Angelina, but that I had no money or cattle in Kakuma. After many nego-

---

[24] Hutchinson, *Nuer Dilemmas*.

tiations with Angelina's father [who remained in Nuerland] over the radio call, they agreed to give me Angelina under the promise that I will pay the full bridewealth when I come to Sudan. Now, the first step is to meet with my father and to negotiate the cows with the father of Angelina. I will also have to get a job so I can buy some cattle and give them to my in-laws.

Due to the lack of *diel* (the descendants of the original settlers of a tribal territory, or as Evans-Pritchard referred to them, 'aristocrats'), relatives and the physical distance from 'home' in Nuerland, as well as lack of cattle and the general impoverishment of refugees, official marriages with the full payment of bridewealth were rare in Kakuma. Most camp marriages were contracted against pledges to repay on return to Nuerland. A similar trend was identified by Christiane Falge among Nuer refugees in Punyido camp in Ethiopia.[25] Although the transfer of some money to the relatives in the camp was usually necessary, this was seen more as a gift for the bride's mother *(pöth)*. This payment did not have to be returned to the family in case of failure to finalise the marriage or divorce. Bridewealth payment was still to be completed in cattle at home in Nuerland, in addition to any money transfers in Kakuma. Thus, for many young men who had relationships in Kakuma and initiated marriages, usually through 'illegal' ways – impregnating girls or taking them without a payment of bridewealth (i.e. 'stealing') – homecoming meant an obligation to repay the loan, i.e. taking the girl with only a small payment or none at all. This was a significant burden for impoverished returnees lacking physical capital. For Yak and other young men this obligation complicated and prolonged settling-in. Since his family wealth had been scattered by war, he desperately looked for a well-paid job and then saved from his salary to acquire cattle rather than invest in land or a house. Most such young men struggled to find resources to complete their marriages and, through lack of cows, some were forced to abandon their previous girlfriends.

Others experienced family pressures to marry upon their return. Kuok explained these generational clashes and dilemmas:

If you are the oldest son, when you come back and reunite with the family, the family wants to marry you off. Young men become the responsible ones and are told that if they want to be seen as serious in the community they have to marry. Some might not accept it; maybe they have changed their attitude towards marriage. They know that they need to have a job in order to secure the future of the wife and children so that they live a good life and have something to eat. But the parents usually do not care about it. These men also might consider further education, and if they get married this will prevent them from going away again.

For young men, *beben cieng* meant meeting family responsibilities and becoming part of the wider *thok duël* and *cieng* network of *cuong* and obligations. While re-establishing *diel* networks was not always possible due to death and dispersal, there was a certain degree of re-imagining and re-interpreting such relations in order to be able to initiate marriage and feel settled. Returnee young men looked for ways to attach themselves to

[25] Christiane Falge, 'The Nuer as Refugees: A Study on Social Adaptation', MA thesis, Addis Ababa University, 1997.

those with whom they established new relations of trust based on shared experience during war and in displacement. Thus, there was a certain redefinition of *diel* and thereby the basis for lineage and power position within that lineage that was taking place.

Those who did find their *thok duël* and *cieng* members often found themselves faced with a dilemma: although they wanted to continue education to be able to better establish themselves, their families expected them to marry if they were the eldest sons.[26] Marriage was another essential part of forging community bonds and the personal place-making process, sometimes at the expense of one's personal aspirations.

Inter-generational tensions also arose around the choice of the brides. On his return to Lɛr in 2006, Kim, a 'lost boy' absent for twenty years, found himself trapped between the desire to be independent and to be part of the family:

> When I came back, my father, who is an old man, told me that now it is time to marry. I still had my plans of pursuing my education and also I had my girlfriend in Kakuma. We met in school and used to study together. She then got resettled to Australia and is now at the university. We promised to marry each other. But when I came to Lɛr, my parents wanted me to marry a local girl. They need a local girl to understand each other. They don't want a town girl who is educated and who might not obey them. I insisted at the beginning that I marry a girl of my choice, and was thinking about my girlfriend. But now I am in a process of marrying a local wife. I don't know her, she is not educated, but my people told me that I will get to love her.
>
> They say in our culture, that the first wife is the family wife. She is married by the family – she becomes the wife of our family, *ciek ciengdan*, because the whole family makes cattle contribution towards bridewealth. This means that she belongs to the family, except in bed, when she belongs only to you. She is also married for your mother, to assist her in the house. I decided to marry the first wife for my mother, and the second one, I will marry from my resources and she will be *my wife*. If my girlfriend in Australia agrees, she will be my second wife.

Kim's narrative reveals the competing values held by returnee young men and their stayee families with regards to concepts of masculinities, parent–son relations and marriage. His concerns also demonstrate the cementing sources of power enjoyed by returning sons and their stayee families. While returnee young men, through their education, might have changed their position of power vis-à-vis their elders, families' control over resources influences young men's preferences. Reliance on family to meet bridewealth obligations has constrained young men in their choice of bride. Nuer men, as polygamists, assign different responsibilities to different wives. Usually, the role of the first wife is to assist the husband's aging parents. Upon arriving home a number of returnee married men coming from Khartoum, East Africa, but also from the USA or Australia, were subject to parental pressure to take a local, second wife.

[26] Marriage among brothers is sequenced according to cattle rights determined by age. Cattle gained from the marriage of sisters is used by their brothers to marry wives and replenish the female reproductive potential of *cieng* due to the departure of their sisters to other households. The younger brothers have to wait their turn until elder brothers are married.

Even those with university degrees and/or positions with international organisations or the Government of Southern Sudan were faced such expectations. An American Nuer male parliamentarian in Juba told me: 'Our Nuer culture is very strong, and we cannot go against it'. Despite the shifting landscape of social and gender relations, settling-in was at times used as a justification for (re)establishing the pre-war status quo.

Conforming to *cieng nuära* customs often clashed with the aspirations of young modern Kakuma-educated men. Tensions around marriage were due to the different experiences of family members during conflict and changed aspirations and ideas of manhood due to their upbringing in Kakuma. They were often baptised and educated whereas their parents had continued the life of *cieng nuära*. This confrontation often expressed itself through differing views on marriage and the role and position of wives. Young Kakuma men frequently valued more equal partnerships, falling in love, kissing (*ciim*), expressing emotions and marrying a girl of their own choice with similar life experiences. Their parents, however, preferred someone whom they could understand and control, typically through physical punishment.

Inter-generational tensions around marriage also related to the management of resources. The elder generation bestowed the responsibility for handling resources and kinship relations on returning sons. Through the payment of bridewealth, marriage was seen as a communal and family matter rather than a personal one. Young Kakuma men with a more individualised approach to family relations found that their families' control over their cattle obliged them to fit in. Parents insisted on marriage in order to replenish and pass on family resources. Kim's father's comment 'Our son is back and now it is time for him to marry. The cows have been waiting for him' typified, the expectations of men who had stayed behind in Lɛr. Their references to 'strong Nuer culture' and the 'inability to go against it' showed how young men were embroiled in the interplay between hegemonic structural constraints and individual agency.

Stayee–returnee (and also inter-generational within both groups) debates around marriage as an institution of social control became sites of struggle in the context of greater economic and social transformations. Through access to paid employment, young men were challenging the control of elders over marriage partners and time of marriage. Yet, although they aspired to a different life and had goals that at times contradicted those of the elders, such was the power of gender asymmetrical ideas embedded in marriage and the beguiling prospect of enhanced status as a responsible man that, in the end, they went along with what was expected of them. Despite acts of resistance and returnee assertions of a different vision of gender relations, dominant ideas of attainment of manhood through marriage resisted change. My findings reveal how change in gender relations is contingent on political, economic and social conditions, the resources available and people's personal preferences and the readiness to embrace it.

Eventually, marriage was on the mind of almost all young men. They had potentially better prospects of marrying in Nuerland due to access to family and lineage networks and their property. In addition, the choice of girls was much greater than in Kakuma and, as educated modern men having access to jobs and money, returnees were seen as desirable husbands (see below). Some of the Kakuma men decided to marry girls whom they had known or befriended in the camp. However, since bride-wealth payments for educated girls were much higher, they struggled to collect and pay for the necessary cattle. When they were unable to find enough resources, or their parents refused to grant permission for marriage, some eloped in order to force parents to agree to the marriage.

Unlike local girls, those from Kakuma girls were frequently perceived as 'unruly', 'spoilt' and 'difficult to control' because of their education and exposure to notions of gender equality. Young men often justified their decision to wed a local girl by blaming their parents. However, women, stayees and returnees alike, saw it differently. Nyajung, a returnee married woman from Kakuma, explained in Nuer:

> The educated men prefer to marry uneducated girls because it is easier to control them. Educated girl cannot be controlled by a man, because she has knowledge. She will not fear to go away and take care of children [through a job]. The man will go away from uneducated girl for good and she will be left without any support.

Women pointed to the education of girls as undermining the men's power and control over women and the fear of losing their position in the family and community. A group discussion with women and girls attending a maternity and health care education programme for midwives in Lɛr confirmed this. Women dismissed the arguments presented by returnee men that there is a lack of educated girls in Lɛr and that young men are pressured into marrying uneducated girls. One pointed out that 'if these men are educated, they could marry alone if they get a job and earn their own money. This should not be a problem'.

When one young returnee man tried to defend his position, a married stayee woman replied as follows:

> This is really a question of power and control over an uneducated girl. Educated girls are more independent and if they are abused, they will complain and run away. They know that they can have their financial independence because they are educated and can get a job. The men prefer to marry an uneducated girl because if the wife is not following their orders they can beat her and she will not complain. Men fear being under the responsibility of the woman and they will fear being controlled [financially] by an educated wife. Also, educated girls will not accept being beaten and abused by uneducated men.

These comments point to the key question of power within social structures and relations. I use here Ortner's model of 'serious games' to describe practice of social relations that embodies agency. She argues that this reflects:

> social life as [being] culturally organized and constructed, in terms of defining categories of actors, rules and goals of the games .... that social life is precisely social, consisting of webs of relationships and interaction between multiple,

shiftingly interrelated subject relations, none of which can be extracted as autonomous 'agents'; and yet at the same time there is 'agency', that is, actors play with skill, intention, wit, knowledge, intelligence.[27]

Power for Nuer women meant the ability to make decisions and their own choices in life, and to have more control over one's self. Some were highly aware of how they internalised their subordination and the ways in which they were dominated by men. However, they often acquiesced in these 'serious games' in order to benefit from them. Even so, cattle-over-blood ideology was being further eroded by the autonomous ways of acquiring wealth and the increase in 'illegal' or 'run-away' marriages to which young women and men often resorted. It was also being under-mined by girls' access to education and their expanding autonomy from men and cattle. Access to knowledge gained through education was perceived by some women as a means of improving their strategic position vis-à-vis men and other women as well as their domestic and communal bargaining positions.

When I asked elders about the old days, almost all said that cows had been more important than women, since they 'married women'. Men had been more powerful than cows as they were in charge of cows and could marry women with them. These views were still upheld among some of the stayee population. When questioned similarly, the responses of returnee women and men were very different. 'Women and men are equal now, we have something called human rights and this means that women and men are equal, because they are both human [beings]', I was told by Gatmain, a young returnee man who had spent ten years in Kenya. 'Women and men are equal in front of God. It is only the lack of knowl-edge that makes us, women, dependent on men,' commented a married woman. Education was seen as an interlocking power in gender rela-tions. However, the disadvantages for women who accessed education further deepened their subordinate position. The educational gap was a source of further subjugation used by men who resisted more balanced gender relations. As was the case in Kakuma, the church's influence in Lɛr was also strong in terms of upholding unequal gender relations. Some quoted the Bible as a source of 'male dominance'. Paul, a university-educated returnee from Uganda, said: 'In Genesis II, it is said that a woman was made out of man's rib. Hence, man is superior over woman and he is in control of her'.[28] Some educated men used their knowledge to improve their social position and gain greater power over both senior men and women. In the eyes of these men, educated girls and women were challenging the established power structures in the community and demanding a stronger and more equal position, something they found unacceptable.

[27] Sherry Ortner, *Making Gender: The Politics and Erotics of Culture* (Boston, 1996), p. 12.
[28] See also Christiana Falge, 'The Cultural Resilience in Nuer Conversation and a "Capitalist Missionary"', in Günther Schlee and Elizabeth E. Watson (eds), *Changing Identifications and Alliances in North-East Africa*, (Berghan Books, 2009), pp. 205–17.

The contradictions in the behaviour, choices and strategies adopted by returnee men reveal that gender identities, ideas and relations are often strategically chosen and shaped. This points to the importance of the context and the general political, economic and social environment in which power and gender hierarchies are defined and practiced.[29] With the changing landscape of larger structures of domination embedded in women's reproductive capabilities and in cattle-based bridewealth ideologies, some men feared losing control over women's sexuality and reproduction and thus their dominance over women. Educated women with access to independent income were perceived as being able and willing to re-define the terms of the conjugal contract, on which *cieng nuära* exchange of goods, services, labour and privileges between husbands and wives were based. The different strategies of marriage returnee young men adopted show that while some were ready to embrace more equal gender relations and division of labour with educated women, others perceived such change as a general loss in their personal and communal status.

Those men who had been displaced and exposed to education and gender mainstreaming for longer periods saw a higher value in (re) shaping the terms of the conjugal contract. They acknowledge that, ultimately, educated and empowered women will be able to improve wellbeing of their households and communities. Those who had been displaced for shorter periods or who had stayed behind perceived the immediate (personal) costs of women's empowerment in the immediate loss of their own status (as men). These contradictions demonstrate that change is also a deeply personal experience that challenges the imagined and experienced community and personal identity.

Girls and young women and choice: marriage as freedom, marriage and freedom

On late afternoons, I usually saw Nyakueth and Nyariek and groups of girls, all elegantly dressed, gathering in places where young men spent their time: on the football field, in local tea and coffee shops in the market or a local disco. Girls laughing and flirting with passing men were also present at celebrations, football matches and community gatherings. Here, the importance of marriage was widely debated among (returnee) girls. Nyakueth, a 20-year-old unmarried woman, was back from Kenya wearing nice clothes and red *khaway* (foreign) hair extensions. 'She will be a new item on the market and will have many offers,' commented Nyayena, a friend of hers. 'She will be able to choose among the men who will try to engage her. Kakuma girls are desirable items, because we are civilised a bit and educated a bit'. Nyakueth was indeed trying to look good. She was wearing her best clothes, had nicely plaited hair and carefully painted nails and toes. When I asked her about what settling-in meant for her, she immediately replied:

---

[29] See Tim Allen (ed.), *In Search of Cool Ground: War, Flight and Homecoming in Northeast Africa* (London and Trenton, NJ, 1996), p. 267.

Marriage. I have been a girl in my father's home for too long. Now that I am back from Kakuma after twelve years away, I am ready to have my [own] home. All my age mates are married, but I am late because I was in education. Now it is time for me to have my own home. I will be really settled when I marry.

Nyariek, who had returned from Khartoum after ten years away, was also debating the options of marriage. She had left Lɛr in 1997 when the conflict intensified. In Khartoum, she finished secondary education, as did her two brothers. Her younger sister stayed at home to assist their mother. Her father, a businessman, wanted Nyariek to finish education and did not mind that she was still unmarried at the age of 24. In March 2007, Nyariek came back to Lɛr and was hired as a teacher-trainer and a teacher in Lɛr's primary school. She stayed in her brother's house together with his youngest wife and her sister. She explained her current situation in fluent English:

Right now, I am also getting ready to be married. There are many men who come to propose: those from Kenya, Khartoum and Lɛr. But I am still waiting and I have not given a green light to any of them. I am twenty-four now and the people worry that I will not marry. All my age mates are married with children already! I have also decided that now it is a good time for me to marry. I want to have a husband and children, but also it is the only way for me to have a position in the community. My people want me to be an MP – but I can only be given a position in the community if I am married and I have children. This is when the people will see whether I am a good mother and a wife. As a girl, you cannot be given a leadership in the community. You can only work either in the school as a teacher or in the hospital [...].

I definitely do not want to marry a man with *gaar* – these men are bad. They do not know anything. They just beat their wives. Also, I want a husband who is educated – maybe go to university [...].

After the marriage, I will continue working. If there is a problem between me and the first wife, I can go and build a separate house somewhere else and the man will be able to come and visit me. It is better for me not to stay with the first wife. Also, I want to have four children, and buy a car, so I can be independent and I can afford to take all the children to school. This is important. Also, if anything happens, I will divorce; if I have a job, I will be able to stay by myself – and not worry about the person who will be providing for me. In this society it is very difficult to divorce. When you are educated, the men will pay many cows for you, maybe even 75 or 100. And then it will be hard to divorce if something happens. It is better to have a job and put some money to the side, so if there is a problem, I can buy cows with my money and return them to the husband.

Due to education and being away, a number of returnee girls were older and still unmarried. In Nuerland girls were married off earlier usually between the ages of sixteen and eighteen. As discussed in Chapter 2, conflict and impoverishment drastically lowered the marriage age for girls. Despite the higher bridewealth for educated girls, impoverished families saw an immediate profit in marrying off their daughters. In post-war Lɛr, girls as young as twelve or thirteen were already in the process of getting married. I witnessed several such cases, especially in rural areas. Older girls were lacking, either having been married off during wars or taken by force by rebels. Thus, most of the returnee girls' age mates in Lɛr were already married and there was a substantial social and family pressure on returnee girls to follow suit. I asked Nyariek how she had managed to remain single for such a long time. She replied: 'As long as you refuse to marry, the family cannot force you. I have been refusing until now. And I will not marry until I finish university. There are very few Nuer women who are educated'. Wearing an elegant skirt and high heels, she balanced an umbrella shading her from the sun. She looked like a city woman, different from those around her.

Nyakueth and Nyariek's narratives illustrate the general desire of returnee girls to find marriage partners. In their view, the post-return process of settling-in was associated with the establishment of a household and a family. A young divorcee in Lɛr explained the benefits of being a (married) woman:

> It is good to have a husband. When you have your husband you have your freedom. I have spent many years in the house of my mother and I was not free there because there were many things that I was asked to do for the family. I wanted to get married and have my own home. When you are married it is good because then you have help. The man does things that he is supposed to do and the woman does things that she is supposed to do. You know, there are things that women cannot do and that's why they need husbands in their lives.

Nyamai was divorced against her will: her former husband had found another woman and wanted to take back the cattle he had paid for Nyamai in order to marry her. He claimed that Nyamai was a loose woman and that she had had affairs with other men. Her two children were taken away from her and given to her husband. She felt that being back at her parents' house did not guarantee her access to resources, decision-making and status in the community. Hence, she finally remarried, to Jay, a young returnee from Kakuma. She got pregnant as quickly as possible in order to strength her position as a married woman and secure her future and continuously associated marriage with freedom.

Nyakueth, Nyariek, Nyamai and other girls recognised their relative weak and dependent position as girls in the community and within the household. Despite being unable to enjoy the freedoms previously guaranteed in Kakuma, some perceived marriage as a opportunity to gain – in theory – independence from their parents and achieve greater autonomy. Through marriage and subsequent procreation, girls achieve womanhood and the rights associated with their higher social position. With the birth of a child, a young wife (*kau*) acquires a status of *ciek*, which awards her rights over property at home, access to land and resources. As we saw in Chapter 5, women's entitlements to land and resources are regulated through men, but with the birth of each child their social position stabilises and becomes more secure and autonomous. Whether or not they had stayed behind or been displaced to Khartoum, girls and women strongly adhered to the embeddedness of gender identity in the institution of marriage.

The status of a married woman guarantees access to rights and privileges within the community, just as Nyariek suggests. If she is to achieve a position as an MP she must first prove that she is a responsible person, which in the case of women means a good wife and mother. Nyariek's interest in marriage was hence linked to wider strategic objectives that she set for herself.

The flipside of marriage and the constraints that it created for women were also recognised by some returnee girls and women. 'When you are a girl you want to marry because you want your freedom. But then you marry and you get yourself into another problem. There is no solution [for women and girls]'.

A married man employed by an international agency told me:

> Girls want to get married because they want to be free from the family. They are eager to get a title of a wife and get their own home. However, they do not realise the pressure of being married and the pressure to bear children afterwards.

Nyayena, like others, recognised that the rights and relative freedom that a woman gained through marriage were dependent on the husband. Nyakuol, a returnee widow described this in Nuer:

> Nuer men are bad [*Wutni nuäri jiäke long*] here. They do not respect their wives, and they can beat you whenever they want, if you have not cooked, or talked back to them, or were too tired to dig the garden; or even if you did not serve his food on your knees. There is nothing you can do about it [because the husband paid bridewealth for you]. The court will always give the right to the man. It is better to stay alone or continue with school for these young girls than get married. Being a Nuer woman [*ciek nuära*] is exhausting!

Female subordination was reinforced through the institution of marriage and the dominant position of the husband attained through bridewealth. The narratives of Nyakuol and Jany (at the beginning of the chapter), in which they spoke of the physical punishment used by husbands, reveal how this subordination was supposed to be maintained within the household. Beating wives made them obedient, honest, hard-working and deferential. This further buttressed a male-constructed gender ideology in which the husband had the authority and was the decision-maker. As elsewhere in Africa, bridewealth was central to structuring gender relations within marriage.[30] 'Once the bridewealth is paid, as a woman you can do nothing. It is like he bought you,' a female elder in Lɛr told me. Bridewealth gave husbands ultimate power over women, and forced women to concede that their husband was their superior. This was manifest in the way women referred to their husbands as *guar* (father), hence acknowledging their position as minors.

Many women and girls recognised these gender hierarchical constraints instilled in marriage and associated it with loss of the relative freedoms returnees had enjoyed in Kakuma. While some girls were eagerly interested in getting married, others fiercely opposed family pressures while seeking a degree of autonomy through education and financial independence.[31] Nyariek's narrative illustrates how returnee (and some stayee) girls and young women were fully aware of their

---

[30] Lovett ibid.

[31] Most returnee girls continued with schooling after their return to Lɛr. There were also some local girls, who persuaded their parents to send them to school.

need to be strategic in their choices of husbands. With their education, exposure to human rights and other cultures, returnee girls like Nyariek had a broader perspective on life beyond marriage. They balanced their options between further education, financial independence through paid employment and making choosing their husbands. Hence, Nyariek, aware of the constraints imposed by marriage manoeuvred, cleverly her limited options. Like other returnee girls, she was looking for a good husband similar to her – educated, worldly, aware of women's rights and in salaried employment. Returnee young women saw the local Nuer men as bad and ignorant, violent and misogynistic. They recognised the importance of being financially independent as a way of gaining greater autonomy from both husband and their own family. This is underscored by Nyariek's insistence on keeping her job after she gets married.

The education that returnee girls gained was seen by their families as having added value and expanding girls' negotiating position. Kuem, in the introduction to this chapter, and Nyariek's narratives confirm that educated girls commanded higher prices than their illiterate age mates. The wars saw families impoverished through the loss of cattle and other property and the high competition for girls among returning and local young men substantially inflated the bride-price. Educated girls' families were now asking up to seventy head of cattle compared to the thirty or thirty-five typically demanded by the western Nuer before the war. Kuem, the 'lost boy' who married a local girl, commented on the additional payments demanded by the bride's family: 'You have to pay for the pen that educated the girl. Also, if the man is educated, he has to pay higher bridewealth since he has better income.' Their high price made them desirable to politicians, high-ranking SPLA officers, wealthy traders and those working for international organisations. They also found husbands among the diaspora Nuer living in Khartoum, East Africa and the west. Nyariek, for example, had a relationship (over email) with a 'lost boy' resettled in the USA. Returnee parents, due to their experiences in displacement and their exposure to the education of girls, saw the long-term benefits of women's empowerment. Yet for those who had stayed behind, and were impoverished as a result of conflict, such education was seen as threatening their position of power. Despite educated women yielding higher bridewealth, their parents were unwilling to relinquish control over their daughters. Education is time-consuming and, in comparison to bridewealth, does not guarantee an immediate pay-off. The parents also worried that that educated and empowered women might take matters into their own hands and negotiate their own choices and preferences and thus undermine the position and preferences of their elders.

Marriage was no longer simply about maintaining lineage and *cieng* alliances, ensuring the continuation of agnatic descent and bringing pride. It was becoming more of an economic process, mediated through educated girls who were providing higher revenues for their parents. Due to substantial losses of property during the conflicts, girls were often seen as the only source of livelihood and wealth. A returnee girl noted:

> Girls are business here; your parents want you to get married so they can get cows from you. They do not care whether you will be beaten or mistreated by the husband. Those of us who were in Kakuma have seen the goodness of education, and many of us prefer to continue with school rather than get married. But the pressure in Sudan from your parents is great. There is also a lot of pressure from young men who want to marry you. They see you as educated and able to contribute to family, and will pay more for you to be their wife.

Educating girls was leading to their commodification. Now, many parents saw the advantage of sending a girl to school, evaluating the future returns that would accrue upon her marriage. The intense competition for such girls led to skyrocketing bride-prices and, in turn, further infringements of girls' rights, as they were compelled to concede to the highest bidder rather marry a man of their choosing. Since young men often could not afford them, they were taken as second wives by older, wealthy men. As Nyariek pointed out, high payments were making it more difficult for women to pursue a divorce, as their families would find it difficult to return the cattle received through bridewealth. This was also the reason why, as Nyariek's narrative illustrates, keeping financial autonomy in the marriage was an important bargaining tool for young returnee women. This was part of the 'serious games', where girls used paid employment as a way to expand their limited autonomy and agency.

Most of my female friends from Kakuma or Khartoum talked about family pressures to marry. Some told stories of their mothers' compliance in arranging the 'stealing' (*kual nyal*) of girls. NyaSunday, a returnee from Kakuma, explained how her mother orchestrated her engagement against her will. She was told to enter a house, after which her mother locked her in. Inside, a man who had been wooing her but whom she had spurned was waiting for her. After he had forced himself on her, NyaSunday was now considered a *keeagh*, shamed by the community and forced to marry her attacker. Other girls reported that if a girl resisted, women would often hold her head so 'the man can work easier on you from behind'. These stories were also confirmed by the men's mothers, who proudly talked about their strategies to 'convince the girl to love the man'. Interestingly, the word 'rape' does not exist in the Nuer language. The act is rather described as 'forcing the woman/girl' or 'taking her by force'. As it is not considered an offence in Nuer customary law, girls thus unable to seek justice in local courts. Before the wars, one a girl's main rights was to choose her husband.[32]

Some girls and young women who were being pressured into marriage devised evasion strategies. Some insisted on continuing education and asked their parents to send them to school. Girls defied marriage by running away with boyfriends of their own choosing to Kenya or Khartoum, which was common already in the 1980s and on the increase in post-war Lɛr, forcing their parents to accept the man by becoming pregnant. During a number of gender awareness workshops that I attended, women and men discussed the impact of forced marriages. They pointed to cases of girls hanging themselves as a result of being forced to marry

[32] Interviews with elders.

men against their will. Although they could only refer to a few recent instances, the fact that such stories circulated shows how girls protested their subordinate position. These strategies, although often seen as further undermining the position of the girl in the community and branding her as 'bad' (*jiäke*), 'loose' or *keeagh* demonstrated the use of their own limited agency to take control of their lives.

These attempts can be interpreted as recovering female agency. Despite their muted voice, through overt and covert actions women and girls found ways to resist male and other female) dominance. This is another example of how girls and women do not consent to subordination, but rather, through their small acts of resistance, show their agency in contesting, stretching and negotiating their narrow autonomies. These acts of resistance reveal that the household is a key site of struggle over gendered norms, interests and choices. As agency is exercised within particular (hegemonic) structures of power, it is often difficult to define and interpret, as it entails culturally and historically specific modes of action.[33] While it is typical to either ignore or romanticise female agency as 'victims or heroines', daily acts of defiance often remain discredited as insubordination and are termed 'bad' or 'behaving like a man'. These acts also demonstrate that some returnee women and girls were willing and able to maintain and expand their empowered status acquired in Kakuma.

Gendered emplacement after return home poses different challenges and constraints for young people. Place-making through marriage was a highly gendered experience directly linked to the practice and negotiation of gender identities and relations. This was part of the transformation and emergence of a post-war community in Lɛr and in Nuerland more broadly. It confirmed how the experience and the existence of a community, as Akhil Gupta and James Ferguson argued, 'is inevitably constituted by a wider set of social and spatial relations'.[34] Marriage remains an important step for young men and women in the passage to full adulthood, expanding their (informal) rights, yet at the same time constraining freedoms acquired and experienced in Kakuma. The diverse practices and experiences of (re)shaping masculinities and femininities employed by returnee young women and men show a rather messy picture of Nuer post-war gender relations.

GENDERED EMPLACEMENT: GENDER RELATIONS IN FLUX

The homecoming of displaced populations provoked debate on what it means to be a woman/man in Nuer community. The moral panic mentioned in Chapter 1 about young people's dress codes spread across southern Sudan, including communities in the Western Upper Nile. Controversy centred around the key ideal of morality, gender and power. This moral panic has also been resisted, especially in Juba, a more a

[33] Hodgson and McCurdy (eds), *'Wicked' Women*, p. 16.
[34] Akhil Gupta and James Ferguson (eds), *Culture, Power, Place* (Durham, NC, 1997), p. 7.

cosmopolitan place with a large influx of international donors, aid and development agencies and returnees from the US, Canada, Australia and Europe. Displaced populations brought with them different cultural habits, including education, styles of dress, religion and manners that collided with gender ideology and stayee identities.

Waraqa and pen versus *gaar* and gun

Returnees, particularly *nei ti cike*, provoked a discussion around alternative forms of gender identities and power relations. Initiation to manhood through education, Christianity and views that were pro-women were confronted by local ideals of *gaar*, *mut* and *ric*, as well as hyper-masculinities based on the gun, participation in the liberation struggle and shared life in the army.

The power of the pen (and paper) was undeniable in enhancing the position of men (and women) in the community. On the road to Adok, I was stopped by an elderly woman, who asked if I could write her a letter allowing her to access money from the local administration. Most widows registered with local authorities received a small stipend from the commissioner's office, but could only do so with documentation. The woman was unable to understand that only the commissioner's office could give her such a magic *waraqa* (paper). Literacy was a highly considered asset.

Educated returnees were confronted by local concepts of masculinities, especially militarised forms of hyper-masculinities. Kuok often complained:

> The power of the pen and the power of the gun are not equal. The people who were in the military in SPLA and had ranks got high positions. They are in charge of things. It is difficult for me, an educated person, to argue with them, because the power of the pen is not respected in Sudan.

The militarisation of Nuer society, and the fact that the bulk of the male population had served in the army, often elevated the power of the gun above that of the pen. Those who had not participated in the military struggle often felt sidelined. 'If you do not fight, they will tell you, "Are you a priest?" If you are a real Nuer, you have to fight,' commented a young returnee father. He added: 'In Kakuma, we learned to discuss issues, but here, this means nothing. If you are a man you have to fight'. Although the new forms of masculinities were often undermined and ridiculed, especially by other men, those who were educated and worldly were becoming more desirable as husbands among the local girls.

Even those in rural areas often expressed their preference for 'educated husbands with a job'. Returnee men often ran into trouble with local girls pressuring them to marry. Girls would come to the homes of such men and then claim that they had had sex with them. 'To play with local girls is dangerous for us [returnee men]. They see our education, they think we have money, and they want to marry you straight away,' explained Jany, a young Kakuma man. The new values that some returnee young men were bringing into the communities were slowly gaining currency among the stayees. As with educated Masaai men and educated and employed Nigerian young men in Ado-Odo,[35] young returnee Nuer men were influencing the (re)negotiation of local concepts of manhood and masculinity, and altering some intergenerational and gender relations. In the process of emplacement and the constant confrontation between competing values held by stayees and returnees, new and different sets of meanings, identities and practices were emerging. As in the case of the Mursi and their movement from one setting to another,[36] in their daily interactions, returnees and stayees were engaged in an active process of creating a community and redefining the terms of *cieng nuära*.

Threatening mini-skirts and agents of change: womanhood reconsidered

Nyajuc, a seventy-something-year-old grandmother, commented on the changed status of girls and women:

> In the past, to be a girl and a woman is to marry. The girl becomes a woman when she is married, the bridewealth is paid and she gives birth to children. But now, girls go to school; they can bring something for the family, not only cows through bridewealth. To be a woman now is not only to be married and give birth to children. A woman has more obligations because of education.

The position of returnee adolescent girls was highly ambiguous. At times they were perceived as threatening, at others as agents of positive change, bringing new concepts of femininities and challenging local and militarised forms of womanhood. Their subtle and more visible actions of daily practice of gendered self were forms of often hidden resistance to existing gender inequalities within their own communities, performed without openly challenging the existing power inequalities. Educated, outspoken, seen as good cooks, being able to take better care of children and contributing to the community through their ability to find paid work, returnee girls and young women were expanding the realm of possibilities and freedoms for women. Notwithstanding their reputation as 'loose', they were often seen as desirable marriage partners due to their education and ability to contribute to household income.

Despite being shamed by stayees and returnee women and men from Khartoum, returnee girls from Kakuma continued to challenge their limited status. Local adolescent girls and younger women envied and emulated their fashion choices and mobility. Now locally available, jeans became the most 'must-have' garments in the market. When I offered to go shopping with my host's daughter, 13-year-old Nyamuc

---

[35] Dorothy L. Hodgson, *Once Intrepid Warriors: Gender, Ethnicity, and the Cultural Politics of Maasai Development* (Bloomington, IN, 2004); Andrea Cornwall, 'To be a Man is More Than a Day's Work: Shifting Ideals of Masculinity in Ado-Odo, Southwestern Nigeria', in L. Lindsay and S. Miescher (eds), *Men and Masculinities in Modern Africa* (Portsmouth, NH, 2003).

[36] See David Turton, 'The Meaning of Place in a World of Movement: Lessons from Long-Term Field Research in Southern Ethiopia', *Journal of Refugee Studies*, 2005, Vol. 18, pp. 258–80.

– who had spent most of her life in Lɛr – immediately wanted to get a pair. At a wedding of a young returnee man both the bride and her bridesmaid (neither of whom had ever left Lɛr) were wearing denim and had red hair extensions. Although returnee girls had to conform to some extent to local expectations, they were also agents of change. During my ten months in Lɛr, I saw increasing numbers of girls riding bicycles, playing sports, attending school, going to discos and moving around freely.

Cosmetics became desirable items for locals, a demand met by Kakuma women selling soaps, body lotions and hair-extensions brought in from Kenya. When I went to Nairobi, they often asked me to bring back new supplies. Fashion style wasWas seen as contributions to change and *wa nhiam*, seeing the local stayee population start to conform to East African and Western standards experienced in displacement or seen on television. These embodied everyday forms of resistance were manifestations of girls' agency and power that they were willing and able to exercise albeit within constrained limits.

Returnee young women were also working as teachers, nurses and community organisers. Adolescent girls were promoting schooling among the local girls. Nyamuc and other women who had stayed in Sudan often commented on the goodness of this:

> When they know something, they will be able to be more respected by the husband and manage independently even if the husband does not support them. I wish I could have had this chance before. These Kakuma girls are better off this way.

Under the influence of other returnee girls (and perhaps me), Nyamuc decided to join an adult education programme run by the Catholic Church. She insisted that her 13-year-old daughter Nyarial continue primary education. They often asked me to help them with homework and quiz them in mathematics and English. Nyarial followed the example of other returnee girls and became determined to succeed in school. Despite her numerous domestic tasks, she was diligent with her homework. 'I want to be like your friend from Kakuma, who knows how to read and write, speaks English and has a job,' Nyarial explained.

The value of education for girls and women was also being slowly recognised by local (male) authorities. On a visit to the Lɛr commissioner, Nyayena, a returnee woman directly asked for land, a job and financial support. She was outspoken. Spotting a mattress in the commissioner's compound, she asked for it: 'I am a returnee and need a bed for my daughter and myself. Can you assist me? Once I get a job, I will pay you back'. The commissioner smiled and told me: 'Returnee women are very different from those who stayed behind. They have been educated and they are not afraid to ask for their rights. They have no fear, are able to represent the community and support their families. They are bringing development for women here'. Although this attestation may have been influenced by my presence, other senior men and women were also acknowledging the social change wrought by returnee women.

As with similar 'wayward', 'dangerous', 'wicked' and 'vagabond' African women, the transgressive behaviour of adolescent Nuer girls was proving pivotal in transforming gender relations and other domains of social life. This was not only through fashion, but also through the desire for schooling. 'Somehow educated', as they referred to themselves, returnee girls and young women enjoyed greater ability to access paid jobs, communicate with outsiders, raise issues with the authorities, expand their choices over husbands and (re)negotiate unequal power relations within the household. Of the few women formally employed in the school, church, hospital and the commissioner's office in Lɛr, all were returnees from Kakuma. Their mothers, and often fathers, who had also spent substantial time in displacement supported their quest for further education. Several returnee women sent their daughters to schools in Bentiu and often talked about the importance of female education. Nyajung commented as follows:

> When they know something, their lives will be better. They will not be easily abused by men. Girls who are illiterate they just accept the beating, but girls who know something are respected by their husbands and in the community. They can also be more autonomous.

Through their emplacement practices, returnee women and girls were reshaping concepts of femininities and bringing about change, even if incremental and more in terms of consciousness rather than actual practice, for other women in Lɛr.

Nyakuma, my (illiterate) host, succinctly summarised the importance of education in changing women's position in the household and in the community:

> Why are there no women in the government? There are only three women in the government, the ones who can read and write. If you do not know how to read and write, you cannot be in the government. Now, women are not equal with men. Women are at home, doing all the work and men are outside working in hospital, government, army and police. This is the culture. In the past, the men had their barn (*luak*), and their responsibility was taking care of cows. Women were in charge of house (*duël*). Now, there are no cows so men sit around. But things will change when girls and boys will go to school together and women know how to read and write. They will come together and be equal, like in your place.

The position of girls in the community was slowly changing due to the spread of Christianity. Churches were promoting an enhanced role for women, and sisters from the Catholic Comboni order were running special education classes and courses for girls and young women. More girls were enrolling in primary classes, as parents realised that educated girls have greater value for the family and community. However, while the institution was promoting girls' access to education, its doctrine was also being skilfully used by men and women to continue to keep women in subordinate positions.

Another sign of women's greater autonomy and awareness of their own interests was the increase in the number who were asking for divorce. As the chiefs in Lɛr commented, this signified, on the one hand, women's growing disobedience, and on the other, their tiredness with 'useless and abusive husbands'. Women were also contesting male privilege by breaking taboos and 'trespassing' gendered spaces by working in public spaces, including the market, hospitals, schools and the government. In the past, women and men ate separately as a sign of respect, but now women openly shared food with related or unrelated men. I also watched an animal sacrifice where, due to the lack of immediate male relatives, a woman was asked to slaughter a cow, a task previously exclusively reserved for men. A new custom was also entering the sharing of bride-wealth, with a cow being given to a female friend of the bride's mother, a custom previously reserved for the male friends of the bride's father.

As women slowly started entering education and work, although still limited, they directly challenged the male breadwinner and men's dominant position. Their acts of transgression – speaking publicly, sitting on chairs on a par with men and participating in decision-making in the community – were signs of transformations taking place in gender relations. As one of the Kakuma widows commented,

> .... now it is much better than before [the wars]. At least we have some women in the government, and now we are invited to speak at ceremonies, and are given [some] our rights. Things are changing slowly here in Lɛr.

Some men were worried about the growing autonomy of women and their own position being rendered useless. Ruan, a young returnee man from Kakuma, once shared the news he had heard on the radio with me: 'I heard that there are special places where women can go and get sperm and then they can get babies by themselves. If this happens women will not need us any longer. We will be useless, and they will be completely independent and free'. This reveals the gender power of men linked to reproduction (and the cattle complex). In these metaphors of women 'getting babies by themselves', Nuer men were expressing their concern of losing power and control over (their) women and children. While reproduction bound women to subordinate positions through the rights over children assigned to the husband who paid cattle, the possibility of women of freeing themselves from this predicament threatened male privilege and their hegemonic position.

'Loose' girls and women thus became agents of change. Whether change was seen positively depended on the position of the different actors whose social power was at stake in (re)negotiation of the gender order. Through some female solidarity and support from some women (and men), girls and younger women were able to exercise their limited agency and subvert some of the strict constraints to their status enshrined in the hegemonic structures of 'our culture' discourse. These actions became 'sites for debate over, and occasionally transformations in, gender relations, social practices, cultural norms, and political-economic institutions'.[37] Ortner's comments on the nature of agency and resistance are insightful here.

[37] Hodgson and McCurdy (eds), *'Wicked' Women*, p. 2.

> The question of adequate representation of subjects in the attempt to understand resistance is not purely a matter of providing better portraits of subjects in and of themselves. The importance of subjects (whether individual actors or social entities) lies not so much in who they are and how they are put together as in the *projects* that they construct and enact. For it is in the formulation and enactment of those projects that they both become and transform who they are, and that they sustain or transform their social and cultural universe.[38]

Thus, the settling-in experiences and aspirations of adolescent girls and women were part of a transformative project that was affecting returnee girls and women as well as those who had stayed behind. The everyday practice that returnee girls and young women have to carefully negotiate contributes to the transformation of themselves and their communities. What it meant to be an adolescent girl and a woman was being questioned, contested and (re)negotiated in post-war Nuerland. While the role of individuals and their agency in bringing about change is pivotal, if it is to become a fully fledged transformation, there needs to be change at the institutional level to support an overall transformation in gender relations.

CHANGING THE LANDSCAPES OF POST-WAR COMMUNITIES

Returnee women and men's reshaping of gender identities also led to the changing the terms of the landscape of social norms of the emerging post-war *cieng nuära*. In this context, some returnee women and men pushed the boundaries of acceptable and proper gender behaviour, showing the fluidity of gender boundaries and contributing, at times, to transformations in gender identities, norms and institutions. Through the emplacement practices they negotiated with those who had stayed behind, returnee young women and men were transforming gender identities, gender discourses of power and terms of exchange and sharing within the household and the wider community. Although not able to benefit from the same opportunities and freedoms as in Kakuma, young women, for example, were nonetheless actively stretching the choices and options available to women in post-war Lɛr. While they were engaged in a place-making project in Lɛr, they were also transforming themselves and their gender identities as a result of emplacement processes. This reflects Stuart Hall's suggestion that, rather than being fixed and stable, identity is a 'meeting point', 'a point of suture or temporary identification – that constitutes and re-forms that subject so as to enable that subject to act'.[39] By adding gender and age, this process reveals how identity, home and subject formation within it are intertwined with agency. It also reveals, I would argue, how new hierarchies of power are being constituted in the context of locality production in post-war South Sudan.

The marriage process proved to be at the core of *beben cieng* and *nyuuri piny*. It was critical for forging new and old community bonds, (re)creating

---

[38] Ortner, *Making Gender*, p. 196.
[39] c.f. Gupta and Ferguson, *Culture, Power, Place*, p. 13.

landscapes of communities, social relations and finding oneself within them. Yet, women and men used their agency to contest, resist and (re) negotiate some of the gender hierarchies and subordinate femininities. While marriage (and procreation) remained associated with full passage to adulthood, most young people also associated it with the process of *nyuuri piny* through creating their own household. Through acts of resistance and practice of their limited agency, both young returnee women and men were bringing change and contesting local gender identities, norms and practices embedded in the institution of marriage. These acts of transgression also demonstrate the ability and the willingness of girls and young women to challenge local concepts of subordinate femininities and male dominance. These acts are also steps towards transforming gender relations in the process of creating a (new) meaning of the community's landscape.

7

Returnees as Visitors and the Nuer Community: Where Do We Go From Here?

DILEMMAS ABOUT SOCIAL LIFE IN FLUX

When I left Lɛr in September 2007, Nyakuol, Kuok and Nyariek were partially settled-in. They had found their relatives and had built huts on their land. Nyakuol opened a small shop in the market, established a garden and her children were going to school. In recognition of her strong leadership skills, she was asked to participate in the SPLM political campaign as a representative for Lɛr. Nyariek, still living with her father, was in the process of getting married. Although she had convinced her father to let her complete primary school, she continued to battle against other restrictions imposed on her. She had to stop playing football and was often reprimanded for wearing short skirts. Kuok was working as a teacher and constructing his *duël*. In 2008, he got married and moved in with his wife. He started teaching his wife reading, writing and English to, as he told me, 'share knowledge and bring her up'.

Nevertheless, Nyakuol, Nyariek and Kuok felt that their social relations and identities were in flux. They were debating the changing gender norms and relations and found it difficult to conform to their families' expectations to behave according to the rules of *cieng nuära*. The *nyuuri piny* of the displaced populations prompted discussions around the transformations of gender relations among the residents of Lɛr and Bentiu, wider Western Upper Nile and other areas in South Sudan.[1] While this book focuses mainly on Lɛr, and to some extent on Bentiu, the tensions between stayees and returnees presented here shed light on changes and continuities of social and gender relations in the aftermath of civil conflict and the repatriation of the displaced. They also reveal the contestations, dilemmas and uncertainties about social life in flux in the context of community- and nation-building, Lɛr being an example of a social lens for other places in South Sudan.

My research demonstrates that anthropological concepts of emplace-

---

[1] While the research for this book focused predominantly on Lɛr and Western Upper Nile area, other reports, research and newspaper articles confirm that gender relations are being questioned in different parts of South Sudan. Currently, there is unfortunately no in-depth research on such dynamics in other areas in South Sudan.

ment and social change during different phases of conflict and displacement shed light on the personal, communal and structural dynamics of
these processes. As Laura Hammond notes, these concepts 'question the
primacy of sedentarist orientations and explore the creation of meaning,
identity, and community in the context of flux and disorder [and they] can
and should be used to investigate what happens to people who return'.[2]
My findings show that processes of emplacement and place-making
affect and engage stayees as much as returnees. By focusing on the aspirations, practices and experiences of settling-in and building a meaning
for both Lɛr returnees and stayees, the study of Nuer displacement engen-
ders the emplacement concept. While my focus was on 'individual and
collective agency as determining elements in the experience of return',[3]
my analysis examines the gendered and generational nature of agency
and how it interplays with institutions and norms in the processes of
social change. I emphasise the fluidity of gender and generational relations and their (re)configuration in different stages of displacement and
emplacement. The complexities of the gendered and generational nature
of these processes have both theoretical and practical implications: they
offer important insights not only for South Sudanese policy-makers and
community leaders, but have wider consequences for all those involved
in South Sudan's nation-building process.

ANTHROPOLOGY OF DISORDER AND SOCIAL THEORY

In the past two decades anthropology has seen a considerable shift
towards examining global processes and movements of people and ideas
across borders and continents. The study of migrant communities, and
refugees more specifically, occupies a major place in anthropological
writings. The twentieth century has been called 'the century of refugees'.
This is evident in the broad body of research examining the experiences
of uprooted populations, violence and warfare. It is now widely acknowledged that such analyses offer new and important insights into a range
of theoretical debates. Migration and displacement have generated new
debates in theories of social change,[4] identity and community formation,
diasporas, globalisation and transnational studies, as well as the newly
emerging sub-field of mobility studies. Refugee studies in particular have
long been identified as a unique 'chance to record the processes of social
change, not merely as a process of transition within a cultural enclave,
but also in the dramatic context of uprootedness, where a people's quest
for survival becomes a model for social change'.[5]

---

[2] Laura Hammond, *This Place will become Home: Refugee Repatriation to Ethiopian*
(Ithaca, NY, 2004), p. 207.
[3] Ibid.
[4] See, for example, N. Glick Schiller and T. Faist, 'Introduction: Migration, Development and Social Transformation', *Social Analysis*, Vol. 53, pp. 1–13.
[5] Barbara Harrell-Bond and Efthixia Voutira, 'Anthropology and the Study of
Refugees', *Anthropology Today*, 1992, Vol. 8, p. 9.

Slowly, albeit with much hesitation, refugee and displacement studies have been accepted as contributing more significantly to anthropology and social sciences. However, they still remain slightly on the margins of what John Davis refers to as:

> comfortable anthropology ... which is concerned with social organizations which represent as working more or less normally, ticking over, with occasional spasms of adjustment – changing pains, as you might say – but in general reasonably autonomous, locally construed arrangements for living which attract the commitment and creativity of those who live in that way.[6]

Another reason for the limited theoretical contributions of refugee studies is due to such research being largely policy focused. Anthropologists interested in the issues of displaced populations usually resort to applied research that has a direct connection to policies, programmes and projects that affect these populations. Recently, the anthropological focus has also shifted from populations affected by displacement to humanitarian institutions and processes involved in the response it. Yet, this engagement with the world of humanitarian actors has not translated into deepening social theory. As a result, refugee, displacement and humanitarian studies display a range of case studies with little theoretical thread to bind them together. An anthropology of disorder or uncertainty as a juxtaposition to 'comfortable' anthropology does, however, offer a range of material and insights for pushing the theorisation of social change in the context of abrupt rupture and continuity that accompanies displaced persons, stayees and their communities.

'HOMEMAKING': IMPLICATIONS FOR THE STUDY OF RETURN MIGRATION

Much of the anthropological debates surrounding refugees and return migration and repatriation policies and programmes have exhibited a sedentarist bias. For a long time anthropologists have bound people to place. As Arjun Appadurai argues, 'natives are not only persons who are from certain places, and belong to those places, but they are also those who are somehow incarcerated, or confined, in those places'.[7] While the place of origin as the real place of belonging for refugees is widely disputed,[8] humanitarian responses to refugee crises still see returning home as the most desired and viable option, or the 'preferred durable solution' in humanitarian terminology. It is the restoration of the natural order of things. This is all the more so in the current anti-immigration climate across much of the world, where migration has increasingly

---

[6] John Davis, 'The anthropology of suffering', *Journal of Refugee Studies* 5(2): 149–61 (1992), p. 149.
[7] Arjun Appadurai, 'Putting hierarchy in its place', *Cultural Anthropology*, 1998, Vol. 3, p. 37.
[8] See Liisa H. Malkki, 'Refugees and Exile: From "Refugee Studies" to the National Order of Things', *Annual Review of Anthropology*, 1995, Vol. 24, pp. 495–523.

become developmentalised and securitised. While access to asylum has been shrinking, returned migrants are seen as the new vehicles for development of their 'homes'.

Yet, as critics of the placelessness paradigm have pointed out, home does have a territorial dimension, and thus return might be the only or the most desired option for many displaced women and men. The theoretical concept of emplacement does not presuppose an internal link between people and place but rather opens up to empirical questioning the types of aspirations, actions and practices that establish a link between people, movement, identity and place.

My research with the people in Kakuma and in Lɛr suggests that *bebeng cieng* and *nyuuri piny* are important elements in emplacement. Emplacement has involved actions and interactions to make not only a place but also a landscape of social interactions feel like home. The connections that people were gradually establishing to place were physical (building a house), economic (getting a job, farming land), social ((re)creating new and expanding other social networks through re-casting kinship relations, through marriage, socialisation and by transforming ties of friendship based on shared experiences) and civic/political (becoming an official in the community and acquiring rights to participate in political and communal life). Emplacement involved negotiating and (re)establishing social relations with those who had stayed behind, migrated elsewhere or forged bonds with previous friends from displacement. As much as displaced people have changed, so too have their homes. This suggests the theoretical concept of homemaking should be widened to include reciprocal processes of piecing together disjointed lives and creating a new place and home.

The experiences of returnees – whether from Kenya, Uganda, Ethiopia or Khartoum –regardless of whether they had returned with the assistance of international organisations, the GoSS or by their own volition, reflect the wisdom of Edward Said, who said that the return home is never an uncomplicated and homogenous experience. Thus, emplacement is a creative process of community formation, relying on old kinship ties and reinterpreting new relationships by transforming ties of friendship into new forms of *maar*. In this way, *cieng* acquires a new sense based on becoming and being part of a community beyond previous kinship bonds and finding one's place within it.

As I have demonstrated, the concept of *cieng* as rooted in social relations rather than merely in a specific place further contributes to discussions of links between place, identity and culture. For the Nuer women and men, as for other agro-pastoralist and mobile populations, movement and thus homemaking was part of their larger history of mobility and livelihoods. Emplacement is a long-term process bound up with social relations of *maar* and the presence of ancestors rather than a specific physical place. In the absence of relatives, or the unwillingness to (re) cast previous kinship relations, it also involved creating new kinship ties, one not necessarily based on blood but rather on previous shared experiences. Thus, as David Turton argues:

to understand how a sense of place becomes bound up with a person's social and individual identity, we must treat place, not as a stage for social activity but as a 'product' of it. Such an understanding of the link between people and place helps us to appreciate that displacement is not just about the loss of place, but also about the struggle to *make* a place in the world, where meaningful action and shared understanding is possible.[9]

The emerging nationalist discourses of South Sudan as a homeland propagated during the war and in refugee camps altered the meaning of home for the Nuer women and men. As a result, home became associated with a specific country, rights, freedoms, territory and boundaries. In the context of global migrations, this book also underscores the fact that, despite the growing understanding of mobile homes, home as attached to a specific place still matters. For refugees in particular, through being denied access to basic rights in most settlement places, home acquires a territorial meaning linked to land and citizenship.

My research is situated within the debates around the gendered and generational nature of home. The contributions from feminist anthropology in deciphering the heterogeneous character of home are especially important here. Based on culturally inscribed notions of maleness and femaleness within, and in relation to, the home space as a site of household, women and men's experiences of losing their home due to displacement and settling-in after their return vary due to gendered and generational obligations and entitlements within the household and the community. This gendered and generational dimension of home as a social field demonstrates the different aspirations and experiences of returning home.

For the Nuer women and men, home as a site of social, economic and political relations is experienced differently depending on age, gender and the stage in their lifecycle, and also on the actual place. Within community and nation-formation practices, some people are piecing their lives and relationships together in the new context, while others create new belonging and homes. For some, mainly educated men, homecoming results in increasing their position and status, whereas for others, mainly women, returning home, to a place where the subordination of women is more explicit, might result in constraining the freedoms they gained in exile. Daily negotiations around changing gender concepts show how emplacement is experienced by individuals and communities in differentiated ways. These insights do not easily translate into humanitarian and post-war development programmes, which tend to rely on more generalisable data and are rarely nuanced. However, insights from detailed ethnographic research on the effects of displacement during its different stages might encourage a more nuanced policy and programming approach to providing assistance.

Due to war-time separation and disjointed and fragmented family lives, homecoming poses several challenges for gender ideologies and norms of

---

[9]   David Turton, 'The Meaning of Place in a World of Movement: Lessons from Long-Term Field Research in Southern Ethiopia', *Journal of Refugee Studies*, 2005, Vol. 18, p. 258.

returnees and stayees. Entering and (re)establishing a web of relations, obligations and expectations infused with *cieng nuära* ideals of femininity, masculinity and gender norms creates challenges of belonging and fitting in, especially for returnee young men and women who grew up in displacement. They arriving with hugely diverse experiences in refugee camps. Separation from family and community created an opportunity for transgressing gender ideology and norms and enlarging a space of freedoms for young women and men. Homecoming did not necessarily mean going back to an imagined past, but rather entering a different set of cultural and social relations, and finding oneself within them.

Different gender norms could be practiced in Kakuma, giving girls and women a more equal status in society, because it was not home. In Lɛr, these ideas and new social practices clashed with *cieng nuära* gender and generational ideologies and the cultural identities of stayees. They revealed the differentiated femininities, masculinities and gender norms emerging as a result of war and displacement. For young women and men, homecoming meant having to obey family and community pressures to be good Nuer girls and respectable women/men. Thus, the social value of what it meant to be a woman or a man in Lɛr was intrinsically linked with *cieng* and home.

This book sheds light on sedentarist assumptions and reveals what happens to place, home, identity and meaning when people move between places. This suggests that the theoretical concepts of home infused with gender and generational ideologies are also key in transforming relations of power and creating (in)equalities. Thus, I see emplacement as a dialectic and negotiation between the displaced and stayees, influenced by their capacities to put themselves and others into a place and the power relations that unequally distribute this capacity.[10] Such analyses demonstrate the fluidity and dynamism of place and offer useful insights fo unpacking the economic, social and political practices and norms that displaced populations employ to transform the (often unfamiliar) place into 'something like home'.

GENDERED DISPLACEMENT, EMPLACEMENT AND IMPLICATIONS FOR THEORIES OF SOCIAL CHANGE

While disruption and often expedited social change frequently accompany displacement, what is less clear is the nature of such change, its directionality and long-term durability. My key concern is to examine the causality between forced displacement and change in social, and primarily gender and generational relations. However, as other authors have shown, studying change and, in particular, identifying the causality of change is one of the most challenging tasks for social scientists.[11]

[10] See S. Jansen and S. Løfving, *Struggles for Home: Violence, Hope and the Movement of People* (Berghan Books (2009), p. 13.
[11] See, for example, Sharon E. Hutchinson, *Nuer Dilemmas Dilemmas: Coping with Money, War and the State* (Berkeley, CA, 1996).

Talking about change does give a partial account of how things are and how they were in the past, but doing change remains more imperceptible. Partly, this is because these changes are usually incremental and often invisible to the actors involved, and even more so to outsiders. It also has to do with actors' strategies, the discrepancy between the official and the unofficial discourse and the gap between say and do. Yet despite the multiplicity of potential sources of change in often chaotic and fluid conditions of war and displacement, such contexts reveal how social relations are negotiated, and in particular how gender relations are constituted, contested and (re)configured in a rapidly changing environment. They enhance our understandings of lived gender and generational experiences and the challenges posed by the (re)negotiation of gender power relations.

The fact that displacement produces changes in gender and generational relations, resulting in new configurations of social relations largely due to its abrupt nature and often traumatic gendered experiences has been widely recognised.[12] While most studies focus on experiences during displacement, resettlement or post-war return, this study looked into social conditions and relations across different stages of displacement and emplacement.[13] I argue that as much as forced displacement, relocation and emplacement affect the reordering of gender relations within different societies, the notions and experiences of home and return often shift the practice of gender relations themselves.

The experiences of women and men described herein demonstrate that war, and war-time displacement, are social conditions that require even more creative and innovative approaches to survival, which often generates social change. Stephen Lubkemann argues that 'as sites of both social reproduction and prolific social production ... warscapes may provide privileged sites within which to theorize processes of social change and innovation'.[14] This is also the case in the context of creating a meaning, life and home, be it temporary in refugee camps or long-term as part of the post-return settlement. The different trajectories of people's displacement and emplacement that I followed reveal the gendered nature of these processes and their implications for gender (and generational) relations of power, identity and practice. While 'emplacement is a continuous process of generating meaning',[15] it also gives an opportunity to (re)define existing social relations, ideas and norms. Hence, what it means to be a Nuer woman/girl or man/boy for stayees and the displaced takes on a different dimension and shows how social relations and identities are variable and changeable. This approach elucidates how changes in gender and generational relations are a continuous process and that gender relations thus need to be examined spatially and temporarily.

[12] See, for example, Doreen Indra (ed.), *Engendering Forced Migration: Theory and Practice* (New York, 1999).
[13] See S. Lubkemann (2008) on the war in Mozambique as another example of a study that explores different stages of war-time displacement.
[14] Ibid.
[15] Hammond, *This Place will become Home*, p. 208.

Yet, as in other situations of socioeconomic change in rural and urban East Africa, the gains and losses of empowerment are not equally redistributed. Some groups suffer greater disempowerment than others. My findings demonstrate how change is intertwined with social values. As the basis of the social value enshrined in the concepts of 'real Nuer men' and 'respectable Nuer girls/women' transform in Kakuma and in Lɛr, those who are unable to achieve these requirements suffer greater disempowerment. Thus, my research questions the debates around men as the dominant gender by emphasising how those men who are unable to fulfil requirements of hegemonic masculinities are marginalised.

Much of the literature on social change focuses on the dialectic between agency and structure.[16] The processes of transformation in Kakuma and in Lɛr reveal how social change is constantly negotiated by individuals, communities, institutions and the state. Yet, the outcome of these negotiations is not linear and thus during the process of social transformations change can be resisted as well as welcomed. The importance of my findings for globalisation theories lies in the types of encounters, negotiations and transformations that take place among the Nuer women and men in the sites of displacement and emplacement. Humanitarian regimes contribute to the increasing globalising processes of social change among affected displaced and stayee communities and produce new hierarchies of power and privilege. While the distinction between local and global becomes even more blurred, the type of local modernities that emerge, including concepts of modern femininities and masculinities or womanhood and manhood, take on their own distinctive forms. They need to be further taken into account in the emergence of 'theory from the South'.

To understand processes of social change, the concept of home is pivotal. While it has been used by policy-makers and those involved in humanitarian assistance quite problematically (often as static and as a safe haven), critical anthropology approaches to homemaking have started to detangle it.[17] The relationships of Nuer women and men to their homes demonstrate how homecoming is neither to a fixed place nor to a fixed past. Home as a myth and its temporal dimension had to be created through practice. This entails particular challenges for the gender and generational relations of those displaced as well as those who stayed behind. The experiences of settling in southern Sudan show that social transformation was central during their different stages of displacement. Thus, as Nina Glick Schiller and Thomas Faist, Nick Van Hear and Steven Castles argue, social transformation is a key category for examining processes of migration and displacement.[18] Such analyses

[16] See Oliver Bakewell, 'Some Reflections on Structure and Agency in Migration Theory', *Journal of Ethnic and Migration Studies* 2010, 36 no. 10.
[17] See, for example Jansen and Løfving, *Struggles for Home*.
[18] N. Glick Schiller and T. Faist, 'Introduction: Migration, Development and Social Transformation'; N. Van Hear, 'Theories of Migration and Social Change', *Journal of Ethnic and Migration Studies* 2010, 36, no. 10, pp. 1531–6; S. Castles, 'Understanding Global Migration: A Social Transformation Perspective', *Journal of Ethnic and Migration Studies* 2010, 36, no.10, pp. 1565–86.

attempt to 'facilitate understanding of the complexity, interconnected-ness, variability, contextuality and multi-level mediations of migratory processes in the context of rapid global change'.[19] In a context where home has changed or ceased to exist, gendered and generational locality production involved not merely learning *cieng nuära*, but rather (re) negotiating gender order, gender identities, aspirations and norms. My analysis allows us to better understand how complex social processes involved in gendered and generational emplacement play themselves out not only on women and men's bodies but also on their social identities, gender institutions and ideology, networks, physical capital and place itself. What emerges is a state of flux of gender norms, ideologies and institutions partially instigated by the returning population that char-acterise the contemporary Nuer communities in Western Upper Nile and are examples for the wider dilemmas in nation-building in South Sudan.

The call towards anthropology of disorder or uncertainty emphasises the dynamics inherent in the homemaking process. Situations of flux pose a challenge for reaching definitive conclusions about the hierarchy of sources as well as the direction of transformations in social relations. Yet, displacement and post-war in-flux environments provide both rich and complex material for identifying and analysing processes of change. The anthropological approach allows also us to underscore the impor-tance of human agency in bringing about change, often through social navigation. Hendrik Vigh argues that:

> the concept of social navigation grants us an alternative perspective on practice and the intersection between agency, social forces and change. By highlighting the *interactivity* of practice and the *intermorphology* of motion, it grants us an analytical optic which allows us to focus on how people move and manage within situations of social flux and change.[20]

While structures, institutions and socio-political and economic contexts of transformations give impetus for social change, individuals and communities have to cope with these new challenges. As the expe-riences of Nuer refugee and stayee women and men show, both those on the move due to displacement and those more immobile have to navigate the terrain of social flux. They respond by (re)negotiating their identi-ties, belonging and social relations within new contexts. How much and what type of change comes about is negotiated between different actors, institutions and diverse axes of power. For those returnees in Ler who had access to greater (social and financial) capital and resources, change in livelihoods and social relations was much greater than for those who were less able. Adolescent girls and young women are faced with partic-ular challenges in the context of locality production upon return as they are often perceived as agents of social transformation, which threaten established gender power relations. Young returnee men, by sharing domestic work and recognising women's equal position, challenge the

---

[19] Castles, ibid, p. 1565.
[20] H. Vigh, 'Motion squared: A second look at the concept of social navigation', *Anthropological Theory* 2009, 9(4): 419–38, p. 420.

concepts of hegemonic masculinities and the types of roles and responsibilities culturally assigned to them.

By analysing the web of power embedded in emplacement processes and capabilities of social navigation, I expand the notions of home proposed by Stef Jansen and Staffan Löfving.[21] They show how 'home-making, un-making and re-making' unfold for people who have to navigate the socially transformative and uncertain conditions generated by conflict and structural violence. The concepts are filled with power differentials and how these processes depend on individual capacities to regulate power but are also regulated by power relations. Yet, as the example of Lɛr residents reveals, this focus needs to be broadened by including effects of these processes on the actors involved (both returnees and stayees, or the displaced and host population) on their power positions and the (re)making of their own gendered selves and their identities.

GENDER THEORIES, DISPLACEMENT AND IMPLICATIONS FOR GENDER-MAINSTREAMING POLICIES

The experiences of Nuer women and men described and analysed here also have implications for the study of gender and gender-mainstreaming approaches in humanitarian and development programmes more specifically. The war-induced displacement setting chosen as a framework for the book allows for a better understanding of the lived gender experiences as well as the (re)negotiation of gender and generational relations. By employing a feminist analysis that centres gender, age and other axes of difference, I break away from men and women's independent experiences of displacement and mobility. I underscore the relational nature of gender and age, which improves our understanding of the continuities and discontinuities of gender practices under rapid social change. This study also emphasises the particular resistance of gender ideologies, despite challenges to the material basis of women's subordination. Even so, the idea of men as being always a dominant gender needs also critical contextualization, for gender asymmetries are fluid and contingent on places in which they occur. Despite changing sources of power, new gender inequalities emerge. Although some women who enjoy access to resources and education as a new basis of power manage to negotiate greater autonomy, those lacking these privileges suffer additional subordination. These findings need to be better integrated in policies and programmes that attempt to bring about gender equality.

These insights also have practical implications. They permit humanitarian organisations to better understand the gender and generational effects of war, displacement and emplacement, feed into the debates on gender, migration and displacement and demonstrate how war and civil conflicts challenge gendered and generational access to, and the nature of, mobility. The war-time trajectories of different women and men

---

[21] Jansen and Löfving, *Struggles for Home*.

reveal that (im)mobility, migration and displacement are not neutral terms and that they are conditioned, among other things, by gender, age, social position and access to resources. In general, men have easier access to migration and thus are able to reap greater benefits from war-time displacement. Women are less mobile due to their social and reproduction roles and as a result often stay behind in conflict zones. Yet some who enjoy influential positions within a community due to their access to resources and social networks were able to access refugee camps. As a result, their autonomy expanded. My findings underscore the diverse experiences and positions of power and privilege between and among women and men. They are also helpful in discerning the links between gender, structure and agency in accounting for (trans-national) movements. They also question the assumption that most refugees are women.

My findings also point to multifaceted reasons for mobility and further problematise the grey area between voluntary and forced migration. As the trajectories of the 'lost boys' show, the reasons for the boys' move-ment were often intertwined between forced and voluntary recruitment, the search for alternative livelihoods, education and opportunities for supporting the family. Some, in their search for education, became refu-gees in Kakuma. These acts of social navigation illustrate how young boys and men often manoeuvred their social conditions and the war environment to reap benefits from displacement. They also demonstrate how communities and individuals deal with extreme circumstances, using their agency and taking advantage of limited opportunities created by displacement. Thus, wars and displacement are not only destructive forces, they can also open up possibilities of change, learning and expan-sion of personal and community resources. Hence, the organisational discourses that typify young people as being powerless victims need to be further questioned. The existing international assistance approaches need to allow for greater scope in the analysis of causes of war-time popu-lation movement.

Much of the migration literature situates women as those who either gain or lose in status and importance within the family due to new economic and social circumstances.[22] Studies in the last few years have revealed more contradictory effects of migration and displacement on gender relations and family dynamics. For example, Nadje Al-Ali's research among Bosnian refugee families and Ruba Salih's investigation of Moroccan migrant women in Italy both show that these dynamics 'have shifted in various directions, accounting for empowerment and increased opportunities, as well as impediment and loss among migrant and refugee women'.[23] For the Nuer women and men, each of the stages

[22] G. Buijis, 'Introduction', in G. Buijis (ed.), Migrant women: Crossing boundaries and changing identities (Oxford: Berg 1993) (pp. 1–19) p. 8.
[23] Nadje Al-Ali, 'Trans- or a-National? Bosnian Refugees in the UK and the Netherlands', in N. Al-Ali and K. Khoser (eds) *New Approaches to Migration? Transnational Communities and the Transformation of Home* (London, 2002), pp. 96–117; Ruba Salih, 'Shifting Meanings of "Home": Consumption and Identity in

of displacement demonstrated a different set of changes to gender order. Although women suffered disproportionately more than men in the warzones, especially due to being targets of ethnicised gender violence and as a result of more restricted access to migration, forced displacement created opportunities for them to contest male privilege. Settling-in and emplacement in southern Sudan was both an empowering and constraining experience for women and men.

Especially useful for gender-mainstreaming programming are insights from gendered effects of war and the experiences of gender-equality awareness-raising programmes in the refugee camps. The dynamics of change in gender relations also shed light on the dynamic, and contradictory, ways in which war and displacement affect gender and generational power relations. War and displacement give rise to multiple forms, both weakened and reinforced, of femininities and masculinities. Male insecurity in times of great turmoil and changing life conditions is common. Thus, it is important that practitioners involved in gender-equality programming for war-affected populations move beyond a monolithic notion of the 'patriarchal violent' man. By closely examining men's experiences in relation to women's, and relative to other men's experiences, we are able to account for fluidity of masculinities and for gender as a constraining concept for both women and men.

War, displacement and the type of gender-mainstreaming assistance offered in Kakuma undermined the traditional material basis for male privilege and introduced new sources of social power and prestige. The authority of senior men was challenged by young educated men, emerging women leaders and women's autonomy. Although humanitarian assistance disempowered some men, the new sources of power were also used to reinforce the status and authority of (educated or militarised) men over (uneducated) women (and other men). Due to their disproportionately greater access to education, younger men's position in the patriarchal bargain (with uneducated women) was, at times, reinforced. Despite increasing calls from academics and some practitioners to critically re-assess the way in which gender has been womanised, sloganised, technicalised and turned into a 'ticking boxes' exercise, the focus on women as primary victims of gender hierarchies remains.

Yet, the impact of war on women was also contradictory – they went beyond being victims. Rather, women had to manoeuvre fluid multidimensional positions during the conflicts. This sheds light on women's agency, resistance and coping strategies in extreme conditions. In the absence of men during war and in displacement, women were pushed towards greater autonomy and self-sufficiency. In post-war South Sudan, opportunities for widening women's autonomy and opening spaces for change are partially due to changing livelihood strategies and the emergence of money and paid jobs as the primary source of income. Experiences in exile and exposure to women's empowerment programmes,

(cont.) Moroccan Women's Transnational Practices between Italy and Morocco', in N. Al-Ali and K. Khoser (eds) (London, 2002), pp. 51–67.

including education, training and gender equality awareness, propagated in refugee camps have contributed to envisaging more equal gender order in postwar communities. This is coupled with new legal norms with gender equality imprinted in the national laws. While some women negotiate their access to land through invoking new national laws, others use their social status (as daughters, wives or widows of influential men). Thus, transformations of gender relations take on new dynamics, even in the context where gender equality programmes sponsored by development organisations are no longer available. Policy wise, at both national and international level, there is a need to (re)consider the negative consequences of male disempowerment in relation to efforts to empower women, and to improve prospects of building a community based on gender justice principles in post-war societies.

REFUGEES AND HOME IN FLUX

In the past decade, there has been a general move at academic, policy, international and national intervention and advocacy level to recognise the complexity of the reasons for people's movement across and within borders. At the same time, by introducing terms such as 'mixed migration', refugees and those displaced due to violent conflict often become invisible in policy, academic research and advocacy.

The focus on war-time displacement is of particular importance due to the urgency and violent effects of war, which tear families and communities apart, and the power politics of international humanitarian enterprises to which displaced women and men are subjected. Violent displacement involves people living on the edge of urban slums or in refugee camps. This creates particular problems, as the deserving poor are faced with the gendering effects of humanitarian assistance. For years, or decades, they live in an out-of-state protection context, in a state of suspension. Such drastic displacement affects women and men, old and young, and changes their lives dramatically. The forced aspect population mobility, whether in the context of displacement or return, is of particular importance for the concepts of homemaking and emplacement. The experiences of the women and men whom I met in Kakuma and in Lɛr testify to this, as well as the type of changes in gender and generational relations resulting from war-time displacement. It is thus time to bring refugees into the focus of researchers and policy-makers by emphasising their particular predicaments.

There are a number of ethical, analytical and theoretical choices as well as consequences and dilemmas related to bringing refugees back into migration studies. As I have tried to demonstrate in this book, the violent aspects of war and displacement have fundamental consequences on people's lives, identities, strategies and hopes. With new displacements in and from, for example, Congo, Mali, South Sudan, Sudan and Syria, it is still, if not more, relevant to talk about refugees and those forcibly displaced.

As I am writing the last paragraphs of this book, South Sudan is experiencing another cycle of violence and wars. There are ongoing inter-community conflicts in Jonglei and Unity and ongoing conflicts on the borders with Sudan. New refugee camps are being created on the borders of South Sudan and forced-out displaced populations from Khartoum continue to arrive in this resource-strapped country. Due to floods, the communities of Lɛr and Nyal are suffering from lack of food. What are the prospects of returning home to Nuer *jäal* in the current post-war environment in South Sudan? Although peace came to Nuer communities in 2005, its lasting prospects are more elusive. Since the independence of South Sudan in July 2011, there have been clashes among southerners and between northerners and southerners. There is also much that needs to be done among the Nuer communities themselves to reconcile and build stable lives.

For now, Kuok has decided to continue with the settling-in process in Lɛr. 'I have finally my home. I am married now and feel that I found my home and my place' he told me over the phone in September 2011. Nyakuol, on the other hand, moved to Juba in search of a better livelihood and educational prospects for herself and her family. The question is, are they all finally home?

What can home offer in view of the current insecurities? How and where can they create their homes and how permanent will they be? What gender relations will they practice and how will they define themselves as gendered individuals within an ever-changing post-war South Sudan? One question that needs further investigation is what position women will occupy in the context of the nation-building processes in South Sudan. How will the diverse claims and experiences of women be accommodated in the emerging South Sudanese nation? While gender remains an important determinant of hierarchies, access to power, livelihoods, resources and privilege, it is increasingly linked to the level of education, status and war-trajectories. For now, communities in Lɛr and Western Upper Nile, and in South Sudan at large, continuously negotiate their homes in flux, with gender intersecting with these axes of difference in shaping power relations within the emerging nation.

Epilogue

On 15 December 2013, fighting broke out between the pro-government forces aligned with President Silva Kiir and opposition groups associated with the former Vice-President, Riek Machar. There are competing narratives about the events of the new conflict. Many commentators dubbed the violence as ethnically motivated, between Dinka and Nuer groups. Yet, this explanation skims over the deeper tensions and the more fragile and complex alliances that emerged as a result of the December crisis. The violence spread from Juba to Unity and Jongolei, and further to Equatoria. At first, Bentiu, Lɛr and Malakal were strongholds of the anti-government forces. However, government forces slowly but surely reclaimed these areas. As a result, Bentiu and Lɛr were razed by both retreating rebels and advancing government forces. By the beginning of February 2014, the United Nations estimated that over 740,000 people had been displaced, with large numbers seeking protection in UNMIS bases. Around 131,000 refugees had crossed into Ethiopia, Kenya, Sudan and Uganda.[1]

The violence that was unleashed came as a shock. As Jok Madut Jok, a founder of the Sudd Institute, argued during a meeting of representatives of South Sudanese civil society in Nairobi held on 10 January 2014,[2] the abruptness of events, how suddenly they erupted, and without warning, was a great surprise. What was also shocking was the speed at which the violence spread, not just from barracks to barracks but from state to state. The viciousness was also a shock, as was the ethnic tone that it rapidly acquired, having previously been contained as an internal military issue.

Yet, as Jok and others at the meeting argued, the events of 15 December were not unexpected for anyone who has been paying attention to South Sudan over the last eight years. Abuse, human rights violations and crimes have long gone unpunished; so far no one has been held accountable in South Sudan. This, as many South Sudanese activists argue, needs to be addressed if peace negotiations are to find a resolution.

The history of this violence goes back to the legacy of South Sudan's

---

[1] UNHCR, 'South Sudan Emergency Situation', 5 February, UNHCR External Regional Update, 2012.
[2] The event was held under the auspices of the Sudd Institute, the South Sudan Law Society (SSLS), the Gurtong Trust, the Open Society Initiative for Eastern Africa (OSIEA), and the Rift Valley Institute's Nairobi Forum.

independence and liberation wars, where factionalism and division had left deep social frictions. While there were numerous promises that, at independence, the wounds inflicted would be healed, little has actually been achieved in terms of reconciliation and healing since the Comprehensive Peace Agreement. Moreover, the SPLM/A was and continues to be in crisis. Built haphazardly, and having absorbed a number of militias, some of which had sided with Khartoum during the civil war and fought with the SPLA, an uneasy coalition was 'formed more by accident than design, creating an unwieldy institution without a central ethos or culture – one that "did not reflect the diversity of the country"'.[3] The violence that ensued was a logical consequence of these factors. However, no one can agree what triggered the fighting on 15 December.

The government's version of events lays the blame on Riek Machar and his alleged attempts at a coup d'état. Others argue that those who were unilaterally dismissed from the cabinet by Salva Kiir in July 2013 thereafter formed an opposition wanting to depose the President. Another interpretation of events 'locates the origin of the crisis purely within disagreements among the Presidential guard, the division of the military known as Division 8 (also known as the Tiger Division)'.[4] These disagreements spread to other units across the country. The last explanation involves the disgruntled officer in the national defence who 'took advantage of the confusion and the crisis to settle old scores, leading to the escalation of the crisis and widespread confusion'.[5] Despite ongoing peace negotiations between the government and the rebels being held in Ethiopia under the auspices of the Intergovernmental Authority on Development (IGAD), the most worrying element of the continuing violence is the lack of options with which to resolve the conflict. The complexity of social, political, economic and military issues need to be looked at from a historical perspective in order to understand the type of solutions that might bring an end to the crisis. The need is for 'a comprehensive process towards restoring peace among all ethnic communities in South Sudan'.

Once again, women became primary recipients of indiscriminate violence and subjected to displacement, yet their voices were excluded at the peace talks in Addis Ababa. At the beginning of February, in response to the destruction of lives, homes and livelihoods across South Sudan, women from various ethnic groups staying in the UNMIS protection site in Bentiu marched twelve kilometres in silence, holding white flags, to the Governor's office. They demanded that displaced women be engaged in peace processes. This initiative was undertaken by displaced Nuer and Dinka women who also sought to open up inter- and intra-community dialogues to address the conflicts in Unity state. 'We are women of peace, we have come together – Nuers, Dinkas and Equatorians – to promote peace and reconciliation', said Aluel Wal Magor, a 40-year old mother of nine. 'We met with the state governor [Dr Joseph Nguen Monytuil] to tell him that we do not buy the idea of being divided along ethnic lines'.

[3] Ibid.
[4] Ibid.
[5] Ibid.

Lɛr and Bentiu no longer exist. They were burned to the ground, reportedly by government forces in the beginning of February 2014. Nyakuol, Nyariek, Kuok and others whom I followed during the research in Kakuma and in South Sudan have become displaced yet again. Some have lost their lives, and some are once again refugees in Kakuma. All have lost everything they built and worked so hard for over the last eight years.

Despite the attempts to sign a peace agreement, the fighting continues; it will be a long time before the residents of Lɛr will be able to go back and start (re)building their lives once again. Their experiences of displacement are not over yet, despite their attempts to settle. Nyakuoth, now a 23-year-old university graduate residing in Nairobi, shared her thoughts about the recent conflict by email. Her words serve as a closing and a new beginning for Nuer residents of Lɛr:

> Lɛr is burnt, and also Gatdor. I have talked to my brother [who was in Lɛr during this time] through satellite phone and he said they are still in hiding, big problems with kids, no food and it's just bad, one has to be even more careful whom your hiding, with people betray each other and kill without mercy. It's anger, envy and hearts full of hate for fellow beings. Only God will make miracles in that country. We hope peace finds us. We [were] born in war, raised in war now going to even be mothers in it [in war]. I am so tired of hoping for peace in that country that I have given up, let it be. I will start my life far away from it, though my heart will always belong there, but I will never wait for it, let it find me walking. I am a [human] being and life must go on. It just hurts so much that people go through the same thing. I had experienced it, and that picture is so fresh in my mind, only death can take it. I pity those crying children with their poor mothers hiding them in those rivers, hoping to see the next day. I hope new generation will emerge soon.

14 May 2014

Bibliography

CITED REFERENCES

Abdi, Cawo, 'Refugees, Gender Based Violence and Resistance: A Case Study of Somali Women in Kenyan Camps', in E. Tastsoglou and A. Dobrowolsky (eds) *Gender, Migration and Citizenship: Making Local, National and Transnational Connections* (London, 2006).

Abu-Sharaf, Rogaia Mustafa, *Transforming Displaced Women in Sudan* (Chicago, IL, 2009).

—*Wanderings: Sudanese Migrants and Exiles in North America* (Ithaca, NY, 2002)

Al-Ali, Nadje, 'Gender Relations and Transnational Ties among Bosnian Refugees', in U. Vuorella and D. Bryceson (ed.) *Forging New Frontiers in Europe: Transnational Families and their Global Networks* (Oxford, 2003).

Alier, Abel, *Southern Sudan: Too Many Agreements Dishonoured*, 2nd Ed. (Reading, 1992).

Allen, Tim (ed.), *In Search of Cool Ground: War, Flight and Homecoming in Northeast Africa* (London and Trenton, NJ, 1996).

Allen, Tim and Hubert Morsink (eds), *When Refugees Go Home* (London and Trenton, NJ, 1994).

Anthias, Floya, 'New Hybridities, Old Concepts: The Limits of "Culture"', *Ethnic and Racial Studies*, 2001, Vol. 24, pp. 619–41.

Appadurai, Arjun, *Modernity at Large: Cultural Dimensions of Globalization* (Minneapolis, IN, 1996).

—'Putting Hierarchy in Its Place', *Cultural Anthropology*, 1998, Vol. 3, pp. 37–50.

Arendt, Hannah, *The human condition* (Chicago: The University of Chicago Press, IL, 1958).

Arop, Madut-Arop, *Sudan's Painful Road to Peace. A Full Story of the Founding and Development of SPLM/SPLA* (BookSurge, 2006).

Assal, Munzoul, 'Rights and Decisions to Return: Internally Displaced Persons in Post-war Sudan', in K. Grabska and L. Mehta (eds) *Forced Displacement: Why Rights Matter?* (London, 2008) pp. 139–58.

Bachelard, Gaston, *The Poetics of Space* (Beacon Press, 1969).

Bailey Sarah, and Simon Harragin, 'Food assistance, reintegration and dependency in Southern Sudan', Overseas Development Institute: London (2009).

Bakewell, Oliver, 'Some Reflections on Structure and Agency in Migration Theory', *Journal of Ethnic and Migration Studies* 36(10), 2010.

—'Repatriation and Self-settled Refugees in Zambia: Bringing Solutions to the Wrong Problems', *Journal of Refugee Studies*, 2000, Vol. 13, pp. 356–73.

Behera, Navnita Chadha, and Meenakshi Thapan (eds), *Gender, Conflict and Migration*, Vol. 3, Refugee Watch Online, 2008.

Berger, Carol, 'The SPLA and Lost Boys', PhD dissertation, University of Oxford, 2010.

BICC, 'Oil Investment and Conflict in Upper Nile State, South Sudan', *Bonn International Center for Conversion Brief* 48, 2013.

Black, Richard and Khalid Koser (eds), *The End of the Refugee Cycle? Refugee Repatriation and Reconstruction* (Oxford, 1999).

Breckenridge, C., S. Pollock, H. Bhabha and D. Chakrabarty, *Cosmopolitanisms* (Durham, NC, 2002).

Buijis, G. 'Introduction', in G. Buijis (ed.), Migrant women: Crossing boundaries and changing identities (Oxford: Berg, 1993), pp. 1–19.

Burr, Millard, and Robert O. Collins, *Requiem for Sudan: War, Droughts, and Disaster Relief on the Nile* (Boulder, CO, 1995).

Butler, Judith, *Bodies that Matter: On the discursive limits of "sex"* (New York, Routledge, 1993).

Callamard, Agnes, 'Flour is Power: The Gendered Division of Labour in Lisongwe Camp', in W. Giles, H. Moussa and P. Van Esterik (eds), *Development and Diaspora: Gender and the Refugee Experience* (Dundas, 1996), pp. 176–98.

Casey, Edward S., 'How to Get from Space to Place in a Fairly Short Stretch of Time: Phenomenological Prolegomena', in S. Feld and K. H. Basso (eds) *Senses of Place* (Santa Fe, NM, 1996), pp. 13–51.

—*The Fate of Place: A Philosophical History* (Berkeley, CA, 1997).

Castles, Stephen, "Understanding Global Migration: A Social Transformation Perspective", *Journal of Ethnic and Migration Studies* 36, no.10: 1565–86, 2010.

Clifford, James, *Routes: Travel and Translation in the Late Twentieth Century* (Cambridge, MA, 1997).

Cock, J., 'Women and the Military: Implications for Demilitarisation in the 1990s in South Africa', *Gender and Security*, 1994, Vol. 8 pp. 152–69.

Comaroff, Jean, and John Comaroff (eds), *Modernity and its Malcontents: Ritual and Power in Postcolonial Africa* (Chicago, IL, 1993).

Cornwall, Andrea, 'To be a Man is more Than a Day's Work: Shifting Ideals of Masculinity in Ado-Odo, Southwestern Nigeria', in L.A. Lindsay and S.F. Miescher (eds), *Men and Masculinities in Modern Africa* (Portsmouth, NH, 2003).

—'Wayward Women and Useless Men: Contest and Change in Gender Relations in Ado-Odo, S.W. Nigeria', in D.L. Hodgson and S. McCurdy (eds), *"Wicked" Women and the Reconfiguration of Gender in Africa* (Portsmouth, NH, 2001).

Cornwall, Andrea, and Nancy Lindisfarne (eds), *Dislocating Masculinity: Comparative Ethnographies* (London, 1996).

Cornwall, Andrea, Elisabeth Harrison, and Ann Whitehead (eds), *Feminisms in Development: Contradictions, Contestations and Challenges* (London, 2007).

Daly, M.W., and Ahmad Sikainga (eds), *Civil War in the Sudan* (London, 1993).

Davis, John, 'The anthropology of suffering'. *Journal of Refugee Studies* 5(2): 149–61 (1992).

de Alwis, Malathi, 'The "Purity" of Displacement and the Reterritorialization of Longing: Muslim IDPs in North-western Sri Lanka', in W. Giles and J. Hyndman (eds) *Sites of Violence: Gender and Conflict Zones* (Berkeley, CA, 2004), pp. 213–32.

Deng, Francis M., *War of Visions: Conflict of Identity in the Sudan* (Washington, DC, 1995).

Deng, Luka Biong, 'Are Non-Poor Households always less Vulnerable? The Case of Households exposed to Protracted Civil War in Southern Sudan', *Disasters*, 2008, Vol. 32, pp. 377–98.

—'Confronting Civil War: A Comparative Study of Household Assets Management in Southern Sudan during the 1990s', *IDS Discussion Paper* 381, Institute of Development Studies, 2002.

Denov, Myriam, and Christine Gervais, 'Negotiating (In)Security: Agency, Resistance, and Resourcefulness among Girls Formerly Associated with Sierra Leone's Revolutionary United Front', *Signs*, 2007, Vol. 32, pp. 885–910.

de Montclos, Marc-Antoine, and Peter Mwangi Kagwanja, 'Refugee Camps or Cities? The Socio-economic Dynamics of the Dadaab and Kakuma Camps in Northern Kenya', *Journal of Refugee Studies*, 2000, Vol. 13, pp. 205–22.

de Waal, Alex, *Famine Crimes: Politics and the Disaster Relief Industry in Africa* (Oxford and Bloomington, IN, 1997).

Duffield, Mark, Jok Madut Jok, David Keen, Geoff Loane, Fiona O'Reilly, John Ryle and Philip Winter, 'Sudan: Unintended Consequences of Humanitarian Assistance – Field Evaluation Study', University of Dublin, Trinity College: April 2000.

Eastmond, Marita, 'Transnational Returns and Reconstruction in Post-war Bosnia and Herzegovina', *International Migration*, 2006, Vol. 44, pp. 141–66.

Eastmond, Marita and Joakim Ojendal, 'Revisiting a "Repatriation Success": The Case of Cambodia', in Black and Koser (eds), *The End of the Refugee Cycle? Refugee Repatriation and Reconstruction* (Oxford, 1999).

ECOS, 'Briefing Note: Instruments to address South Sudan's Petroleum Legacy Issues', European Coalition on Oil in Sudan, Utrecht, 2011.

—'Sudan's Oil Industry – Facts and Analysis', www.ecosonline.org/news/2008/south_sudan_villagers_environment_suffer_from_oil_boom/.

Eggers, Dave, *What is the What?* (San Francisco, CA, 2006).

El-Bushra, Judy, 'Transforming Conflict: Some Thoughts on a Gendered Understanding of Conflict Processes', in S. Jacobs, R. Jacobson and J. Marchbank (eds), *States of Conflict: Gender, Violence and Resistance* (London, 2000) pp. 66–87.

Elharaway, Samir and Sara Pantuliano, 'Land Issues in Post-Conflict Return and Recovery', in J. Unruh and R. Williams (eds), *Land and Post-Conflict Peacebuilding* (London, 2013) pp. 115–20.

El Jack, Amani, 'Gendered Implications: Development-Induced Displacement in the Sudan', in P. Vandergeest, P. Idahosa and P. Bose (eds) *Development's Displacements: Ecologies, Economies and Cultures at Risk* (Vancouver, 2007).

Enloe, Cynthia, 'Feminism, Nationalism and Militarism: Wariness without Paralysis?', in C.R. Sutton (ed.), *Feminism, Nationalism and Militarism* (Washington, DC, 1995), pp. 13–34.

Essed, P., G. Frerks and J. Schrijvers (eds), *Refugees and the Transformation of Societies: Agency, Policies, Ethics and Politics* (Oxford, 2005).

Evans-Pritchard, Edward E., *Nuer Religion* (Oxford, 1956).

— *Kinship and Marriage among the Nuer* (Oxford, 1951).

—*The Nuer: A Description of the Modes of Livelihood and Political Institutions of a Nilotic People* (Oxford, 1940).

Fábos, Anita H., *'Brothers' or Other? Propriety and Gender for Muslim Arab Sudanese in Egypt* (Oxford, 2008).

Falge, Christiane, 'The Cultural Resilience in Nuer Conversation and a "Capitalist Missionary"', in Günther Schlee and Elizabeth E. Watson (eds), *Changing Identifications and Alliances in North-East Africa* (Berghan Books, 2009), pp. 205–17.

— 'The Nuer as Refugees: A Study on Social Adaptation', MA thesis, Addis Ababa University, 1997.

Faria, Caroline, 'Gendering War and Peace in the South Sudan: the Elision and Emergence of Women', Association of Concerned Africa Scholars, Vol. 86, 2011.

Feld, Steven, and Keith H. Basso (eds), *Senses of Place, School of American Research Press* (Santa Fe, CA, 1996).

Ferguson, James, *Expectations of Modernity: Myths and Meanings of Modern Life on the Zambian Copperbelt* (Berkeley, CA, 1999).

Fitzgerald, Mary Anne, *Throwing the Stick Forward: The Impact of War on Southern Sudanese Women* (Nairobi, 2002).

Flick, Uwe, *An Introduction of Qualitative Research* (London, 2002).

Gable, Eric, 'The Funeral and Modernity in Manjaco', *Cultural Anthropology*, 2006, Vol. 21, pp. 385–415.

Gagnon, G. and John Ryle, 'Report of an Investigation into Oil Development, Conflict and Displacement in Western Upper Nile', 2001.

Geertz, Clifford, *The Interpretation of Cultures: Selected Essays* (New York, NY, 1973).

Geschiere, Peter, *The Witchcraft of Modernity: Politics and the Occult in Postcolonial Africa* (Charlottesville, VA, 1997).

Ghorashi, Halleh, 'Giving Silence a Chance: The Importance of Life Stories for Research on Refugees', *Journal of Refugee Studies*, 2008, Vol. 21, pp. 117–32.

Giles, Wenona, 'Public and Private Constructions of Gendered Violence in Ethnic National Conflict', *Engendering Forced Migration* ed. D. Indra (Oxford, 1999), pp. 83–93.

Giles, Wenona and Jennifer Hyndman, *Sites of Violence: Gender and Conflict Zones* (Berkeley, CA, 2004).

Glick Schiller, N., and T. Faist, 'Introduction: Migration, Development and Social Transformation', *Social Analysis*, 2009, Vol. 53, pp. 1–13.

GoSS, 'The Interim Constitution of Southern Sudan', December 2005, www.chr.up.ac.za/undp/domestic /docs/c_SouthernSudan.pdf.

GoSS and SPLA, *Comprehensive Peace Agreement*, Government of Sudan and Sudan People's Liberation Army, 9 January 2005, Nivasha, Kenya, www.unmis.org/english/cpa.htm.

Grabska, Katarzyna, 'Lost Boys, Invisible Girls: Stories of Marriage across Borders', *Gender, Place and Culture*, 2010, Vol. 17, pp. 479–97.

Gupta, Akhil, and James Ferguson (eds), *Culture, Power, Place: Explorations in Critical Anthropology* (Durham, NC, 1997).

Hale, Sondra, 'Feminist Method, Process and Self Criticism: Interviewing Sudanese Women', in *Women's Words*, S. Berger Gluck and D. Patai (eds) (New York, NY, 1991), pp. 121–36.

Hall, Stuart, 'Introduction: Who Needs "Identity"?', in S. Hall and P. du Gay (eds), *Questions of Cultural Identity* (London, 1996).

—'Old and New Identities, Old and New Ethnicities', in A.D. King (ed.) *Culture, Globalization and the World System* (Basingstoke, 1991).

Hammond, Laura, *This Place will Become Home: Refugee Repatriation to Ethiopian* (Ithaca, 2004).

—'Examining the Discourse of Repatriation: Towards a More Proactive Theory of Return Migration', in R. Black and K. Koser (eds), *The End of the Refugee Cycle? Refugee Repatriation and Reconstruction* (Oxford, 1999).

Hansen, Lene, and Louise Olsson (2004). 'Gender and Security' Special Issue, *Security Dialogue* 35(4), London: SAGE Publications.

Harding, Sandra (ed.), *Feminism and Methodology* (Bloomington, IN, 1987).

Haraway, Donna, 'A Manifesto for Cyborgs: Science, Technology, Socialist Feminism in the 1980s', *Socialist Review*, Vol. 80, pp. 65–107.

Harir, S. and T. Tvedt (eds), *Short-Cut to Decay: The Case of the Sudan* (Uppsala: The Scandinavian Institute of African Studies, 1994).

Harker, John, 'Human Security in Sudan: The Report of a Canadian Assessment Mission', January 2000.

Harrell-Bond, Barbara, *Imposing Aid* (Oxford, 1986).

—'Response to Kibreab', *Journal of Refugee Studies*, 2004, Vol. 17, pp. 27–8.

Harrell-Bond, Barbara, and Efthixia Voutira 'Anthropology and the Study of Refugees', *Anthropology Today*, 1992, Vol. 8, pp. 6–10.

Harragin, S. and C. Chol, The Southern Sudan Vulnerability Study, Nairobi: Save the Children (UK) 1999.

Hirsch, Eric and Michael O'Hanlon, *The Anthropology of Landscape* (Oxford, 1995)

Hodgson, Dorothy L., *Once Intrepid Warriors: Gender, Ethnicity, and the Cultural Politics of Maasai Development* (Bloomington, IN, 2004).

—*Gendered Modernities: Ethnographic Perspectives of Modernity/Modernities, Gender and Ethnography* (New York, NY, 2001).

Hodgson, Dorothy L., and Sherry McCurdy (eds), *"Wicked" Women and the Reconfiguration of Gender in Africa* (Portsmouth, NH, 2001).

Horst, Cindy, *Transnational Nomads: How Somalis Cope with Refugee Life in the Dadaab Refugee Camps of Kenya* (New York, NY, 2006).

Human Rights Watch, *Sudan, Oil, and Human Rights* (New York, NY, 2003).

—'Famine in Sudan 1998: The Human Rights Causes', www.hrw.org/reports/1999/sudan/SUDAWEB2.htm#P374_19682 (accessed February 2014), 1999.

—*Civilian Devastation: Abuses by All Parties in the War in Southern Sudan* (New York, NY, 1994).

Hutchinson, Sharon E., "Peace and Puzzlement: Grass-roots Peace Initiatives between the Nuer and Dinka of South Sudan", in Günther Schlee and Elizabeth Watson (eds), *Changing Identification and Alliances in North-east Africa*, Vol. II (New York and Oxford: Berghahn Books, 2009), pp. 49–72.

—'Gendered Violence and the Militarization of Nuer and Dinka Ethnic Identities', University of Wisconsin-Madison, Cultural Pluralism Research Circle, 2000.

—'Nuer Ethnicity Militarized', *Anthropology Today*, 2000, Vol. 16, pp. 6–13.

— 'Death, Memory and the Politics of Legitimation: Nuer Experiences of the Continuing Second Civil War', *Memory and the Postcolony: African Anthropology and the Critique of Power* ed. R. Webner (London, 1998) pp. 58–71.

—*Nuer Dilemmas: Coping with Money, War and the State* (Berkeley, CA, 1996).

—'Rising Divorce among the Nuer, 1936–1983', *Man*, Vol. 25, 1990, pp. 393–411.

Hyndman, Jennifer, *Managing Displacement: Refugees and the Politics of Humanitarianism* (Minneapolis, 2000).

Hyndman, Jennifer, and Malathi de Alwis, 'Beyond Gender: Toward a Feminist Analysis of Humanitarianism and Development in Sri Lanka', *Women's Studies Quarterly*, 2003, Vols. 3–4, pp. 212–26.

Indra, Doreen (ed.), *Engendering Forced Migration: Theory and Practice* (New York, NY, 1999).

International Crisis Group (ICG), *God, Oil and Country, Changing the Logic of War in Sudan* (Brussels, 2002).

Itto, Anne, 'Guests at the Table? The Role of Women in Peace Processes', Conciliation Resources, www.c-r.org/our-work/accord/sudan/women.php, 2006.

Jackson, Michael, *The Politics of Storytelling: Violence, Transgression and Intersubjectivity* (Copenhagen, 2006).

Jacobs, S., R. Jacobson and J. Marchbank, *States of Conflict: Gender, Violence and Resistance* (London, 2000).

Jansen, Bram J., 'Between Vulnerability and Assertiveness: Negotiating Resettlement in Kakuma Refugee Camp, Kenya', *African Affairs*, 2008, Vol. 107, pp. 569–87.

Jansen, Stef, and Löfving Staffan, *Struggles for Home: Violence, Hope and the Movement of People* (Berghan Books, 2009).

Jayawardena, Kumari, *Feminism and Nationalism in the Third World* (New York, NY, 1986).

Johnson, Douglas, *Nuer Prophets: A History of Prophecy from the Upper Nile in the Nineteenth and Twentieth Centuries* (Oxford, 1994).

—*The Root Causes of Sudan's Civil Wars* (Oxford, 2006).

—'The Sudan People's Liberation Army and the Problem of Fractionalism', in C. Clapman (ed.), *African Guerrillas* (Oxford, 1998) pp. 53–72.

—'Destruction and reconstruction in the economy of the Southern Sudan', in S. Harir and T. Tvedt (eds), *Short-Cut to Decay: The Case of the Sudan* (Uppsala: The Scandinavian Institute of African Studies, 1994).

—'Twentieth century civil wars', in John Ryle et al. (eds), *The Sudan Handbook* (Woodbridge, James Currey, 2011).

—'The Nuer civil wars', in Günther Schlee and Elizabeth Watson (eds), *Changing Identification and Alliances in North-east Africa*, Vol. II (NY and Oxford: Berghahn Books, 2009), pp. 31–48.

Jok, Madut Jok, 'War, Changing Ethics and the Position of Youth in South Sudan', in J. Abbink and I. van Kessel (eds), *Vanguards or Vandals: Youth, Politics and Conflict in Africa* (Leiden, 2005).

—*War and Slavery in Sudan* (Philadelphia, 2001).

—'Militarism, Gender and Reproductive Suffering: The Case of Abortion in Western Dinka', *Africa*, 1999, Vol. 69, pp. 194–212.

—'Militarization and Gender Violence in South Sudan', *Journal of Asian and African Studies*, 1999, Vol. 34, pp. 427–42.

—*Militarization, Gender and Reproductive Health in South Sudan* (New York, NY, 1998).

Jok, Madut Jok, and Sharon E. Hutchinson, 'Sudan's Prolonged Second Civil War and the Militarization of Nuer and Dinka Ethnic Identities', *African Studies Review*, 1999, Vol. 42, pp. 125–45.

JRS Kakuma, 'Gender Cases in the JRS Safe-Heavens, Statistics 2003–2006', Jesuit Refugee Services Kakuma Report, 2006.

Kabeer, Naila, *Power to Choose* (London, 2000).

—*Reversed Realities Gender Hierarchies in Development Thought* (London, 1994).

Kagwanja, Peter M., 'Ethnicity, Gender and Violence in Kenya', *Forced Migration Review*, 2000, Vol. 9, pp. 22–25.

—'"Power to Uhuru": Youth Identity and Generational Politics in Kenya's 2002 Elections', *African Affairs*, 2006, Vol. 105, pp. 51–75.

Kandiyoti, Deniz, 'Bargaining with Patriarchy', *Gender and Society*, 1988, Vol. 2, pp. 274–90.

—'Gender, Power and Contestation: Rethinking Bargaining with Patriarchy', in C. Jackson and R. Pearson (eds) *Feminist Visions of Development: Gender Analysis and Policy* (London, 1998).

Kani Edwards, Jane, *Sudanese Women Refugees: Transformations and Future Imaginings* (New York, NY, 2007).
Keen, David, *Conflict and Collusion in Sierra Leone* (Oxford, 2005).
Kibreab, Gaim, 'Access to Economic and Social Rights in First Countries of Asylum and Repatriation: A Case Study of Eritrean Refugees in Sudan', in K. Grabska and L. Mehta (eds) *Forced Displacement: Why Rights Matter?* (London, 2008).
—'Pulling the Wool over the Eyes of the Strangers: Refugees Deceit and Trickery in Institutionalized Settings', *Journal of Refugee Studies*, 2004, Vol. 17, pp. 1–26.
—'Rethinking Household Headship among Eritrean Refugees and Returnees', *Development and Change*, 2003, Vol. 34, pp. 311–37.
Kiggen, J., *Nuer-English Dictionary* (London, 1948).
Kunz, Egon, 'Exile and Resettlement: Refugee Theory', *International Migration Review*, 1981, Vol. 15, pp. 42–51.
Kurimoto, Eisei, 'Civil war and regional conflicts: the Pari and their neighbours in south-eastern Sudan', in Katsuyoshi Fukui and John Markakis (eds), *Ethnicity and Conflict in the Horn of Africa* (London, 1994)
Kurimoto, Eisei and Simon Simonse (eds), *Conflict, Age and Power in North East Africa* (London, 1994).
Lal, Jayati, 'Situating Locations: The Politics of Self, Identity, and "Other" in Living and Writing the Text', in D.L. Wolf (ed.), *Feminist Dilemmas in Fieldwork* (Boulder, CO, 1996), pp. 185–.
Leonardi, Cherry, '"Liberation" or Capture: Youth in Between "Hakuma", and "Home" During Civil War and its Aftermath in Southern Sudan', *African Affairs*, 2008, Vol. 106, pp. 391–412.
Lindsay, Lisa A., and Stephan F. Miescher (eds), *Men and Masculinities in Modern Africa* (Portsmouth, NH, 2003).
Lobban, Richard A., Robert S. Kramer and Carolyn Luehr-Lobban, *Historical Dictionary of the Sudan* (Lanham, MD, 2002).
Loizos, Peter, 'Displacement Shock and Recovery in Cyprus', *Forced Migration Review*, No. 33, 2009, pp.40–42.
London, Charles, 'The Forgotten Children of Sudan', Refugees International, 2003, www.refintl.org/content/article/detai/1071 (accessed November 2008).
Long, Lynellyn D., and Ellen Oxfeld (eds), *Coming Home? Refugees, Migrants, and Those Who Stayed Behind* (Philadelphia, NJ, 2004).
Lovett, Margaret, '"She Thinks She's Like a Man": Marriage and (De)constructing Gender Identity in Colonial Buha, Western Tanzania, 1943–1960', in D.L. Hodgson and S. McCurdy (eds), *"Wicked" Women and the Reconfiguration of Gender in Africa* (Portsmouth, NH; Oxford; Cape Town, 2001).
Lubkemann, Stephen, *Culture in Chaos. An Anthropology of the Social Condition in War* (Chicago, 2008).
LWF Kakuma, 'Gender Report 2005–2006, Kakuma Refugee Camp', Lutheran World Federation Field Report, 2006.
Malkki, Liisa H., 'National Geographic: The Rooting of Peoples and the Territorialization of National Identity among Scholars and Refugees', *Cultural Anthropology*, 1992, Vol. 7, pp. 24–44.
—*Purity and Exile: Violence, Memory, and National Cosmology among Hutu Refugees in Tanzania* (Chicago, 1995).
—'Refugees and Exile: From 'Refugee Studies' to the National Order of Things', *Annual Review of Anthropology*, 1995, Vol. 24, pp. 495–523.
Marriage, Zoë, 'The Comfort of Denial: External Assistance in Southern Sudan', in *Development and Change*, 2006, Vol. 37(3), pp. 479–500.
Martin, Susan F., *Refugee Women*, (Maryland, 2004).
McCallum, Judith, and Alfred Okech, 'Small Arms and Light Weapons Control and Community Security in Southern Sudan: The Links between Gender Identity and Disarmament', *Regional Security, Gender Identity, and CPA Implementation in Sudan*, (Ontario, 2008).
McSpadden, Lucia A., 'Negotiating Masculinity in the Reconstruction of Social Place: Eritrean and Ethiopian Refugees in the United States and Sweden', in D. Indra (ed.), *Engendering Forced Migration: Theory and Practice*, (New York, 1999), pp. 242–61.
—'Contemplating Repatriation to Eritrea', in L. D. Long and E. Oxfeld (eds), *Coming*

Home? Refugees, Migrants, and Those Who Stayed Behind (Philadelphia, NJ, 2004), pp. 34–49.

Michrina, Barry P., and Cherylanne Richards, *Person to Person: Fieldwork, Dialogue, and the Hermeneutic Method* (Albany, NY, 1996).

Mills, Mary Beth, *Thai Women in the Global Labour Force: Consuming Desires, Contested Selves* (New Brunswick, New Jersey: Rutgers University Press, 2002)

Minear, Larry, ed., *Humanitarianism Under Siege. A Critical Review of Operation Lifeline Sudan* (Trenton, NJ, 1991).

Minh Haa, Trin, *Woman, Native, Other: Writing Postcoloniality and Feminism* (Bloomington, IN, 1989).

Mohanty, Chandra T., 'Under Western Eyes: Feminist Scholarship and Colonial Discourses', *Feminist Review,* 1987, Vol. 30, pp. 61–88. See Chandra T. Mohanty, 'Categories of Struggle: Third World Women and the Politics of Feminism', in C.T. Mohanty, A. Russo and L. Torres (eds) *The Third World Women and the Politics of Feminism,* (Indiana University Press, IN, 1991).

Moore, Henrietta, *Space, Text, and Gender. An Anthropological Study of the Marakwet of Kenya* (New York, NY, 1996).

—*A Passion for Difference. Essays in Anthropology and Gender* (London, 1994).

Moussa, Hellen, *Storm and Sanctuary: The Journey of Ethiopian and Eritrean Women Refugees* (Dundas, 1993).

Nordstrom, Carolyn, *Girls and Warzones: Troubling Questions* (Uppsala, 1997).

Nordstrom, Carolyn, and Antonius C.G.M. Robben (eds), *Fieldwork Under Fire: Contemporary Studies of Violence and Survival* (Berkeley, CA, 1995).

North, Liisa L., and Alan B. Simmons, *Journeys of Fear: Refugee Return and National Transformation in Guatemala* (Montreal, 1999).

Nyaba, Peter A., *The Politics of Liberation in South Sudan: An Insider's View* (Kampala, 1997).

Nyberg-Sørensen, N., N. van Hear and P. Engberg-Pedersen, 'The Migration-Development Nexus: Evidence and Policy Options; State of the Art Overview', *International Migration,* 2002, Vol. 40, pp. 3–71.

Ong, Aihwa, *Flexible Citizenship: The Cultural Logics of Transnationality* (Durham, NJ, 1999).

Ortner, Sherry, *Making Gender: The Politics and Erotics of Culture* (Boston, MA, 1996).

Ortner, Sherry, and Harriet Whitehead, *Sexual Meanings: The Cultural Construction of Gender and Sexuality* (Cambridge, 1981).

Pantuliano, Sara, *Uncharted Territory: Land, Conflict and Humanitarian Action* (Rugby, 2009).

Daphne Patai, 'US Academics and Third World Women: Is Ethical Research Possible?', in S. Berger Gluck and D. Patai (eds) *Women's Words: The Feminist Practice of Oral History* (New York, 1991), pp. 137–53.

Pearson, Ruth, Ann Whitehead and Kate Young, 'The Continued Subordination of Women in the Development Process', in K. Young, C. Wolkowitz and R. McCullagh (eds), *Of Marriage and the Market,* 2nd ed. (London, 1984).

Pilkington, Hilary, and Moya Flynn, 'From "Refugee" to 'Repatriate': Russian Repatriation Discourse in the Making', in R. Black and K. Koser (eds), *The End of the Refugee Cycle: Refugee Repatriation and Reconstruction* (Oxford, 1999) pp. 171–97.

Porteous, J. Douglas, 'Home: The Territorial Core', *Geographical Review,* 1976, Vol. 66, pp. 383–90.

Powles, Julia, 'Life History and Personal Narrative: Theoretical and Methodological Issues Relevant to Research and Evaluation in Refugee Contexts', *New Issues in Refugee Research Working Paper* 106, UNHCR, Geneva, 2004.

Riaka, L.G., 'Miss Malaika is a Threat to Southern Sudanese Cultures', *Sudan Tribune,* 7 December 2007.

Richards, Paul, 'New War: An Ethnographic Approach', in P. Richards (ed.), *No Peace, No War: An Anthropology of Contemporary Armed Conflicts* (Oxford, 2005).

Richmond, Anthony, 'Sociological Theories of International Migration: The Case of Refugees', *Current Sociology,* 1988, Vol. 36, pp. 7–25.

Ringera, K.L., 'Excluded Voices: Grassroots Women and Peacebuilding in Southern Sudan', PhD thesis, Department of Human Communication Studies, University of Denver, 2007.

Rolandsen, Øystein, *Guerrilla Government. Political Changes in the Southern Sudan during the 1990s* (Uppsala, 2005).

Rose, Gillian, *Feminism and Geography: The Limits of Geographical Knowledge* (Minneapolis, MN, 1993).

Ryle, John, Justine Willis, Suliman Baldo and Jok Madut Jok (eds), *The Sudan Handbook* (Oxford, 2011).

Sahlins, Marshall, *Tribesmen* (New Jersey, 1968).

Said, Edward, *Out of Place: a Memoir* (New York, 1999).

Salih, Ruba, 'Shifting Meanings of "Home": Consumption and Identity in Moroccan Women's Transnational Practices between Italy and Morocco", in N. Al-Ali and K. Khoser (eds), *New Approaches to Migration? Transnational Communities and the Transformation of Home* (London: Routledge, 2002) pp. 51–67.

Schechter, James, 'Lost Boys: Governing Sudanese Refugees in a UNHCR Camp', PhD thesis, University of Colorado, 2004.

Schipper, M., *Imagining Insiders: Africa and the Question of Belonging* (London, 1999).

Schrijvers, J., 'Fighters, Victims and Survivors: Constructions of Ethnicity, Gender and Refugeeness among Tamils in Sri Lanka', *Journal of Refugee Studies,* Vol. 12, no. 3, pp. 307–33, 1999.

Sen, Amartya K., 'Gender and Cooperative Conflicts', in I. Tinker (ed.) *Persistent Inequalities. Women and World Development* (New York, NY, 1990), pp. 123–49.

Sen, Samita, 'Motherhood and Mothercraft: Gender and Nationalism in Bengal', *Gender and History*, 1993, Vol. 5, pp. 231–43.

Shandy, Dianne, *Nuer-American Passages: Globalizing Sudanese Migration* (Florida, 2007).

—'Transnational Linkages between Refugees in Africa and in the Diaspora', *Forced Migration Review*, 2003, Vol. 16, pp. 7–9.

Silberschmidt, Margrethe, 'Disempowerment of Men in Rural and Urban East Africa: Implications for Male Identity and Sexual Behavior', *World Development*, 2001, Vol. 29, pp. 657–71.

SPLM, Protecting Rights and Strengthening Resilience of the Civilian Population in Bahr el Ghazal Region OLS: 31 May 1999.

SSCCSE, 'Key Indicators for Southern Sudan', Southern Sudan Centre for Census, Statistics and Evaluations, Juba, 2011.

SRRA Database and Monitoring Unit, SRRA Annual Assessment Report, November 1998.

Strathern, Marilyn, *The Gender of the Gift* (Berkeley, CA, 1988)

Sudan Tribune, 'South Sudan Villagers, Environment suffer from Oil Boom', 5 March 2008.

—'Dilemmas of South Sudanese and Culture', 15 October 2008.

Tuan, Yi-Fu, *Space and Place: The Perspective of an Experience* (Minneapolis, 1977).

Turner, Simon, 'Angry Young Men in Camps: Gender, Age and Class Relations among Burundian Refugees in Tanzania', *UNHCR Working Paper* No. 9, 1999.

—'Vindicating Masculinity: The Fate of Promoting Gender Equality', *Forced Migration Review*, 2000, Vol. 9, pp. 8–12.

—'The Barriers of Innocence: Humanitarian Intervention and Political Imagination in a Refugee Camp for Burundians in Tanzania', PhD Dissertation, Roskilde University, 2001.

Turshen, Meredeth, and Clotilde Twarigaramariya, *What Women Do in Wartime: Gender and Conflict in Africa* (London, 1998).

Turton, David, 'The Meaning of Place in a World of Movement: Lessons from Long-Term Field Research in Southern Ethiopia', *Journal of Refugee Studies*, 2005, Vol. 18, pp. 258–80.

UNDP, *Human Development Report: Overcoming Barriers: Human Mobility and Development* (New York, NY, 2009).

UNHCR, 'UNHCR Country Operations Profile: South Sudan' (Geneva, 2013), www.unhcr.org/pages/4e43cb466.html.

—'UNHCR Global Appeal 2012–2013 South Sudan' (Geneva, 2012).

—UNHCR policy on refugee protection and solutions in urban areas (2009).

—'South Sudan Emergency Situation', 5 February, UNHCR External Regional Update, 2012.

UNHCR Kenya, 'Evaluation of UNHCR's Returnee Reintegration Programme in Southern Sudan', Report of the United Nations High Commissioner for Refugees Policy and Evaluation Services (PDES), (Geneva, 2008).

—*Handbook for the Protection of Women and Girls* (Geneva, 2008).

—'Statistics of the Kakuma Camp Population' (2007).

—Country Operations Plan for Kenya (2006).

Unruh, J. and R. Williams (eds) *Land and Post-Conflict Peacebuilding* (London, 2013).

Utas, Mats, 'Building a Future? The Reintegration and Remarginalisation of Youth in Liberia', in P. Richards (ed.), *No Peace, No War: An Anthropology of Contemporary Armed Conflicts* (Oxford, 2005).

—'Sweet Battlefields: Youth and the Liberian Civil War', PhD Dissertation, Uppsala University, 2003.

Van Hear, Nick, 'Theories of Migration and Social Change', *Journal of Ethnic and Migration Studies* 36, no. 10, pp. 1531–6 (2010).

—'Editorial Introduction', *Journal of Refugee Studies*, 1998, Vol. 11, pp. 341–9.

Verdirame, Guglielmo, 'Human Rights and Refugees: The Case of Kenya', *Journal of Refugee Studies*, 1999, Vol. 12, pp. 54–77.

Vigh, Hendrik E., 'Motion squared: A second look at the concept of social navigation', *Anthropological Theory* 9(4): 419–38, (2009).

—Social Death and Violent Life Chances', in C. Christiansen, M. Utas and H.E. Vigh (eds), *Navigating Terrains of War: Youth and Soldiering in Guinea-Bissau* (New York, NY, 2007).

Voutira, Eftihia, and Barbara E. Harrell-Bond, 'In Search of the Locus of Trust: The Social World of the Refugee Camp', in E.V. Daniel and J. Chr. Knudsen (eds), *Mistrusting Refugees* (Berkeley, CA, 1995).

Walby, Sylvia, 'Post-Post-Modernism? Theorizing Social Complexity', in M. Barrett and A. Phillips (eds), *Destabilizing Theory: Contemporary Feminist Debates* (Cambridge, 1992) pp. 31–52.

White, A. M., 'All the Men are Fighting for Freedom, all the Women are Mourning their Men, but some of us carried Guns: A Raced-Gendered Analysis of Fanon's Psychological Perspectives on War', *Signs*, 2007, Vol. 32, pp. 958–984.

Whitehead, Ann, 'Women and Men; Kinship and Property: Some General Issues (1)', in R. Hirschon (ed.) *Women and Property, Women as Property* (Kent, 1984).

—'I'm Hungry, Mum: The Politics of Domestic Budgeting', in Kate Young, Carol Wolkowitz, Roslyn McCullagh (eds), *Of Marriage and the Market: Women's Insubordination Internationally and its Lessons* (London, 1981).

—'Some Preliminary Notes on the Subordination of Women', *IDS Bulletin*, 1979, Vol. 10, pp. 10–13.

Willems, Roos, 'Embedding the Refugee Experience: Forced Migration and Social Networks in Dar Es Salaam, Tanzania', PhD Thesis, University of Florida, 2003.

Willis, Justin, 'Who put the 'Y' in the BYDA? Youth in Sudan's Civil Wars', in B. Trudell et al. (eds), *Africa's Young Majority* (Edinburgh, 2002).

Wolf, Diane L., 'Situating Feminist Dilemmas in Fieldwork', in D.L. Wolf, *Feminist Dilemmas in Fieldwork* (Boulder, CO, 1996).

Yuval-Davis, Nira, *Gender and Nation* (London, 1997).

Zarkov, Dubravka (ed.), *Gender, Violent Conflict and Development* (New Delhi, 2008).

Zetter, Roger, 'Reconceptualizing the myth of return: continuity and transition amongst the Greek–Cypriot refugees of 1974', *Journal of Refugee Studies*, 12(1), 1–22 (1999).

ADDITIONAL SOURCES

Abbink, Jon, 'Being Young in Africa: The Politics of Despair and Renewal', in J. Abbink and I. van Kessel (eds), *Vanguards or Vandals: Youth, Politics and Conflict in Africa* (Leiden, 2005).

Abdi, Cawo, 'Diasporic Lives and Threatened Identities: Gender struggles of Somalis in America', PhD thesis, University of Sussex, 2006.

Al-Ali, Nadje, 'Loss of Status or New Opportunities? Gender Relations and Transnational Ties among Bosnian Refugees', in U. Vuorella and D. Bryceson (eds), *The Transnational Family: New European Frontiers and Global Networks* (Oxford, 2002).

—'Trans- or a-National? Bosnian Refugees in the UK and the Netherlands', in N. Al-Ali and K. Khoser (eds), *New Approaches to Migration? Transnational Communities and the Transformation of Home* (London, 2002) pp. 96–117.

Allen, Tim, and David Turton, 'Introduction', in T. Allen (ed.) *In Search of Cool Ground: War, Flight and Homecoming in Northeast Africa* (Trenton, NJ, 1996) pp. 1–22.

Amadiume, Ifi, *Male Daughters, Female Husbands: Gender and Sex in an African Society* (London, 1987).

Arnold, Matthew B. and Chris Alden, 'This Gun is our Food: Demilitarising the White Army Militias of South Sudan', *Norwegian Institute of International Affairs Working Paper* 722, 2007.

Bartolomei, Linda, Eileen Pittaway and Emma Elizabeth Pittaway, 'Who Am I? Identity and Citizenship in Kakuma Refugee Camp in Northern Kenya', 2003, *Development – Journal of Society for International Development*, Vol. 46, pp. 87–94.

Berman, Marshall, *All That is Solid Melts into Air. The Experience of Modernity* (New York, NY, 1982).

Beswick, Stephanie, *Sudan's Blood Memory: The Legacy of War, Ethnicity, and Slavery in South Sudan* (Rochester, NY, 2006).

Boserup, Ester, *Women's Role in Economic Development* (London, 1989).

Boyden, Jo, and Joanna D. Berry, *Children and Youth on the Front Line: Ethnography, Armed Conflict and Displacement* (Oxford, 2004).

Brun, Catherine, 'Making Young Displaced Men Visible', *Forced Migration Review*, 2000, Vol. 9, pp. 10–12.

Callamard, Agnes, 'Refugee Women: A Gendered and Political Analysis of the Refuge Experience', in A. Ager (ed.), *Refugees: Perspectives on the Experience of Forced Migration* (New York, NY, 1999) pp. 196–214.

Camino, Linda A., and Ruth M. Krulfeld (1994) *Reconstructing Lives, Recapturing Meaning: Refugee Identity, Gender, and Culture Change.* (Gordon and Breach Publishers: Basel).

Campbell, Elisabeth, 'Urban Refugees in Nairobi: Problems of Protection, Mechanisms of Survival, and Possibilities for Integration', *Journal of Refugee Studies*, 2006, Vol. 19, pp. 396–41.

Christiansen, Catrine, Mats Utas and Henrik E. Vigh (eds), *Navigating Youth, Generating Adulthood: Social becoming in an African context* (Uppsala, 2006).

Cockburn, Cynthia, 'The Continuum of Violence: A Gender Perspective on War and Peace', in W. Giles and J. Hyndman (eds), *Sites of Violence: Gender and Conflict Zones* (Berkeley, CA, 2004) pp. 24–45.

Connell, Robert W., *Masculinities*, 2nd Ed. (Berkeley, CA, 2005).

—*The Men and the Boys* (Cambridge, 2000).

Cowan, Jane, *Dance and the Body Politic in Northern Greece* (Princeton, NJ, 1990).

Crisp, Jeff, 'No Solutions in Sight: The Problem of Protracted Refugee Situations in Africa', *CCIS Working Paper* 68, University of California, 2002.

Crosby, Alison, "To Whim Shall the Nation Belong? The Gender and Ethnic Dimensions of Refugee Return and Struggles for Peace in Guatemala," in Liisa L. North, and Alen B. Simmons (1999), *Journeys of Fear: Refugee Return and National Transformation in Guatemala* (McGill-Queen's University Press: Montreal Kingston, London, Ithaca, 1999).

Deng, Francis M., *The Dinka of the Sudan* (Prospect Heights, IL, 1972).

Deng, Luka Biong, 'Famine in the Sudan: Causes, Preparedness and Response: A Political, Social and Economic Analysis of the 1998 Bahr Al Ghazal Famine', *IDS Discussion Paper* 369, Institute of Development Studies, 1999.

de Vriese, Machtelt, 'Refugee Livelihoods A Review of the Evidence', UNHCR EPAU Report, Geneva, 2006.

Dolan, Chris, 'Repatriation from South Africa to Mozambique – Undermining Durable Solutions?', in R. Black and K. Koser (eds), *The End of the Refugee Cycle: Refugee Repatriation and Reconstruction* (Oxford, 1999) pp. 95–109.

Eastmond, Marita, 'Luchar y Sufrir-Stories of Life and Exile: Reflections on the Ethnographic Process', *Ethnos*, 1996, Vol. 61, pp. 231–50.

El-Bushra, Judy, 'Gender and Forced Migration: Editorial', *Forced Migration Review*, 2000, Vol. 9.

Ellis, Stephen, *Mask of Anarchy: The Destruction of Liberia and the Religious Dimension of an African Civil War* (New York, NY, 2001).

Elson, Diane (ed.), *Male Bias in the Development Process* (Manchester, 1991).

Elson, Diane, and Ruth Pearson, 'The Subordination of Women and the Internationalization of Factory Production', in K. Young, C. Wolkowitz and R. McCullagh (eds), *Of Marriage and the Market: Women's Subordination in International Perspective* (London, 1982), pp. 144–66.

Enloe, Cynthia, *Bananas, Beaches and Bases: Making Feminist Senses of International Politics* (Berkeley, CA, 1989).

Faria, Caroline, 'Contesting Miss Sudan', *International Feminist Journal of Politics*, 2010.

Geertz, Clifford, *Local Knowledge: Further Essays in Interpretive Anthropology* (New York, 1983).

—*Words and Lives: The Anthropologist as an Author* (Stanford, CA, 1983).

George, Sheba Mariam, *When Women Come First: Gender and Class in Transnational Migration* (Berkeley, CA, 2005).

Giddens, Anthony, *Modernity and Self-Identity: Self and Society in the Late Modern Age* (Stanford, CA, 1991).

—*Social Theory and Modern Sociology* (Stanford, CA, 1987).

Gough, Kathleen, 'Nuer Kinship: A Re-examination', in T.O. Beidelman (ed.), *The Translation of Culture: Essays to E.E. Evans-Pritchard* (London, 1971), pp. 79–122.

Grabska, Katarzyna, 'Brothers or Poor Cousins? Rights, Policies and the Wellbeing of Refugees in Egypt', in K. Grabska and L. Mehta Lyla (eds), *Forced Displacement: Why Rights Matter?* (London, 2008).

Gramsci, Antonio, *Selection from the Prison Notebooks*. Q. Hoare and G. Nowell-Smith (ed. and trans.) (London, 1971).

Hodgson, Dorothy L., '"My Daughter belongs to the Government Now": Marriage, Masaasi, and the Tanzanian State', in D.L. Hodgson and S. McCurdy (eds) *"Wicked" Women and the Reconfiguration of Gender in Africa* (Portsmouth, NH, 2001).

Holt, P.M., and W. M. Daly (eds), *A History of the Sudan: From the Coming of Islam to the Present Day*, 5th ed. (New York, NY, 2000).

Holtzman, Jon D., 'Dialling 911 in Nuer: Gender Transformations and Domestic Violence in a Midwestern Sudanese Refugee Community', in N. Foner, R. Rumbaut and S.J. Gold (eds), *Immigration Research for a New Century*, (New York, 2003) pp. 390–408.

—'*Nuer Journeys, Nuer Lives: Sudanese Refugees in Minnesota* (Boston, MA, 2000).

Hondagneu-Sotelo, Pierrette, *Gendered transitions: Mexican experiences of Immigration* (Berkeley, CA, 1994).

Hohwana, A, and F. De Boeck (eds), *Makers and Breakers: Children and Youth in Postcolonial Africa* (Trenton, NJ, 2005).

HSBA, 'No Standing, Few Prospects: How Peace is failing South Sudanese Female Combatants and WAAFG', *The Sudan Human Security Baseline Assessment*, Brief No. 8, September 2008.

Human Rights Watch, 'Kenya: Protect Somali Refugees', www.hrw.org/en/news/2008/11/13/kenya-protect-somali-refugees (accessed 13 November 2008).

Hutchinson, Sharon E., 'Relations between the Sexes among the Nuer: 1930', *Africa*, 1980, Vol. 50, pp. 371–87.

Hyndman, Jennifer, 'Managing Difference: Gender and Culture in Humanitarian Emergencies', *Gender, Place and Culture*, 1998, Vol. 5, pp. 241–60.

Jacobsen, Karen, 'Introduction: Refugees and Asylum Seekers in Urban Areas: A Livelihoods Perspective', *Journal of Refugee Studies*, 2006, Vol. 19, pp. 273–86.

Jaji, Rosemary, 'Masculinity on Unstable Ground: Young Refugee Men in Nairobi, Kenya, *Journal of Refugee Studies*, 2009, Vol. 22, pp. 177–94.

Jamal, Arafat, 'Minimum Standards and Essential Needs in a Protracted Refugee Situation: A Review of UNHCR Programme in Kakuma', Evaluation and Policy Analysis Unit, UNHCR, Geneva, 2000.

James, Wendy, *War and Survival in Sudan's Frontierlands: Voices from the Blue Nile* (Oxford, Oxford University Press, 2009).

Janzen, John, 'Illusions of Home in the Story of a Rwandan Refugee's Return', in D.

Long and E. Oxfeld (eds), *Coming Home? Refugees, Migrants, and Those Who Stayed Behind* (Philadelphia, NJ, 2004).

Kaiser, Tania, 'Participation or Consultation? Reflections on a "Beneficiary Based" Evaluation of UNHCR's Programme for Sierra Leonean and Liberian Refugees in Guinea, June–July 2000', *Journal of Refugee Studies*, 2004, Vol. 17, pp. 185–204.

Kaldor, Mary, *New and Old Wars: Organized Violence in a Global Era.* 2nd edition (Cambridge, Polity, 2006).

Kelly, Raymond, *The Nuer Conquest: The Structure and Development of an Expansionist System* (Ann Arbor, MI, 1985).

Kibreab, Gaim, 'Revisiting the Debate on People, Place, Identity and Displacement', *Journal of Refugee Studies*, 1999, Vol. 12, pp. 384–410.

—'The Myth of Dependency Among Camp Refugees in Somalia', *Journal of Refugee Studies*, 1993, Vol. 6, pp. 384–428.

Korac, Maja, 'Gender, Nationalism, Ethnic-National Identity Crisis: The Case of the Former Yugoslavia', in W. Giles, H. Moussa and P. Van Esterik (eds), *Development and Diaspora: Gender and the Refugee Experience* (Dundas, 1996) pp. 87–99.

Kuhlman, Thomas, 'The Economic Integration of Refugees in Developing Countries: A Research Model', *Journal of Refugee Studies*, 1991, Vol. 4, pp. 1–20.

Kulusika, Simon E., (1998). *Southern Sudan: Political and Economic Power Dilemmas and Options* (London: Minerva Press).

Lammers, Ellen, 'War, Refugee and Self: Soldiers, Students and Artists in Kampala, Uganda', PhD thesis, University of Amsterdam, 2006.

Lejukole, James, 'Changes in Family Gender Roles Among the Southern Sudanese Refugee Families in Cairo', MA thesis, The American University in Cairo, 2000.

Lesch, Ann, *The Sudan: Contested National Identities* (Bloomington, IN, 1998).

Loescher, Gil, Edward Newman, James Milner and Gary Troeller (eds), *Protracted Refugee Situations: Political, Human Rights and Security Implications* (New York, 2008).

Malkki, Liisa H., 'Speechless Emissaries: Refugees, Humanitarianism, and Dehistoricization', *Cultural Anthropology*, 1996, Vol. 11, pp. 377–404.

Marcus, George E., Ethnography in/of the world system: the emergence of multi-sited ethnography, in George E. Marcus, *Ethnography through thick and thin*, pp. 79–104 (Princeton: Princeton University Press, NJ, 1998).

Massey, Doreen, *Space, Place and Gender*, (Cambridge, 1994).

Matsouka, Atsuoko, and John Sorenson, 'Eritrean Canadian Refugee Households as Sites of Gender Renegotiation', in D. Indra (ed.), *Engendering Forced Migration: Theory and Practice*, (New York, NY, 1999).

Monsutti, Alessandro, 'La migration comme rite de passage: la construction de la masculinité parmi les jeunes Afghans en Iran', in: C. Verschuur, F. Reysoo (eds), *Genre, nouvelle division internationale du travail et migrations*, Cahiers genre et développement, no. 5, (Paris: L'Harmattan, 2005), pp. 79–186.

Moore, Henrietta, *Feminism and Anthropology* (Cambridge, 1988).

Moro, Leben Nelson, *Oil, conflict and displacement in Sudan.* PhD thesis, University of Oxford, 2008.

Morokvasic, Mirjana, 'Birds of Passage are also Women', *International Migration Review*, 1984, Vol. 18, pp. 886–907.

Moser, Carol, and F. Clark, *Victims, Perpetrators or Actors? Gender, Armed Conflict and Political Violence* (London, 2001).

North, Liisa L., 'Fear and Hope: Return and Transformation in Historical Perspective', in L. North and A.B. Simmons (eds), *Journeys of Fear: Refugee Return and National Transformation in Guatemala* (Montreal, 1999).

O'Brien, Donald C., 'A Lost Generation? Youth Identity and State Decay in West Africa', in R. Werbner and T. Ranger (eds), *Postcolonial Identities in Africa* (London, 1996).

Omaar, Rakiya, and Alex de Waal, *Components of a Lasting Peace in Sudan: First Thoughts* (London, 1993).

Ortner, B. Sherry, 'Is Female to Male as Nature Is to Culture?', in M. Zimbalist Rosaldo and L. Lamphare (eds), *Woman, Culture, and Society* (Stanford, CA, 1974).

Ossome, Lyn, 'Cultural Fundamentalism: Abduction, Confinement and Sexual Violence against South Sudanese Women and Girls in Kakuma Refugee Camp,

Kenya', Unpublished Field Report, 2006.
Pessar, Patricia R., 'Engendering Migration Studies: The Case of New Immigrants in the United States', *American Behavioural Scientist*, 1999, Vol. 42, pp. 577–600.
Phizacklea, Annie, (ed.), *One Way Ticket: Migration and Female Labour* (London, 1983).
Piot, Charles, *Remotely Global: Village Modernity in West Africa* (Chicago, IL, 1999).
Pittaway, Eileen, and Linda Bartolomei, Unpublished Fieldtrip Report to Kenya and Thailand, 2002.
Powles, Julia, 'Refugee Voices – Home and Homelessness: The Life History of Susanna Mwana-uta, an Angolan Refugee', *Journal of Refugee Studies*, 2002, Vol. 15, pp. 81–102.
Prince, Ruth, 'Popular Music and Luo Youth in Western Kenya: Ambiguities of Modernity, Morality and Gender Relations in the Era of AIDS', in C. Christiansen, M. Utas and H.E. Vigh (eds), *Navigating Youth, Generating Adulthood: Social becoming in an African Context* (Uppsala, 2006).
Richards, Paul, *Fighting for the Rain Forest: War, Youth and Resources in Sierra Leone* (Oxford, 1996).
—(ed.), *No Peace, No War: An Anthropology of Contemporary Armed Conflicts* (Oxford, 2005).
Rowe, Martin, 'Performance and Representation: Masculinity and Leadership at the Cairo Refugee Protest', Paper presented at the 4th Annual Forced Migration Post-graduate Student Conference, University of East London, March 2006.
Ruay, Deng Akol, *The Politics of Two Sudans: The North and the South* (Uppsala, 1994).
Samuelson, M., 'The Disfigured Body of the Female Guerilla: (De)militarization, Sexual Violence, and Redomestication, *Signs*, 2007, Vol. 32, pp. 833–56.
Scroggins, Deborah, *Emma's War: Love, Betrayal and Death in the Sudan* (London, 2002).
Small Arms Survey, 'The Militarisation of Sudan: A Preliminary Review of Arms Flows and Holdings', Sudan Issue Brief: Human Security Baseline Assessment No. 5, April, 2007, www.smallarmssurvey.org/files/portal/spotlight/sudan/Sudan_pdf/SIB%206%20militarization.pdf.
Smith, Merill, *Warehousing Refugees: A Denial of Rights, a Waste of Humanity* (Washington, DC, 2004).
Sommers, Marc, 'Peace Education and Refugee Youth', in J. Crisp, C. Talbot and D.B. Cipollone (eds), *Learning for a Future: Refugee Education in Developing Countries* (Geneva, 2001) pp. 163–216.
Strathern, Marilyn, *Women in Between: Female Roles in a Male World: Mount Hagen, New Guinea* (London, 1972).
Taylor, Charles, 'Modern Social Imaginaries', *Public Culture*, 2002, Vol. 14, pp. 91–125.
Tripartite Agreement, 'Tripartite Agreement between the Government of the Republic of Kenya, the Government of the Republic of Sudan and the United Nations High Commissioner for Refugees for the Voluntary Repatriation of Sudanese Refugees in Kenya Back to the Sudan', 12 January 2006.
Turshen, Meredeth, 'The Political Economy of Rape: An Analysis of Systemic Rape and Sexual Abuse of Women during Armed Conflict in Africa', in C. Moser and F. Clark (eds), *Victims, Perpetrators or Actors? Gender, Armed Conflict and Political Violence* (London, 2001) pp. 55–69.
—'UNHCR Manual on a Community Based Approach in UNHCR Operations' (March, 2008), www:unhcr.org/refworld/docid/47da54722.html.
UNMIS 'Comprehensive Peace Agreement', UN Mission in Sudan (2006), www.unmis.org/English/cpa/htm.
Utas, Mats, 'Agency of Victims: Young Women in the Liberation Civil War', in A. Hohwana and F. De Boeck (eds), *Makers and Breakers: Children and Youth in Postcolonial Africa* (Trenton, NJ, 2005), pp. 53–80.
Verdirame, Guglielmo, and Barbara E. Harrell-Bond, *Rights in Exile: Janus Faced Humanitarianism* (Oxford, 2005).
Weiss, Brad, *The Making and Unmaking of the Haya Lived World: Consumption, Commoditization, and Everyday Practice* (Durham, NC, 1996).
Werbner, Richard, *Postcolonial Subjectivities in Africa* (London, 2002).
Yuval-Davis, Nira, and F. Anthias *Woman-Nation-Gender* (London, 1989).

Index

abortion 17, 31
access to education 5, 23, 83–4, 95
  boys' 50
  girls' 44, 75, 84, 95, 102
access to jobs 93
access to land 131, 134, 140, 149
  women's 126, 131, 137, 148, 150
access to livelihoods 134, 141, 143
  women's 133, 137, 140–2
access to resources 131, 145
  women's 137–8, 148
'after-fire' fieldwork ix, 10
Age, Gender, and Diversity
  Mainstreaming (AGDM) 77–80
agro-pastoralism 25, 32, 36–7, 108, 120,
  130
aid dependency 32, 76, 120–1
aid industry 14
aid workers 72–3
Akol, Lam 33
Al-Bashir, Omar 40
Angelina 94, 170
animal sacrifice 134, 153, 186
anthropology 10, 190–1
anti-immigration 191–2
Appadurai, Arjun 109, 191
Arab fighting 36, 57
Arabic
  culture 106, 117, 146, 165
  language ix, 106
  traders 117
arranged marriages 90, 91–2, 166
  see also forced marriages

behaviour, concept of proper 154, 164
beben cieng (returning home) 105–6,
  155, 167, 170, 187, 192 *see also*
  homecoming
Bentiu 112, 117, 203, 205
Bol 87–8, 95, 115
Bor massacre 34, 34 n.26
boy soldiers 39, 41, 50
  training camps, Ethiopia 3, 40, 49, 52
boy-run households 42

bridewealth 4, 43, 45, 61, 90, 148, 152,
  156–7, 169, 172, 178, 183
  accumulating ('running after cows')
  169
  increase due to education 90, 173
bull boys (unscarified men) 81
Bul Nuer 34, 35, 37 n.40, 46, 115

Cairo viii, 164
cattle 174
  herding 25
  movement (*rwil*) 25
  'of money' 157, 169
  'over blood' 156–7, 168, 174
  raiding 34, 59
  wars 34–5
child mortality 30, 60 n.95
Christianity 5, 11, 22, 24, 134, 185
  christianisation 81
cieng (home or community) 11, 96,
  128–9, 130–1, 132, 155–6, 192–3
  see also community
civil war 41
  first 1 n.1, 29
  second 1, 25
colonialism 4, 11, 22, 48, 66, 142
community 85–6, 88, 96, 109, 137, 139,
  176
  codes 34, 45
  creating new bonds 135–6, 155, 168
  estrangement 139, 164
conflict 50, 57, 59, 63, 69, 74
  violence 28, 47
conjugal bargain 20, 96, 175
consumerism 77
Cornwall, Andrea 88, 96
courts 92, 139, 166
cultivation 96, 120, 141–3, 146–7
cultural adjustment 162
culture 11, 52, 82, 96–7, 158–9, 172
  identity 21
  returnee 3–4
  threat to 4, 24, 95, 101, 122, 161
    see also cieng

Cuol, Gordon Kong 33
cuong (pl. *cung*; rights) 156, 170 *see also* rights

Dak 24, 162
Dau 121–2
diaspora 37, 66, 149
Dinka 29, 33–4, 60, 121–2, 130
disempowerment 86
displacement 5–6, 19–20, 22, 24, 36–7, 81, 101–2, 122–6, 195
    gendered 6, 8, 37–8
    generational 8
    irreversibility of process 123
    war-time 38
division of labour 43, 85, 149
    gendered 8, 9, 24, 26–7, 146–9, 161–2, 175
divorce 61 62, 147, 176–7
Dok Nuer 10, 38
domestic violence 14, 54, 88, 91, 99–100, 158, 163
dress codes *see also* fashion 92, 123
    returnees 3, 3 n.3, 123
drought 25, 31, 121
duël (mud/grass hut) 15, 119, 129

educated wives 90, 100
education 79, 81, 74
    access to *see under* access to education
    commodification 179–180
    primary school 144–5, 152
    refugee camp 3, 41, 42, 75, 75 n.17
    status 171, 173
    value 82, 83, 89, 179, 184, 185
Egypt 7
elders 48, 50, 83
    decrease in respect for 96, 120
    undermining of 84, 86
emasculation 47, 54, 85–6, 88, 163
emplacement 109, 110, 114, 115, 124, 163, 190, 192 *see also* settling-in
    activities 12, 110
employment market 140, 141
ethics 14 n.33, 17–18 *see also* positionality
Ethiopia 40, 40 n.45
ethnicity 29, 33, 45
    fluid notion 45
    identity 46, 47, 69, 160
Evans-Pritchard, Edward 9, 129

family 53, 60, 95, 100
    responsibilities to 50, 159, 160, 170
    (re)unification 115, 126, 130, 135, 147
    wife 171
fashion *see also* dress codes 1, 66, 153, 164, 183–4

hair extensions 153, 164, 175, 184
female headed households 6, 22, 147, 148, 150
feminist analysis 10, 15, 18–19, 193, 198
food shortages 31
forced marriage 79, 92, 100, 180 *see also* arranged marriages

Gadet, Peter 37, 37 n.40, 46
Garang, John 29, 33, 48–9
Gatbel 136, 148
Gatchang 15, 49
Gatleak 136, 137
Gatmai 161, 174
geer ro (change) 12, 20
gender 4, 18
    mainstreaming programmes 22–3, 68, 77, 93, 200
    statistics 42, 43 n.52, 80
gendered division of space 43, 90, 146, 156, 160, 161–2
gendered emplacement 150–1, 155, 157, 181
gender norms 7, 22, 93, 95, 166, 194
    female identity 44, 58
    male identity 20, 22, 61
    identity 21–4, 43, 48, 62–3, 68, 80, 163, 167, 187
    transgressions 161, 185–6
gender violence 46, 54, 57, 80
    kidnap 34, 46
    rape 46–7, 53, 61 n.99, 72, 78, 117, 180
    targeting women and children 34, 45, 45 n.57, 57
generational change 4, 122, 166, 172
girls *see also* young women 78, 89
    chastity 43, 164
    mobility restrictions 43, 167
    returnees compared to stayees 89, 164, 165–6
Gladys 163
globalisation 23–4, 67, 196
government (*kume*) 7, 11, 28, 84, 138, 169, 185, 186, 204
Government of Southern Sudan (GOSS) 42, 112, 114, 126, 131–2, 138, 139
    Structures 117, 147
Greater Upper Nile 1, 10, 42
guns 47–8, 52, 53, 58, 123

home 103, 107, 110, 116
    as private space 129
    concept of 3, 108, 128
    fears and disappointment about 92, 116
    myth of 124–5
    nostalgia 115–6
    sedentarist assumptions 106, 191–2, 194

see also cieng
homecoming 106, 124–5, 133, 140, 149–50, 194
  ceremony 134
  feeling lost 105, 154
  see also beben cieng
households 44, 50, 61, 93–4, 134, 156
humanitarianism 7, 12–14, 68, 75, 77, 103, 120
Hutchinson, Sharon 9, 45, 81
hypermasculinities *see under* masculinities

in flux 5, 20–1, 23, 24, 115, 155, 189
inheritance 100
insecurity 40, 51, 60, 78, 108, 112
inter-ethnic violence 22, 23, 33, 35, 47, 59, 112
internally displaced 7, 102, 139
international aid 162
International Committee of the Red Cross (ICRC) 40
International Organization for Migration (IOM) 114
inter-war period 32
intra-ethnic fighting 32
invisible girls 25, 29, 38, 42, 44
Islamic codes 5

Jal, Emmanuel 50 n.71
Jany 153–4, 155, 158, 159
Juba, South Sudan capital 3–4, 78, 105

Kakuma refugee camp *see under* refugee camps
Kenya 38, 68, 68 n.7, 70, 70 n.10, 75, 76
  culture 97, 98
Khartoum 37
  government 7, 34
Kiir, President Silva 203, 204
Kim Jial 39–40, 114, 159, 169, 171
kinship (*maar*) 32, 95, 130
  fictive 130, 136
  ties 135, 160
Kong 92, 97
Kuem 152, 154, 162
Kuok 1, 3, 8, 21, 49, 76, 83, 105–6, 114, 116, 122, 123, 126–7, 135, 136, 140, 144, 145–6, 162, 168, 182, 189, 202, 205
Kuoth divinity 28 n.1, 35

labour market, women's entry into 143, 145, 148
land 129, 131, 138
  access to *see under* access to land
  laws 138, 139
  rights 129, 131, 138
  title 138, 139
language ix, 79, 123

Lɛr 1, 12, 118–20, 144, 203, 205
  destruction 37, 46, 119
Lɛr County Land Commission 138
life stories methodology 15–16, 22, 81
literacy 141
  importance of 95, 182
  rates 31 n.7
livelihoods 51, 102, 108, 112
  access *see under* access to livelihoods
  strategies 141–2
local girls' attitudes 158, 166, 182
Lokichoggio refugees 40
Lony 64, 76
'lost boys' 39–40, 42, 77, 81, 90, 91
  resettlement to USA 40, 41–2, 41 n.47
Lutheran World Federation (LWF) 13, 73, 78

Machar, Riek 29, 33, 33 n.18, 34 n.29, 35–6, 46, 52, 152, 152 n.1, 152 n.2, 203, 204
Madut Jok, Jok 34, 203
male authority, undermining of 22
manhood 48, 51, 52, 81
  age mates (*ric*) 48, 49, 83
  initiation (*gaar*) 34 n.29, 48, 49–50, 52, 52 n.77, 81, 158
  spears (*mut*) 48, 53, 153, 154
marriage 59, 60, 62, 90–1, 96, 160, 168, 169, 176, 187, 188
  against pledge 170
  bridewealth *see under* bridewealth
  marriageable age 61, 176
  marrying with cows 88, 122
  pressure to marry 90, 170, 180
  transfer to husband 45, 155
masculinities 29, 44, 47–8, 53, 63, 85, 88
  alternative 53, 54, 83, 159
  hypermasculinities 48, 53, 85, 88, 182
maternal mortality 30
Matip, Paulino 35, 46
men
  as guardians of culture 98–9, 100
  real Nuer 49, 84, 127–8, 154, 160, 163, 196
Mengistu, Haile Mariam 40, 41
migration literature 127, 199
military training 40, 41, 44, 48–9
militia attacks 31, 36
missionary organisations 39
modern identity 92, 163
modernity *see also* culture, threat to 21, 23, 66–7, 70
monetarisation 142
moral panic 3, 4, 21, 24, 165, 181–2

Nairobi refugees 36 n.35, 41, 44, 68
national homeland 62, 107, 131
nationalism 48, 54, 85, 99, 131, 193

nation-building 7, 113, 132, 165
NGO workers 14, 72, 73
Ngundɛng Bong 28 n.1
northern traders 117, 146
Nuer 9, 11 n.27, 29, 34
    customs 17, 67, 100, 153
    hospitality 133
    identity 12, 159
    language ix, 11
    way of life 76, 81, 85, 95, 146
Nuer-Dinka relations 36, 99
Nuer girls' duties 163–4
Nuerland 23, 62, 76, 101, 160
Nyabol 133, 134
Nyachan 144, 145
Nyadak 47, 58, 94
Nyajuc 60–1, 141, 183
Nyajung 135, 137, 139, 173, 185
NyaKlang 58, 90
Nyakuma 15, 185
Nyakuol 1, 8, 21, 67, 74, 93, 104, 114,
    116, 119, 122, 126, 131, 135, 138,
    143–4, 148, 166–7, 178, 189, 205
Nyakuoth 39, 39 n.42, 70, 90, 112, 114,
    205
Nyakwong 135, 144
Nyal 162
Nyaluak 152
Nyamai 78, 88–9, 92–3, 177
Nyamead 37
Nyamuc 142–3, 164, 183, 184
Nyapiliny 17, 137
Nyapiny 104–5, 115, 126, 148
Nyariek 1, 3, 8, 21, 28, 164, 176, 189, 205
NyaSunday 115, 122, 180
Nyatap 136
Nyayena 145, 155, 175, 184
Nyuuri piny (settling-in) *see under*
    settling-in

oil industry 29, 118
    ecological impact 118
ongoing conflict 69, 202
Operation Lifeline Sudan (OLS) 31, 32,
    74 n.15
orphans 41, 42

patriarchal bargain 94, 200
peace agreement, 2005 1, 69
peace-building 36
    women's roles 59
permanent place 104, 131
place-making 107, 109, 171, 181, 190
polygamy 84, 132, 163, 171
positionality 10, 13, 14 *see also* ethics
post-war situation 23, 143, 148
power 24, 74, 100, 173–4, 198
    power relations 12, 19, 92

reconnecting with friends 12, 110

Raan 75
rain (*tot*) 25, 27, 152
rebel groups 40, 41
Red Army 40, 49, 51
refugee camps 39, 81, 101
    Ethiopia 38
    Kakuma 3, 12–13, 36, 39, 64, 68, 76,
        78
    Khartoum 5, 124
    post-2013 204–5
    Uganda 38
refugee camp life 114
    gender training 79
    headcounts 74
    income generating opportunities 5,
        74
    laws 70
    organisation 69, 73, 74
refugee protection areas 80
refugee repatriation 123 *see also*
    repatriation
religion 76
    beliefs 73, 83, 174
    church 76–7, 83, 165
repatriation 69, 94, 104, 106–7, 111, 113
    difficulties 126
    journeys 105, 111
    process 111
reproduction 60, 61, 175, 177, 186
    roles 60
    taboos 60, 60 n.96
reproductive power 157
research methods 10–11, 15
resettlement 14, 43, 72, 115
    difficulties finding work 126, 141, 146
returnee girls 110, 184 *see also* girls
    transgressive behaviour 161, 164,
        165, 185–6
returnees 7, 94, 114, 124, 138, 192
    Ethiopian returnees 109
    tensions with stayees 124, 134, 158,
        160, 172
rights 157, 180 *see also cuong/cung*
    citizenship 66, 78, 133
    human 46, 78, 87, 174
    women's 64, 79, 86, 90, 148–9
Ruan 111, 186
Rubkona 15, 39, 112, 117

Sarah 96, 100, 130
scarification *see under* manhood
seasonality 25
    seasonal migration 36
settling-in 12, 126, 133, 148, 159, 160,
    168, 176, 187 *see also* emplacement
sexual services 53, 57, 60
social change 4, 11, 19–20, 96, 167,
    194–5, 196
social change theory 190–1
social emplacement 150, 159, 161

social networks support 120–1
social relations between boys and girls
   160, 175
social status 5, 132
   boys' 5
   girls' 145, 150, 164, 166
   married women's 60, 132, 176, 177
   men's 60
South Sudan viii–ix, 1, 2, 4, 7, 9, 12, 13,
   23, 26, 27, 30, 31, 33, 42, 52, 54,
   68-9, 82, 95, 102, 111–12, 127,
   131, 136, 139, 143, 149–50, 165–6,
   187–90, 197, 200, 201–5
   independence 7, 33, 131
South Sudan Independence Movement
   (SSIM) 33 n.19
South Sudan Liberation Movement/
   Army (SSLM/A) 49, 54
Southern Sudan Defence Force (SSDF)
   35
space 108
statistics 30–2
   repatriation 69, 111–2
   conflict violence 31, 35
   displacements 6, 36, 36 n.35, 40, 68,
   203
stayees 21, 121, 142, 161
storytelling 18, 28, 43
Sudanese Armed Forces (SAF) 117
Sudan People's Liberation Army/
   Movement (SPLA/M) 1, 3, 32–3, 40,
   189, 204

Thudan 138
Tito 140
Tot 77, 81, 84, 86
Turkana 14, 68 n.5
   community 69
Tut 157–8

United Nations (UN) 64, 92, 94,
   105
   as father 85–6

presence in Western Upper Nile
   117–18
UNHCR 3, 13, 39, 40, 64, 70, 72, 73, 76,
   78
   registering refugees 72 *see also*
     refugee camp life
   refugee regulation 66, 72
Unity State 1 n.1, 36 *see also* Western
   Upper Nile
   changes following war 117, 119
unmarried girls 132, 137, 176
USA 37, 42
   migration to 42 *see also* lost boys

visitors (*jiääl*) 133

Wanten 51–2, 84, 116, 160
war of educated 33, 34–5, 45
wedding ceremony 152, 154
Western Upper Nile 1, 9, 23, 27, 29,
   33–4, 36–9, 52, 58, 111, 116–18, 121,
   169, 181, 189, 197, 202 *see also* Unity
   State
widows 137, 138, 140, 149, 150, 151
women
   access to employment 22
   as bearers of tradition 62–3, 166
   as mothers of the nation 7, 60, 132
   becoming 'real men' 127, 145, 148,
     149
women combatants 56–7, 60 n.97
women traders 146
women's agency 61, 63, 90, 97, 181
women's organisations 79
women's subordination 6, 18–19, 20, 22,
   23, 24–5, 87, 98, 141, 165, 167, 174,
   178
women's training 79, 93
World Food Program (WFP) 14, 76

Yak 98, 115–16, 169–70
young women 164, 183 *see also* girls
youth agency 44, 51, 157

EASTERN AFRICAN STUDIES

These titles published in the United States and Canada by Ohio University Press

Revealing Prophets
Edited by DAVID M. ANDERSON
& DOUGLAS H. JOHNSON

*East African Expressions of
Chistianity*
Edited by THOMAS SPEAR
& ISARIA N. KIMAMBO

The Poor Are Not Us
Edited by DAVID M. ANDERSON
& VIGDIS BROCH-DUE

Potent Brews
JUSTIN WILLIS

Swahili Origins
JAMES DE VERE ALLEN

Being Maasai
Edited by THOMAS SPEAR
& RICHARD WALLER

Jua Kali Kerya
KENNETH KING

Control & Crisis in Colonial Kenya
BRUCE BERMAN

Unhappy Valley
Book One: State & Class
Book Two: Violence & Ethnicity
BRUCE BERMAN
& JOHN LONSDALE

Mau Mau from Below
GREET KERSHAW

The Mau Mau War in Perspective
FRANK FUREDI

*Squatters & the Roots of Mau Mau
1905-63*
TABITHA KANOGO

*Economic & Social Origins of Mau
Mau 1945-53*
DAVID W. THROUP

Multi-Party Politics in Kenya
DAVID W. THROUP
& CHARLES HORNSBY

Empire State-Building
JOANNA LEWIS

*Decolonization & Independence in
Kenya 1940-93*
Edited by B.A. OGOT
& WILLIAM R. OCHIENG'

Eroding the Commons
DAVID ANDERSON

Penetration & Protest in Tanzania
ISARIA N. KIMAMBO

Custodians of the Land
Edited by GREGORY MADDOX,
JAMES L. GIBLIN & ISARIA N.
KIMAMBO

*Education in the Development of
Tanzania 1919-1990*
LENE BUCHERT

The Second Economy in Tanzania
T.L. MALIYAMKONO
& M.S.D. BAGACHWA

*Ecology Control & Economic
Development in East African
History*
HELGE KJEKSHUS

Siaya
DAVID WILLIAM COHEN
& E.S. ATIENO ODHIAMBO

*Uganda Now • Changing Uganda
Developing Uganda • From Chaos
to Order • Religion & Politics in
East Africa*
Edited by HOLGER BERNT
HANSEN & MICHAEL TWADDLE

*Kakungulu & the Creation of
Uganda 1868-1928*
MICHAEL TWADDLE

Controlling Anger
SUZETTE HEALD

Kampala Women Getting By
SANDRA WALLMAN

*Political Power in Pre-Colonial
Buganda*
RICHARD J. REID

Alice Lakwena & the Holy Spirits
HEIKE BEHREND

Slaves, Spices & Ivory in Zanzibar
ABDUL SHERIFF

Zanzibar Under Colonial Rule
Edited by ABDUL SHERIFF
& ED FERGUSON

*The History & Conservation of
Zanzibar Stone Town*
Edited by ABDUL SHERIFF

Pastimes & Politics
LAURA FAIR

*Ethnicity & Conflict in the Horn
of Africa*
Edited by KATSUYOSHI FUKUI &
JOHN MARKAKIS

*Conflict, Age & Power in North
East Africa*
Edited by EISEI KURIMOTO
& SIMON SIMONSE

*Propery Rights & Political
Development in Ethiopia & Eritrea*
SANDRA FULLERTON
JOIREMAN

Revolution & Religion in Ethiopia
ØYVIND M. EIDE

Brothers at War
TEKESTE NEGASH & KJETIL
TRONVOLL

From Guerrillas to Government
DAVID POOL

Mau Mau & Nationhood
Edited by E.S. ATIENO
ODHIAMBO & JOHN LONSDALE

*A History of Modern Ethiopia,
1855-1991*(2nd edn)
BAHRU ZEWDE

Pioneers of Change in Ethiopia
BAHRU ZEWDE

Remapping Ethiopia
Edited by W. JAMES,
D. DONHAM, E. KURIMOTO
& A. TRIULZI

*Southern Marches of Imperial
Ethiopia*
Edited by DONALD L. DONHAM
& WENDY JAMES

A Modern History of the Somali
(4th edn)
I.M. LEWIS

*Islands of Intensive Agriculture in
East Africa*
Edited by MATS WIDGREN
& JOHN E.G. SUTTON

Leaf of Allah
EZEKIEL GEBISSA

*Dhows & the Colonial Economy of
Zanzibar 1860-1970*
ERIK GILBERT

*African Womanhood in Colonial
Kerya*
TABITHA KANOGO

African Underclass
ANDREW BURTON

In Search of a Nation
Edited by GREGORY H. MADDOX
& JAMES L. GIBLIN

A History of the Excluded
JAMES L. GIBLIN

Black Poachers, White Hunters
EDWARD I. STEINHART

Ethnic Federalism
DAVID TURTON

Crisis & Decline in Bunyoro
SHANE DOYLE

*Emancipation without Abolition in
German East Africa*
JAN-GEORG DEUTSCH

*Women, Work & Domestic
Virtue in Uganda 1900-2003*
GRACE BANTEBYA
KYOMUHENDO & MARJORIE
KENISTON McINTOSH

Cultivating Success in Uganda
GRACE CARSWELL

*War in Pre-Colonial
Eastern Africa*
RICHARD REID

Slavery in the Great Lakes Region
of East Africa
Edited by HENRI MÉDARD
& SHANE DOYLE

The Benefits of Famine
DAVID KEEN